PURITY *of* HEART
and
CONTEMPLATION

PURITY *of* HEART *and* CONTEMPLATION

—— A ——

Monastic Dialogue
Between
Christian and
Asian Traditions

EDITED BY
BRUNO BARNHART
AND JOSEPH WONG

CONTINUUM
New York • London

2001

The Continuum International Publishing Group Inc
370 Lexington Avenue, New York, NY 10017

The Continuum International Publishing Group Ltd
The Tower Building, 11 York Road, London SE1 7NX

Library of Congress Cataloging-in-Publication Data

Purity of heart and contemplation : a monastic dialogue between Christian and Asian traditions / edited by Bruno Barnhart and Joseph Wong.
      p.   cm.
   ISBN 0-8264-1348-X
   1. Monastic and religious life – Comparative studies. 2. Asceticism – Comparative studies. 3. Contemplation – Comparative studies. I. Barnhart, Bruno, 1931- II. Huang, Yuese.

BL631 .P87 2001
291.6′57 – dc21

                                                      2001037248

Contents

Acknowledgments

The symposium and this book which it has brought forth have involved a broad collaboration. The prior of New Camaldoli, Father Raniero Hoffman, and the whole monastic community, provided consistently warm and thoughtful hospitality for the large group of participants. The monks put up with the many extra tasks and the unusual daily schedule with patience and good humor. The invited participants deserve thanks—whether those who did the hard work of writing a paper and preparing it for publication, those who responded to the presentations, or those who moderated the sessions.

The symposium could not have taken place without the help of several generous donors, particularly Patrick Tsim and Thomas Ho. Publication of this book has been made possible largely through the generosity of a European foundation which prefers to remain unnamed.

Indispensable assistance in editing the manuscript was given by oblates Jeffry B. Spencer, Paula Huston, Laura Morland, and Lynne Clarkin, and by New Camaldoli monks Cyprian Consiglio, Bede Healey, Mark Mahoney, and Augustine Murray.

Foreword

The Heart of Dialogue

THOMAS G. HAND, S.J.

The papers in this book were presented during a remarkable week of inter-faith dialogue held at New Camaldoli Hermitage, Big Sur, California, from June 25 to July 1, 2000. Geographically, the setting for the international symposium was both symbolic and naturally superb. Built on a mountain-side rising up from the Big Sur coast, the monastery looks down on the Pacific from an elevation of thirteen hundred feet. Since it is a totally non-violent place, not only the redwood and oak trees, but also the quail, jays, foxes, deer and, hidden in the hills, even the mountain lions were our close companions all during the week. One truly symbolic element was that dur-ing the whole time we never once saw the ocean itself. Night and day it was covered by a sea of low-lying cloud. Sometimes the fog would rise all the way up to the monastery and make mystery of everything. In general, though, we were in the bright sun above the clouds. Only on the last morning did the deep blue ocean and the white breakers on the coast reveal themselves. The symbolism comes from both East and West. The East loves the "cloud sea." One of the special attractions of the Yellow Mountains in central China is the cloud sea and its sense of mystery. In the Judeo-Christian tradition the deepest mysteries of reality are in and above the clouds which veil our world. To rise into and above the cloud of unknowing is to ascend into higher, even the Highest Truth. All during the week of dialogue we were touching this Truth and being mutually enlightened. We were riding on the clouds of each tradition: Hindu, Buddhist, Taoist, Confucian, and Judeo-Christian. Taoists often picture their fully realized sages, the Immortals, as riding the clouds. Each participant in the symposium was certainly elevated above our ordinary cloudy way of seeing reality by the enlightening energy of the group.

Another feature of the geography of the hermitage was an accurate meta-phor of the event. Both physically and symbolically the background of the monastery stretches across the whole American continent to Europe and the Near East with its long tradition of Christian monasticism. In front, all the monastics and others gathered for the dialogue were facing across the "Peaceful Ocean" to China, Japan, even to India and the whole East.

This means that the representatives of the East—Hindu, Buddhist, Taoist, and Confucian—were from their side facing West. This meeting was pacific, broad and deep. When the first missionaries went and faced Japan they sometimes cast down the Buddhist "idols." Nowadays the idols that tumble are those of illusion and attachment, so as to reveal the purity of heart shining out from all spiritual traditions.

The depth of the dialogue was immensely promoted by the rich hospitality and profound liturgies of the Camaldolese monks. Also, the silent sitting we did together made us of one heart like nothing else. The energy of place, people, and program was amazingly effective, to say the least.

The word "energy" is deliberately used to describe the movement of dialogue. Energy, formed by Aristotle from *en* and *ergein* and meaning "at work," is appropriate, because the Spirit was certainly at work in each presenter and in all the respondents and discussants. Using a Chinese character, the whole dialogue took place in the realm of *hsin* (or *xin;* Japanese *shin*). The short discussion we had about how to translate this Chinese ideogram into English highlighted the quality of the energy movement and indicates how a person can best read these papers. They are to be read with one's whole *hsin*.

For many years *hsin* was usually translated as Mind (with a capital "M"). But anyone who knows Chinese or Japanese knows that this is too restrictive a rendering. Lately many translate it as "heart/mind" or even as "psyche." The point is that *hsin* is an extremely big, all-encompassing word. Besides meaning the physical heart and the vague "heart of a person," it also refers to all the interior faculties and activities of the human person: intuiting, conceptualizing, reasoning, willing, imagining, and emoting of all kinds. As the papers of this compilation were presented, all the powers of our psyches were activated. Academic as it was, the symposium was much more. The whole *hsin* (heart/mind) of each of us was touched and transformed.

These chapters can be read with academic eyes, but it is the hope of the Camaldolese Institute for East-West Dialogue and of all the members of the symposium that they also be read with the eye of the heart, in its full and rich meaning, and that lives will be reshaped.

The general theme of the whole project can easily and surely carry us beyond the merely academic, valuable as it is. The theme was taken from the Sermon on the Mount: Blessed are the *pure of heart,* they shall *see* God. Purity of heart leading to contemplation speaks to the mind, heart, psyche, and life of every human being. It was certainly no mere coincidence that the symposium was held at a hermitage/monastery dedicated to the Immaculate Heart of Mary, and that it ended on this very patronal feast day itself. Another rendition of this title of Mary is the Most Pure Heart of Mary (Ch. *chwen hsin;* Ja. *jun shin*). This was the gift, to some degree, that we all returned home with. Our very psyches were purified and changed. Again, it is with this in mind that we offer this collection of papers on purity of heart leading to contemplation.

On the last day it was remarked that the future of Christian spirituality is to be found in dialogue such as we had just had. It would seem that true and holistic dialogue is an important, even essential movement for the revitalization of all the spiritual paths of our global village.

Preface

The Dialogue in Its Monastic Setting
DAVID STEINDL-RAST, O.S.B.

Context makes all the difference. A fish on dry land quickly comes to realize this fact. But the women and men who wrote the pages you are about to read were in their element; they took to the monastic environment of the symposium like fish to water. In this book their papers stand without the context in which they were shared. While there remains much you will enjoy, your enjoyment will be more vivid if your imagination can supply the missing context—New Camaldoli Hermitage, its daily rhythm, its setting high above the Pacific, its romantic white-robed monks, the somewhat less romantic symposium participants, and their interactions during one of those weeks that linger long in one's memory and keep sparkling.

Start by imagining a fountain surrounded by banks of fragrant herbs. There is sagebrush and there is lavender, representing two different cultures related to this spot. The velvety aroma of sagebrush native to these hills evokes memories of the tribes that lived on this land for five thousand years—Esalen and Salinas Indians. They used sagebrush in their sacred rituals and smudged themselves with its fragrant smoke. The fresh scent of lavender native to the Mediterranean coastlands, so similar in climate to the Big Sur coast, recalls the past of the monks who came across the sea to found this monastery. For centuries monks of their order had perfumed altar cloths and linen chests with lavender back in Italy. They also used its refreshing scent for products of their ancient *farmacia*. Here now, while bees are busy among the purple spikes, the fountain freshens the air that makes the fragrances of sage and lavender rise and mingle one with the other.

What an incredible exuberance, a fountain in this semi-arid area; what a powerful symbol, what a gift. We know that this water is preserved and circulated back; still, the image remains one of superabundance. The heart of a medieval monastery was a cloister garden; the monks called it *Paradise*. In the middle of that paradise splattered a fountain. Here, too, in this new foundation, eight hundred years and the breadth of an ocean and the width of a continent removed from the medieval Camaldoli, the symbols of paradise and fountain have found a new embodiment. Here, too, they form the hub of the monastic complex, a center of stillness at the intersection of busy walkways. Monks who sit on the benches surrounding this fountain can listen to quail calling from covey to covey and to the shrieks of bluejays above the *cantus firmus* of the fountain's sound and the humming of bees. The message of this music is: peace.

During the week of the monastic dialogue between Christian and Asian traditions, the symbol of the fountain in the Garden of Eden took on an added significance. It brought to mind a passage from the book of Genesis: "A river flowed from Eden to water the garden, and from there it divided to make four streams" (2:10). Participants experienced every day the reality behind this biblical metaphor: the streams of the spiritual traditions that water the world flow from one and the same source. To the four corners of the Earth they flow out, yet all who drink from them can taste the flavor of their common origin.

The lively discussions that followed the papers gathered in this volume tapped again and again a source which all spiritual traditions share, no matter how much they differ one from the other. Long ago, that source sprang up at the fountainhead of each tradition, but it still springs up to-day, this living water of the *garden enclosed* (Song of Songs 2:12), in the heart of each practitioner. The women and men who had been invited to this international symposium were not all monastics, but all of them were practitioners—*scholar practitioners*. Their papers, printed here, maintain high scholarly standards, yet their authors are not interested in academic trivia. Their central concern is spiritual practice. That is why their papers are anything but dry. In the lively exchanges which these papers called forth, one could always hear the sound of the fountain *that makes the garden fertile,* the *well of living water* (Song 4:15). This is why, despite all differences of terminology (at times aggravated by heavy accents), all spoke the same language.

Between monastics and other practitioners runs only a blurred demarcation line; between practitioners and mere adherents of a given tradition stretches a chasm. A practicing Buddhist and a practicing Christian have little in common with those of their own tradition who do not practice what they profess; to each other, however, these two practitioners are close in spirit. Monastics are practitioners who have found their physical home in a monastery. This is a rare blessing, and it is getting rarer in our time. Yet, at the same time, householders who find their spiritual home in a monastery are increasing in numbers. "Oblates" Benedictines call these men and women who formally commit themselves to membership in an extended monastic community. New Camaldoli counts ten oblates for every monk who lives in the monastery. In some other monasteries the proportion is even higher. The number of oblates is growing faster than that of monks. The implications are far reaching and the consequences difficult to predict.

This was a frequent topic of informal conversations at the symposium. The shifting proportion between householders and monastics is of concern to both Buddhist and Christian practitioners in America, though the two traditions are moving toward each other from opposite directions. Until recently, it was widely assumed that Buddhism in America would remain a lay movement. Yet, more and more American Buddhist monastics are rising to prominence, among them outstanding women. Many of the teachers who brought Buddhism from Asia are passing on their leadership roles to their most dedicated American disciples, and those are not infrequently monastics. Through books, lectures, and the media, the impact of women like Pema Chodren or Thubten Chodron—to name but two examples—is considerable.

These two examples could be matched by the names of, say, Gunilla Norris or Esther de Waal, oblates who have done as much as many monks to call attention to the significance of Christian monasticism for householders. While Christian practitioners are discovering that the spiritual riches of monastic tradition are not the exclusive property of monastics, Buddhist practitioners are becoming aware of the unique role monastics play in preserving and transmitting the tradition of their practice. Several of the Buddhist participants at the symposium had just a few days earlier attended a large gathering of American Buddhist teachers. There, in the presence of H.H. the Dalai Lama and with his backing, the importance of monasticism for American Buddhists had been acknowledged "for the first time," they said. Future spiritual practice in America, both Christian and Buddhist, might well be predominantly a lay movement in the secular desert for which monasteries—few and far between—serve as spiritual watering-holes. Here the archetypes of paradise and fountain merge with that of the oasis.

It made all the difference that the Dialogue between Christian and Asian Traditions of which this book is a tangible fruit was a monastic dialogue—that it focused on topics central to monastic traditions East and West and, above all, that it took place at a monastery. The rhythm of the monastic day was the rhythm of this symposium. The silence of the monastery was the matrix for the Dialogue. This is the reason why our exchanges were indeed a heart-to-heart sharing. Words that do not come out of silence are merely chitchat. The day started at dawn with the monks chanting Vigils. Chant does not break the silence; chant lets the silence come to word—like the trickling of water or the sound of wind in the pines. There was much talking during the day, but little small talk. During breaks and at meals the discussions that followed the reading of each paper continued full force in smaller groups. But many participants felt that the deepest communication took place when we were silent together.

After Vespers each evening, the monks walked in procession to the Lady Chapel to sing the ancient *Salve Regina* before an icon of Mary with the

Christ-child. One must experience this brief ritual to feel how image and melody together make one's heart ready to let itself down into the ultimate mothering silence. Right afterward, all were invited to return to the octagon of the Chapel to practice sitting meditation in silence for half an hour. The high-domed, dimly lit space, stark empty except for the stone cube of the altar in the center, gives one the feeling of a *Zendo*—all the more so, as many were sitting upon cushions on the floor. Here, if anywhere, it was brought home to us that silence unites. We drank it in deep drafts like crystal-clear water from a shared cup.

Interreligious dialogue becomes a different reality in a monastic setting. Shared practice gives it a new actuality. When silence is the matrix for dialogue, the partners do not start out from positions set over against one another; rather, they start out from a shared position. Starting from their common ground, they proceed to compare their respective peculiarities. This kind of dialogue between traditions holds great promise for increased cooperation and understanding, because a deep communality is present from the outset.

By a most significant synchronicity, the first day of the symposium was the charter signing day for the United Religions Initiative (URI), a breakthrough event in the history of our planet. This grassroots initiative was stimulated by the troubling fact that the world community has a United Nations but still lacks a United Religions. Is not the struggle for peace on earth a religious one? Shouldn't religion be united, too? Those who think so created URI.

The garden with its fountain was less an image of *paradise lost,* in those days of the symposium, than an anticipation of *paradise re-created.* In twelve places around the globe practitioners joined in signing the Charter of the United Religions Initiative on June 26, 2000; the monastery at Big Sur was one of these places. With the sense of crossing a decisive threshold the monks and their scholarly guests talked about the significance of this day. Someone noticed that URI sounds like "you are I"—another unplanned coincidence, we were told. "Love thy neighbor as thyself" (Lev 19:18; Mk 12:31) does not suggest an effort to love one's "you" *as if* the "other" were oneself; it takes for granted that there is no other. On the deepest level we are one. My love for you as neighbor simply acknowledges the fact that you are I. All who practice their faith (whatever faith it may be) live by this truth.

Living this truth is not always as easy as it was during that week at New Camaldoli. Hospitality is the celebration of a communion based on the you-are-I insight. The smallest kindness to a stranger on a commuter train is hospitality in this sense, no less than volunteer work at a soup kitchen or a demonstration for the rights of an ethnic or sexual minority. But there are times when hospitality becomes pure celebration—in the sense in which *service* means not only table waiting, but also liturgy. During the symposium, the prior of the hermitage wore his kitchen apron no less festively than his priestly vestments. The service offered by the monks was all the more impressive for being so well hidden. To make a large conference run smoothly—housing, transportation, and a thousand minor details—is a formidable task. The monastic community rose to this task with radiant gracefulness.

Memorable conversations took place on an afternoon of hiking. The land below the hermitage descends for some thousand feet straight down to the Pacific. There are no houses in sight. The level surface of the ocean appears to rise steeply up to the horizon, so that the coastline with its white foaming breakers seems to form a deep trench between descending land and ascending sea. The land above the shelf on which the monastery is built continues to rise for several thousand feet. The vistas from these slopes are breathtaking. We walked on dusty, narrow fire roads shaded for stretches by tall ponderosa pines. Their bark, warmed by the sun, fills the air with fragrance and in their needles the summer breeze makes a music no instrument can imitate. High up near a small lake generations of native women used to grind acorns, a staple food for tribes who migrated seasonally between their camps in the hills and their fishing spots near the hot springs on the coast below. Only their mortar holes remain. Cut into a huge rock near the lake and polished smooth by millennia of use, they are shaded by live oak trees, old enough to still have seen the last survivors of that vanished world.

When you read a paper about mystical experience, imagine it being discussed on a walk under oak trees and pines; this context will make it lighter. When you read about Taoist alchemy, think of it as a topic of conversation at the cookout under the pepper trees. Picture the more formal exchanges after each paper as characteristically informal—all on a first name basis, no titles, no pretense—and full of surprises. Moments of surprising insight light up in my memory: a Buddhist monk looks up to the crucifix above the blackboard and remarks, "If this is not the First Noble Truth ("Suffering is all-pervasive"), what is it?" A young Camaldolese monk whom we had mostly seen with stacks of dirty dishes joins in the formal discussion at a crucial point and clarifies with ease an obscure passage in Plato's *Timaeos*. (Humility was more often displayed than discussed; appropriately so.) A Buddhist abbot and poet reads Psalms in his own English version and Christian monks find themselves more deeply moved thereby than they ever were by reciting them in choir. A Benedictine monk reveals himself as a first-class actor, playing Thomas Merton in the dramatic reading of a paper written with surprising imagination. Many participants considered it the greatest surprise of the symposium that one speaker did not go beyond the allotted time! There never seemed enough time for papers or discussions. The exchanges were always at their liveliest and many hands were still raised, when time was up.

The deepest sharing, though, took place at times of silence—at the silent sitting after Vespers and at a special Interfaith Prayer Service. At other times, too, some of the most memorable messages came across without words. By merely observing the way a young Taoist practitioner sat upright I learned to be doubly alert to my own tendency to slouch and slump. Often a Chinese character scribbled on the blackboard and briefly explained taught more than a torrent of words. But in this Interfaith Prayer Service the silence itself became the teaching; words fell away like husks falling from the sweet kernel when it is ripe. There were still symbols in this silence—candle flame, charcoal glow, smoke of incense rising, water. There was still the sound of bell and gong, giving voice to Western and Eastern traditions in turn. The bell ringing out in a pattern of ever-widening circles of sound; the gong humming with a resonance that draws itself back into itself until it reaches the innermost center of silence—the same silence to which the song of the bell finds its way beyond the beyond; the *same,* because silence is one. And being one, silence unites.

Walking out into the open after this service I felt one not only with all who had shared the experience, but with the swallows feeding their fledglings in a nest above the chapel door, with the lizards doing push-ups on the sun-warmed rocks, with Mr. Blue (the cat on the prowl) for whom swallow and lizard are potential supper. What made this privileged plot of ground appear like Eden was not that *the lion* lay *down with the* lamb—it didn't (witness the cat and the birds)—but that, nevertheless, there was peace. As I listened once again to the splatter of the fountain, I remembered what one Buddhist had said at this symposium: "I learned a lot about the Bodhisattva path from Christians." I remembered what a Jesuit had said somewhere else: "Those Buddhists will make a Christian out of me yet!" And I remembered, above all, the story which a Hassidic Rabbi had told at one of the earliest monastic interreligious dialogues, half a century ago. The story had become a reality, then, in the telling; to me it seemed to have become reality again at this moment. That is why I am retelling it here as a closing to this foreword and an opening to the book itself.

A rabbi and his close disciples celebrating the Sabbath together had reached such a pitch of ecstatic peace that the rabbi sent one of the students: "Quick, go to the window to see if the Messiah has come!" The scout returned disappointed: "Out there everything is going on as always. Nothing has changed." "But Rebbe," another student questioned, "If the Messiah had come, would you have to look out the window? Wouldn't you know it in here?"—"Oh, in here," the rabbi answered, "In here the Messiah *has* come!"

Introduction

BRUNO BARNHART, O.S.B. CAM.,
AND JOSEPH H. WONG, O.S.B. CAM.

The Background

A Pivotal Moment

This book is the fruit of an exchange between representatives of Asian monastic traditions and Christian monks and nuns at New Camaldoli. The dialogue event, along with several similar meetings in recent years, is a striking historical sign.

This intentional dialogue between religious traditions is something new. It corresponds to the unique moment in history which is our own time, the turn of the millennium. This time has been called the era of the emergence of a *global consciousness*.[1] In the Roman Catholic Church, the event which has, above all others, characterized this historical turning point is the Second Vatican Council. It was in the documents of this council that the church manifested a decisive turning toward the world, toward contemporary culture and—most important for us here—toward the other religious traditions.

Among the world's religious traditions, it is those of the East—the great Asian traditions of Hinduism, Buddhism, and Taoism—which have been of particular interest to Western monks.[2] Asia is the original homeland of monasticism; the Asian traditions of asceticism and of contemplative spirituality can be traced back many centuries before the time of Christ—and centuries more before the beginning of Christian monasticism. For over a thousand years, European Christianity lived in nearly complete isolation from the great Asian traditions. Then, during the past five hundred years, missionaries carried Christianity to the East—with limited success. During the second half of the twentieth century, the Asian religions came to the West,[3] and began to exert a deep influence upon the contemplative spirituality of Europe and North America. The present dialogue is a moment in this new interaction between East and West on the level of contemplative life.

The one fundamental orientation which is common to these practitioners of the different traditions is the spiritual quest:[4] a commitment to "seeking God," in the words of St. Benedict, to the pursuit of liberation, or of

1

nirvana, or union with the divine Absolute. Today, however, a second axis appears, perpendicular to that movement of spiritual progression, of self-transcendence and divine union. It is the "lateral" dimension of dialogue, of intentional interaction with other spiritual traditions.

Interreligious dialogue presupposes a solid grounding—experiential as well as doctrinal—in one's own tradition. Those who have been able to participate in the dialogue from such a position have tasted its fruits. Among the most important of these is a deeper grasp of one's own "Mystery," a deeper and more differentiated understanding of the essential core of one's faith and journey. At the same time, paradoxically, one may discover a level of solidarity and communion which crosses all of the boundaries that divide humanity today. Beyond all that can be comprehended from where one stands, one becomes aware of participating in an all-embracing process. A new world is coming to be, and it is characterized by global interaction.

Monastic Dialogue

One consequence of the new openness to the world's religions on the part of the Roman Catholic Church which emerged in the Second Vatican Council has been an official encouragement to monastic men and women to engage in dialogue with representatives of the monastic traditions of the other religious traditions.[5] This task has been taken up by Benedictine monks in Europe and America.[6] The Camaldolese have joined energetically in the dialogue, stimulated largely by the entrance of Father Bede Griffiths and his South Indian Ashram, Shantivanam, into the congregation.

During the past forty years a wide variety of Asian religious traditions have established themselves in North America. It is not surprising that this diverse Asian spiritual presence is especially evident in California. The monks of New Camaldoli, the hermitage on the Big Sur coast of central California, have through the years had frequent contact with practitioners of the Zen Buddhist tradition. Hindu influence has come mostly through Bede Griffiths, in his visits to Big Sur and in his writings.

Origin of the Symposium

The present symposium is a fruit of the interest and energy of Father Joseph Wong, a Chinese from Hong Kong, theologian and monk of New Camaldoli. The presence of the Chinese traditions of Taoism, Confucianism, and Chan Buddhism, unusual in Asian-Christian dialogue events until now, is due to Joseph Wong's personal connections and his efforts. The symposium was the first major event held by the Camaldolese Institute for East-West Dialogue, of which Joseph is the founder. Rev. Heng Sure, of the Institute for World Religions in Berkeley, was of great assistance in bringing together the participants from the Chinese traditions.

The Participants and the Program

The Vision

Joseph Wong's initial idea was a broad monastic encounter between Christian monastics and practitioners of the major Asian spiritual traditions: Hindu, Buddhist, Taoist, and Confucian. Dialogue between Hindus and Christians has been going on for several decades,[7] and Buddhist-Christian dialogue is well established.[8] Interaction between Christian monastics and the Chinese traditions of Taoism, Confucianism and Chan Buddhism, however, is only in its beginnings. The symposium is a landmark particularly in this area of dialogue.

The Participants

We wanted to create a *monastic* symposium; that is, not only an exchange focused upon a subject which is central to monasticism, but one in which the intellectual communication was grounded in contemplative practice. In aiming at a balance and integration of spiritual practice and disciplined scholarship, both monastic and academic scholars were invited. Participants included both those who presented papers and the "discussants" who responded to the papers.[9] On the Christian side, the Camaldolese Benedictine participants were, of course, most numerous. Three members of the Institute for World Religions in Berkeley represented the Chan Buddhist tradition. The Benedictine "Monastic Interreligious Dialogue" was represented by its two principal officers and other past and present members. Pascaline Coff, John Borelli, David Steindl-Rast, Thomas Hand, and Thomas Matus brought to the symposium an extensive experience of East-West dialogue. In addition to Joseph Wong, two other Chinese-born scholars were present: Professors Chung-ying Cheng and Liu Xiaogan.

The Program

The program continued for five busy days, with four separate presentations and discussions each day. Each forty-minute presentation was followed by the response of the designated "discussant" and then by a general discussion. All of this was carried on within the framework of the daily monastic program of prayer and meditation. Scriptures from the various traditions were read at evening prayer. In the middle of the week, evening prayer was celebrated in the form of an interfaith service, with a more ample selection of readings from Eastern and Western traditions. This liturgy incorporated the Indian ritual of *arati* (blessing with flame), a Native American blessing of the four directions of the earth, and the chants of Shantivanam (the South-Indian ashram of Bede Griffiths). There was much lively interaction outside the more formal sessions. Participants remarked again and again on the freshness and vitality they experienced during these days. Brother David and Father Tom Hand have both been able to convey something of this flavor of the week.[10]

Purity of Heart—Contemplation

We chose as topic of the symposium a double theme: *Purity of Heart and Contemplation*. The participants presenting a paper were asked to treat one or both of the two terms, or to discuss the close link between them. Although "purity of heart" and "contemplation" may seem typical Christian terms, these ideas, expressed in a variety of terms, are central to most Asian religious traditions. Regarding the second theme of the title, confusion may arise when the words "contemplation" and "meditation" are used interchangeably. A working distinction between the two terms may help: We shall consider meditation as a *practice* preparatory to the *experience* of contemplation.[11] While meditation usually involves an effort of concentration, contemplation is a direct intuitive seeing, using spiritual faculties beyond discursive thinking. However, Asian traditions tend to use the term "meditation" to include what Christian tradition would call "contemplation," and the two terms are not used consistently by different authors in this book. Here we shall briefly sketch the historical development of the double theme "purity of heart—contemplation" in the Christian monastic tradition, and then point out its importance in various Asian traditions, along with the consistently intimate relation between the two terms.

The relevance of the theme of purity of heart among Christian monastics can be seen clearly in a recent book, *Purity of Heart in Early Ascetic and Monastic Literature*. The book is a collection of essays, written mainly by Benedictine monks and nuns, to commemorate Sister Juana Raasch, O.S.B. (1927–74), who had led the way with her research on the topic of purity of heart in early Christian monastic writings.[12] Among the early Greek Fathers, the conjunction of the ideas of purity of heart and contemplation originated with Clement of Alexandria, who proposed two basic stages of spiritual life: ascetic practice (*praxis*) and contemplation (*theoria*). The goal of ascetic practice is to arrive at *apatheia* (which can be translated as "passionlessness" or "freedom from passion"), so that one can contemplate God with a serene and clear mind.[13] Origen adopted and developed Clement's two stages of spiritual life into three stages by further distinguishing between two grades of contemplation: contemplation of created things and contemplation of God.[14]

The division of the spiritual life into two major stages was brought into the monastic circle by Evagrius Ponticus. He followed the Platonic division of the soul into three parts: rational, irascible, and concupiscible.[15] The latter two are also called the passionate part of the soul and are understood as the source of resistance and repulsion on the one hand, and of desire and attraction on the other. However *apatheia,* the goal of ascetic practice, does not signify the suppression of passions; rather, it means integration of attractions and repulsions in a tranquil personality. It is necessary to purify the passionate part of the soul so that the rational part may devote itself to contemplation. Thus ascetic practice consists in combating passionate "thoughts," or vices, and cultivating virtues.[16] Evagrius points to *agape* (love) as the link connecting *apatheia* and contemplation: "Now this *apatheia* has a child called *agape* who keeps the door to deep knowledge of the created universe."[17] Although in his work *The Praktikos* Evagrius employs almost exclusively the term *apatheia* for the goal of ascetic practice, in his other writings he uses the more biblical expression "purity of heart" for the same purpose.[18] The idea of "purity" often appears in the expression "pure prayer," which means an encounter with God without the mediation of image or concept.[19]

Borrowing much of his teaching on this topic from his master Evagrius, Cassian consistently renders *apatheia* by the biblical expression "purity of heart." He presents purity of heart as the nearer "goal" (Gk. *skopos*) of the monastic life, while indicating the "kingdom of God" as its ultimate "end" (Gk. *telos*).[20] Cassian's "purity of heart" has a range of meaning, including *apatheia,* or freedom from harmful passion,[21] tranquillity of mind,[22] stability of mind,[23] chastity,[24] etc. In particular, Cassian identifies perfect purity of heart with *love* as described by Paul in his letter to the Corinthians (1 Cor 13:4–7).[25]

Cassian also follows his monastic predecessors in describing the intimate interdependence of ascetical maturity and deepening spiritual insight:[26] "Therefore, if you wish to prepare a sacred tabernacle of spiritual knowledge in your heart, cleanse yourselves from the contagion of every vice and strip yourselves of the cares of the present world."[27] He also writes: "If you wish to attain to a true knowledge of Scripture . . . you must first hasten to acquire a steadfast humility of heart. . . . For it is impossible for the impure mind to receive the gift of spiritual knowledge."[28] For Cassian, spiritual knowledge or contemplation means, above all, true understanding of Scripture, which is a gift of the Holy Spirit. It is interesting to note that in this passage Cassian equates "humility of heart" with purity of mind, as an indispensable condition for receiving the gift of spiritual knowledge.

Relying on Jesus' promise in his Sermon on the Mount, "Blessed are the pure of heart, for they shall see God" (Mt 5:8), Cassian believes that in the world to come, the saints will enjoy the "contemplation of divine things in perpetual purity of heart."[29] What we are striving to do, here and now, in attaining purity of heart so as to experience contemplation, is simply an anticipation of eternal life. Thus the intimate connection between purity of heart and contemplation is ultimately based on Jesus' own teaching.

Commenting on this beatitude Gregory of Nyssa asserts that, since God lives in inaccessible light, his divine nature is incomprehensible and ineffable. The words of the Gospel do not mean, therefore, that one will have a direct vision of God when the soul's eye has been purified.[30] However, God has imprinted upon our heart the very image of his own glorious nature. This image, unfortunately, often lies hidden under foul coverings. If one's heart has been purified, one will see the image of the divine nature reflected in the beauty of one's own soul.[31] At this point, Gregory offers the apt metaphor of the *mirror*: "Though people who see the sun in a mirror do not gaze at the sky itself, yet they see the sun in the reflection of the mirror no less than those who look at its very orb."[32] Gregory employs the same images of mirror and the sun in his *Commentary on the Song of Songs*: "Thus, the mirror represents in its own being whatever is placed before it. So too the soul, when cleansed by the Word from vice, receives within itself the sun's orb and shines with this reflected light."[33] In Gregory's use of this metaphor of the mirror, there is a close connection between being "cleansed" and the "shining" forth of the light and beauty of the divine image. Thus the metaphor of the mirror admirably expresses the relationship between our two themes of purity of heart and contemplation.

The comparison of the human heart or mind to a mirror is found in almost all the major religious traditions. Thus, for example, Lao Tzu asks the question: "In polishing and cleansing your profound mirror—can you do it so that it has no blemish?"[34] By "profound mirror" (*hsuan-chien*) Lao Tzu means the heart or mind, which, if kept clean and shining, will reflect Tao present in all things. In another chapter of the *Tao-te-ching*, Lao Tzu gives the following exhortation: "Attain utmost emptiness; maintain complete stillness. The ten thousand things rise together. And I contemplate (*kuan*) their return. All things flourish, each returning to its root."[35] Here "emptiness" and "stillness" refer to the inner state of the mind, which is necessary for "contemplating" things as they rise from and return to their ultimate source and root—Tao. Thus, "emptiness," or nonattachment, and "stillness" are different expressions of purity for Lao Tzu.

Chuang Tzu, likewise, compares the sage's mind to a mirror. He points out that water, when it is still, gives back a clear image of beard and eyebrows. Chuang Tzu continues: "And if water in stillness possesses such clarity, how much more does most pure spirit. The sage's mind in stillness is the mirror of heaven and earth, the glass of the ten thousand things."[36] Like still water, a tranquil mind can serve as a mirror to reflect heaven and earth and the myriad things on earth, perceiving the presence of Tao in all things. In the well-known colloquy on "fasting of the mind," Chuang Tzu states: "Tao gathers only in emptiness. Emptiness is the fasting of the mind."[37] Just as the mind, when it is pure, can reflect Tao as present in all things, it is only when the mind is empty or nonattached that it can be the habitation of Tao.

In Chan or Zen Buddhism also the mind is compared to a mirror.[38] One of the aims of this school is to come to possess the "mirror mind" or "enlightened mind." William Johnston comments: "Just as the pure and polished mirror is completely transparent, receiving everything into itself without distortion and reflecting all objects as if they were appearing in it for the first time, so the enlightened mind is completely receptive and filled with wonder, seeing everything as if for the first time." The "mirror-mind" is also called "no-mind." One attains this "no-mind," as Johnston suggests, by becoming *mu,* that is, by keeping one's mind totally open and never fixed on any particular object, not even on itself.[39] With the understanding of the "mirror mind" as "no-mind," purity means "self-emptying."

The Yoga system, one of the classical schools of Indian philosophy, forms the basis of much of Hindu spirituality. In the *Yoga Sutra,* Patanjali defines Yoga as "the cessation of the modifications of the mind."[40] The object of meditation and other ascetic practices is to still the mind so that the pure absolute spirit (*purusha*) may become manifest in one's consciousness. In order to achieve this goal, classical Yoga proposes an eight-step discipline, starting with moral restraints and observances, progressing through meditation techniques, and arriving at the final stage of "one-pointedness" (*samadhi*).[41] When the yogi attains the stage of *samadhi,* there occurs the complete cessation of the modifications of the mind. Through the "illumination" (*prajna*) spontaneously experienced at this stage, the yogi experiences his or her true nature as pure consciousness, which is free of all material attributes.

Thus, in the Yoga system "one-pointedness" and "illumination" (*samadhi* and *prajna*) are comparable to purity of heart and contemplation, respectively. They are the fruits of a twofold purification: moral purification through ethical observances, and mental purification through meditational practices. The image of the mirror is applicable here also. Consciousness is reflected best in a pure heart, or a "mirror mind," so to speak. Here again, we meet the limit of the applicability of the metaphor of "mirror" for the mind: illumination in the Yoga system is an unmediated oneness with Consciousness Itself. Useful as it is, the image of the mirror is to be transcended in the nondual experience of most Asian traditions. The image will come to an end also in the Christian tradition: "For now we see in a mirror, dimly, but then we will see face to face" (1 Cor 13:12).[42]

The Common Quest

The thirty people who gathered at the hermitage for those June days were drawn together by a deep confluence of interests, and—not only the monastic participants—by a common experience, a common quest, the sense of a shared journey. Brother David Steindl-Rast has brought out this strong commonality among the practitioners in his Foreword.

The spiritual journeys of a Buddhist, a Taoist, and a Christian monk are different. But the word "journey" already expresses a commonality. So do the words "monk," "monastic," "practice," "meditation." Is it possible to further illuminate this broad area of common practice and common experience by developing a common language in which to express it?

The related themes "purity of heart" and "contemplation" were chosen for the symposium because of their centrality in the monastic quest, but also because of their universality. These two themes offer a meeting point, an area of spirituality which is shared by all the traditions involved. But there are other words, other features which further define the landscape of this area of commonality. As we briefly develop some of these themes, we shall sketch some central lines of continuity which relate the different essays in this book. The ten themes which follow may be seen as an unfolding of the implications of "purity of heart—contemplation."

1. The Journey

Common to the spiritual traditions of humankind is an awakening to the knowledge that *this is not all:* that there is somewhere to go. Common to all the essays which follow, therefore, is a spiritual quest, a journey. This journey is intrinsic to monasticism, and in its progression is the meaning of monastic life and practice. While the journey or process is described in different terms in each tradition, there is an essential sameness about these descriptions, for it is the same human being who is journeying, the same human structure in which the transformation takes place. We shall see also that there are strong convergences in the understandings of the journey's goal.

We shall encounter many different expressions of this journey: the discovery of one's true identity, of one's true self, restoration of the image of God, acquisition of the likeness of God, return to one's true nature, to innocence, to the chaos which is completeness, unity and harmony (Crowe); human development, growth (Healey), the transformation of desire (Healey and Freeman), final integration (Merton-Funk), a progression from baptismal to eucharistic life (Barnhart).

2. Paradox and Mystery: Beyond the Rational Known

The monastic journey is an experience of *liminality:* a sojourn outside the boundaries of normal human and religious life. Here lies an epistemological truth as well. The journey may lead one outside the boundaries of "normal" consciousness and thought—as, after all, does faith itself. We shall frequently encounter in these essays a "knowing in unknowing," alongside a new symbolic depth in the visible things that surround us. We shall also encounter rude paradox, the inversion of common wisdom and apparently of common sense. We shall meet the "holy fool" (Leighton), who belongs not only to Zen but to Christian monastic tradition. The boundaries both of human reason and of human knowing itself will be challenged. The realization of nonduality involves "unknowing" as well as paradox, the *coincidentia oppositorum.*

Apophatic theology,[43] while it remains central to Eastern Christianity, has often been forgotten in the West; its recovery today[44] is catalyzed by contact with the Asian traditions. While the apophatic way is well represented in our papers, particularly in those by Buddhist authors, the kataphatic[45] or positive way appears particularly in the work of Laurence Freeman and Bede Healey, writing of the transformation—rather than the extinction—of desire. From this perspective the spiritual journey appears as a progressive education of desire from a fixation upon visible and particular objects—persons or things—to a freedom which is a participation in the divine Absolute.

Kevin Hunt, writing of "doubt" and of the "Great Doubt" in Zen Buddhism, points to an interior crisis which involves a radical challenge to one's rationality. Here the paradox is experiential, intensely personal. Though experienced in very different cultural and historical contexts in Asian Buddhism and in Western Christianity, we may expect the challenge to the self, the invitation to self-transcendence, to be very similar.

3. Desire and Detachment

The spiritual journey is driven by a single, all-embracing desire. Yet the spiritual journey is understood almost universally as a path of detachment. This notion will surface again and again in almost every one of the papers. We have already spoken of the two ways: negative and positive.[46] Monastic—and traditional—spirituality tends to appear as predominantly a way of renunciation; today there is widespread interest in a recovery of the "positive" tradition of seeking union with the divine Absolute through the natural things that surround us—and through the positive activity of our own "natural" energies.

A spirituality of *desire,* encountered in the two essays in the book's final part, is not something new in Christian tradition. One finds it in St. Augustine and then at the heart of the monastic spiritual theology of the West which culminates in Bernard and in William of St. Thierry in the twelfth century. Desire is at the heart of the world's spiritual traditions, but almost always in a negative sense, within a spirituality of detachment or renunciation, of liberation from the "passions."[47] Detachment is the key to purity of heart, according to the principal traditions.

4. Meditation

Silent meditation is a primary meeting place of East and West today. During the symposium, the daily times of common meditation were experienced by many as times of a wordless communion deeper than the verbal exchanges could take them. "Meditation" has taken on a new meaning—and a new importance—for many people in the Western world during the past half-century, under the influence of the Asian spiritual traditions. Meditation, in this ancient sense, is not the rational reflection, the mental activity which the word has long denoted in the West, but a quiet centering, a movement into an interior simplicity and unity. *Zazen, transcendental meditation, centering prayer, Christian meditation, vipassana* have become familiar terms in Western spirituality. Silent meditation, a descent into the depths of consciousness and self, has assumed a new primacy in the spiritual life. Within the diversity of forms of meditation which we shall encounter in this book, one will find the same essential simplicity. Three of our Buddhist papers (Verhoeven, Heng Sure, Cook) and two of our Taoist papers (Liu, Crowe) concentrate on the practice of meditation, which is central to these two traditions. It is a component, however, of nearly every one of the paths which are described in this book.

5. Contemplation

The practice of meditation leads, the traditions tell us, to the experience of contemplation. *Samadhi, nirvana,* nondual consciousness, "seeing the One," divine union: the traditions offer many expressions for the supreme state of human consciousness. It is helpful to think of contemplation as *nondual consciousness,* though this language is not familiar in the West. We can understand this as the transparency of the transformed or liberated self, the natural luminosity of the realized person. Purity of heart—according to a Christian tradition which finds echoes in many of the other traditions—is the doorway and essential precondition of contemplation. Contemplation, in turn, is inseparable from love or compassion.

Hinduism and Buddhism have developed complex systems of contemplative practice and precise classifications of the varieties of contemplative consciousness and experience. In Christian tradition, baptismal initiation—the birth of the new self—may be seen as the basic contemplative or unitive experience (Barnhart). Contemplation and faith are two sides—light and dark—of the same reality, the same experience. Laurence Freeman finds in Simone Weil what seems an extension of "contemplation" not only into prayer but into study. It is essentially the practice of "attention" which opens the human spirit to divine union. Here we can see a close analogy to the role of meditation in the Asian traditions.

6. Nonduality

Meditation, as we have described it, is a descent into the depths or center of the human person which are characterized by *nonduality;* contemplation is the experience of this nonduality. This concept is central to the great Asian traditions of Hinduism, Buddhism, and Taoism.[48] This is the supreme idea which is at the heart of the "perennial philosophy,"[49] and probably it is the point of strongest contrast with the consciousness of the West—particularly of the modern secular West. From this point, however, Christian theology and spirituality may be opened to their intrinsic depth and fullness.[50] *Advaita, samadhi, satori, sunyata, nirvana, Tao:* these primary words at the heart of the Hindu, Buddhist, and Taoist traditions are different expressions of the central mystery of nonduality.

Nonduality is strongly present—whether explicitly or implicitly—in each of our Buddhist and Taoist papers, as well as in Vrajaprana's presentation of raja yoga. In Joseph Wong's paper, nonduality underlies the resonances between Chuang Tzu and Meister Eckhart. It is Eckhart—frequently seen as close to the Buddhist viewpoint—who is the clearest and most audacious exponent of nonduality among Christian writers. The reality, however, is abundantly present beneath the surface of the New Testament and of the more contemplative currents of Christian theology. Its Christian expressions, Barnhart suggests, differ largely from those of the Asian traditions, and follow an "incarnational" trajectory.

Nonduality appears under many different guises in the papers, particularly in the accounts of the Asian traditions. It is implicit in the *samadhi* attained through meditation (Vrajaprana, Verhoeven, Cook), in the *satori* and "becoming love" of Skudlarek, in the experience of the One in the Taoist tradition recalled by Liu ("keeping the One"), Crowe and Wong ("knowing the One," "seeing the One"), as well as in Eckhart's "breaking through" into the depths of God beyond knowledge and love (Wong) and in the return to the stillness and unity of the primal chaos (Crowe). It is implicit in the Confucian harmony and integration of the person (Corcoran) and in the *point vierge* of Sufism (Merton, Funk). Christian baptismal initiation is presented by Barnhart as an experience of a new birth into nonduality: an experience of "identity" in both senses of the word. Further, nonduality is experienced "horizontally" as well, in the koinonia or communion of the Christian disciples.

7. Heart, Center

In our primary theme "purity of heart," a center of the human being has been posited from the beginning. To the center denoted by the biblical term "heart" (*lev, kardia*) correspond more or less the terms in other traditions which refer to a point of ultimate depth, a point of equipoise between opposites, a single root of the human person, a meeting place of body, soul, and spirit. Thomas Matus brings our attention to this point in the Hindu tradition. Like Cyprian Consiglio (in "The Space in the Lotus of the Heart"), he finds here not only the meeting place of the Divine and the human, but also of the different religious traditions. The *point vierge* of Mary Margaret Funk's conversation with Thomas Merton directs us to the same central place of nonduality and fullness. As Norman Fischer concludes his introduction to his versions of the Psalms by bringing us to "this human heart before you now," we encounter the mystery of the person from a different side—within this world and its trouble and affliction—challenging every ideal of a tranquil spiritual realization beyond life's pain and diminishment.

8. Self and Self-Transcendence

Western spiritualities have usually been marked by the analytical bent of the Western mind, understanding the human person in terms of distinct faculties of senses, intellect, and will, and losing sight of the unity and integrity of the human person. Contact with the East today brings with it a renewed sense of the person as a whole: of the self. Transcendence of the ego-self, realization of the divine Self: this is the common denominator, the central axis of the spiritual journey which lies beneath the different expressions in these essays. Self is transcended "vertically" through interior participation in the divine Absolute. Self is transcended "horizontally" in relationship with other human beings, in community.

The classical spiritual ways of Hinduism and of Buddhism are clearly centered in a transcending of the ordinary self, or "ego." For the Hindu ascetic, the renunciation of this individual self is the way to realization of the *Atman,* or unitive and universal divine self. A Buddhist may refuse to recognize the reality of even such a transcendent self. Taoist masters will speak of the bringing of the self into harmony, unity, and its original simplicity, and Confucians will speak of self-cultivation. In Christianity, self-transcendence is understood to be rooted in the death and resurrection of Christ and in baptismal rebirth. Self-transcendence presents special problems—and perhaps a special promise—in the context of extreme individualism which is the modern Western world.

In reflecting on this journey of self-transcendence, we inevitably come to the controversial question of an anthropology: *who* is it that journeys? This is a central concern; all of our papers orbit around this human subject whose fulfillment, paradoxically, is in self-transcendence. In the very first of John Cassian's *Conferences,* Abba Moses responds to the basic need of the seeker for a goal: a conception, an image, a myth that indicates the way that is to be traveled. If *purity of heart* is the goal that Moses firmly points out, this is a modification of the person, of the subject, the self. We shall encounter many different expressions for this "subject." It is Buddhism which often carries the paradox of self-realization through self-transcendence to its extreme by denying the reality of any self. Here, in the apophatic nonduality of Buddhism, we shall encounter the strongest contrast with the "personalism" of the Judeo-Christian tradition and of the West.

Besides the traditional spiritual perspectives, we shall find in the essays that follow also some psychological approaches (sociological aspects of the person are hardly touched upon). We shall encounter a wide variety of expressions for the experience of the ultimate ground or subject: to see into one's own nature, to attain the true mind, the Buddha nature, to be a Buddha, to know one's self as mirror, to return to true nature, to become a whole person, to become the pure-hearted adept, the true person, the image of God, the one Son of God, to realize one's god-nature, to attain the true self, the embodied self, to realize the *point vierge* as the center of one's person and as a state of purity of heart, to become the new self, new person, the unitive self. Or, in a Western conception with an Eastern resonance, to become the true poet who is empty of identity (Freeman, quoting John Keats).

If "Self/Person" is at the center of the contrast—or complementarity—of the spiritual traditions of East and West, it is also the pivot of the evolution of these spiritualities from their "classical" forms into the present-day context. This is particularly true in the modern West, with its unparalleled emergence of the individual.

9. Wholeness and Multidimensionality

Does the world of the spirit have an intrinsic shape? Sister Vrajaprana offers such a basic template from the tradition of ancient Hinduism, as she presents the four yogas—*raja, jnana, bhakti,* and *karma* yoga—as the cardinal points of an all-embracing pattern. Here we may discern the outline of that human fullness which lies at the end of every spiritual path, and for which we have already encountered a variety of metaphors.[51] The ways of spiritual practice and progress which Vrajaprana outlines suggest also the intrinsic form of the human person: the figure of spiritual practice points to the structure of an anthropology. The papers will pursue one or another of these ways: the way of bodily practice (bowing: Heng Sure), the way of meditation (Verhoeven, Cook, Liu), the way of desire and its transformation (Healey, Freeman), the way of study (Simone Weil in Freeman). Christianity, because it tends to be defined by the Word and enclosed within verbal and conceptual structures, can glimpse once again its own intrinsic fullness in this inclusive vision of the spiritual world which derives from the ancient Hindu tradition.

Cyprian Consiglio's sketch of the three worlds of matter, soul/mind, and spirit extends this anthropological paradigm into a cosmic perspective. Wholeness characterizes the goal of Taoist practice (see Liu, Crowe) as well as that of psychotherapy (Healey); sometimes the paradigm is that of a harmonization within the person of the three spheres of body, mind, and spirit. We shall need, however, to reflect upon these ancient paradigms in the context of the world and the person of today. Has a further dynamism—within history and within the person—emerged in recent centuries which must be taken into account?

10. The Word

Finally, we must introduce a term which is common to only "one side" of the dialogue: to Judaism, Christianity, and Islam. If nonduality, or "The One," is the invisible center of the Asian traditions, it is the divine *Word* which is central to the traditions of Judaism, Christianity, and Islam. Christian monastic spirituality has been centered in the Word.[52] "Purity of heart" itself is a phrase taken from the Gospel of Matthew.[53] Inseparably joined to this divine Word are the basic and enduring conceptions of a personal God and of the human person, and of a relationship of faith and love as the context of the spiritual journey. Word implies *event,* and therefore meaning in *history.*

If the symposium contributions from the Christian side hardly reflect this primacy of the Word, this is largely because of the nature of the dialogue. Thomas Matus finds Sri Yukteswar expressing his yogic teachings in the language of the Bible. William Skudlarek considers Jesus' command, "Do not judge ... " from the perspective of Buddhist nondual consciousness. Barnhart points out that a Christian monastic theology is challenged today to integrate the revealed divine Word and the divine "nonduality" which is participated at the core of the human person. The one sustained treatment of the biblical Word during the symposium was Zen teacher Norman Fischer's presentation of his translations of selected psalms: the "music of enlightenment." Here was a real meeting of Asian and Judeo-Christian traditions, of meditation and the Word, in the experience and the words of a poet.[54]

The Dialogue

Levels of Dialogue

What was envisioned was a monastic dialogue between Christianity and the great Asian traditions of Hinduism, Buddhism (in its different currents), Taoism, and Confucianism, on the promising common ground of "purity of heart and contemplation." Actually, as we have seen, the situation is more complex. There are usually also one or more interior dialogues going on within an author's thought, and these may or may not become conscious and explicit in the presentation. This will be likely for a Westerner who is presenting an Eastern tradition, whether this person is doing so "from the outside" or has long been personally committed to the Eastern path. In addition to the conscious dialogue with another tradition, as we have seen, each of the participants is engaged in an inner dialogue between the classical expressions of their own tradition and contemporary spiritual experience— theirs and that of others.

Thomas Matus pointed out the distinction between *interreligious* and *intrareligious* dialogue: "the dialogue I carry on within myself, between a faith I share with others who believe as I do, and the experiences I receive through contact with persons who believe differently."[55] The symposium participants were experiencing both these conversations simultaneously, during much of the week.

In the final discussion, Father Thomas also distinguished four different levels of interreligious dialogue: shared life, shared action, theological exchange, and participation in another religious experience. The week of the symposium involved for the thirty participants a sharing of life, of meditation and worship, as well as an intense and extended theological exchange. For many of us it was an occasion of sharing our personal religious experience in conversation with someone who is walking on a different path.

The Matter of Dialogue

Some authors undertake a dialogue explicitly within their papers, by comparing figures or texts in two traditions. Others remain within one (usually their own) tradition, while suggesting or inviting comparison with another tradition. One paper (Barnhart) attempts an overall view of the influence of the Asian traditions on Christianity. Another (Freeman) follows a continuum of meaning through a number of texts from different traditions.

A frequent contrast that emerges in the papers is that between the unitive or "nondual" vision of the Eastern traditions (particularly Buddhism and Taoism) and the "dualistic" consciousness of the West—particularly of the modern West. (Nondual consciousness is also found in the mystical traditions of Christianity, but most Christian expressions of nonduality differ from those of the Asian traditions because of the incarnational dimension which characterizes them.) Often the confrontation is explicit. At other times it is audible in the background. The focus of the contrast may vary from morality to meditation to spiritual experience and its expression. A related comparison is between a spirituality of interior experience and an external religion of law, authority, and dogma.

Francis Cook contrasts Zen Buddhism, as a way of the transformation of consciousness centered in meditation and paying relatively less attention to external morality, with a Christianity which is concerned first and foremost with conformity of belief and behavior—and imposes this conformity with institutional authority. Martin Verhoeven contrasts a Buddhist spirituality which is unmediated and grounded entirely within the individual with a Christianity which relates to God as an external reality and relies on divine revelation and divine grace as external mediations.

Heng Sure contrasts the bodily realism of Chan Buddhist practice (specifically the practice of bowing) with modern Western attitudes for which such a practice is inconceivable.

Paul Crowe contrasts the positive Taoist conception of chaos—as a creative primal fullness—with the negative biblical view of chaos as a primal disorder upon which creation imposes an order. Implicitly here, a holistic Asian consciousness is contrasted with a dualistic Western mindset. Donald Corcoran contrasts a negative anthropology of Western Christianity—and a corresponding negative contamination of the Western notion of humility—with the positive view of the human person and positive teaching of self-cultivation in Confucianism.

Norman Fischer, a Zen Buddhist teacher of Jewish origin and a poet, speaks from within a complex web of contrasts. He poignantly expresses the tension which he feels between the luminous simplicity and tranquillity of Buddhist nondual consciousness and the passionate intensity and chiaroscuro of the biblical tradition, specifically of the Psalms. Buddhism's conclusive silence is contrasted with the urgency of speech, of language, with the passionate cry of the psalmist. There emerges not only a dialogue between Buddhist and biblical traditions, but between all the ancient spiritual traditions, on the one hand, and, on the other hand, contemporary human experience with its frequent meaninglessness and darkness, with its absence of God and sometimes—as in the Holocaust—with its raw, naked evil. He finds the Psalms, with their turbulence and darkness, more resonant with this experience than an Eastern passionlessness. Here one also feels a tension between the cool impersonality of the classical ascetic traditions and the acutely sensitive humanity, the intense subjectivity and imagination of the emergent individual. For Norman Fischer, it is because of this peculiar human experience of today that interreligious dialogue has become an urgent necessity. After explaining how he came to work on the Psalms, Fischer concludes,

> I feel that in our period it is the challenge of religious traditions to do something more than simply reassert and reinterpret their faiths, hoping for loyal adherents to what they perceive to be the true doctrine. Looking back at the last century, with its devastating wars and holocausts and the shock of ecological vulnerability, I have the sense that religious traditions must now have a wider mission, and it is in recognition of this mission, I believe, that interreligious dialogue becomes not only something polite and interesting, but also essential. I have come to feel, after working for many years intimately with many people along the course of their heartfelt spiritual journeys, that traditions now need to listen to the human heart before them as much and more than they listen to their various doctrines and beliefs.... [56]

Beneath the surface of the conversation which is this book, one may discern two great axes of dialogue. They are suggested in these words of Norman Fischer. Between East and West there is developing a dialogue of nondual consciousness with an objective divine revelation—the *One* with the *Word*. Across the wide gap that extends from the "axial time" of the birth of our classical religious traditions to our present moment emerges a further dialogue which is more difficult to name. In the simplest of terms—as a first approximation—it is the dialogue of spiritual tradition itself with the emerging person, with a humanity—individual and collective—which is awakening to self-consciousness at the center of a world in transformation. Today we awaken also to our own role—and our responsibility—in this transformation.

For the Reader

The order in which the papers appear in this book corresponds in general to the order of their presentation at the symposium. The Asian traditions are presented first, followed by the Christian (and Western) expressions. Within this framework the order is primarily historical: older traditions appear first. Among the different expressions of a given tradition, the "pure" treatments are presented first, followed by the comparative studies. A brief introduction will be found at the beginning of each Part.

The reader need not feel obliged to follow the order of the papers in the book, since each is essentially complete in itself. The widest panoramas are offered by Vrajaprana (from a Hindu perspective), by Barnhart (from a Christian perspective), and by Consiglio (from both Hindu and Christian viewpoints). One may choose to begin the journey in familiar territory, or through being introduced to a tradition to which one comes with fewer preconceptions. To experience the richness and depth of this encounter, however, one will do well, finally, to read all of the contributions. Altogether, it is quite a banquet.

Part I

HINDUISM

Hinduism is not a single distinct and coherent religion; the word has come to denote a wide spectrum of spiritual traditions of the different peoples of India. The traditions of India can, however, claim a certain primacy among the world's religions. It is in this fertile human soil that, over two thousand years ago, the spiritual aspiration had already manifested itself with the most luxuriant variety and with an unsurpassable depth and intensity. Our presentations of "Hindu" spirituality can only suggest something of these developments.

Pravrajika Vrajaprana presents the spiritual journey as a quest of the "kingdom" as one's true identity—a royal (divine) identity. The four "yogas" are paths responding to the individual temperaments of the seekers, but they also sketch out an anthropology, a paradigm of the fullness of humanity. Purity of heart is identification with the *Atman,* or true self. Contemplation is equivalent to *samadhi,* or divine union. This first presentation communicates both the breadth and the depth of experience that characterized this sunrise of the human spirit, marking out for us the dimensions of the country in which our subsequent encounters will take place.

Thomas Matus examines the Yogic tradition of Hinduism, with reference to its recent interaction with the spiritualities of the West. He chooses two texts from different strata of the tradition which present Yoga as "a way of the heart and to the heart, in view of the recognition of God in ourselves." The way is one of devotion, of "abiding in the heart." Once again, salvation is understood as a realization of one's own true nature—but also as vision of all other beings in God. This realization does not remove a person from the common human condition, from ordinary life.

Cyprian Consiglio studies the vision of Bede Griffiths, a contemporary Christian monk who spent much of his life in India, engaged in a dialogue between Hindu Vedanta and Christianity. The focus is particularly upon Griffiths's "tripartite anthropology": his conception of the human person as constituted by body, soul, and spirit and thus as integrating within itself all reality. Of particular interest is Griffiths's notion of *spirit,* the unitive ground of all created reality in which body and psyche, or matter and consciousness, are united.

The presentations of Vrajaprana and Cyprian Consiglio—to recall Brother David's metaphor—seem to place us in an original Paradise of human spirituality, with four rivers flowing from its center. It is as if—Bede Griffiths might say—all the possibilities of human spiritual realization had already emerged in this lush spiritual garden five hundred years before Christ. The diverse ways and their abundance are summed up in the term "Yoga." Thomas Matus focuses upon one of these ways: that of *bhakti* yoga, the way of devotion (emphasized also by Vrajaprana). Here his concern is with the "center": the human center which is the heart. Cyprian Consiglio also arrives at the heart-center, corresponding to the "human spirit." He proposes "the space in the lotus of the heart" as the common center, the meeting place of religions. These opening presentations from the Hindu tradition have sketched out for us the great dimensions of spiritual life and fixed the center of that spacious universe: the human heart.

1

Regaining the Lost Kingdom

Purity and Meditation
in the Hindu Spiritual Tradition

PRAVRAJIKA VRAJAPRANA

Long ago in ancient India there lived a king who ruled over the magnificent city of Smritinagar, which in Sanskrit means "the city of memory." One day the king—an avid and excellent hunter—left his kingdom before dawn to go hunting alone. He rode through his extensive lands and, crossing the borders of his kingdom, entered into a dense forest. As he rode through the forest, a snake suddenly slithered across the path; the horse reared and the king was thrown violently to the ground. The king lay unconscious for many hours; the horse returned riderless to the kingdom.

When the king finally awoke, he had no idea who he was or where he was. Since he was dressed in hunter's attire he assumed he must be a hunter who had lost his way. He made himself a rough dwelling and lived as a hunter. Yet despite his excellence in hunting, he was dissatisfied. He somehow didn't *feel* he was a hunter. He was also troubled by a recurring dream: in this dream he lived in a magnificent palace surrounded by riches, attended by his courtiers and cherished by his loving queen and children. But then he'd wake and find himself lying in the dirt of his hovel.

One day the hunter-king met a merchant in the forest and decided to tell him of his recurring dream. The merchant said, "Ah, I see you want to be rich! You should become a merchant like me—then you can be rich and buy yourself a kingdom!" The king thought the advice was good and went to the city with his deer skins to sell them in the market. Unfortunately, the king was an abysmal merchant and soon became bankrupt. He returned to the forest and the recurring dream continued.

Next the king met a soldier. Hearing his dream, the soldier told him that he should become a soldier; with martial skills he could simply take a kingdom by force. But when the king tried to enlist, he was told that he was too old and flabby to be a soldier.

Disheartened, the king finally encountered a *sadhu*—a wandering Hindu holy man—in the forest. "Where have you been, your majesty?" the *sadhu*

23

exclaimed. "The entire kingdom has been looking for you!" The king was baffled by these words and said, "I don't know what *you're* talking about but I *am* having this strange dream!" When he recounted his dream, the *sadhu* understood what had happened.

"Have no fear, my child," said the *sadhu,* "I can make your dream come true! All you need to do is to hire a white horse with a silver saddle. Ride into the neighboring kingdom of Smritinagar and proclaim yourself the king of Smritinagar." The king looked doubtful, so the *sadhu* added, "My austerities have given me the power to confer hypnotic speech. By my will, everyone who hears your words will believe you."

The king was a pious man and had faith in the *sadhu's* words. He hired a horse with a silver saddle and rode into the kingdom. He was apprehensive when he ran into a contingent of soldiers, but nevertheless said, "I am the king of Smritinagar!" To his astonishment, the soldiers dismounted and bowed low before him. His faith in the *sadhu's* words increased considerably. As he rode into the city proclaiming his identity, the king was greeted everywhere with jubilation. Soon he saw the palace looming ahead of him and then his memory returned. He realized that he really *was* the lost king of Smritinagar. Regaining his kingdom, the king lived happily and reigned wisely for a long, long time.

Every religious tradition has its teaching stories, and this one nicely illustrates two of Hinduism's primary tenets: first, that we are heirs to a glorious kingdom and second, that we are suffering from a spiritual amnesia which prevents us from claiming it.

How was the kingdom lost and how can it be regained? Hinduism says that we can't *really* lose our kingdom. Just as the king never really *lost* his kingdom—it was waiting for him all the time—our spiritual kingdom lies in the depths of our hearts and awaits our arrival.

Like the king, most human beings try doing the wrong things in order to regain what we instinctively sense we've lost. As Huston Smith once said, "Everyone possesses a God-shaped hole in the heart." Unfortunately, the human *modus operandi* is to try to fill that hole with the wrong shape—whether a healthy shape in the form of satisfying relationships, cultural and intellectual achievements and social activism, or an unhealthy shape in the form of addictive behaviors and injurious human relationships.

Our kingdom *appears* to be lost because of *maya*—ignorance of our true nature. Ignorance is removed through knowledge, and knowledge comes through meditation. But, without purification of the heart, meditation is a lost cause and spiritual attainment is impossible. This is Hinduism's basic equation for purity and meditation. As Swami Vivekananda said, "The Kingdom of Heaven is within us, but only the pure in heart can see the King."[1]

A quick caveat: There are many schools of Hinduism and giving them adequate representation within this short space isn't feasible. The views I present will lean heavily toward the Vedanta school—that is, the nondualistic philosophy of the Upanishads, Hinduism's most ancient and sacred texts. In the context of Hinduism, nondualism, or monism, means the philosophy which affirms the oneness of the individual soul, God, and the universe.

If God's kingdom lies within us, why are we unaware of it? Hinduism says that *maya* causes a spiritual amnesia which clouds our understanding and prevents us from knowing who we really are.

Who *are* we? While we appear to be limited mortals, we live, move, and have our being in Brahman—the infinite, transcendent Reality. Further, the very core of our being—the Atman—is divine and one with Brahman. The Atman isn't a little chunk of Brahman; the Atman *is* Brahman in all its infinite fullness. God within us is called "Atman" out of semantic necessity, but there is no essential difference between Atman and Brahman.

What artificially separates the Atman from Brahman is the body-mind complex. Maya makes us identify with our psychophysical characteristics rather than with our real nature which is pure, perfect, blissful, and ever free. Our true nature, the Atman, is untouched by birth and death, sorrow and delusion, hatred, fear, or any other human limitation.

Maya, like the king's amnesia, makes us forgetful of the divine treasure already in our possession. "The Lord created the senses to turn outward," the Katha Upanishad says, "hence we look outside instead of seeing the Atman within. Rare is the person who, longing for immortality, turns away from externals and beholds the Atman within."[2] When a Hindu reads John 1:5—"The light shineth in darkness and the darkness comprehended it not"—he or she will identify this as the veiling power of maya obscuring the divine light of the Atman.

The world we see around us is nothing *but* Brahman, but we see it through the prism of maya. It's a distorted vision, like an image in a funhouse mirror. The world that we see is circumscribed by time, space, causality, and by our mind's own limitations. "Nothing hinders the soul's knowledge of God as much as time and space," Meister Eckhart said, "for time and space are fragments whereas God is one!"[3]

This world of maya may not be *ultimately* real, but it's nevertheless real enough in our daily experience. I can't pretend that if I stub my toe it doesn't hurt; I can't pretend that if someone says something mean to me I don't react. In order to progress on our spiritual journey, we have to acknowledge our immediate reality with care, intelligence, and the quality that Cassian so greatly prized, discernment. Only then will we have access to higher levels of reality; only then will we be able to escape maya so that we *can* regain our kingdom. And that is where the practices of purification and meditation come in.

In Cassian's first conference, Abbot Moses says that while our ultimate goal is the kingdom of God, our attention must be placed on the immediate direction which takes us to our goal. He said: "Our objective is purity of heart...for without this the goal cannot be reached...you have purity of heart for an objective and eternal life as the goal."[4]

For serious Hindu practitioners these words ring sound and true. Purity is an absolute prerequisite in Hindu spirituality. It doesn't matter whether you're a dualist or nondualist, it doesn't matter to which philosophical school you belong, purity is seen as the basic requirement for an authentic spiritual life. In Hinduism purity and meditation are inextricably linked—either they go together or they don't go at all. It's really a pity that in the West the practice of meditation, which is strongly associated with Hinduism, is known and popular while its necessary counterpart, purity, is given precious little attention.

How does Hinduism define purity? The Atman is pure, perfect, and free, unaffected by desires and free from the vagaries of the body and mind. The more we identify with the Atman, the purer we are; the more we identify with the urges of the body and moods of the mind, the less pure we are.

For this reason Hinduism has always placed great importance on sexual restraint or *brahmacharya,* which literally means "the state of dwelling in Brahman"—that is, living in such a way that the mind remains identified with Brahman/Atman. Sexual desire intrudes powerfully on the body and mind: one who is in the grip of sexual passion becomes completely identified with the body, and the mind becomes a helpless hostage to its demands. Self-restraint—particularly sexual self-restraint—strengthens the body, mind, and, naturally, character. The more we face down desires, the more control we gain over the body-mind complex and the more peaceful our minds become. As the Bhagavad Gita says: "Those whose senses are not restrained have neither spiritual understanding nor the capacity for meditation. There is no peace for those who cannot meditate, and without peace, where is happiness?"[5]

I've singled out sexual desire since it's the most powerful, but in fact *all* desires and all attraction to sense pleasures make us identify ourselves as psychophysical beings rather than Spirit. Our senses, unless consciously restrained, will go out toward sense objects, "carrying away the mind," says the Bhagavad Gita, "as a gale tosses about a ship at sea."[6]

Developing purity is one of the central objectives of Hindu spiritual practice, and every major yoga—that is, spiritual path—puts great emphasis on its attainment. The word "yoga" comes from two different Sanskrit verb roots and has two different but complementary meanings: one is "concentration" and the other is "joining" or "yoking"—that is, yoking oneself to the divine. Unfortunately, when Westerners say "yoga" they usually mean hatha yoga—a technique of strengthening the body and increasing its longevity which has little to do with traditional meditation practices.[7]

Hinduism has historically recognized the need to provide various spiritual paths for differing psychological temperaments. Some people are predominantly emotional while others are intellectual. Some are active while others are contemplative. Rather than trying to cram various psychological dispositions into a one-size-fits-all religious approach, Hinduism has provided a spiritual path or yoga for each predominant temperament. While these paths of attainment have existed and have been practiced since ancient times, it was only in the nineteenth century that Swami Vivekananda formally systematized them into the four major yogas. Each yoga has a different approach for gaining purity while consistently stressing its necessity in spiritual practice.

Those who are predominantly emotional are suited for the path of devotion, or *bhakti yoga*. Those who are led by the head rather than the heart and have a powerful, discriminating intellect are qualified for the path of *jnana yoga*, the path of knowledge. *Karma yoga*, the path of selfless action, is for those with an active temperament, and those who are naturally contemplative are fit for the path of *raja yoga*, the royal path of meditation.

Every yoga results in regaining the divine kingdom and each yoga complements every other yoga. These yogas are not airtight compartments: they are meant to strengthen each another and build upon one another. No one is exclusively intellectual, emotional, active, or contemplative. While everyone has certain predispositions, the yogas are meant to balance one another so that our entire personality can be pulled into spiritual life.

Apart from purity and meditation, every yoga follows the two basic steps of withdrawing the mind from whatever is finite and relative, then focusing it on what is infinite, real, and absolute. These two steps call for two qualities which are indispensable in spiritual life: detachment from the finite and yearning for God or the Infinite.

Detachment doesn't mean indifference or coldness. These characteristics spring from egotism and self-centeredness, not spirituality. Real detachment is freedom from desires, freedom from our lower impulses. Hand in hand with detachment comes *attachment* to God or to the Atman. Unless we feel drawn to something higher, we won't be able to push away lower impulses. And unless we make an effort to subdue lower impulses, we won't succeed in drawing close to the divine.

Since every yoga utilizes meditation to a greater or lesser degree, I'll begin with *raja* yoga, the path of meditation. It's also in *raja* yoga where the issues of purity and its effect on meditation come into focus most clearly.

Raja Yoga—The Path of Meditation

For Hindus, meditation is not a relaxation technique—it's an intense and concentrated search for the divine reality within. According to Patanjali—the ancient sage and author of the *Yoga Sutras*—meditation is "an unbroken flow of thought toward the object of concentration"[8] and has been compared to an unbroken, steady stream of oil when poured from one vessel to another. In *raja* yoga, the object of meditation can either be the impersonal, formless Reality or a personal form of God.

But what happens when we sit to meditate? Once the mind is quiet and the externals are turned down, random messages start popping up from the subconscious. We suddenly remember where we left the keys or we create the perfect retort for yesterday's argument. While we tend to take these shortcomings personally, it's a universal human phenomenon and one that Patanjali thoroughly investigated.

Patanjali's *Yoga Sutras* are the first known attempt to systematize Indian psychology. In this classic text he has famously defined yoga as "control of the *vrittis* (thought-waves) of the mind."[9] The goal of *raja* yoga is to control these vrittis—our thought-waves—so that the Atman can be experienced, unimpeded by our ignorance and limitations.

Raja yoga's classic metaphor is that of a lake: When the surface of the lake is calm and tranquil, the bottom of the lake can be clearly seen. When the lake's surface is lashed into waves, the water becomes muddy and the lake bottom can't be seen. The bottom of the lake represents the Atman, the water is the mind, and the waves are the vrittis. If the vrittis are controlled, the mind will remain placid so that the Atman can shine forth in its own splendor. When the vrittis are under our control, we'll be able to uncover the treasure within us; we will regain our lost kingdom.

But to control the vrittis we must completely overhaul the mind itself and *that* means effecting a complete transformation of character. As St. Paul said in his Epistle to the Romans: "Be ye transformed by the renewing of your mind." As with everything else in spiritual life, easier said than done!

According to Hindu psychology, every thought and act creates a subtle groove in the mind called a *samskara*. This impression remains embedded in the mind, in either a faint or deeper form. The more the same thoughts and actions are repeated, the deeper the groove becomes. The aggregate of these grooves forms our character. As water when directed into a narrow canal gains force, so repeated thoughts and actions create behavior patterns that are nearly irresistible in their power.

In order to be freed from the undertow of desires, the whirlpool of vrittis has to be subdued into one steady, calm vritti—into one unwavering thought-wave toward God or the Atman. And this, in fact, is what meditation is.

Freedom from the slavery of desire is the basic requirement for attaining purity of heart. The method *raja* yoga provides for achieving this is the practice of the moral virtues which were formulated by Patanjali in his *Yoga Sutras*. Since ancient times these virtues have been considered the essential groundwork necessary for a serious spiritual life.

Patanjali divided moral conduct into two categories, *yama* and *niyama*. Yama consists of nonviolence, truthfulness, nonstealing, chastity, and the nonreceiving of gifts. Niyama consists of cleanliness, contentment, austerity, study, and devotion to God.[10] It is assumed that these virtues will be practiced not only physically but mentally as well.

By following these purificatory disciplines we gain inner freedom—freedom from our desires and the impulses that pull our attention away from God, deflecting us from our spiritual quest. Trying to meditate without practicing these disciplines is like swimming in the ocean through a bed of seaweed: You can't swim in any direction if your legs are entangled; it's all you can do just to tread water. Similarly, if our minds are entangled in a nest of lower impulses—our individual tangle of samskaras and desires—our minds won't be free to move in a spiritual direction. But if we can gain control over our minds, then we can swim away freely.

Desires in and of themselves are not the problem. As long as we have a body and mind, desires of one sort or another will arise and flow into the mind. The Bhagavad Gita says, "As water flowing into the ocean leaves the ocean undisturbed, so desire enters the mind of the wise person, leaving the mind undisturbed."[11] If a desire enters the mind and we think about it without acting upon it, the samskara created is much weaker than the samskara created when we choose to act upon it. Further, the more we practice *not* acting upon our desires—not even mentally dwelling upon them—the more attenuated the desires become.

It is only with the highest spiritual realization that samskaras are finally destroyed. Like seeds which have been burnt, samskaras can never sprout again after this most profound of spiritual experiences. But since this lofty state is *extremely* rare, the immediate aim of *raja* yoga is to weaken the samskaras so that meditation is possible.

Before this can happen, however, the mind must first be withdrawn from external objects and then fixed on a center of spiritual consciousness within. This concentration or fixing of the mind has been compared to a bird returning to its nest. Once the mind stops reaching out for sense objects and rejects unrelated thoughts, the mind develops a natural inwardness. This inwardness allows meditation—when unwavering, prolonged, and concentrated—to deepen into an utterly complete absorption which makes union with God, *samadhi,* possible.

Before this exalted experience, we've only had a concept of God or the Atman. With samadhi, the true nature of what we've meditated upon shines forth. This experience is more than "perception"—it is direct and immediate knowledge unimpeded by the mind's limitations. With this experience, we're eternally and perfectly free. We have touched the divine within our hearts. We have regained our lost kingdom.

Bhakti Yoga—The Path of Love

The goal of *bhakti* yoga, the path of devotion, is to develop such intense, one-pointed love for God that no distance is left between the lover and the Beloved. The state of union that the *raja* yogi achieves through meditation, the *bhakti* yogi attains through wholehearted devotion.

The beauty of *bhakti* yoga is that it utilizes the faculties and desires we already have: Everyone has the capacity to love and everyone has a deep need to be loved. *Bhakti* yoga harnesses the power of love and focuses that power into a path for God-realization.

As our yearning for God increases, our attraction for sense pleasures and ego-gratification decreases. St. John of the Cross said that "the soul, by restraining its rejoicing as to things of sense, is restored from the distraction into which it has fallen through excessive use of the senses, and is recollected in God."[12] Sri Ramakrishna made a similar equation: "The less you are attached to the world, the more you love God."[13]

Bhakti yoga implies a dualistic relationship with a personal aspect of God. Yet as we read in the *Narada Bhakti Sutras*—one of the classic texts of Hindu devotion—as our love for God grows, we become increasingly aware that the God we are worshiping is really our own Self, our own real nature.[14]

The personal aspect of God that the devotee chooses to worship is called the *Ishta,* the Chosen Ideal. The Ishta that we worship may be a divine incarnation such as Krishna or Jesus or Buddha, or the Ishta may be a god or goddess such as Shiva or Vishnu or Durga. This doesn't mean polytheism, however; just as there are many aspects in a limited human being, so there are infinite aspects of Brahman. Hindu gods and goddesses are the infinite Brahman, seen from different angles through varying human lenses.

Hindus share with Christians the belief that God incarnates for the sake of humanity. The Sanskrit word for incarnation is *avatar,* which literally means "coming down"—that is, the descent of God into the world in tangible form. "When goodness grows weak, when evil increases, I make myself a body," the Bhagavad Gita says. "In every age I come back to deliver the holy, to destroy the sin of the sinner, to establish righteousness."[15]

Proponents of *bhakti* yoga suggest adopting a particular relationship (*bhava*) toward one's Ishta. These relationships are: (1) *shanta,* a peaceful, philosophic relationship with God; (2) *dasya,* the relationship of a servant to a master; (3) *apatya,* the attitude of a child toward the mother or father;

(4) *sakhya,* the relationship between friends; (5) *vatsalya,* the attitude of a parent toward a child; and (6) *madhura,* the relationship between the lover and the beloved.

As we can see, these relationships cover the entire gamut of human experience and move in an ascending order from the relationship offering the least emotional involvement to the relationship that is the most absorbing and intimate. From ancient times Hindu spiritual teachers have understood that for a devotee to having a meaningful relationship with God, one standardized approach could never work for everyone. This deeply personal issue has therefore always been left to the devotee and his or her guru, spiritual teacher.

The aim of *bhakti* yoga is simple—to develop an increasing love for God as well as an increasing awareness of God's love for us. To do this, the devotee practices constant recollectedness of God. One of the easiest and most effective ways of doing this is through *japa*—the repetition of a mantra. Hindus delight when they discover that Cassian, St. Catherine of Genoa, as well as the author of the *Cloud of Unknowing* and many others came to the same conclusion.

St. Paul's instruction to "pray without ceasing" finds particular resonance with Hindu practitioners. I suspect many Christians would be astonished to discover how many Hindus have found *The Way of a Pilgrim* profoundly inspiring; for Hindus, that pilgrim is a prime example of one who is *japa siddha*—perfected through japa.

Bhakti yoga uses the purifying technique of japa to cleanse the mind of its lower tendencies. By constantly infusing the divine name into the mind, the mind's dark cellar eventually becomes cleansed—the way you'd clean an inkwell by repeatedly flushing fresh water into it.

Prayer also has a significant role in the Hindu tradition. Like the Lord's Prayer, the Abhyaroha and Gayatri mantras have been a source of inspiration, meditation, and illumination for thousands of years.

Spontaneous prayers are equally—if not more—efficacious. If God is our very own, nearer than the nearest and dearer than the dearest—our own true Self—then we don't need to follow any formula to talk to him (or her). Just as we unburden our heart to our closest friend or ask our mother to fulfill our needs—knowing full well that she will—so should be our prayers to God.

Prayer is one of the most effective ways of concentrating the mind and giving it a godward turn. There's no way the mind can wander if it is focused in heartfelt prayer. We can't fall asleep or reenact yesterday's argument. The very act of prayer narrows the mind's focus to touch base with God.

Prayer is also a powerful purifying agent: when we pray for others we lessen our self-centered interests. One traditional Hindu prayer is: "May all be happy. May all be free from disease. May all realize what is good. May none be subject to misery." Further, even before beginning meditation, one is supposed to send out thoughts of peace to people everywhere in the world.

When we pray for those spiritual qualities that bring us closer to God such as devotion or purity or desirelessness, our prayers are answered. "Ask, and it shall be given you; seek, and ye shall find; knock, and it shall be opened unto you" is a profound truth for all spiritual seekers. Prayer, when wholehearted and deeply felt, cuts through the desires that tie us to worldliness.

A prayer that is a real cry of the heart to God bangs on the door of spiritual awakening. That door *must* open when the banging is fervent and incessant. As Sri Ramakrishna said, "If a devotee prays to God with real longing, God cannot help revealing himself to him."[16]

Worship is another essential spiritual practice in *bhakti* yoga. While prayer involves—at least at the beginning—*asking* of God, worship is *giving* to God. For that reason worship is often seen as the stage after prayer. Human nature being what it is, we generally put ourselves and our needs first. But when real love arises, the heart expands; then we find it more fulfilling to give rather than to receive. That is worship.

What we give doesn't matter; it's the attitude with which we give that is critical. "Whatever a person gives me in true devotion—fruit or water, a leaf or flower—that I will accept, the devout gift of the pure-minded," says Sri Krishna in the Bhagavad Gita.[17] Christ's praise for the widow and her offering of two mites resonates here. In worship there's neither bargaining nor bartering; we neither want nor expect anything. We give out of the fullness of love simply because we need to express our love.

Included in worship is ritual—the symbolic actions that express the mystic relationship between the devotee and God. Ritual is a particularly effective devotional method since it involves the total human being—body, intellect, and emotion. While ritual has often been dismissed as meaningless rote activity, the purpose of ritual is to express through action the truth that words cannot express.

The real feeling that Hindu ritual evokes, however, is intimacy with God. The worshiper doesn't think of God's power or glories. The worshiper sees only the sweet form of the divine Beloved, graciously gazing at him or her. The goal of worship—as with meditation—is divine communion. Through the process of worship, the devotee feels increasingly closer to God until the point of communion is attained.

All these methods—prayer, worship, japa, as well as other devotional practices such as sacred music, holy reading, keeping holy company, and pilgrimage—lead the devotee to the constant recollectedness of God's living presence within the heart. With this, the culmination of *bhakti* is reached. Then lover and Beloved become one and the lost kingdom is regained.

Karma Yoga—The Path of Dedicated Action

Bhakti yoga assures us that the Lord lovingly accepts whatever we offer with devotion. But just as we can offer flowers and fruits, love and adoration, so we can offer our actions and *their* fruits. "Whatever you do, whatever you eat, whatever you offer in sacrifice, whatever you give in charity, whatever austerity you perform—do that as an offering to me," says Sri Krishna in the Bhagavad Gita.[18]

Karma yoga is the path of dedicated, selfless action. The goal of *karma* yoga is to transform work from a bondage into a means for spiritual realization. While *karma* yoga is specifically meant for those with an active temperament, *all* spiritual seekers are advised to use the methods of *karma* yoga since every human being is continually engaged in action; even thinking is an action. Work is a necessity of the human condition; *karma* yoga teaches us how to transform work into a sacrament.

The word *karma* comes from the verb *kri,* "to do," and refers to both action and the effects of action. By observing the human condition, Vedanta has formulated the sequence of events concerning karma as a kind of cyclic chain reaction: At ground zero we face, as a result of maya, ignorance of our true nature. Like the hunter-king, we're suffering from amnesia. Ignorance leads to desire (the God-shaped hole in the heart which we fill with all the wrong things); desire leads to action, karma. (The hunter-king, feeling dissatisfied, tries to do things—sell skins or become a soldier—to assuage his misery.) Karma—that is, action and its inescapable effects—leads to rebirth. With rebirth comes the inevitability of death, limitation, suffering, bondage, and more karma.

Karma is normally binding because action is coupled to desire; we act to fulfill some desire, either conscious or unconscious. *Karma* yoga breaks the powerful link between desire and action. This is done in one of two ways: either by working for work's sake alone or by offering the results of our work to God. Either way the mind is purified by removing desire for the results of our actions. "To work alone you have the right, and not to the fruits thereof," says the Bhagavad Gita. "Do not allow longing for the results to be the motivating force of your actions and do not allow yourself to be attached to indolence."[19] This teaching is the real anthem of *karma* yoga, both for those who follow the path of the Impersonal as well as for those who worship a personal God.

The first method of *karma* yoga—work for work's sake—is for those who relate to the impersonal Reality, Brahman. These *karma* yogis must train themselves to do good simply because it is good to do good.

The second method of *karma* yoga is for those who feel drawn toward a personal aspect of God. Here the devotee offers the results of all actions to God. For the *karma* yogi inspired by devotion, the goal is to work with no personal motivation since every action and every thought is an offering at the altar of the beloved Lord. This *karma* yogi has, as had Brother Lawrence, "no other care... but faithfully to reject every other thought *that he might perform all his actions for the love of God.*"[20]

For all *karma* yogis, work is worship. Whether we're sitting in the shrine or working on the septic tank, the subjective feeling is the same. It's all worship. No work by itself is either menial or lofty; when work becomes a prayer, every action becomes noble.

I know an elderly monk who for many years was stationed in our hospital in Benares, India. Especially in the hospital's early years, the conditions were very difficult; there were only a handful of monks to look after a vast number of extremely ill patients. No equipment, no supplies, scant funding, and little sleep. This monk would clean and bathe the patients every day, wiping away their excrement with his own hands. One day as he went from patient to patient, the pail containing the excrement got increasingly heavy, so by the time he finished one round, he found it easier to bear the weight by carrying the pail on his head. A brother monk, seeing him with his rather unseemly load, said to him in a joking way, "Are those the temple's worship articles you're carrying on your head?" To which the monk immediately shot back, "Yes, as a matter of fact, they *are!*" This is the attitude of a true *karma* yogi: all work is holy.

What distinguishes *karma* yoga from other yogas is its twofold movement: first, inward to the divine source, then outward to service and action. While other yogas take the mind and focus it inward, *karma* yoga takes the mind inward only to have it go outward again—for worship in the form of work.

This two-part movement distinguishes *karma* yoga from mere social work. Unless the mind is purified and drawn inward first, the outward activity can easily degenerate into ego-driven social activity. In order for the work to be *transformed* into worship rather than mere busyness, the inwardness and alertness produced by meditation has to be present at all times.

During the past century, Hinduism has taken on a new dimension by emphasizing social service as *karma* yoga. This movement was spearheaded by Swami Vivekananda in the late nineteenth century. During the twentieth century, this ideal was accepted and embraced by other traditions within Hinduism. While Hinduism has always proclaimed the divinity of the soul and the oneness of existence, it was Vivekananda who linked this philosophy to social service: to worship God one should serve humankind, the living God standing before us. "The yogi who sees me in all things and sees all things in me, never becomes separated from me, nor do I become separated from him," says Sri Krishna in the Gita. "The yogi who, established in unity, worships me who dwells in all beings, that yogi abides in me."[21] If the highest expression of yoga is seeing God dwelling in the hearts of all, then true worship is offering service to humankind.

Through the path of work, the *karma* yogi uses everything at his or her disposal to bring the mind back to its divine center. The *karma* yogi aims to make the method so perfect that the means and the end become one. The result is complete communion, the regaining of the lost kingdom.

Jnana Yoga—The Path of Knowledge

Jnana yoga, the path of knowledge, is for spiritual seekers whose intellects are more powerful than their emotions. *Jnana* yoga asserts that ignorance of our divine nature is the only obstacle to spiritual realization, and knowledge alone can remove this obstacle. "Knowledge" in this context does not refer to an intellectual understanding but to the direct experience of the Atman.

Knowledge of the Atman is referred to as "Self-knowledge" in Vedanta since it means knowing the real "me"—knowing the reality underlying my existence. Since this reality and the reality underlying the world are not different, Self-knowledge and the knowledge of Brahman are one and the same.

Jnana yogis use the intellect to carve a path through maya to freedom and perfection. While intellectual knowledge is not the goal, the intellect can nevertheless be an incisive instrument to slice through the veil of maya. "The Self, deep-hidden in the hearts of all beings, does not shine forth," says the Katha Upanishad. It is realized only by the sharp, refined intellects of those who can experience the subtle Reality.[22]

The "sharp, refined intellect" essential for *jnana* yoga is a direct consequence of purity of heart. Purity of heart means being freed from the pull of lower impulses; as long as impulses and desires pull the mind away from the Atman, the intellect isn't free to cut the bonds of maya. And there isn't much of an inclination to do so. The intellect cannot become sharp if it's pulled in opposite directions.

To sharpen a knife, you must carefully pull the knife again and again in the same direction. Change the direction, the blade is ruined. In the same way, the intellect is sharpened by not allowing it to be blunted by desires. "If you purify your soul of attachments and desires," says St. John of the Cross, "you will understand things spiritually. If you deny your appetite for them, you will enjoy their truth, understanding what is certain in them."[23] Several millennia earlier, the Katha Upanishad said: "When all the desires clinging to the heart are destroyed, then a mortal becomes immortal and attains oneness with Brahman."[24]

Jnana yoga has four preliminary requisites that proceed in an ascending order—each requisite allowing the following requisite to be possible. The first and most fundamental requirement for *jnana* yoga is discrimination (*viveka*) between the real and the unreal, the everlasting and the transitory. Shankara, India's greatest exponent of nondualism or Advaita Vedanta, defined discrimination as the deep conviction that Brahman is real and the world is illusory.[25] This isn't to say that the world doesn't exist; it *does* but its existence is dependent upon Brahman—the only unchanging reality.

The second requirement of *jnana* yoga is detachment or dispassion (*vairagya*)—a turning away of the mind from sense pleasures. And, as we have seen before, renouncing sense pleasures is synonymous with purity of heart. Discrimination produces (hopefully) detachment because discrimination makes us realize that worldly pleasures can bring us no lasting fulfillment. As discrimination produces detachment, so detachment empowers discrimination. It's no use discriminating between the real and the unreal unless we have the desire to shun the unreal. Shankara's renowned text, the *Vivekacudamani,* says that with detachment, the spiritual seeker shuns the illusory "as from the droppings of a crow."[26] St. John of the Cross mentions a dual process very similar to the one mentioned here: "A bird caught in birdlime has a twofold task: It must free itself and cleanse itself. And by satisfying their appetites, people suffer in a twofold way: They must detach themselves and, after being detached, clean themselves of what has clung to them."[27]

The third requirement is a collection of six virtues which begins with tranquillity.[28] Once we have detached the mind from sense pleasures by continually being aware of their inherent defects, tranquillity comes. The mind, reined in from the senses, is then free to abide in Brahman. Self-control, the second virtue, is controlling the sense organs. Without controlling the mind, there is little point in controlling the sense organs. It only leads to frustration. Unless both are present, real concentration is impossible.

Mental poise is the third virtue, and it means not allowing the mind to be swayed by anything external. St. John of the Cross offers the same instruction: "Strive to preserve your heart in peace; let no event of this world disturb it; reflect that all must come to an end."[29]

Forbearance, the fourth virtue, means enduring all afflictions without anxiety or complaint. This means externally as well as internally: We can't be said to be practicing forbearance if our irritation and resentment are felt but not expressed. With mental poise and forbearance, the *jnana* yogi is immune to external provocations as well as mental anxieties. Faith, the fifth virtue, is the unwavering conviction that the words of the scriptures and the spiritual teacher are true and lead to the realization of Brahman. Again, without practicing the previous virtues, we can't gain the conviction that our spiritual life is authentic and that the words of the scriptures and the teacher are true. This isn't blind acceptance; it's a deep conviction based on our own experience of spiritual life. Unless we develop this deep conviction, spiritual progress isn't possible. As long as our conviction wavers, the mind won't have the necessary strength to practice serious spiritual disciplines. The final virtue, concentration, means not babying the mind by allowing it to be lulled in idle thoughts; concentration means having the higher portion of the mind fixed in Brahman.

With these six virtues firmly in place, we can reach the fourth prerequisite of *jnana* yoga, longing for liberation. Liberation means freedom from the bondage of ignorance which engenders egotism and identification with the body. Once ignorance is removed, Brahman is revealed. The bondage of ignorance is so powerful, however, that only the most intense desire for freedom will break its chains. Longing for liberation is a *burning* desire for freedom—a desire so intense that Vedanta literature compares it to a person whose hair is on fire desperately seeking water to quench the flames. This person has no other interest, no other desire, no other thought, no other goal.

Cultivating the four spiritual requisites makes the student fit for the fundamental practices of *jnana* yoga—the classic triad of hearing the truth (*shravana*), reflecting on the truth (*manana*), and having unbroken meditation on the truth of Brahman (*nididhyasana*).

First, we must hear the truth of the scriptures from a qualified teacher. Second, we need to reflect—think of Brahman constantly and through that gain a deep conviction about the truth of Brahman. Finally, we must meditate—which means having a constant, unbroken stream of meditation upon Brahman. Unbroken meditation, practiced for a long period of time, brings samadhi, divine union.

Every yoga has samadhi as its ultimate goal. What is this experience? It's impossible to say since it has been defined by the Upanishads as "that which words cannot express and the mind cannot reach." But what Shankara describes in the *Vivekacudamani* is worth repeating here. The disciple, having wholeheartedly followed the instructions of his/her teacher, goes into deep samadhi. Having returned to a normal plane of consciousness, the disciple says "out of the fullness of his/her joy":

> The ego has disappeared. I have realized my identity with Brahman and so all my desires have melted away.... What is this joy that I feel? Who shall measure it? I know nothing but joy, limitless, unbounded! ...
>
> My mind fell like a hailstone into that vast expanse of Brahman's ocean. Touching one drop of it, I melted away and became one with Brahman. And now, though I return to human consciousness, I abide in the joy of the Atman....
>
> Now, finally and clearly, I know that I am the Atman, whose nature is eternal joy.[30]

This experience, Hinduism says, is the goal of human life, the highest attainment. Attaining that divine kingdom within our own hearts, we will realize that the kingdom had been waiting for us the whole time. As Meister Eckhart said, "When the Kingdom appears to the soul and it is recognized, there is no further need for preaching or instruction: it is learnéd enough and has at once secured eternal life. To know and see how near God's Kingdom is, is to say with Jacob: 'God is in this place and I did not know it.' "[31]

2

Heart Yoga:
A Comparison of Two Texts

Pratyabhijna–hridayam
(Kashmir, eleventh century) and
Kaivalya–darsanam
(West Bengal, nineteenth century)

THOMAS MATUS, O.S.B. CAM.

These two texts, distant from one another in time and space, exemplify in their underlying similarities the continuity of Yogic teachings in Hinduism. The author of the *Pratyabhijna-hridayam* was Rajanaka Kshemaraja, disciple of the great Kashmiri-Shaiva master Abhinavagupta, a contemporary of St. Romuald.[1] The *Kaivalya-darsanam* was written in English, at the end of the nineteenth century, by Swami Sri Yukteswar Giri (1855–1936), a monastic disciple of the great lay Yogi, Lahiri Mahashaya of Benares. Sri Yukteswar, in turn, became the guru of Paramahansa Yogananda. In common the two texts have their literary genre—a commentary on a series of Sanskrit *sutras* or aphorisms—and their conception of Yoga as a way *of* the heart and a way *to* the heart, to enable us to recognize God in ourselves. An external link between the texts is offered by the editors and translators of the earlier text, who like the nineteenth-century Bengali sage were intent on discovering a "scientific" understanding of religion.

Both authors were, of course, Hindus, but our reflection on the two texts aims at opening a dialogue between Hindus and Christians. This dialogue is to be both "interreligious" and "intrareligious."

Dialogue Starting from Within

Although "interreligious dialogue" in the Catholic Church did not begin with the Second Vatican Council's declaration *Nostra Aetate,* the council did clarify the ecclesial character of the dialogue. The declaration's title spoke of the church's "relationship with non-Christian religions," and the key word

39

was "relationship." While Christians since the time of Justin Martyr have considered that the charity of Christ might bring them into contact and hence dialogue with individual adherents of other faiths, in Vatican II the church itself was relating to other religions as social realities. One of the consequences of this new understanding has been the series of contacts between Catholic ecclesiastics and prominent representatives of other faiths: the pope meeting the Dalai Lama, for instance. Such contacts have borne good fruit, but if interreligious dialogue were this and nothing else, it would mean little for the spiritual progress of its participants, much less for that of humanity.

Since the council, the most important development in the relationship among different faiths has been at the grass-roots level: the dialogue between simple believers of different faiths or among searchers for spiritual truth on different paths. When I meet another person of faith who believes differently than I do, and I discover, alongside our differences, many similarities in our respective ways of believing, I am drawn into a dialogue not only with that person but also with myself. As I carry on an external conversation with persons of another faith, an internal dialogue is taking place: I learn to see reality through their eyes, to walk in their shoes, and to feel with them the common human need for absolute truth and wisdom. While I remain faithful to the tradition I have received, I can no longer see it by itself, in splendid isolation, since I see it in relation to other, different traditions.

Some would call this the "intrareligious dialogue," an exchange from faith to faith within the souls of both participants in an external dialogue. On both levels, God is present. As Jacques Dupuis has said,

> The principal agent of interreligious dialogue is the Spirit of God, who is present in the traditions on both sides and who animates the partners in dialogue. It is the same God who works saving deeds in human history and who speaks to human beings in the depths of their hearts. The same God is both "Totally Other" and the "Ground of Being" of all that is; the transcendent "beyond" and the immanent "in the depths"; the Father of our Lord Jesus Christ and the Self at the center of the self. The one and the same God is contemplated in ecstasy, whose realization may flow forth from "enstasis"; the same is affirmed by cataphatic theology and inferred by apophatic mysticism.[2]

The inner dialogue, then, reflects the nature of every human experience of God: a paradox, or perhaps a necessary rhythm, of ecstasy-enstasis, of going beyond and going within, like *prana-apana,* breathing in and breathing out.

My own experience of this rhythm and of the intrareligious dialogue began with reading, at age fourteen, the *Autobiography of a Yogi,*[3] of Paramahansa Yogananda (1893–1952), a monk of the Giri order of Swamis. His book introduced me to the Bhagavad Gita, the Upanishads, and other

Hindu and Buddhist texts, which were then (in the mid-fifties) beginning to be available in inexpensive, paperback editions. Three years later I was at Occidental College in Los Angeles, a half-hour's walk from Yogananda's monastic center on Mount Washington. I often joined his disciples in meditation, and a year later I received initiation into Kriya Yoga, a technique that unites *pranayama* (control of breath and energy), *pratyahara* (control of the senses), and meditation on the centers of consciousness (metaphorically termed "lotuses") along the cerebrospinal axis. This practice is similar to those known among the Shaiva mystics of Kashmir a thousand years ago, but Yogananda inherited it from a line of Bengali spiritual masters, whose lives he narrated in his autobiography, especially that of his own guru, Swami Sri Yukteswar of Serampore (1855–1936).

Yogananda came to the United States in 1920 at the age of twenty-seven. He began to present his form of Kriya Yoga as a "scientific technique of God-realization," in the hopes that pragmatic Americans would be attracted by the adjective "scientific." They were attracted, and in great numbers they attended his public lectures and received Kriya Yoga initiation from him. But Yogananda soon discovered that Americans were not so coldly pragmatic and technologically minded as he thought, and so he began to reveal the real secret of his practice, which was a way of the heart, an exercise of the breath accompanied by devotion, feeling, and intense longing for the face-to-face vision of God.

Yogananda was the first Hindu teacher of Yoga who lived for several decades in the West. In addition to his famous *Autobiography,* praised by Thomas Mann and translated into a score of languages, he wrote a number of books and articles, including extensive commentaries on the New Testament, serialized in the periodicals of the "Self-Realization Fellowship" he founded in California in 1925. Yogananda aimed consciously at the inculturation of Yoga in America (without, of course, using the term "inculturation"), and to this end he made frequent references to the Bible in his teachings, included the invocation of Jesus Christ in his prayers, and avoided much of the Sanskrit jargon with which other gurus salted their lessons. Whatever may be said of his blending of Hindu thought (especially Vedanta philosophy) with borrowings from liberal Protestantism, he deserves to be recognized as one of the most authentic bearers of the Yoga message. For him, Yoga was essentially a practice of meditation leading to *samadhi* or total absorption in God. His concern was to offer Westerners, formed in rationalistic thought and in the Cartesian-Newtonian paradigm, a "scientific method of meditation"; yet those who committed themselves to his formation found him a demanding teacher whose chief concern was to train them in the affective ways of *bhakti.*[4]

Yogananda spoke of the highest state of Yoga meditation both as "divine ecstasy" and as "cosmic consciousness," bringing into play the paradoxical language of the mystics: the reality experienced is both within and without (*interior intimo meo, superior supremo meo,* as St. Augustine said), and so the experience itself is both an expansion and a concentration of consciousness, an all-embracing vision of the cosmos, and an intense focus on God at the center of the soul. Having attained this state, the Yogi is *jivanmukta,* "freed while living," liberated from all entanglement with nature and from nature's delusion and seduction, *maya,* while yet living in the flesh, the cosmos, and time,[5] and carrying on a normal human existence. In other words, Yoga is paradoxically a way of *viyoga,* of "unyoking" the soul from its space-time limitations, so that the Yogi may become *yuktesvara,* "yoked to the Lord" and united with God, just as much at home in the cosmos as God is, in whom the cosmos lives, moves, and has its being.[6]

"Yukteswar" is of course the name of Paramahansa Yogananda's guru, the author of the *Kaivalya-darsanam,* which we are examining in this paper.[7] His book, written in 1894 before he entered the *swami* order, is essentially a commentary on eighty-four Sanskrit sutras from an unidentified source; one may suppose that he composed them himself. He compares them with texts from the Bible (mostly the New Testament), cited both as proof of the universality of his teachings and in view of his project of a "Yoga for the West" which later would be propagated by his disciple Yogananda.[8]

Models of Western Yoga

After Yogananda, numerous other Yoga teachers migrated from India to the West, although few of them shared his dedication to monastic life and his insistence on the affective (*bhakti*) dimension of Yoga. The propagation of Yoga in the West has made it a permanent feature of Western culture and by no means a negative one.

In India, *Yoga* is the generic term for any sort of dedicated spiritual practice. In the West, even those who limit their contact with it to a few hours each week at a gymnasium or other health facility eventually discover the spiritual implications of "doing Yoga." A great number of them find in Yoga a framework for spiritual practice that their own Christian or Jewish formation seems not to have offered them. Some, of course, substitute Yoga for Christianity or Judaism; others, perhaps the majority, feel that Yoga is compatible with their inherited religion, and practice both. A small but significant number of persons, having undergone an intense, paranormal experience of the sort often termed "spiritual emergency,"[9] turn to Eastern disciplines of the Yoga type (about which they may have had no previous knowledge) and discover in them an explanation for their state and a way of resolving it positively. Finally, there are those who adopt some form of Yoga or Buddhist meditation with the conscious intent of participating at the personal level in the church's dialogue with other spiritual traditions; their motivations are those of a deeply nurtured and well-instructed Christian faith.[10]

To this wide range of motivations for practicing Yoga corresponds an equally wide range of models. The first is that of Yoga as physical training; in the minds of many Westerners, the postures (*asanas*) and other bodily exercises of Hatha-Yoga (*pranayama*, etc.) are "Yoga" *par excellence*.[11] Sometimes the Yoga label is used to package a series of exercises that have little or no basis in the ancient texts. In other cases, while the emphasis is on the physical discipline, the traditional spiritual orientation is preserved, and the *asanas* are taught as propaedeutic to meditation, as in the works of B. K. S. Iyengar.[12]

A second model, often associated with Yogananda, is that of Yoga as a total religious experience. The *disciplina arcani* with which his disciples have surrounded the teaching of his meditation technique (Kriya Yoga), along with the severe admonition not to modify it in any way, has conferred upon the technique much of the aura of a sacrament. Perhaps the majority of adherents to his Self-Realization Fellowship regard the organization as their church and exclusively attend the worship services it offers. However, there are also a significant number of Catholics among Yogananda's followers who consider Kriya Yoga an adjunct to their traditional practices of Christian prayer and sacramental worship.

These latter can also be grouped with those Christians who, without dissociating themselves either exteriorly or interiorly from their ecclesial communities, find in Yoga a framework or formative discipline into which they consciously infuse a Christian meaning, both through their inner devotion to the God of the Bible and through their search for practical methods, delineated by Christian writers of the past, which have some affinity with India's various forms of Yoga. In India one can find several examples of this model: Bede Griffiths, for example, while not showing preference for any particular Indian technique or discipline, favored the use of Yoga practices at Saccidananda Ashram, Shantivanam, and encouraged his disciples to teach them.[13] In the West we have the example of another Benedictine monk, John Main, who in the last years of his life promoted a simple and essentially Christian meditation practice, which personal contact with a Hindu Yoga teacher had suggested to him and which he later developed through the study of Christian monastic literature, especially the writings of John Cassian.[14] At a greater distance, culturally speaking, from Yoga but with implicit (and sometimes explicit) references to it, we find various forms of meditation inspired and guided by the anonymous fourteenth-century classic *The Cloud of Unknowing* (e.g., "Centering Prayer" and similar approaches to a new contemplative practice).

Finally, a fourth model of "Western Yoga" is exemplified by those Christian believers, many of them members of monastic communities, who engage in Yoga or Zen practice in the spirit of interfaith dialogue. While not employing Eastern forms of meditation as their exclusive spiritual practice, they participate willingly in these disciplines for shorter or longer periods, often in Hindu ashrams or Japanese Zendos. Outstanding in this group of Christian meditators is David Steindl-Rast, a Benedictine monk who has been at the forefront of Buddhist-Christian dialogue in North America for many years.[15] Pierre-François de Béthune, the secretary general of the Benedictine-Cistercian dialogue commission (D.I.M.-M.I.D.), guided the preparation and publication of an important document that touches on these issues: "Contemplation et Dialogue Interreligieux."[16] De Béthune has also helped to organize several "spiritual exchanges," which have brought together Christian monastics with those of Buddhist or Hindu traditions in the monasteries of Europe, India, and Japan.

Yoga from West to East

Obviously the fourth model is preferred by Christians in countries like India, where even the most open and ecumenically committed individuals among them are concerned to convey a clear image of their Christian identity. But in Asia, outside the Christian milieu, one is currently witnessing a paradox: Yoga and similar practices are being exported from the West and reimported into the countries of their origin.

Yogananda is again an example of this. Having founded the Self-Realization Fellowship in California, he returned to India and united his followers there in the Yogoda Sat-Sangha Society, which he placed under the direction of his American organization. But even before him, most of the protagonists of the nineteenth- and early twentieth-century revival of Hinduism were men profoundly influenced by Western educational experience. Ram Mohan Roy, Mahatma Gandhi, Rabindranath Tagore, Pandit Nehru, Sarvepalli Radhakrishnan, and Sri Aurobindo (a distant cousin of Yogananda) were all formed according to European, especially British, cultural paradigms, and only as adults did they recover their Indian linguistic, cultural, and religious heritage.[17]

Today in India, the promotion of new industrial enterprises, the neo-capitalist market economy, and fashionable consumer tastes among the younger generations of Indians have created conditions of spiritual need analogous to those in the West. With the general loss of traditional values and the yielding of religious customs to pragmatic concerns in the context of secular society, access to authentic gurus has become more and more difficult. At the same time, increasing literacy has created a reading market whose demand for literature on Yoga is satisfied in part by the publications that abound in the West. Finally, Hindus themselves desire the transformation of their hallowed techniques into forms more practical for persons who engage daily in nonagricultural work or whose daily rhythms, in any case, are modified by urban influences, even in village and countryside.

Returning to the Sources of Yoga

The best known source of yogic doctrine and practice is the *Yoga Sutras* of Patanjali. Here let me examine a few of Patanjali's aphorisms, especially those seldom quoted in popular Yoga textbooks.[18]

Yogananda named his principal meditation technique "Kriya Yoga," and claimed that it represented the highest form of Raja Yoga, the "royal path" followed by Yogis since the time of Bhagavan Krishna. The same claim has been made for other practices, but in any case the term harks back to the Yoga-Sutras and seems to imply very ancient origins. The Yoga-Sutras speak of Kriya Yoga in the second book, *Sadhana-pada* (Yoga-Sutras 2,1): "Asceticism, study of one's tradition, and abandonment to the Lord constitute practical Yoga." Note my translation: Kriya Yoga="practical Yoga." The word *kriya* can simply be taken as a synonym for *karma,* in the generic sense of "action." In this context, the word denotes those actions that a Yogi performs in preparation for *samyama,* the meditative process of *dharana, dhyana,* and *samadhi.* Thus the expression seems to refer to Yoga as outward practice, hence "practical Yoga." On the other hand, the term *kriya* in many ancient Vedic texts bears the specific, technical sense of "ritual action," practices and gestures associated with the offering of sacrifice. In the Upanishads and especially in Tantric literature, ritual action is consistently interiorized, and Yoga practices in turn become substitutes for *yajna* and the sacrificial fire-rite.

It is important to note that the three terms "asceticism, study of one's tradition, and abandonment to the Lord" are identical with the last three *Niyama* precepts (Yoga-Sutras 2,32). According to the rules of ancient rhetoric, the end implies the whole, and hence a concluding phrase or expression stands as a summation of an entire text. This is quite clear in the ancient commentary attributed to Vyasa (the name is the same as that of the legendary author of the Bhagavad Gita). On the one hand, Vyasa defines Yoga itself by its ultimate end, *samadhi,*[19] and on the other, he shows Yama-Niyama to be more than just a preliminary phase that can soon be left behind.[20] The ethical underpinnings of Yoga are a constant in every phase of its practice, and even though reaching the goal entails going beyond ethical obligations, the accomplished Yogi is expected to incarnate all the values inherent in Yama-Niyama.

The final term in both Kriya Yoga (Yoga-Sutras 2,1) and Niyama (2,32) is "abandonment to the Lord," described in the commentaries as "the offering of all actions" and "the surrendering of one's whole nature" to the Supreme Teacher (cf. 2,45). This abandonment leads to the "perfection of *samadhi*" (ibid.) and hence of Yoga itself. It has often been noted that this particular precept is a departure from the supposedly "atheistic" (better, "nontheistic") nature of Sankhya philosophy, the conceptual framework around which Patanjali constructed his Yoga system. While it is true that Sankhya does not presuppose the existence of a Supreme Being, the practice of Yoga has from time immemorial found its natural context within the practice of religion and devotion. *Bhakti,* "devotion," as a particular yogic "path" (*marga*) is more than just an optional variant of the basic Yoga; it is intrinsic to its practice even for those who by nature are more inclined to follow the path of wisdom (*jnana*) or of action (*karma*). When Yoga practice takes the place of ritual worship, it retains the affective spirit of the ancient rites. Hence Patanjali and his earliest commentators are agreed that Yoga is not to be identified with the "techniques." It is not a cold, "scientific" procedure performed by a detached observer. It requires a devotional attitude that, when present, contains within itself the essence and perfection of Yoga as a whole.

The renewal of Hindu thought and practice in the nineteenth century reaffirmed this understanding of Yoga. One contribution to this renewal was represented by the line of gurus to whom Paramahansa Yogananda paid homage in his *Autobiography of a Yogi,* particularly Swami Sri Yukteswar of Serampore. The latter's essay, *Kaivalya-darsanam,*[21] proposes to mediate between the traditional language of Yoga mysticism and the language of the Bible, which the author cites from the familiar King James Version. In addition to the English Bible, other Western philosophical sources seem to influence Sri Yukteswar's understanding of the Judeo-Christian Scriptures: perhaps Spinoza and Berkeley, although he cites neither of them. He ends his book, however, with a direct quotation of the poet Sir Walter Scott.

Sri Yukteswar frequently borrows expressions from the Bible and from English poetry in translating Sanskrit philosophical terms: *parambrahma* becomes "the Eternal Father, God,"[22] while *cit* is rendered "Omniscient Feeling."[23] Thus from the metaphysics of *advaita,* nonduality, we are abruptly transferred into the sphere of affective relations. The human being is "the likeness of God" (Sri Yukteswar cites Gen 1:27) and reflects the divine nature of thought as feeling. This same feeling, through its intrinsic power, becomes "love" in the manifestation of the universe. Cosmic causality is effected through *pranava-sabda,* translated not only by its Sanskrit equivalent *aum* (*om*) but also by the Johannine terms "Word" and "Amen."[24] The Bengali sage concludes: "This manifestation of the Word (becoming flesh, the external material) created this visible world. So the Word (*Amen, Aum*), being the manifestation of the Eternal Nature of the Almighty Father or His Own Self, is inseparable from and nothing but God Himself; as the burning power is inseparable from and nothing but the fire itself," and he proceeds to quote Revelation 3:14 and John 1:1, 3, 14.[25] Finally, Sri Yukteswar completes his "trinitarian" interpretation of the One and its emanations with the terms *premabija* (literally, "seed of love"), *kutastha caitanya* ("highest consciousness"), and *purushottama* ("supreme person"), gathered together under the biblical name "Holy Spirit." This is "Life" itself and "Light," whose "rays" are the individual persons, *purushas,* or "sons of God."[26]

Having further elaborated, after the manner of Sankhya, a universal schema of emanations, Sri Yukteswar analyzes the human person, the individual *purusha* or "son of God" as an embodied being, structured concentrically in five layers or *kosas.* The innermost or highest layer of embodiment is that of the *citta,* translated not by the usual term "thought" but as "heart," the "seat of bliss, *ananda.*"[27] The goal of human existence is the heart's emergence from the darkness of ignorance into the light of God.

> In this state, all the necessities having been attained and the ultimate aim effected, the heart becomes perfectly purified and, instead of merely reflecting the spiritual light, actively manifests the same. Man, being thus consecrated or anointed by the Holy Spirit, becomes Christ, the anointed Savior. Entering the kingdom of Spiritual Light, he becomes the Son of God.

Sri Yukteswar is speaking the language of the Gospel of John (he cites Jn 14:11: "Believe me that I am in the Father and the Father in me."), but his metaphysical understanding of the ultimate end remains that of India's nondualistic Vedanta thought.

The Sanskrit verses analyzed in chapter three of Sri Yukteswar's essay, called "*Sadhana,* The Procedure," adhere closely to the themes of the *Sadhana-pada* of Patanjali's sutras.[28] The opening verse of the former is practically identical with that of the latter, except that two key terms are altered. In the first place, what Patanjali calls Kriya Yoga Yukteswar calls *yajna,* "sacrifice." This is, of course, in accordance with the interpretation of *kriya* as "ritual action" rather than as "action" or "practice" in general. Furthermore, Patanjali's *Isvara-pranidhana* ("abandonment to the Lord") becomes *Brahma-nidhana,* translated not as "abandonment to the Absolute" but as "the practice of meditation on *Aum.*" The terms *Brahman* and *Aum* may seem more impersonal than *Isvara;* however, since Sri Yukteswar repeatedly refers them to the biblical concepts of "the Eternal Father," "the Word," and the "Spirit," their sense still implies the relationship of love and hence the primacy of *bhakti* in the practice of Yoga.

Tapas ("penance, religious mortification") is not so much active asceticism as "evenmindedness" and "patience both in enjoyments and in sufferings." *Svadhyaya* "consists of reading or hearing spiritual truth, pondering it, and forming a definite conception of it." Although Sri Yukteswar retains the traditional understanding of *svadhyaya* as "studying the sacred writings of one's own tradition," he also extends its meaning in the direction of "self-study": "forming of an idea of the true faith about Self, that is, what I am, whence I came, where I shall go, what I have come for, and other such matters concerning Self."[29]

The following pages further elaborate the understanding of *Brahma-nidhana* and meditation on *pranava-sabda* (*aum*) as an exercise of *bhakti*. The "Holy Sound" is manifested spontaneously in the human heart as *sraddha* (literally, "faith"), which Sri Yukteswar calls "the heart's natural love." Convinced as he is that all human beings tend spontaneously to a holy life, Yukteswar affirms that this natural love, when not repressed or turned away from its proper end, union with God, brings about health in body and mind and makes one seek "the Godlike company of the divine personages," that is, gurus and spiritual teachers.[30] Faith and devotion in the heart of the Yogi are developed by attachment to a guru or by remembering and meditating on the virtues of the saints.[31]

The fourth chapter of Sri Yukteswar's essay bears the Sanskrit title *vibhuti,* whose literal meaning in the present context ought to be "the successful issue [of the sacrifice]" but which Yukteswar translates "Revelation," the name given in many English Bibles to the last book of the New Testament, the Apocalypse. In fact, he elaborates an allegorical interpretation of John's vision of the Son of Man (see Rev 1:9–20), in which the "seven stars" and "seven golden candlesticks" are identified with the *cakras* or centers of consciousness that the Yogis discover within the body through their practice of *pranayama* and meditation on the *pranava-sabda*.[32]

Sri Yukteswar paraphrases his final sutra ("Knowledge of evolution, life, and dissolution thus leads to complete emancipation from the bonds of *Maya,* delusion. Beholding the self in the Supreme Self, man gains eternal freedom") in terms that again echo the Johannine books of the New Testament, and he adds a quote from Revelation 3:21: "To him that overcometh will I grant to sit with me in my throne, even as I also overcame, and am set down with my Father in his throne." But it is with a stanza of English-language poetry that he concludes his book: "Love rules the court, the camp, the grove, / The men below and the saints above; / For love is heaven and heaven is love."[33] This is more than "the noblest sentiment of a poet," says Sri Yukteswar; it is "an aphorism of eternal truth."[34] Bhakti Yoga is hence a universal practice that transcends religious particularism; however, Sri Yukteswar does affirm that the particular Yoga practices described in his book (and transmitted under the name of Kriya Yoga by his disciple Yogananda) serve to "cultivate" love and develop it to the point that the Yogi finds an authentic guru, "becomes baptized in the holy stream, and sacrifices his Self before the altar of God, becoming unified with the Eternal Father forever and ever."[35]

I have summarized at length the essay of Yogananda's guru, because I believe it is an excellent example of how a contemporary Hindu might approach both interreligious dialogue and the teaching of Yoga to a Western audience. Many readers, both Hindu and Christian, might describe Sri Yukteswar's approach as "syncretism," and for some this would be a compliment, while for others it would imply a negative judgment. The word is too controversial, at a time when not only traditional Christians but also Hindus are redefining their identity not in relation but in total opposition to other religious identities. Let me suggest that, rather than calling it "syncretism," we could see Sri Yukteswar's use of biblical terminology in speaking of Yoga as an essay in what Christian theologians are accustomed to call "inculturation." Indeed, the Bengali sage yields nothing of his metaphysical and spiritual principles, and he confidently affirms the universal validity of India's Yoga. But at the same time, he is convinced that "eternal truth" has been and can always be expressed through other languages, with other terms, and thus Yoga can be mediated to those who live in other cultural contexts.

A Source of Kriya Yoga in the Mystics of Kashmir

When, after theological studies, I began research for a degree in history of religions, one of my primary concerns was to find earlier sources for Kriya Yoga, antecedent to the Bengali masters of Yogananda's lineage.[36] I discovered these sources in a series of Sanskrit texts from medieval Kashmir, published at the beginning of the twentieth century and slowly being translated into French, Italian, and English. The greatest of the Kashmiri mystics was Abhinavagupta (a contemporary of St. Romuald), and his were the writings I studied most, in comparison with those of the Orthodox mystic, St. Symeon the New Theologian (949–1022), as a basis for my dissertation. Abhinavagupta's chief disciple was Kshemaraja, who gave us the other text—the *Pratyabhijna-hridayam*—that we are examining here.

The edition I use was published by Adyar Library, a branch of the Theosophical Society, but the book itself was edited by a German Indologist, Emil Baer, and his translator into English, Kurt F. Leidecker.[37] The publisher inserted the entire Sanskrit text, with beautifully readable Devanagari characters, into the translation; fully half the volume is devoted to the meticulous philological and interpretive notes. What I can offer here is much less than what the text would merit, only a brief summary and a focus on some particular passages, which should be sufficient for the purposes of our dialogue.

A word about the title: literally, it means "The Heart of Recognition." The word *hridayam*, "heart," has a double meaning: first, the text offers the "heart" or secret essence of the Kashmiri school's mystical doctrine, and second, it guides the student on the way of the heart or the central path, where God is known. The term *pratyabhijna* is the name of the school itself, meaning "recognition," since Abhinavagupta and his disciples taught that God is to be recognized as the One Existent in all existing souls and beings.

As I mentioned above, the literary genre of the text is similar to that of Sri Yukteswar's: a commentary on a series of Sanskrit aphorisms, purporting to be traditional but composed by the author himself. Kshemaraja's intent was different, however, since he did not pose the question of dialogue with another religion. Nevertheless, the Kashmiri sage proceeds on an assumption like that of the Yogi of Serampore: that theoretical and philosophical differences are ultimately a question of words and concepts, not of substance. Kshemaraja uses a theatrical metaphor. The theories and principles of the various systems and schools are like the "roles" of an actor, a series of disguises that the actor himself,[38] in this case the *Atman* or spirit, does not confuse with his true essence.[39]

Likewise for Kshemaraja as for Yukteswar, the One Existent, in whom the universe (*visva*, literally, "the All") exists, is understood as *caitanya, cit,* or *citi,* terms roughly synonymous, translatable as "consciousness."[40] Permit me, as I paraphrase Kshemaraja's text, to use Sri Yukteswar's terminology, in this case, "Omniscient Feeling." The common tradition justifies the affective overtones of the Bengali's English terminology, since the One is never a coldly neutral and detached consciousness, but rather a divine Being who contemplates self in a rapture of love, and therein generates the All. *Cit,* in fact, is most often used in compound nouns with another root, especially *ananda,* "bliss," hence the Ultimate is *cidananda,* "Conscious Joy" and hence "All-knowing Love."[41] A similar term is *prakasananda,* "Blessed Light,"[42] although this refers more to the state of one who has realized, or "recognized," the nonseparation of the individual self from the Divine Self.

For both of our authors, salvation is in fact a realization, a *prise de conscience,* of the true nature of one's own existence and that of all other beings as existing in God. According to Kshemaraja's Sutra 16, "When [*Cidananda* is] attained, salvation in one's lifetime means lasting acquisition of the condition in which *cit* is . . . [one's] only self—let the body and the other [physical constituents] still be noticeable."[43] Kshemaraja does not doubt that the universe is real, although it is a realm of bondage. The condition of bodily existence is neither illusory nor evil; hence it is possible to achieve salvation while remaining in the common human condition. This is the state called *jivanmukti,* "liberation while living."[44]

Nevertheless, it is true that Kshemaraja's treatise is of a more technical and philosophical nature, and its general tone might be perceived as "colder" than Sri Yukteswar's. It must be remembered that the former's writings were intended for a narrower readership, a circle of disciples who were committed practitioners of Yoga, whereas Sri Yukteswar aimed at reaching the common reader, in line with the project of "Yoga for householders," dear to his own guru Lahiri Mahasaya. One must look to the whole Kashmiri tradition, above all to Abhinavagupta, to find the central role of "devotion," *bhakti,* underlying Kshemaraja's exposition of the way to liberation.[45]

The chief means to this end, recognition of union with "All-knowing Love," is the discovery of the "center," *madhya.* More precisely, Kshemaraja speaks of "opening" the center,[46] and the author's commentary elaborates the sense of this expression in accordance with traditional Yoga doctrine. The center is both the "heart" (Kshemaraja uses the term *citta,* which we have seen translated as "heart" by Sri Yukteswar), and the "central channel," which can be identified with the *susumna-nadi* spoken of in *Kaivalya-darsanam* and many other texts. The metaphor suggests not so much a physical object or organ as a dynamic process, a path of energy that both rises upward and tends toward a transcendent center. Kshemaraja presupposes the doctrine of the five-level embodiment found in the Upanishads and of central importance in the essay of Sri Yukteswar, but in addition, he elaborates a system of categories listed in seven pentads or groups of five.[47]

From ancient times, the experience of yogis has in general included the moment of renunciation, not only of that which impedes the recognition of nonseparation from God, but even of the effort and practice of Yoga itself. This is the moment of what, in terms of theology, might be called "grace." Kshemaraja alludes to this moment, citing a text of the Kashmiri tradition:

> When, O [Divine] Mother, men renounce completely all the activities of *manas* [the mind] and thus their dependence [on outward means] ends in flames, because they devote themselves to the activity of the organ of those that are saved [i.e., the heart]—they experience, through your power, that highest state which flows with the nectar of never-weakening, imperishable happiness.[48]

In other words, when the Yogi abandons all outward practice except that of abiding in the heart, God then manifests as Mother, the giver of ever-new joy. Another quotation, this time from the great *Vijnanabhairava Tantra,* expresses the same thought: "He who has his eyes fixed closely on the [space] of the heart, penetrates into the center of the lotus cup, and excludes all else from consciousness, will, O Beautiful One, partake of supreme joy."[49] The worship of the Divine Mother is an archaic and pre-Aryan element in Hinduism, just as is Yoga itself.

Having taken up the study of the Kashmiri Yoga tradition in search of clues to the sources of Yogananda's Kriya Yoga, I was a bit disappointed to have found hardly a word in Kshemaraja about meditation on the primordial sound, *pranava* or *om,* a practice deemed essential by Sri Yukteswar. However, among the annotations to the *Pratyabhijna-hridayam* I did discover a reference to another text of Kshemaraja, his *Siva-sutra-vimarsini* or "Commentary on the Shiva Aphorisms," where he elaborates a comparison of the various pentads or groups of five in his system of categories with the letters of the Sanskrit alphabet, the Devanagari script.[50] Note that "letters" in the Sanskrit tradition are not the written characters but the phonemes; they are elementary sounds, metaphorically termed "seeds," potential manifestations of the infinite sound or *pranava*. Kshemaraja finds a primary sonic pentad in the series of pure vowels and semi-vowels (*a, i, u, r, l*) which, when aligned with the five breath-energies of Yoga tradition, corresponds perfectly with the basic *pranayama* taught by Yogananda.

The tradition of Abhinavagupta and Kshemaraja centers around the worship of the One Absolute as Shiva, manifested in the feminine triad of his *saktis* (consorts); and the same divine One was also honored by Lahiri Mahasaya, a Brahman and the guru of Sri Yukteswar. It is interesting to note that Yukteswar's beloved disciple Yogananda, a Kshatriya (i.e., one of the warrior caste), introduced into his Yoga meditation the devotion to Bhagavan Krishna, an avatar of Vishnu. This intra-Hindu syncretism is very common in both traditional and modern Indian piety. It may have been Yogananda himself who introduced the mental recitation of the *Bhagavata-mantra* (*Om namo Bhagavate Vasudevaya*—"I adore the Lord Vasudeva [=Krishna]") as an overlay upon the chief *pranayama* practice of Kriya Yoga.[51] This interweaving of devotional prayer and technique, and the free modification of the external practice, have apparently been forgotten by some of the more rigid disciples of Yogananda, who tend to insist dogmatically that the *Kriya* technique may never be altered.

A Last Word

In spite of the church's interreligious dialogue and the movement toward a "re-inculturation" of Yoga in the East through borrowing from the West, all religious groups in India are regrettably being touched by fundamentalist and fanatical sentiments, leading to the reaffirmation of whatever is deemed traditional and authentic against all forms of innovation and contamination from other sources. The inherited religious identity, consequently, is held up in sharp opposition to all other faiths. With these motives some Indian neo-fundamentalists proclaim: "Keep Yoga out of the [Christian] convents and the Bible out of the [Hindu] ashrams!" This slogan, of course, is on the lips of Christians as well as of Hindus; here we have an excellent example of the perverse "ecumenism" that often favors convergence between extremists of opposed traditions. In Hinduism, it should be remembered, those who assume a fundamentalist and discriminatory stance can lay no claim to a "conservative" or traditional position, since Hindu and Buddhist tradition in India have left humanity an exemplary legacy of interreligious tolerance and reciprocal exchange that dates back well before the beginning of the common era.

Most of the polemics about the use of Yoga outside Hindu orthodoxy are too abstract, in that they often prescind from both personal experience and the knowledge of traditional written sources. My own reading of the sources and my personal experience assure me that it is possible to use Yogic means to the Christian end, union with God through Christ in the Spirit, because ultimately Yoga itself implies both incarnation and sacrifice, two essential dimensions of the Christ-mystery. When Yoga is practiced as a way of the heart, it moves to and from that center where humanity and divinity are one mystical person: the heart of Jesus. If Yoga is practiced as a sacrifice, in view of realizing love, then not only is it Christian; it is also universal.

3

The Space in the Lotus of the Heart

The Anthropological Spirit
in the Writings of Bede Griffiths

CYPRIAN CONSIGLIO, O.S.B. CAM.

Father Bede Griffiths was an Oxford-educated English Benedictine monk, an author and a spiritual leader, and a prominent, internationally known figure in the arena of interreligious dialogue. Through the study of the sacred writings from many of the world's religions, he sought to find the one Source common to all religion.[1]

The Immanent Mystery

At the beginning of his autobiographical work *The Golden String,* written before his move to India in 1955, Griffiths had written of his awakening to what he called the "mystery of existence." This awakening had come to him through the experience of nature, an experience that he felt to be best expressed and interpreted by the words of the Romantic poets that he had always loved so much—Wordsworth, Shelley, and Keats.

> Wordsworth taught me to find in nature the presence of a power which pervades both the universe and the [human mind].[2] Shelley had awakened me to the Platonic idea of an eternal world, of which the world we see is a dim reflection. Keats had set before me the values of "the holiness of the heart's affections and the truth of the imagination." These were for me not merely abstract ideas but living principles, which were working in me over many years and which I tried to comprehend in a reasoned philosophy of life.[3]

These ideas lay dormant in Griffiths during his years as a monk in England, but were reawakened specifically after his move to India, where he discovered that this intuition of his favored poets was the common faith of Indian culture, and had been for countless centuries. This "power which pervades the universe and the human mind" had been revealed in the Vedas centuries before the birth of Christ; the eternal world of Plato that Shelley had suggested to him was something that had been intuited by the seers of the Upanishads; and Keats's "truth of the imagination" was the primordial truth that hearkened back to the very roots of human experience.

The Threefold Universe

According to Griffiths, the great insight that the Vedic philosophers had come to was an understanding of the threefold nature of reality, that the world is at once physical, psychological, and spiritual. These three realms of reality are always interdependent and interwoven. In other words, according to Vedic philosophy, every physical reality has a psychological aspect, and both the psychological and physical realms have an underlying reality which is the source of both other realms—spiritual reality. The Vedic philosophers never separated these aspects.[4] Griffiths claims that this understanding of the threefold nature of the world

> ...underlies not only the Vedas but all ancient thought. In the primitive mind (which is also the natural mind) there is no such thing as a merely physical object. Every material thing has a psychological aspect, a relation to human consciousness, and this in turn is related to the supreme spirit which pervades both the physical world and human consciousness.[5]

This integrated understanding of the universe was "typical of the whole ancient world which had emerged out of the mythological world of more ancient times." Griffiths called this unitive vision of reality

> ...the Oriental view of the universe, which is in fact, the view of the "perennial philosophy," the cosmic vision which is common to all religious tradition from the most primitive tribal religions to the great world religions, Hinduism, Buddhism, Islam, and Christianity.[6]

Griffiths asserts that up through the Middle Ages (500–1500 c.e.), in China, India, and the Islamic world as well as in Europe, a creative synthesis had been achieved and was maintained in which the physical, psychic, and spiritual worlds were integrated. Economic, social, political and cultural orders were all conceived as a harmonious unity in which each human being was related to nature, to one's fellows, and to the Divine. According to Griffiths this unitive vision began to be lost at the Renaissance:

> After [the Middle Ages] this creative synthesis began to disintegrate. The Reformation and the Renaissance, the "Enlightenment" and the French Revolution, the Russian and the Chinese Revolutions, are all stages in this process of disintegration.[7]

Griffiths also accused Protestantism of breaking up the organic unity of the mystical body of Christ, rationalism of setting the human mind free from the divine, and communism of depriving humans beings of their basic liberty and enslaving them to the material world.[8] Consequently, in our times we have now inherited a mind-set that separates matter from mind, and separates matter and mind from the Supreme Reality, from God.[9] Especially the West suffers from the disease of the merely rational mind that " ... causes us to see [matter, mind, and spirit] as separate from one another, to imagine a world extended outside of us in space and time, and the mind as something separate from the external world."[10]

Griffiths saw far-reaching consequences for the West slowly regaining this original and ancient vision, this perennial philosophy, through depth psychology and modern physics. It is specifically the application of this worldview to human nature that is the subject of this paper. Though there are no specific references to Aldous Huxley in Griffiths's writings, and it is quite possible that Griffiths uses "Perennial Philosophy" in the standard Western sense of Aristotelian/Thomistic thought, it is equally possible that it is Huxley's version of the Perennial Philosophy that Griffiths has in mind, as will become clear from further exposition of Griffiths's thought below. Huxley, coincidentally, in his introduction to Christopher Isherwood's translation of the Bhagavad Gita, makes the statement that the focus of Indian religion "is also one of the clearest and most comprehensive summaries of the Perennial Philosophy ever to have been made."[11] He states it in four points. First: "the phenomenal world of matter and of individualised consciousness—the world of things and animals and [human beings] and even gods—is a manifestation of a Divine Ground within which all partial realities have their being." Second: human beings are capable of realizing the existence of the Divine Ground "by a direct intuition [that is] superior to discursive reasoning," a knowledge that unites the knower with that which is known. Third: human beings possess a double nature, "a phenomenal ego and an eternal Self, which is the inner person, the spirit, the spark of divinity within the soul." Fourth: the end and purpose of human life is to identify oneself with this eternal Self and "so to come to unitive knowledge of the Divine Ground."[12] It is the third point that leads us specifically into Bede Griffiths's anthropology, and the connection between the three realms and human nature.

Just as all created reality has a spiritual, psychological, and material dimension, so each human being is spirit, soul, and body. It is this tripartite anthropology that became the core of Griffiths's teaching and writings. This is not the typical Western way to speak of Christian anthropology. We do not normally distinguish spirit from soul, but speak of the human person as either body and soul or body and spirit, though we do speak of the "spiritual soul." For example, the Catechism of the Roman Catholic Church says:

> Sometimes the soul is distinguished from the spirit.... This does not introduce a duality into the soul. "Spirit" signifies that from creation [human beings] are ordered to a supernatural end and that [one's] soul can be gratuitously raised ... to communion with God.[13]

Griffiths, among others, found this anthropology lacking. On the one hand Griffiths saw the need always to distinguish between the spirit and the soul, between the spiritual and the psychic; on the other hand he saw the need to specifically understand and accentuate the importance of the spiritual realm, and so bring the other two realms to their fruition. Once, in a presentation just before his death, he said, "The body, mind, and spirit are the main focus of all my thinking presently; we have to integrate these three levels of reality that exist at every moment."[14]

Griffiths claimed that this view of the human person as body, soul, and spirit was fundamental in the Bible and very clear in St. Paul.[15] As body, human nature is part of the whole physical universe. It evolves out of the physical universe, from matter and life. As soul (*psyche*), humanity is the head of the universe; it is, in a sense, matter coming into consciousness and forming an individual soul. But then, like matter itself, that soul has the potential to open to the *pneuma*, the spirit, which is the point where the human spirit opens onto the Spirit of God.[16]

Wisdom of the Vedanta

This awakening came for Griffiths, as noted above, through his study of the Vedanta. That discovery then opened him to see this anthropology latent in Judeo-Christian theology as well. Let us review the exposition of certain aspects of Hinduism which Bede used to explain this worldview. In Hindu theology there are many different ways to speak about the Godhead. Let us examine two of the most basic ones.

At first glance Hinduism appears to be polytheistic, but ultimately all the gods (in Sanskrit *devas*) are manifestations of the one God, the Supreme One. There are generally three different names given for this Supreme Being. The first and most typical is *Brahman*. The word *Brahman* roughly means the Fullness or the Ultimate, the reality behind everything. A second name for this ultimate reality is *Atman*. Whereas *Brahman* has the nuance of reality, *Atman* has the nuance of essence. *Atman* is the Spirit *within* everything. This is the aspect we will delve into more below. A third name for God is *Purusha*. This is the personal God, God as the Person, the Supreme Person.[17]

Another way to express this same reality is to say that *Brahman* is manifested at three different levels. First, God is *Nirguna Brahman,* the ultimate transcendent mystery beyond all word or thought, infinite transcendent reality, God without qualities or attributes, beyond everything that can be

conceived. Then there is *Saguna Brahman,* God *with* attributes and related
to the universe. In this sense God is conceived of as Creator, source of all reality, consciousness and existence, and Lord and Saviour.[18] As the Chandogya
Upanishad says: "The universe comes forth from Brahman and will return
to Brahman. Verily, all is Brahman."[19] In *Return to the Center,* Griffiths
equates this view with the Trinity:

> The Father is *nirguna* Brahman, the naked Godhead, the abyss of Be-
> ing, the divine darkness, without form and void, the silence where
> no word is spoken, where no thought comes, the absolute nothing-
> ness from which everything comes, the not-being from which all being
> comes, the One without a second, which is utterly empty yet immea-
> surably full, wayless and fathomless.... The Son is *saguna* Brahman,
> the Word through which the Father receives a name, by which he is
> expressed, by which he is conceived.... In the Son the whole creation
> comes forth eternally from the Father.[20]

Finally, as mentioned above, God is *Atman,* manifested as indwelling
in each person and each thing. Again, it is this aspect, *Atman,* God as indwelling Supreme Spirit, that is the focus of this paper. *Atman* is the spiritual
aspect of the three interpenetrating realms of reality, beyond the physical and
the psychological. *Atman* is also each human being's highest and truest self,
the self that is ultimately one with the Supreme Self. God as *Atman* dwells in
each person as one's own inner spirit, as one's own *Atman.* This is the Spirit
of God in the human person, the Spirit of God's Self-communication.[21]

The Sanskrit word *Atman* is usually translated as "self." It is derived from
two Sanskrit roots that mean "to move constantly" and "to pervade."[22]
At various times the word *Atman* means wind, breath, oneself (reflexive
pronoun), body, essence, controller, and principle of intelligence.[23] This is
a striking similarity to the Hebrew *ruah* and the Greek *pneuma,* so it is
not without justification that Griffiths equates this *Atman* with the Judeo-
Christian notion of spirit.

One can discern three different uses of the term *Atman* in Hindu theology.
These nuances of the word *Atman* correspond to nuances found in Pauline
and general Christian use of the word *pneuma,* or spirit: God the Holy Spirit
(in Christianity, the Third Person of the Holy Trinity); the apportioned[24]
indwelling Spirit given to each person by virtue of grace; and, finally, one's
own spirit, what some call the "natural spirit" or the human spirit. So in
Hindu thought there is first of all the *Paramatman,* the "Supreme Being"
or "Supreme Self," referring specifically to the Godhead. Griffiths equates
this sense, the Great Self, with the Christian concept of the third person
of the Christian Trinity, God the Holy Spirit. *Paramatman,* the Supreme
Spirit, is beyond word and thought. This *Paramatman* is also present in each
human being in the depth of his or her being. This is a second nuance to

the word *Atman*—the Spirit of God *in* a human being.[25] This sense seems to correspond to the notion of apportioned Spirit common to both the Hebrew and Christian Scriptures, and a concept that is specifically Pauline, as we shall see later. In a third nuance, *Atman* can also refer to the human being's *own* spirit,[26] "spirit" as an anthropological element. This usage of spirit is suggested in Pauline literature when he refers to "your spirit" or "my spirit."[27]

Meditation is of course essential for the Upanishadic teachers.

> One who meditates upon and realizes the Self discovers that everything in the cosmos—energy and space, fire and water, name and form, birth and death, mind and will, word and deed, mantram and meditation—all come from the Self.
>
> ... Those who meditate upon the Self and realize the Self go beyond decay and death, beyond separateness and sorrow. They see the Self in everyone and obtain all things.
>
> Control the senses and purify the mind. In a pure mind there is a constant awareness of the Self.[28]

In meditation one detaches consciousness from the body and senses. Here is Father Bede explaining his own approach to meditation:

> In meditation I try to let go of everything of the outer world of the senses, the inner world of thoughts, and listen to the inner voice, the voice of the Word, which comes in the silence, in the stillness when all the activity of body and mind cease.[29]

Then, as meditation deepens, one detaches consciousness from all the layers of mind, ultimately to reach the state of *turiya*, dreamless sleep, in the depths of the unconscious where one is aware of neither body nor mind. At this stage every trace of individuality is removed and the meditator realizes pure being, Brahman, the ground of existence, the essence of every created thing:

> Simultaneous with this discovery comes another: this unitary awareness is also the ground of one's own being, the core of personality. This divine ground the Upanishads call simply *Atman*, "the Self" spelled with a capital to distinguish it from individual personality.... In all persons, all creatures, the Self is the innermost essence. And it is identical with Brahman: our real Self is not different from the ultimate Reality called God.[30]

The classic example of this teaching is in the Chandogya Upanishad where a father tells his son over and over again through many examples how the *Atman* is everywhere, the hidden essence that merges with all things. At one point the father compares the *Atman* to salt dissolved in water and says:

> It is everywhere, though we see it not.
> Just so, dear one, the Self is everywhere,
> Within all things, although we see him not.
> There is nothing that does not come from him.
> Of everything he is the inmost Self.
> He is the truth; he is the Self supreme.
> *You are that, Shvetaketu; you are that.*[31]

It is this last line—in Sanskrit, *Tat tvam asi! You are that!*—that is arguably the most famous of the Upanishadic literature. Griffiths says that "this is the record of the decisive moment in Indian history, the discovery of the identity of the *Brahman* and the *Atman.*"[32] This is the experience that underlies all subsequent Hindu thought. Another famous image, "the space in the lotus of the heart," comes from the same Upanishad. (The "city of Brahman" here refers to the human body.)

> In the city of Brahman is a secret dwelling, the lotus of the heart. Within this dwelling is a space, and within that space is the fulfilment of our desires. What is within the space should be longed for and realized. As great as the infinite space beyond is the space within the lotus of the heart.[33]

Spirit and Soul

The next necessary step is to distinguish spirit from soul. In Hindu anthropology this is done with the same word *Atman* and a different prefix—*jiva.* The *jivatman* is the individual self or the soul, the Ultimate Reality in an individual.[34] It is the individual self as opposed to the Great Self, but it is not the individual spirit; Griffiths and Sharma both say the term is equivalent to our notion of "soul." Griffiths employs the sense used by late Vedic and Sanskrit literature, referring to the *jivatman* as the "lower self" or the self with a small "s." Here "soul" includes the senses, the mind, the ego, and the intellect, all separate components in Hindu psychology—in Sanskrit the *indriyas, manas, ahamkara,* and *buddhi* respectively. The intellect (*buddhi*) is of special importance because it is at the point of the intellect, which is our capability for self-transcendence, "where we can go beyond ourselves." To humanity, by virtue of the soul and its intellect, belongs the psychological world which stands between the spiritual world of heaven and the material world of earth.[35] It is important to note, however, that the conscious mind is only one aspect of the *jivatman;* it is a complex organic structure in which many other levels of the mind exist—the subconscious, unconscious, preconscious, and higher forms of consciousness. Together they embrace the whole world of consciousness.[36]

But always, beyond the lower self or soul (*jivatman*) of each human being, there is the higher self, the *Atman,* which is actually the true Self, "the Self of our striving." This higher self Griffiths equates with the human spirit, hence quoting and paraphrasing verse 6:5 of the Bhagavad Gita to read

> With the help of your spirit (*paramatman*) lift up your soul (*jivatman*): do not allow your soul to fall. For your soul can be your friend, and your soul can be your enemy. A person's soul is a friend when by the spirit one has conquered the soul; but when one is not lord of one's soul then this becomes one's enemy.[37]

What is to be noted here is the dynamic between the soul and the spirit. The spirit is the force or vitality of the soul's striving toward perfection. But the soul can be the enemy to the spirit; the lower self can be an enemy to the true or higher self. The soul stands between the *Atman* and the world of senses, passions, and activity. It is the soul with its intellect that makes the choice either to turn toward the world and the body, or toward the Spirit within and live by the Spirit's law. It is this function of the soul to choose between the world of sense and activity and the world of the Spirit that Griffiths uses to make the connection to biblical, specifically Pauline, thought. With the translator Zaehner he points out that according to St. Paul to live by the Spirit is to live by the Holy Spirit within, and to live by the flesh is to live by one's natural feelings. This latter Paul calls *anthropos psychikos,* i.e., a person of the soul, the former *anthropos pneumatikos,* i.e., the person of the Spirit.[38]

Atman and Spirit

The *Atman* is the point of meeting between God and the human person. The *Atman* is our real Self, and when body and soul are under the control of the inner *Atman* we are *yukta* (integrated), "realized," or *anthropos pneumatikos* in Pauline vocabulary. When we are thus realized, the Spirit of God meets the human spirit. This is the goal of yoga:

> [Yoga is]...a means of union, union of the powers of the body in harmony, union of body and soul in harmony, union of body and soul with the inner Spirit. But this is only attained when body and soul are "sacrificed" to the Spirit.... This is the death the body and soul have to undergo, the sacrifice of their autonomy, their surrender to the inner Spirit.[39]

What then is the relation of the individual *Atman,* the human spirit, to the *Paramatman,* the Spirit of God? This is where language breaks down because later Hindu spirituality, especially under the influence of Shankara, also has the concept of *advaita*—nonduality. It is a typically Western way of approaching the problem to point out that there are three notions of *Atman:* God-as-spirit, God-as-indwelling-Spirit, and one's own spirit. To a Hindu, this does not necessarily matter. Even though we are pointing to *Atman* as being at once the essence of the Supreme Being and as abiding in the individual soul, to the Hindu they are "not two." The basic ideal of the relationship between the individual soul (*jivatman*) and *Brahman* is identity between the Supreme Spirit and the vital spirit. The Supreme Spirit enters the human body as the individual *Atman.* On entering the body the *Atman* is its vital force, directing the functions of its organs, becoming one with the different senses. As well, the *Atman* is the intelligent principle in a person. Still, to the Hindu, ultimately the individual *Atman* is nothing other than the Supreme *Atman.* The goal of life is to realize that one's true nature is one with the *Atman.* So a Hindu can say "I am Brahman." (Also, "You are that.") Of course, in Hindu thinking this entails a *jivatman* transmigrating from one body to another until the individual soul increases enough in knowledge to be freed from the cycle of birth and death (*karma*) by overcoming ignorance.[40] This liberation (*moksha*) is only achieved, this ignorance overcome, by realizing one's true nature, precisely by realizing one's identity with the *Atman.*

While Christianity does not, of course, accept the notion of the transmigration of souls (reincarnation), the discovery of the Self has definite resonances with the language of our own mystical tradition. Griffiths explains:

> ... in the normal understanding, as seen in the *advaitic* school [the school of non-duality], the individual self is identified with the Supreme Self. "I am Brahman." "Thou art that." It is an identity with the Absolute. That is a genuine and profound mystical experience without a doubt. By contrast, in the Christian understanding the human spirit is never identified with the Spirit of God.[41]

Again Huxley's explanation helps, too:

> The Hindu categorically affirms that "thou art That"—that the indwelling *Atman* is the same as *Brahman.* For Orthodox Christianity there is not an identity between the spark and God. Union of the human spirit with God takes place—union so complete that the word "deification" is applied to it; but it is not a union of identical substances. According to Christian theology, the saint is "deified," not because *Atman* is *Brahman,* but because God has assimilated the purified human spirit into the divine substance by an act of grace.[42]

Whereas the Hindu understands union with God by identity ("I am Brahman"), Griffiths taught that the uniquely Christian insight is that the

Godhead is a communion of persons. He points specifically to the Trinity as the example of this. Hence we look forward not to "union by identity" but "union by communion":

> ...in love we go out of ourselves, we offer ourselves to another, each gives [oneself] to the other but you don't lose yourself in the other, you find yourself. That is the mystery of communion in God and with God—the Father and the Son become a total unity and are yet distinct, and that is true of [human beings] and God as well. We are one, and yet we are distinct. There is never a total loss of self. In consciousness there is pure identity, but in love there's never pure identity because love involves two, and yet the two become one. That's the great mystery. It's a paradox.[43]

Hence, the Indian metaphor of the ocean and the droplet that re-merges with the ocean "is not adequate":

> You can say the drop merges in the ocean, but you can also say the ocean is present in the drop. . . . In the ultimate state the individual is totally there, totally realized, but also in total communion with all the rest.[44]

Still there are distinct resonances with Christian mystical language and a valuable insight offered from this Eastern understanding.

> This is the great discovery of Indian thought, the discovery of the Self, the *Atman,* the Ground of personal being, which is one with the *Brahman,* the Ground of universal being. It is not reached by thought; on the contrary, it is only reached by transcending thought. Reason, like the self of which it is a faculty, has to transcend itself.[45]

This, then, is the goal of all holy discipline; to discover, to realize that my ultimate self is one with the Great Self. As for the meaning of this relationship between the Great Self and the individual self, Griffiths gives no systematic treatment except to say that the two, the individual spirit and the Supreme Spirit, meet at the still point, in the heart. When they really meet they are no longer two. The *Paramatman* is present in each human being in the depths of one's own spirit. The human spirit meets the Spirit of God and we experience God's presence; when we enter into the depths of our soul, or rather the depths of our own spirit, we discover the depths of God, the Lord dwelling within us.[46] The human spirit is a dynamic point, the point where the human being is open to God.[47] This is the point of human self-transcendence. When we respond to grace we open to the divine. Griffiths also resonates with the thought of Karl Rahner (whom he said he "admired more than anyone else") and specifically with Rahner's idea of the "supernatural existential."

[Rahner] says that in every human being there is the capacity for self-transcendence. Beyond our body, [note again the same language] beyond the normal faculties of the soul, we are open to the transcendent reality. That capacity is in us at all times, and it can grow and become total, so it is possible for the human being to give [oneself] totally to God.[48]

In another place, Griffiths goes so far as to link up Rahner's supernatural existential, *Atman,* the *pneuma,* and Buddha nature!

In Christian terms we would say you have your body, your physical organism, and you have learned to control a great deal of that energy: you have your psychological organism, senses, feeling, imagination, reason, will and then you go beyond your body, beyond your psyche to your pneuma, your spirit, the Atman in Sanskrit, and there you open to the Divine, the transcendent, the Infinite...what St. Francis de Sales called "the fine point of the soul," the point which Karl Rahner mentions as the point of self-transcendence....It is in every human being. It is what is called the Buddha nature.[49]

One other Christian writer to echo this understanding is the Zen master Lassalle, who writes that "Zen leads [one] into the realm of the pure spirit. The pure spirit, which knows neither psyche nor body, is God. The long journey of Zen meditation leads to that place."[50]

When we resist grace we fall from that point of the spirit to the psyche, that is, the soul with all of its faculties and powers.[51]

... [T]hen we become subject to the powers of this world, the demonic powers as well as other powers. But at that point of the spirit is the Self within all beings. At the still point within my spirit meets the Spirit of God....[52]

The Fall of Genesis then takes on a new meaning:

The Fall is our fall into this present mode of consciousness, where everything is divided, centered on itself and set in conflict with others. The Fall is the fall into self-consciousness, that is, into a consciousness centered in the self which has lost touch with the eternal ground of consciousness, which is the true Self.[53]

In a sense, the reflective consciousness is the source of all sin and misery, but it is also the source of salvation:

...the reflective consciousness turned away from the eternal light of Truth and began to concentrate on [humanity] and nature. The marvels of modern science and technology, the transformation of the world and of human society, which we have witnessed, are the fruits of this reflective consciousness centered on [humanity] and nature. But the cost of it has been the alienation of [human beings] from [their] true [selves], from the Ground of being, of truth and morality, and now they are exposed to all the destructive forces which this has released.[54]

Bede's Anthropology Today

Let us examine some reasons why this anthropology is important. First of all, it is an antidote to dualism. By dualism is meant here the notion that the soul is trapped in the body as in a tomb, and the corollary that the body is somehow bad while the soul is good. Not simply adding another element to a scattered, unintegrated view of the human person, this tripartite anthropology is wedded to an understanding of the three interpenetrating realms of reality—the spiritual, the psychic, and the material. Far from the notion of casting off the body for the liberation of the soul, this view points toward integration; the truly enlightened person is one who is in tune with all these aspects of reality, sensitive not just to the material, and not just to the psychic, but also to the spiritual, to the incipient sacredness of created matter. This is a profoundly Christian idea: created things, material and psychic, find their fulfillment in the spiritual. This seems to me to be the deepest meaning of the Transfiguration, the Resurrection, and the Ascension of our Christ.

The second reason why this distinction is important is that it points out to Christians and non-Christians alike that there is something beyond the psychic realm. For a generation attracted to the New Age phenomena of astrology, channelling, occult practices, and even angels, it is important to point out that these things are *psychic* phenomena. While the common practice is to call these things spiritual, they are not properly of the spiritual realm: they are still created things of the psychic realm that need to be brought farther, to the realm of the spirit. The use of hallucinogenic drugs, through which people claim to have had spiritual awakenings, indeed opens areas of the unconscious and even higher forms of consciousness, and breaks ego boundaries and unlocks secrets. But these are not spiritual things per se—they are still in the realm of the psychic. And these psychic powers are neutral often, but also sometimes are evil. Either way, there needs to be a movement beyond the realm of the psyche, to the spiritual, the realm beyond all phenomena.

Christians, too, are in an age that seems fascinated yet again with visions, locutions, and so-called charismatic gifts. These may indeed be manifestations of authentic spiritual blessings (or not), but either way they are still in the realm of psychic phenomena and there must be a movement beyond, to the realm of the spirit. One thinks of the warnings of St. John of the Cross not to long for these phenomena but to press on into the darkness to the *nada*. This is the realm of the spirit.[55]

The next reason I think this notion of spirit is important is that we are in the process of recovering our mystical tradition in the West, and this cannot be done without a reappreciation of the apophatic. This is the realm of the spirit, the way of unknowing, the way of darkness, where there are not clear-cut answers but an invitation to surrender to the mystery. I am particularly attracted to the Orthodox writer Evdokimov's "... apophatic anthropology leading to an apophatic theology."[56] The mystical tradition, contemplative prayer, calls us to our own "apophatic depths," to our real and truest self. Perhaps it is Christianity's lack of nurturing of our own apophatic, mystical, contemplative tradition that causes so many to be attracted to the spiritualities of the East, specifically Hinduism or yoga, and the many forms of Buddhism. There are very real and good experiences happening to people through the benefit of these practices, and they are available in our own tradition as well, but we are not offering them because we do not understand them.

On the other hand, to distinguish the spiritual from the psychic also gives a new appreciation for the *psychic realm itself*. It is my experience that we Christians are terribly afraid of the psychic realm. I am not calling for an increase of dabbling in the occult! But one monk I know insists that it is because Christianity has not paid enough attention to the psychic realm that psychology has replaced Christianity as the spirituality of the West. I am learning more and more that good psychology is good theology. We need not be afraid of the journey into the unconscious, the subconscious, or higher states of consciousness. We need not be afraid of the psychic realm or psychic phenomena. All these things are part of the created order, and can and must be brought into submission to the higher realm, the realm of the spirit.

Perhaps the most profound implication of Father Bede's view, one of which I have become personally convinced, is that it provides a wonderful meeting point for dialogue with other spiritual traditions. It is undeniable that the seers of the Upanishads, the Buddha and his followers, and the Sufi and Hebrew mystics have all had a very real, and in many ways very similar, experience of mystical presence brought about by meditation and the inner journey. Perhaps we could agree on this "spirit," this mysterious apophatic depth, as a starting point, if we could share experiences and stories at this depth before engaging in doctrinal debates, and therefore go from the known to the unknown.

Finally, the significance and power of this notion of the human spirit can be felt in a phrase used both by Hindus and Buddhists: *the space in the lotus of the heart.*

Within that space is the fulfilment of our desires. What is within the space should be longed for and realized. As great as the infinite space beyond is the space within the lotus of the heart.[57]

There is something wonderful inside of us, a meeting point with the Divine, the place where God ignites a spark, implants the Word, breathes into us the breath of life. We are meant for God because God's image has been imprinted in the very depth of our being. The Hindu tradition calls this depth of our being the space in the lotus of the heart.

Purity of Heart

We shall now make some connections between Bede Griffiths's anthropology and the Christian notion of purity of heart, with specific reference to the *Praktikos* of Evagrius of Pontus. In the tradition of the Greek Christian Fathers, purity of heart is associated with *apatheia,* passionlessness. For Clement of Alexandria, for example, *apatheia* is the absence of passions (*patheia),* passions being not just emotions in general, but pointless, irrational reactions. One has reached a state of *apatheia* when one is in full possession of the affective faculties under divine contemplation, so that any disordered emotions are resolved in a state of abiding calm. For Evagrius there is a progression from *ascesis* (asceticism or praxis) to *apatheia* to *agape* (being both love of God and love of neighbor). *Apatheia* is a relatively permanent state of deep calm resulting from the integration of the emotional life under the influence of *agape.*[58] Tugwell explains that it is not emotionlessness that Evagrius is trying to inculcate but "a state of harmony in which all our faculties are doing precisely what they were created to do, so that they do not disturb our equilibrium or hinder the proper clarity which the mind should have."[59]

There is a striking similarity here with Griffiths's own language, though when he speaks of this same state it is in the context of meditation and yoga. Note that yoga means both "union" (or "integration") and the steps by which one approaches that union or integration. To return to our original formula, the spirit or *Atman* is the point of meeting between God and the human person. The *Atman* is our real Self, and when body and soul are under the control of the inner *Atman* we are *yukta* (integrated), "realized." This is where Bede makes the connection to the *anthropos pneumatikos* in Pauline vocabulary. When we are thus realized, the Spirit of God meets the human spirit. This is the goal of yoga:

> [Yoga is]...a means of union, union of the powers of the body in harmony, union of body and soul in harmony, union of body and soul with the inner Spirit. But this is only attained when body and soul are "sacrificed" to the Spirit.... This is the death the body and soul have

to undergo, the sacrifice of their autonomy, their surrender to the inner Spirit.[60]

This sacrifice of autonomy is connected with release from the grip of the ego; one becomes *yukta,* integrated, when spirit, soul, and body are in right relationship, with the spirit as the guiding element. It is only when the spirit takes the lead that our faculties can do "precisely what they were created to do." Again employing his tripartite anthropology, Griffiths explains in *New Creation in Christ* that we have the body, the physical organism, and we have the soul, the psyche, which is the psychological organism. And at the center of the psyche is the ego:

> that which in Sanskrit is called *ahamkara,* the "I-maker." The psyche is very limited, but beyond it is the spirit, the *Atman* which is the point of self-transcendence. At that point body and soul go beyond their human limitations and open to the infinite, the eternal, the divine.[61]

Using the creation myth of Genesis, Griffiths explains that the human body and soul were intended from creation to respond to the Spirit within, and if Adam and Eve had not fallen they would have grown in body and soul to an ever deeper relationship with God, and all of creation would have been as it was intended. But instead of responding to the Spirit within they centered on the ego, "a separated self, separated from God, from others and from the universe." And thus human beings are trapped in the psyche because "we are all centered in this ego."[62] He explains in *River of Compassion* that there is a physical, a psychological, and a spiritual level to all human action, and while the body and mind are necessarily involved in every action, behind them is the Spirit, the *Atman,* which is meant to be the force, the motivator of every action:

> If the spirit is free from the chains of selfishness and has rid itself of egoism, and if the mind is free from any ill will, then no evil can be conceived. The action will come from the Spirit within and that cannot be evil.[63]

The most obvious means of freeing the spirit from the chains of this selfishness and ridding it of egoism is meditation. Speaking of the use of the mantra, for instance, Griffiths says that its function is to

> recollect the soul, to bring it back to its center and unite the whole person—body, soul, and spirit—with the Spirit of God.... Meditation is passing beyond your body and soul into that point of the spirit.[64]

Meditation, and indeed all Christian practice, is a way of "going beyond the ego and opening to the Spirit, and then allowing the Spirit to transform us,"[65] and again, "The aim of asceticism is to realize the spirit within."[66]

Thus for Evagrius, "Apatheia is the very flower of ascesis."[67] Similar to Evagrius's notion of equilibrium, Griffiths explains that, once one has realized the spirit within,

> one will not be affected by what happens to the body and what happens to the soul. Or rather, one may be affected, one may feel it, but one will not be overcome by it. And that is what is being aimed at.... In all the suffering of the body and the soul, there is always the presence of the Spirit which remains unchanged, above the conflict.[68]

It is important to note that for the Christian meditation is not a self-powered cure. While the union involves the uniting or integrating of all aspects of our own being, the union is primarily with God. "We cannot transform ourselves," Griffiths says, but when we go beyond the ego and open to the Spirit, we allow the Spirit to transform us.[69] In *New Vision of Reality* he speaks directly about Gregory of Nyssa's "concept of *apatheia*, passionlessness, which (Gregory) relates to purity of heart," as being the effect of divine grace: "One does not become passionless and then find God, but God himself enables one to free oneself from passion and attain to this purity of heart."[70]

> Then, when one is freed from passion, anger and desire and as the mind becomes controlled, one reaches the state of inner stillness. At the same time the real self, which controls the body, the mind and everything else, makes itself known.[71]

Evagrius writes that the proof of *apatheia* is when "the spirit begins to see its own light, when it remains in a state of tranquility,"[72] and Griffiths explains that the end of meditation is a "process of unifying all the faculties of the soul at the point of the spirit where they are permeated by the light of truth." The result, for Evagrius, is *agape*, selfless love: "Agape is the progeny of apathcia."[73] Thus for Griffiths:

> the moment we go beyond the ego, beyond its rational consciousness, we enter the non-dual consciousness where we see everybody and everything as distinct but not separate.[74]

Thus, Bede Griffiths's use of the tripartite anthropology is directly connected to purity of heart through his understanding of the ego as the trap at the center of the psyche, and through his understanding of the end of meditation. Through meditation, we go beyond the ego to find ourselves motivated by the Spirit within, which can keep us in a state of equilibrium, in right relationship with the Spirit of God who guides all our actions: "You will guide me by your counsel and so you will lead me to glory."[75]

We shall end with this quote from *River of Compassion* which sums up our thoughts on Bede Griffiths's use of the tripartite anthropology, and its relation to purity of heart:

> There are three levels in all human action: physical, psychological and spiritual. The body and the mind are engaged in all, but behind them both is the *Atman*, the Spirit, and ultimately every action comes from the Spirit of God ... If the spirit is free from the chains of selfishness and has rid itself of egoism, and if the mind is free of any ill will, then no evil can be conceived. The action comes from the Spirit within and that cannot be evil.[76]

Part II

BUDDHISM

Our Buddhist contributions represent two successive phases of a single, highly focused tradition of contemplative spirituality. Chan Buddhism is believed to have been initiated by Bodhidarma when he brought Dhyana Buddhism from India to China at about 500 C.E. Chan Buddhism moved to Japan around 1300 C.E., becoming Zen. The strong central thread of continuity which joins all of these papers is the quest for enlightenment, or nondual consciousness.

Martin Verhoeven (Chan) insists upon the necessity of practice as a basis for enlightenment. The journey is a return to our true nature, "Buddha-nature," "self-nature." The fullness is within oneself, and not to be attained through the mediation of any external power. Heng Sure (Chan) concentrates upon the bodily practice of bowing, which is not understood—and often regarded with aversion—in the modern West. Through bowing, the self-concept may gradually disappear, opening the way to nondual consciousness. Nicholas Koss (Chan) finds similarities between the enlightenment experience of the Chan Buddhist Sixth Patriarch, Hui-neng, and the experience which is expressed in the fourteenth-century English Christian *Cloud of Unknowing*.

Francis Cook (Zen) discusses the place of *purity* in Buddhism from its beginnings through its development into Mahayana and finally Zen forms. Impurity is a matter of perception and of consciousness. Through meditation, one may arrive at the state of *sunyata* (emptiness), in which the illusory duality of pure and impure disappears. Zen, stressing the practice of meditation rather than moral improvement or intellectual development, shows relatively little concern for purity. William Skudlarek (Zen) considers Jesus' command, "Do not judge . . . ," in relation to the nondual consciousness of Zen Buddhism. For a Christian, he proposes, sitting in *zazen* can be one way of surmounting the dualistic consciousness which is compelled to judge, and of coming to an experiential realization of the all-embracing love of God.

Taigen Dan Leighton discusses the anomalous figures of the Zen tradition. In the Mahayana Buddhist tradition, Maitreya, the archetypal bodhisattva, is taken as a model for the purity of heart which expresses itself in loving-kindness and in a simplicity which can appear foolish. Along with Zen monks who exemplify this Maitreyan simplicity and foolishness (Hotei, Hanshan, and Ryokan), he recalls the monks cited by Dogen who stood out for the excellence of their practice and the altruism of their behavior while violating monastic regulations. Exact observance of rules does not suffice to bring a person to purity of heart. Rather, "the monastic procedures . . . serve as a cauldron for guiding the practitioner toward actualizing the inner spirit of the pure heart." Kevin Hunt brings us back to the Christian monastic tradition, where he considers the perennial theme of temptation and trial in the light of the Zen Buddhist conception of the "Great Doubt."

Corresponding to "purity of heart" in the essays of Martin Verhoeven and Heng Sure is *practice*. The stern logic of purification demands an integrity of life on all its levels down to the most earthly. Heng Sure, indeed, regards this integrity of practice "from below," from the viewpoint of the bodily practice of bowing and prostration. Corresponding to "contemplation" in this same tradition of Chan Buddhism is the goal of pure nondual "original mind" or "buddha-mind," a goal which is also the inner principle of the way. Contrasting with the practical logic of the way is Nicholas Koss's presentation of Hui-neng as "gifted," enlightened gratuitously and suddenly. Enlightenment, or nondual consciousness (primary for all three presentations), appears in this essay in its splendid autonomy, free of conditions—even the condition of consistent practice. The strength of Chan Buddhism appears, then, as a paradoxical union of (1) a consistent logic of practice leading to purity and thus to enlightenment, with (2) the perfect and unconditioned principle of "original mind": infinite consciousness without duality.

The Zen Buddhist tradition appears as an unswerving path of the transformation of consciousness, a way of return to the absolute nonduality of "original mind" through meditation. In the four presentations of Zen, nondual consciousness consumes all dualities: the dualities of morality (Cook), of judgment (Skudlarek), of law and lawbreaking (Leighton), of the experience of light and darkness, certainty and doubt, along the path (Hunt). During a discussion, Professor Cheng recalled the verse from the Diamond Sutra that is said to have catalyzed Hui-neng's enlightenment. Here is the heart of this Chan-Zen tradition:

> One should bring forth the thought
> that dwells nowhere.

4

Glistening Frost and Cooking Sand

Unalterable Aspects of Purity
in Chan Buddhist Meditation

MARTIN J. VERHOEVEN

Talking about food won't make you full,
babbling about clothes won't keep out the cold.
A bowl of rice is what fills the belly;
it takes a suit of clothing to make you warm.
And yet, without stopping to consider this,
you complain that Buddha is hard to find.
Turn your mind within! There he is!
Why look for him outside?[1]

Historically, Buddhism has had a revitalizing effect on the religious traditions of the countries and cultures it has encountered and vice versa. This salutary phenomenon shows every sign of repeating in the West. Nowhere is this more evident than in the burgeoning interest in and popularity of Buddhist forms of meditation practice. This paper seeks to briefly map out a commonality of approach to spiritual knowledge derived from practice (especially contemplative) that undergirds a broadly shared spiritual worldview of East Asia and much of South Asia. The Asian religious orientation is essentially orthopraxic, and built upon certain common ideas about the nature of spiritual experience and ultimate goals.

I offer for consideration a translation from the Chinese of one section from the *Shurangama-sutra* (*leng-yan jing*) called "the Four Unalterable Aspects of Purity" (from which the two phrases in the title, "glistening frost" and "cooking sand," are taken). I then refer specifically to two Chan Buddhist monks: Han Shan from the sixteenth century, and Xu Yun from the mid-nineteenth and early twentieth century. Though widely divergent in time, both demonstrate remarkable similarity in their understanding and practice of meditation. Both also allude to and take guidance from the same *Shurangama-sutra* which details the methods, purposes, pitfalls, and psychophysical states associated with Chan meditation.

In brief, the text lays out a precise and explicit formula for the proper cultivation of meditation—one that begins in four aspects of "purity," develops into deepening levels of concentration (*samadhi*), and culminates in wisdom (*prajna*, or insight). Without an exact and diligent adherence to this formula, the text warns of incomplete, unreliable, and even dangerous results.

The paper is meant to be suggestive and exploratory. The text and biographical anecdotes invite discussion on a number of possible implications for other contemplatives, and more specifically, for those engaged in incorporating Buddhist meditation techniques into non-Buddhist theologies and faith traditions.

Background

Early Buddhism emerged from an Indian religious matrix that had evolved and transformed by the Buddha's time into sects of ascetics, mystics, and renunciants who sought for spiritual truth beyond the long-established authority of the brahmin priests. These *sramanas* (from Sanskrit root *sram,* "to make effort, do austerities") were well-established by the time of Buddha's birth. They were less inclined to invoke external gods than to look for "god" within. Union with, or more accurately, "return to" the "divine" was to be achieved less through external ritual than by an inward transformation. This internal emphasis represented a shift from ritualized acts of worship, sacrifice, and devotion to increasing focus on a search for the sacred force within all things.

Increasingly the ultimate reality of the external world of the senses came to be seen as ephemeral, illusory; the locus of truth, more to be found in an eternal spark of the divine (*brahman*) that was in the soul of all beings. The prime concern became then "knowledge/insight" into abiding truth (*dharma*), accompanied by release or liberation (*moksha*) from the cycle of *samsara* (in Sanskrit, "keeping going")—the endless chain of births, deaths, and rebirth.[2] *Dharma,* the basis of all Indian religions, was both descriptive and prescriptive, cognitive and normative. It meant simultaneously "the way things really are," past the veil of illusion (*maya*), and the way we should act, in accord with the eternal and universal moral code.

Desire born of ignorance was the cause of karma. So, some form of seeing through the illusion of the world and mastering one's actions (*karma*) was essential to attaining *moksha* and entry into the "divine." Liberation was achieved through "right practice" consisting of yoga, meditation, ascetic discipline. But practice alone was deemed insufficient. Proper learning under the guidance of a "good teacher" (*kalyanamitra*), a friend in the good life and one who stimulates to goodness/virtue, along with rigorous study of the religious classics, completed the spiritual curriculum. Theory and practice mutually intertwined: theory without practice proved sterile; practice without theory, blind.

The cultivators who pursued these paths—*munis,* or *sramana*—were wandering renunciants who practiced asceticism to overcome limitations of the world and meditation to discipline their minds. They "went forth" (*pravrajya*) from home and family, and to further avoid attachments to worldly possessions and relationships, continually moved, often retiring deep into the forest where they gathered fruits and vegetables. Buddhism both drew on and expanded upon this underlying shared tradition, especially in the Chan school.

In China, Chan Buddhist meditation (shortened from *ch'an-na,* a transliteration of the Sanskrit *dhyana*), referred to collectedness of mind or meditative absorption (*samadhi*) in which all dualistic distinctions are eliminated—I/you, subject/object, Buddha/ordinary being. It is important to note that this *samadhi* was not considered a "state" or "trance," i.e., an altered state of consciousness induced by sensory and/or dietary deprivation and the like. Rather, it was seen as a natural and fundamental acuity which was temporarily "lost" through neglect, scatteredness, delusion, and the leading of an unexamined habit-reflexive life. The Chinese Chan master Hui Neng thus defined "sitting in Chan" as an unimpeded nonarising of any state of mind regardless of the state's good or evil character. Chan, he explained, was simply not grasping any external mark, and not being confused inwardly.

> ...The ability to cultivate the conduct of not-dwelling inwardly or outwardly, of coming and going freely, of casting away the grasping mind, and of unobstructed penetration, is basically identical with the [meaning of] *Prajna Sutra....* If you attach to externals, your mind will be inwardly confused. If you are free from externals, your mind will be inwardly unconfused. The original nature is naturally pure, in a natural state of concentration. Confusion merely arises because states are seen and attended to. If the mind remains unconfused when any state is encountered, that is true concentration.[3]

Sometimes called "stilling one's thoughts," or "stopping the mad mind," the methods and results were also nondual, hence the saying: "when the mad mind stops, that very stopping is enlightenment." Through a direct enlightenment-experience (Chinese, *wù;* Sanskrit, *bodhi*) which removed the cloud of passion (Chinese, *yu;* Sanskrit, *klesa*) from the mind, Chan enabled people to see themselves in their true state. Chan offered an intuitive method of spirituality, aiming at the recovery of the Buddha-nature present in all sentient beings. Thus, the "goal" of meditation was no goal, no aim—what the texts refer to as "attaining nothing to attain."

Paradoxical and enigmatic rhetoric abounds in the Chan tradition. We encounter such seemingly contradictory expressions as "going far away means returning," "attaining nothing to attain," "adding by subtraction," and "true emptiness is just wonderful existence." These occur not as pranks, but as principle: if all have the Buddha-nature, intrinsic and potentially complete, then any effort to acquire spiritual wisdom from outside would be useless and errant. The *Shurangama-sutra* compares this vain external quest to the foolish man, "riding a donkey looking for a donkey." Just as the moon's reflection appears perfectly formed only in an absolutely still pond, so does one's "original face," the Buddha-nature or self-nature, shine forth unobstructed in a still and empty mind.

In Chan meditation, then, the goal is simply nonattachment, the "mind that nowhere dwells...nowhere attaches," not because nonattachment leads *to* something else, but because nonattachment *is* the original ground. A simple Chan verse expresses this subtle flavor:

> With one thought unproduced, the entire substance manifests;
>
> When the six organs [eyes, ears, nose, tongue, body, and mind] move, one is covered in clouds.

So meditation unites *both* means and ends. The threefold practice of virtue, concentration, and insight (*sila, samadhi, prajna*), is presented as sequential for teaching purposes. In practice, however, the three are simultaneous. The actual activity of meditation is itself merely an expedient, "a finger pointing at the moon," or a "borrowing of the false to find the true." The Chan master Hui Neng thus admonished his students against getting attached even to their sitting meditation:

> The door of sitting in Chan consists fundamentally of attaching oneself neither to the mind nor to purity; it is not nonmovement. You should know that the mind is like an illusion, and therefore there is nothing to which you can become attached.[4]

More mystically inclined contemplatives expressed this realization as "melting snow washes itself away with itself."

This calls attention to a potential and perhaps significant divergence between Christian prayer, even contemplative prayer, and Buddhist meditation. Because meditation is simply rediscovering what is always present, though occluded by ignorance and grasping, the methods of practice are characteristically *via negativa*; the aims are distinctively "empty." The basic human disposition, what is called the "fundamental self-nature," is presumed to be "originally pure in itself, neither produced nor destroyed, complete in itself...it is Buddha; apart from this nature there is no other Buddha." Because it is inborn and inalienable, we cannot lose it, nor can it be taken away. Its capacity is "vast and great, encompassing the Dharma-realm...its function to know all; all is one; one is all....If you recognize your self-nature, in a single moment of enlightenment you will arrive at the stage of Buddha."[5]

Prayer, at least in the conventional sense, and within the theological constructs of the Judeo-Christian tradition, implies a dualism and wish: it is both possible and desirable to address the Divine, and the Divine can and will respond. God in the Bible is characterized as "you who answer prayer" (Ps. 65:2). Moreover, communication with God is largely mediated "through Jesus Christ" (Rom 1:8) and made possible through the role of the Spirit (Rom 8:26–28; Gal 4:6). All of this would be seen as unnecessary and potentially as a hindrance to a Chan Buddhist meditator.

In Chan, the acquisition (or recovery) of ultimate truth and wisdom is im-mediate (literally, *not* mediated). It is realized through a "Way" of practice recognized as correct and efficient. This "Way" aims especially at the reclamation of a state of mind-and-heart—the "mind of the sage" (*xin*) characterized always by emotional equilibrium, and unobstructed by any sense of separation between "this" and "that." An ordinary person and a Buddha differ only in a single thought; one need not wait—the moment you "see your nature," you immediately recognize your original mind and become Buddha. This famous passage from the *Sixth Patriarch's Sutra* conveys this essential Chan truth:

> Unenlightened, the Buddha is a living being. At the moment of a single enlightened thought, the living being is a Buddha. Therefore, you should know that the ten thousand dharmas totally exist within your own mind. Why don't you, from within your own mind, suddenly see the true suchness of your original nature!?[6]

The acquisition or recovery of such knowledge or insight, moreover, is really self-generated, that is to say, emanating from within one's own mind and true nature. Thus, the metaphor of *catalyst* (where an agent precipitates, provokes, or inspires a reaction without itself being altered by the reaction) serves as a better descriptive image than "transmission." Hence the famous passage from the *Dhammapada*:

> No one saves us but ourselves,
> No one can; no one may.
> We ourselves must walk the Path;
> Buddhas only show the Way.

"Salvation," then, is indwelling and self-accomplished through an interrelated three-step exercise of virtue, meditation, and insight.

Aspects of the above epistemological formula appear throughout the Asian religious traditions. For example, Taoism speaks of cultivating the mind (*xin*), regarding it as the repository of perceptions and knowledge—it rules the body, it is spiritual and like a divinity that will abide "only where all is clean." Thus the *Kuan Tzu* (fourth to third century B.C.E.) cautions that "All people desire to know, but they do not inquire into that whereby one knows." It specifies:

> What all people desire to know is *that* (i.e., the external world),
> But their means of knowing is *this* (i.e., oneself);
> How can we know *that*?
> Only by the perfection of *this*.[7]

The "perfection" mentioned above refers to the cultivation of moral qualities and in Buddhist terminology, the elimination of "afflictions" (*klesa*) such as greed, anger, ignorance, pride, selfishness, and emotional extremes. It seems less an alteration of consciousness than a purification and quieting of the mind. Mencius talks of obtaining an "unmoving mind" at age forty, again referring to the cultivation of an equanimity resulting from the exercise of moral sense. He distinguished between knowledge acquired from mental activity and knowledge gained from intuitive insight. This latter knowledge he considered superior as it gives noumenal as well as phenomenal understanding. Indeed, the whole of education for Mencius consisted of "recovering this lost mind"—recapturing the intuitive faculties that in the stress of life have been led or allowed to go astray. Chuang Tzu spoke of acquiring knowledge of "the ten thousand things" (i.e., of all nature) through virtuous living and practicing stillness: "to a mind that is 'still' the whole universe surrenders."[8] Even Confucius's famous passage concerning the highest learning (*da xue*) connects utmost knowledge of the universe to the cultivation of one's person and the rectification of one's mind.

Again, though important distinctions apply in any comparison of these three traditions, they all begin with and proceed along a shared path: self-cultivation. All take as the first step along this path a preliminary purity or moral rectitude, and each entails some form of "quietism"—the stilling of the mind, of thoughts, the gathering in of consciousness (in various degrees and forms from tradition to tradition). Moreover, all three locate the Way, or Tao, or Buddhahood, as present within and realized through the perfecting of one's own nature.

Thus, Buddhist meditation is not supplication or reaching out or up (as in *elavare mentes ad deum* ("lifting up one's mind/heart to God"), but a purposeful and deliberate *not* reaching out, not seeking. It is a re-turn, a turning back of attention, which in Chan is called "returning to the root; going back to the source," achieved not by any conscious rumination or visualization, but through "letting go." The Chan practitioner is delving back through the successive stages or layers of consciousness until he/she gets back to, or more accurately, reawakens to, the intrinsic unity of the entire Dharmarealm. It is the details and potential hazards of this "return" that the *Shurangama-sutra* addresses.

The *Shurangama-sutra* (*leng-yan jing*) was translated into Chinese by Paramiti in 705 C.E. at Zhr Zhr Monastery. The text is held in great esteem in Mahayana countries of East Asia. In China, the Sutra was ranked in popularity and importance with the Lotus, Avatamsaka, and Prajnaparamita Sutras. It was and remains favored by Chan meditators as it maps out the mental phenomena experienced by practitioners, the causes of those states, and the difficulties that arise from attachment to the phenomena and misinterpretation of them. In short, it catalogues and classifies spiritual experience and the underlying causes of those experiences—and most importantly, how to steer one's way through this challenging terrain of the mind to enlightenment, how to transmute consciousness into wisdom.[9]

The sutra speaks of the original mind as consisting of "a wonderfully bright, fundamental enlightenment—the enlightened perfect substance of the mind which is not different from that of the Buddhas of the ten directions." It then outlines in detail the "return"—a systematic unraveling of the "false self" (*skandhas*)—and exposes the subtle delusion and attachments that obscure this pure, bright nature.

This meditative journey is neither vague nor imprecise. The various levels of attainment are treated almost clinically, not left to the imagination or to subjective "feelings" of mystical union and epiphanic breakthroughs. Moreover, the rectification (purity of heart) is not accomplished metaphorically through ritual purification and ceremony; it takes place directly and existentially. The *Shurangama-sutra* presents four "unalterable aspects of purity"—the elimination of all actions, thoughts, and of even traces of lust, taking life, stealing, and deception—as prerequisites for correct meditational practice. The text for this teaching begins with Ananda asking the Buddha how to set up a *Bodhimanda* (literally "place/space of enlightenment") and how to rescue and protect living beings sunk in the suffering of *samsara*. The Buddha responds. Key passages of the text follow:

> The Buddha told Ananda, "You constantly hear me explain in the Vinaya that there are three unalterable aspects to cultivation. That is: collecting one's thoughts constitutes the precepts; from the precepts comes samadhi; and, from samadhi arises wisdom. These are called the three non-outflow studies. Why do I call collecting one's thoughts the precepts? If living beings of the six paths of any mundane world had no thoughts of lust, they would not have to follow a continuous succession of births and deaths. Your basic purpose in cultivating is to transcend the wearisome dust. But if you do not forsake your thoughts of lust, you will not be able to get out of the dust. Even though one may have some wisdom, and the experience of Chan concentration, one is certain to enter a demonic path if lust is not ended....[10]

The Buddha then elaborates on the demonic states of mind and corresponding false claims made by people who lose the way to enlightenment. He also
provides a vivid analogy to drive home the point that careful purification is
a *sine qua non* of attaining enlightenment:

> Therefore, Ananda, cultivators of dhyana samadhi who do not restrain
> their lust, are like someone who cooks sand in the hope of getting rice.
> After hundreds of thousands aeons, it will still be hot sand. Why?
> Because it wasn't rice to begin with; it was only sand.

Any awakening, however wonderful, not grounded in thorough purification,
cannot reach the Buddha's nirvana. One will continue to revolve in the six
paths of unenlightened existence. The cleansing must penetrate mental and
physical, emotional and intentional, dimensions of the personality, to the
point of becoming artless. Thus, the Buddha cautions:

> You must cut off lust intrinsic to both body and mind—then get rid of
> even the aspect of cutting it off. At that point you have some hope of
> attaining the Buddha's bodhi.

The sequence is repeated for the three other aspects of purity. Taking life,
even in animal forms, not only cuts off the roots of one's own kindness and
compassion, but creates "debts" that pull one back into samsaric existence.
Thoughts and deeds of stealing, including hoarding and overconsumption,
lead to ego-inflation and the amassing of debts—both obstructions to liberation. Efforts at meditation will prove futile, "like someone who pours
water into a leaking cup, hoping to fill it. He may continue to pour for
aeons as many as motes of dust, but in the end the cup will not be full."
Finally, deception, "claiming to have attained what you have not attained,"
in other words, advertising one's own spiritual achievements and powers
in the hope of acquiring fame and followers, completes the list of the four
unalterable aspects of purity. The Buddha ends his exhortation to Ananda
with the famous line, "the straight mind is the Bodhimanda."

In summary, the Buddha reemphasizes the absolute necessity of purity
of heart, right at the outset of the meditative quest, for "when the beginning is not true, the end will be a tangle." If the meditator's mind is as
"straight as lute strings, true and genuine in everything they do," then the
Buddha guarantees that such people will "realize the Bodhisattvas' unsur-
passed knowledge and enlightenment." This, then, constitutes the heart of
meditation: stilling the thoughts or quieting the mind, which in turn depends
on purity, and leads to wisdom. The *Dhammapada* puts it succinctly:

> By oneself evil is done, by oneself one is defiled. Purity and impurity
> belong to oneself, no one can purify another.... You yourself must

make the effort, the Buddhas are only teachers. . . . Through meditation wisdom is won, through lack of meditation wisdom is lost. . . . [11]

One "must first be as pure as glistening frost," in these four aspects of mind and body. In the *Shurangama-sutra,* the Buddha concludes by reiterating the pivotal teaching of Buddhism: Seek nothing extraneous; do not look for enlightenment in appearances or outside the self-nature. Or as the Chan poet Han Shan rhetorically asked,

> Turn your mind within! There he is!
> Why look for him outside?

Later, the *Shurangama-sutra* delineates the various states that can occur as one penetrates via meditation the five *skandhas* (psycho-physical elements of "self"). If "you cannot recognize these states when they appear," the text points out, "it is because the cleansing of your mind has not been proper," and you will be engulfed. You might "feel satisfied after a small accomplishment," or misconstrue a preliminary meditation level for arhatship or Buddhahood. In short, says the text, "you might mistake a thief for your son." And yet, even these entanglements and impediments occur not so much from without as from within. As my own meditation teacher observed, "basically there are no obstructions; whatever *you* cannot see through and let go of will obstruct you." Conversely, when there is unblemished purity of heart, then the meditation (*dhyana*) is awakened and aware, free of delusion and snares,

> . . . your mind tallies with the mind of the Buddhas, Bodhisattvas, and Great Arhats and you will abide in profound purity, discover truth and return to the source.

Han Shan (1546–1623)

At age nineteen, Han Shan ("silly mountain") "abandoned all worldly things to practice Chan in order to realize the wonder of the mind." But by his twentieth year he discovered, "When I began my Chan practice, I did not know how to control my mind and was not at ease." After some initial instruction he was able to deeply enter meditative concentration. He writes,

> One day after taking rice porridge, I went for a walk as usual and suddenly while standing entered the state of Samadhi. I did not feel the existence of my body and mind. There was only a great brightness, round and full, clear and still like a huge round mirror. All the mountains, rivers and the great earth appeared therein . . . I could not find my body and mind in the brightness; I composed these verses:

When in a flash the mad mind halts, inner organs
And all outer objects are thoroughly perceived.
As the somersaulting body hits and shatters space,
The rise and fall of all things are viewed without concern.

Thereafter, there was a still serenity within and without my body; no
hindrance was met from any sounds or forms. Just then all my former
doubts disappeared.... [12]

Lacking any teacher to confirm or contradict his awakening, "I opened
the *Shurangama-sutra* to verify my experience." He studied it for eight
months to gain comprehension of "its profound meaning without having
a single doubt left." So important was this sutra that measured and tested
his meditation experience that he later dedicated himself to writing *The
Thorough Meaning of the Shurangama-sutra* as a guide to future students
of Chan meditation. He continued to lecture on it for the rest of his life.

Han Shan's reasoning reflects a recurring concern in the Chan tradition:
the hindrances and errors that too often occur when the practitioner has not
completely purified his/her mind prior to attempting prolonged and serious
meditation. He wrote,

At present those who practice Chan are gathering on the mountain;
some achieve stillness of mind in a flash of thought and thereby
experience great comfort [when suddenly all feelings and passions
vanish]. It is regrettable that while sitting on the clean white ground
[i.e., while realizing this state of cleanness] they consider it unique
and refuse to forsake it, not knowing that it will become a Dharma
hindrance.... This is called the barrier of the known. [13]

Han Shan here echoes the great Chinese Chan master Hui Neng who taught,
"the door of sitting in Chan consists fundamentally of attaching oneself
neither to the mind nor to purity." Both hearken back to the *Shurangama-
sutra* which insists that even the notion of purity and nonattachment can
become an obstruction, and advises that one must "get rid of even the aspect
of cutting it off." Han Shan quotes unspecified "ancient masters" who said:

You may reach the state of *Bright Moon in the cold, deep pond,* or
that of the *Sound of the Bell in the stillness of the night,* without that
state being disrupted by contact with swelling water or rising waves
and without deficiency even in the midst of the loud beat and peal; but
you are still on this shore of birth and death. [14]

Han Shan called up a number of Chan stock phrases that illustrate this
subtle form of self-delusion and Chan "sickness." He wrote, "This is called
'Holding fast to the top of the pole with one's arm' or 'the silent immersion

into stagnant water.'" For Han Shan, the *Shurangama-sutra* laid out an indispensable map for Chan meditators, one that kept them from grasping at minor attainments. For those who have experienced "the lightning flash of dhyana by chance," he wrote, the sutra humbles and makes clear that what they took for the perfection of wisdom, was really "only trifling with the shadow of consciousness." Han Shan lamented that this kind of overestimation and eagerness for attainment "is a sickness which is as common these days as it was in former times."

Xu Yun (1840–1959)

Xu Yun ("Empty Cloud"), a living legend in his own time, is considered one of the great Chan adepts of China. In many ways his life so mirrored that of Han Shan that he acquired the nickname "Han Shan come again/returned." Both monks generated a wave of enthusiasm among all classes of people. They followed lives of alternating hermiticism and worldly engagement, yet all the while lived close to the edge as simple and humble monks. Both shunned publicity and self-glorification, refusing comforts, avoiding fame, devoted to reconstructing temples and monasteries. Xu Yun preferred to live in a cowshed out-of-doors rather than indulge himself in even the simple comforts of the monks' quarters. He would often come to a new place with a single walking staff, do his work, and leave with the same staff as his sole possession. Like all great Chinese Chan masters he laid stress on the nonabiding mind which is beyond reach of all conditioned relativities, even as they arise within it.

By his thirty-first year he was already renowned for his meditation skills, living deep in the mountain wilds subsisting on pine needles and mountain stream water. His hair and beard grew over a foot in length and his eyes shone with a piercing radiance that more often than not frightened people. He wrote:

> ...I had many unusual experiences...deep in the mountains and marshy land, I was not attacked by tigers or wolves, nor was I bitten by snakes or insects. I neither craved for human sympathy nor took the cooked food normally eaten by people. Lying on the ground with the sky above me, I felt that the myriad things were complete in myself; I experienced a great joy as if I were a deva [god] of the fourth dhyana heaven. Since I had not even a bowl myself, I experienced boundless freedom from all impediments. Thus my mind was clear and at ease and my strength grew with each passing day. My eyes and ears became sharp and penetrating and I walked with rapid steps as if I were flying. It seemed inexplicable how I came to be in such a condition....As there were mountains to stay on and wild herbs to

eat, I started wandering from place to place and thus passed the year oblivious of time.[15]

Not until he came upon an old Chan master, Yang-jing, on the Hua-ding peak of Mt. Tien-tai, did he get "correction" for his "weak spot," as he later came to describe it. This correction was based on the *Shurangama-sutra*. The old master asked Xu Yun,

> "Are you a monk, a Taoist, or a layman?"
> "A monk," I replied.
> "Have you been ordained?" he asked.
> "I have received the full ordination," I replied.
> "How long have you been in this condition?" he asked. As I related my story, he asked, "Who instructed you to practise in this way?"
> I replied, "I did it because the ancients attained enlightenment by means of such austerities."
> He asked, "You know that the ancients disciplined their bodies, but do you know that they also disciplined their minds?"
> He further added, "As I see your current practice, you are like a heretic and entirely on the wrong path, having wasted ten years' training. If, by staying in a grotto and drinking water from mountain streams you managed to succeed in living ten thousand years, you would only be one of the ten classes or Rishis (immortals) listed [in the "fifty false states"] in the *Shurangama Sutra* and still be far away from the Tao. Even if you managed to advance a further step, thus realizing the "first fruit" you would only be a "self-enlightened fellow" (Pratyeka buddha)....If your method merely consists of abstaining from cereals and in not even wearing trousers, it is only a quest for the extraordinary. How can you expect such a practice to result in perfect enlightenment?"

Thus the Master "pierced my weak spot right to the core," admitted Xu Yun, and so he bowed to the old master, and begged him for instruction.

With the *Shurangama-sutra* as his guide, Xu Yun cultivated Chan for years. In his fifty-sixth year, he apparently broke through with his practice. The details of that enlightenment are telling in regards to the importance of the Shurangama teachings to his attainment. Here, in his own words, he describes an event that occurred during a twelve-week meditation retreat:

> One evening after the set meditation period, I opened my eyes and suddenly perceived a great brightness similar to broad daylight wherein everything inside and outside the monastery was discernible to me. Through the wall, I saw the monk in charge of lamps and incense urinating outside, the guest monk in the latrine, and far away, boats plying on the river with the trees on both its banks—all were clearly

seen....The next morning I asked the incense-monk and the guest-monk about this and both confirmed what I had seen the previous night. Knowing that this experience was only a temporary state I had attained, I did not pay undue regard to its strangeness.[16]

He continued his meditation and only later did, as he put it, "the mad mind come to a stop." He was able to "cut off my last doubt about the Mind-root and rejoice at the realization of my cherished aim." He credits the *Shurangama-sutra* with instilling in him the importance of purity and the consequent dispassion it instills. "If I had not remained indifferent to both favorable and adverse situations," he reflected, "I would have passed another life aimlessly and this experience would not have happened."

It might prove instructive to briefly look at two contemplatives from the Catholic tradition for comparison and contrast. St. Romuald (952–1027), founder of the Camaldolese Order, in his *Brief Rule,* gives instructions for mental cultivation reminiscent of the Buddhist masters in its simplicity, self-sufficiency, and focus: "Sit in your cell as in paradise," he writes, "put the whole world behind you and forget it. Watch your thoughts like a good fisherman watching for fish." (In Chan, interestingly, one "watches" what is *not* the thoughts.) He sympathetically understands how the mind can wander, how elusive can seem the goal of spiritual success. "Do not give up," he exhorts, "hurry back and apply your mind to the words [of the Psalms] once more." St. Romuald locates the source and sustenance of the path to be followed and the goal to be reached in God. He writes,

> Realize above all that you are in God's presence, and stand there with the attitude of one who stands before the emperor. Empty yourself completely and sit waiting, content with the grace of God, like the chick who tastes nothing and eats nothing but what his mother gives him.[17]

Only here do we begin to detect a subtle variance or different "flavor" between a Christian contemplative and Chan Buddhist meditator. We need only to substitute the word "Buddha" for "God" to highlight the differences between this and the Chan approach. Implicit in St. Romuald's language is a distinction, a certain degree of separation, between the seeker and God, here likened to the relationship between ruler and subject or mother and child.

Notably, both Buddhist teachers and St. Romuald concur in the virtue of "emptiness." They seem to diverge, however, on its function and content. Where "emptiness" for the Chan adept means not seeking anything, not looking outside, for the Camaldolese monk the call to "empty yourself" raises an expectation and longing. The emptiness of Benedictine humility gives rise to trust in God, in hope of being uplifted. There is an implicit understanding that self-emptying will be rewarded with "food" through the grace of God. "Empty" in the Buddhist sense, one might say, is intrinsic; in the Camaldolese, instrumental. Moreover, where the Buddhist would assert "no one saves you but yourself," St. Romuald would likely insist that salvation derives from God, and to imagine otherwise is arrogance and delusion. And yet, in both, "salvation" comes from outside the constructed (false) self. But in such seeming coincidence lies critical difference: Romuald's salvation depends on a dualism; the Buddha's does not. Where Romuald's emptying prepares the way for hope in God's restorative power, in Chan the emptiness of no-thought is the Buddha, or as the Sixth Patriarch said, "The nondualistic nature is the Buddha-nature."[18]

This contrast stands out in greater relief if we look at another Camaldolese contemplative, Blessed Paul Giustiniani (1476–1528). Giustiniani founded the Camaldolese Hermits of Monte Corona in 1520 and contributed valuable insights and reflections on the mystical path toward the goal of "the soul united with God." Central to the mystic quest is his concept of "self-knowledge" through humility, whereby we know our own worthlessness in order that we may cease loving ourselves and thus return to God. It is a given in this analysis that human beings are helpless and receive all of their strength and insight from God's love. Giustiniani writes, "Lord Jesus, you who are the light without which nothing can be illuminated."[19]

For Blessed Giustiniani, Christians are creatures dependent upon God, yet superior to all material creation: this is their dignity. At the same time, they are sinners separated from God: this is their "abasement." And from this admixture of dignity and abasement comes the realization of their all-encompassing need for God, as their state of inborn sinfulness "proves their inability to attain God through their own efforts." This contrasts with the Buddhist premise that "all beings equally possess the Buddha-nature; all can become Buddha."

Moreover, where in Buddhism the recovery of that intrinsic enlightenment is im-mediate, in Giustiniani the lifting up to God's sublimity can only come through the mediation of Jesus Christ. In other words, the solution and purification lies outside; the return is other-dependent. Where obstacles to enlightenment in Buddhism both arise and are erased from within, in Giustiniani's Christianity impediments stem from an inherited fallen state, their removal is only effected through an external agent. "Jesus Christ, true God and true man, removed all impediments," writes Giustiniani.

> ... now that our debt is paid, now that our souls have been purified in the font of baptism, there remains no obstacle to our ascent to God. Let us rise to the Father, through the Mediator between God and men.[20]

The fuller import of the contrast can be seen when we compare the following passage from the *Dhammapada,* and Blessed Giustiniani's meditation:

> No one saves you but yourself,
> No one can; no one may.
> You yourself must walk the Path;
> Buddhas only show the Way.

If I depended upon myself alone, I could never rise from it [the "mire of iniquity"]....Who will pick me up, restore me, purify me? Who will bring back my innocence and tranquillity? My soul, hope in the Lord; put your trust in Him, for He lifts up those who fall....I am your servant and your creature: Your Son has redeemed me through his blood.[21]

Yet, one should be wary of overdrawing the differences. Parallels and correspondences abound between many Christian mystics and Chan Buddhist meditators. This remarkable passage from Giustiniani on the dangers of "ecstasies, visions, revelations" bears an uncanny resemblance to similar warnings that one finds in the *Shurangama-sutra*. Moreover, in both instances, the underlying cause of such demonic inspirations lies in hidden self-love, overweening pride. Giustiniani's long meditation on the "perfect and true path to salvation" deserves full quotation:

> Our hidden self-love brings forth all manner of illusions: ecstasies, visions, revelations, prophecies, abstinences impossible to human strength, the experience of Christ's sufferings such as the wound of the side or the stigmata, knowledge acquired without study, speaking in strange languages, the desire to be damned for the love of Christ, extraordinary seeking of humiliation, sublime confessions, fasting from all food except the Blessed Eucharist, vigils beyond human strength, unduly prolonged meditations, knowledge of others' secret thoughts, miracles, and cures. All these marvels are, in some instances, nothing but the work of him who said—and would like to induce us to say: "I shall be like God," and I shall do what He does....I think that these saints inspired by Lucifer are much more numerous, or rather much better known and more admired by the world, than the true saints, who do nothing in order to be known by the world, but who prefer to remain hidden. Christ's true servants love God totally and themselves not at all. So sheltered are they by humility that they are known to God only, not to men.[22]

The *Shurangama-sutra* describes a nearly identical condition afflicting meditators who desirous of self-aggrandizement and notoriety

> ...claim to have attained what they have not attained, to have won certification when they have not been certified. Perhaps they seek to be foremost in the world—the most venerated and superior person...all

in order to elicit the recognition and reverence of others, and because
they are greedy for offerings. These *icchantikas* destroy of the seeds of
Buddhahood just as surely as the tala tree is destroyed if it is chopped
down ... such people sever their good roots and lost their knowledge
and insight.... [23]

True Bodhisattvas and arhats, concludes the Buddha, never say of themselves, "I am actually a Bodhisattva," or "I am truly an arhat." All of this
amounts to nothing more than "deluding and confusing people."

Implications and Questions

While Chan Buddhist meditation and Christian contemplative life share
much in common, significant areas of difference exist as well. At the risk
of oversimplifying, one might say that Buddhism in its core teaching holds
that all living beings can become Buddhas and are in fact endowed with this
altogether pure and wholesome innate capacity unconditionally; that this
highest state of enlightened wisdom and nirvana can and must be reached
primarily through one's own efforts, and only secondarily by "other-power"
(i.e., through the inspiration of exemplary conduct and vows provided by
paragons of self-cultivation like Buddhas, Bodhisattvas, arhats, teachers,
etc.); and, that any sense of dependency, needing or seeking "outside" the
self-nature leads to obstructions and a continuous succession of births and
deaths. Moreover, fundamentally and ultimately the distinction between
"self-power" and "other-power" is illusory in the Chan Buddhist view.

Christian mystics, on the other hand, hold that one can live eternally
with God, or "be united to God ... totally absorbed in God ... like a faithful
servant, may enter into that joy, that I may wholly lose myself"[24] (though it
remains unclear and doubtful that such absorption means to actually become
God). They believe that the restoration of that life with the Father requires
God's grace and Jesus Christ's mediation, and only in a very limited sense
one's own efforts. Further, they believe that depending on oneself ensures
failure, and risks "sinking deeper and deeper" in sin and error. Only humility
can lead to the necessary trust in God; and only penance "gives us access
to His divinity." The message is one of hope and longing, union with God
and pliant submission: "for God wills that sinners should be converted and
should live eternally once they have done penance."[25]

If successful Chan meditation requires the practitioner to be "as pure
as glistening frost"—to "avoid everything extraneous" and not desire or
pursue any external powers, or harbor any expectation of results, rewards,
or divine deliverance—what does Buddhist meditation mean for someone
from another faith tradition whose overarching theology favors strong belief in external reliance and redemption? Is it necessary, or even possible,

to suspend deeply held ideas of dependency, innate depravity, and sinfulness in order to practice Buddhist meditation? To what extent might certain dogmatic and doctrinal beliefs distort and reify the Chan practice of nonattachment into something aversive like loss of grace or arrogant self-love? How can one "let go, release one's hold," yet remain a servant of God, completely dependent on His will and love? How would one reconcile the competing notions of "all living beings can become Buddha" with the pride of Lucifer who says "I shall be like God"? If one stands in need and hope of salvation, "stuck in the mire of iniquity," how can one be "pure as glistening frost"—seeking nothing, grabbing at nothing, desiring nothing?

Anything that encourages the impulse to have an "attainment," or even fosters a wish to be absorbed into eternal divine life, would be seen as extraneous and potentially dangerous from a Chan perspective. Are there parallels in the Christian traditions of contemplatives that could bridge these and other apparent differences? If so, does this suggest a spiritual topography that cuts across time and tradition? If not, what are the uses and limitations of Buddhist meditation for non-Buddhists, or eclectic seekers?

In short, one must ask what are the implications of selectively borrowing a particular meditative practice and isolating it from its larger context—a context that gives meditation not only unique meaning and profound purpose, but which incorporates important safeguards against its misuse. Many current and popular antinomian portrayals of Chan are misleading and inaccurate, as the *Shurangama-sutra* and other Chan scriptures demonstrate. Chan is clearly much more than simply sitting; it has its own epistemology, exacting prerequisites, and well-defined outcomes. Clearly, one can and should meditate without creeds, doctrines, and dogmas as we understand those terms in the conventional Western sense. But can one meditate *with* them?

Perhaps the differences between Chan Buddhist meditation and Christian contemplation may prove to be trivial and tangential. The two may in fact converge over time, over practice, on some deeper level of the mind-ground. But if the *Shurangama-sutra* is correct in its insistence that when the beginning is off by just a little, the end will be a tangle, then these issues deserve closer attention. Otherwise we might be, as the Buddha put it, foolishly "cooking sand in hope of getting rice."

5

Cleansing the Heart

Buddhist Bowing as Contemplation

REV. HENG SURE

The nature of the worshipper and the worshipped is empty and still,
This *Bodhimanda*[1] of mine is like a pearl in Indra's net;
Shakyamuni Buddha manifests within it.
My body appears before Shakyamuni,
Bowing at his feet, I return my life in worship.

Buddhist Bowing Contemplation Verse

Contemplating the nature of mind is a hallmark Buddhist occupation. The Buddha called the mind "a monkey" and "a wild horse." The monkey mind calculates and schemes, chases thoughts of self and others, clings to rights and wrongs, and quarrels over me and mine. The wild horse mind loves to run away into fantasies and false thoughts, to wander far without warning, and to return when it pleases. It is difficult to break the wild horse mind to the saddle of mindfulness and discipline.

To the Chinese, both feeling and thinking are represented by a single written character *xin*, which we will translate as "heart/mind."[2] So the first half of our topic, "purity of heart," viewed from a Buddhist perspective, would be more accurately expressed as "purity of heart/mind."

To assume that the mind of a meditator automatically rests in a state of permanent purity is to never have tried to meditate. Random, discursive thoughts rise and fall without cease, like waves on water. Purity of heart/mind is not a product that one attains like a possession, rather it is a process, a practice. From the perspective of practice we might begin by replacing the noun "purity" with the infinitive "to purify," or employ the gerund form, "purifying," to indicate the dynamic and continuous nature of purifying the heart/mind. One purifies the heart by emptying out its cluttered thoughts and turbid emotions, over and over. Purifying requires letting go of attachments, "truing" or rectifying thoughts, and reining in desire's appetites.

Contemplation in Both Movement and Stillness

The Buddha's teaching in essence presents a variety of methods to accomplish purifying the mind. Chan meditation emphasizes two methods to calm the monkey and to tame the wild horse: *shamatha* and *vipassana*. *Shamatha* in Chinese is *zhi*, "stopping," and *vipassana* is *goan*, "contemplating."[3] A skilled Chan meditator employs these two techniques in turn to direct the mind and body into progressively deeper levels of awareness and insight. "Stopping and contemplating" are not limited to seated meditation; ideally, one uses *gongfu*, or skill, in both activity and in stillness.

Both aspects of Purity of Heart/Contemplation appear with a characteristic Buddhist flavor in "stopping and contemplating." "Stopping" means to neither engage thoughts nor discriminate among them but simply to empty them out; sweep them away, and cleanse the mind as you would polish a mirror. Tang Dynasty Master Shenxiu (600–706) wrote a verse that describes this process:

> The body is a Bodhi tree,
> The mind a mirror-stand bright.
> At all times wipe it clean—
> Let no dust alight.[4]

"Contemplating" complements "stopping." Here the task is not to sweep thoughts away, but instead to mindfully observe each thought as it rises and falls in the mind. Such watchfulness reveals the nature of thoughts, emotions, afflictions, and habits.

Used with diligence and discretion, "stopping and contemplating" gradually reveal the mind's constant pursuit of dualities, discriminations, and emotional attachments. Once purified of defilements, the mind can return to its inherent stillness and purity; one can realize the goal of Chan meditation: "understanding the mind and seeing the nature" (*mingxin jianxing*). The enlightened mind is fundamentally still and pure. Thus, Master Hui Neng (638–713) replied in verse to Master Shenxiu:

> The body's not a Bodhi tree,
> Nor mind a mirror-stand bright,
> Basically there's not one thing:
> Where can dust alight?[5]

Here, "dust" refers to Basic Afflictions: greed, hatred, stupidity, pride, and doubt. Afflictions reinforce an illusory sense of self; from the view of self comes arrogance based on the perceived existence of "me and mine." The arising of arrogance—and of its flip-side, inferiority or low self-esteem—creates myriad related delusions, karma, retribution and its suffering. The Buddha's project, in general, aims to replace the distorted view of self with a direct perception of things as they really are. Replacing the view of an illusory self with a proper view brings suffering to an end. Bowing, or making prostrations, by reducing the centrality of me and mine, is an effective method for bringing into focus a more accurate description of the reality of "not self."

Meditation masters practiced bowing as an active counterpart to seated meditation. Bowing has many purposes; perhaps its primary psychological function in the Buddhist context is to dispel arrogance and to transform the affliction of pride. Master Chengguan (737–839), the Tang Dynasty exegete, in his commentary to the *Flower Adornment Sutra,* explains "bowing in respect to all Buddhas," the first of Samantabhadra Bodhisattva's Ten Practices and Vows:

> When one bows in respect to all Buddhas, a feeling of reverence arises in your heart, and animates your actions and speech. You express this feeling by bowing to all Buddhas. The practice gets rid of both obstacles of arrogance and ego. When respect arises, you deepen your "good roots" of reverence and faith.[6]

Here Master Chengguan explains a psychological effect of bowing. He places his point of reference inside the mind of the practitioner as he or she bows to the Buddha. Chengguan says that body, mouth, and mind experience a feeling of respect. The feeling of respect multiplies the awareness of the sacred presence around and within the worshiper. The obstacles of arrogance and ego diminish as bowing reduces affliction and increases good qualities. The *Avatamsaka* contemplations used when "bowing in respect to all Buddhas," according to Samantabhadra Bodhisattva, constitute a unique feature of bowing in Buddhism.

A close examination of the theory and practice of bowing in Buddhism reveals a highly esteemed Dharma-door long considered indispensable to awakening. As we will see below, bowing has a history in Buddhist monastic liturgy as old as the sangha, or Buddhist community itself. Why then have scholars of Buddhism paid so little attention to bowing?

Westerners in their first encounter with Buddhism typically assume that Buddhist practice is synonymous with sitting meditation.[7] This view persists despite the reality that the most common Buddhist practice in Asia from the third century C.E. was, and still is, bowing to the Buddha. Scholarly literature in English on the subject of Chinese Buddhism in particular has tended to focus on meditation and philosophy, to the exclusion of devotional practice. Eric Reinders in his article "The Iconoclasm of Obeisance: Protestant Images of Chinese Religion and the Catholic Church" substantiates the lack of materials by Western scholars about Buddhist bowing and obeisance. Reinders traces the European Protestant Iconoclasts' aversion for physical gestures of deference and asks whether the quarrel in Europe arising from the Reformation has been projected onto Asian religions.[8] Judith Lief suggests that the reasons why Westerners find bowing difficult are complex:

> As Westerners we tend to think of prostrating as a gesture of defeat or abasement. We think that to show someone else respect is to make ourselves less. Prostrating irritates our sense of democracy, that everyone is equal.... On one hand we want to receive the teachings but on the other we don't really want to bow down to anyone or anything.[9]

One of the reasons for Buddhism's current rapid growth in the West may be because meditation seems egalitarian, and free of dogma; it makes no demands of faith or adherence to a creed. Bowing, on the other hand, seems inherently unequal, undemocratic, humiliating, and submissive. Because bowing takes one to the earth, it appears unsanitary and superstitious; it conjures up the taboos of idolatry and graven images. From a Gospel-based, logocentric perspective, bowing is mere ritual, i.e., not textual. It masks the real thing—doctrine. Moreover, given cultural values of individualism and the ethos of equality, bowing seems to replace self-determination with servility.[10]

And yet, this marginalization of bowing constitutes a relatively recent trend. As we shall see in a brief comparative look at bowing as praxis in other religions, prostrations have figured prominently across the world's religious landscape. Whereas in Buddhism it opens a path to *samadhi* and liberation, bowing takes on different faces in other faiths. The comparisons and contrasts nonetheless are revealing and shed light on an ancient practice that could infuse the contemporary interfaith dialogue with new meaning.

Comparative Bowing Practices

Bowing is by no means unique to Buddhism; it constitutes a ubiquitous practice across the spectrum of organized religions. In the Middle Eastern and Hellenistic traditions, beginning with the Ugaritic and Accadian religions of ancient Babylon, we discover a kinship—in language, liturgy, and doctrine—between Babylonian and Semitic bowing practices. Babylonian texts, Hebrew scriptures, and the Qur'an explain bowing in similar fashion.

Accadian letters from the sixteenth century B.C.E. appear in the archives of the royal palace of Babylon at Ugarit that mention bowing: "At the feet of my lord I bow down twice seven times from afar."[11] Jewish literature reveals an almost identical reference where vassals in the Amarna letters write, "At the feet of the king... seven times, seven times I fall, forward and backward." And in Gilgamesh, the founding literary epic of Babylonian civilization, we find, "When they had slain the bull, they tore out his heart, placing it before Shamash. From afar, they bowed down before Shamash."[12]

In Judaism we find a highly developed, normative and codified system of bowing spanning the centuries from the Hebrew scriptures to the Kabbalah.[13] In the Hebrew scriptures, *hawa* used exclusively in the Eshtaphal stem, and *hishtahawa*, mean "to prostrate oneself," and "to worship." *Hawa* is cognate with the Ugaritic *hwy* to bow down. In Exodus 24:1 we find, "Come up to YHWH ... and bow low from afar." Moses and his companions are expected to appear before the Lord and to prostrate themselves before him in accordance with accepted rules of ceremony. In the Torah the saga of the Israelites' wandering includes the episode with the Golden Calf. God in his wrath prepares to destroy them for their failure to bow. He tells Moses, "I have seen this people and it is a stiff-necked people." In Ezekiel God calls the Israelites "impudent children and stiff-hearted." The stiffness indicates inflexibility and unwillingness to bow. They are externally "stiff-necked" and internally, "stiff-hearted."

Talmudic literature praises Individuals such as Rabbi Akiva (second century C.E.), who performed bowing as a personal practice of humility.[14]

In a long section of the *Mishneh Torah, the Laws of Prayer,* chapter 5, Moses Maimonides defends his practice of excessive bowing. Where a common person bows only at the opening and closing of the central prayer sequence, the High Priest bows at the beginning and the end of every blessing within the sequence. Maimonides says that all of these bows should be bowed so far that all the joints in the spine are loosened and one makes oneself like a rainbow.[15]

The Spanish Kabbalist mystical masterpiece, the *Zohar,* in its *Tahanun* recension, contains penitential prayers that were recited daily in prostrate form. The *Zohar* calls this section *Nefitat Appayim,* "falling on one's face."[16]

In Islamic worship the *salat,* a ritual prayer or divine service, is an expression of humility which was considered as the attitude to the Deity most befitting humanity. The etymology of *salat* is transparent, from the Aramaic root *sl* which means "to bow, to bend, to stretch." *S'lota* is the stative form, which means the act of bowing. In the Qur'an the *salat* is very frequently mentioned along with *sakat;* the two are obviously considered the manifestation of piety most loved by Allah.[17]

It is said, "The nearest a creature is to Allah is when he is prostrating, and that is the meaning of the saying of Allah: "And prostrate thyself and come near!"[18]

The highest goal of the *salat* is complete absorption in the Deity by humiliating oneself. Sufyan al-Thawri is reputed to have said, "If a man does not know humility, his *salat* is invalid."[19]

The recitation of the Qur'an itself is associated with prostration. Bowing, moreover, is used as a means of healing; it can cleanse one of grievous sins.

Thus it is not surprising to find that Islamic literature praises a paragon of bowing: It is related from Ali b. Abdallah b. Abbas that he used to perform a thousand prostrations every day, and they used to call him "the Prostrator."[20]

Rules for bowing in Eastern Orthodox Church worship are ordered "fittingly and reverently," as set forth in the books of the divine services, and particularly in the church *Typicon*. The presence of rules that prescribe making prostrations at special times testifies to the universal presence of bowing within standard Eastern Orthodox devotions. The full prostration is seen either as penance or as an act of deepest reverence. However, on celebrations and festive occasions, the liturgy omits prostrations to the floor.

Making prostrations is Orthodox Christianity's standard form of religious worship. Orthodox monks on Mt. Athos cultivate personal bowing practices in their cells in marathon sessions that last for hours, even all night. While bowing is generally practiced in monasteries, Orthodox Christian laymen who have zeal are permitted to pray on their knees in church and to make full prostrations whenever they wish, excepting those times when the Gospel, Epistle, Old Testament readings, Six Psalms, and sermon are read.[21]

In Roman Catholicism's *Rubrics of the Roman Catholic Breviary and Missal* there are instructions for priests, ministers, prelates, and canons on when to kneel, genuflect, or sit, and also how to uncover the head and how to bow profoundly.[22]

The Desert Fathers of Egypt practiced bowing as mortification and as punishment, as well as to praise the Lord. St. Francis of Assisi's humility brought him close to the ground. At his deathbed he instructed the monks to remove his clothes and lay his dying body on the bare ground inside the Portiuncula, the tiny chapel beloved of Francis. He wished to be close to the earth as his spirit returned to the creator.

Dominicans have the inspiration of St. Dominic who often used to pray by throwing himself face down on the ground and saying, "God, be merciful to me a sinner" (Lk 18:13). He would quote the repentant words of David (2 Sam 24:17) in Psalm 43 ("My soul is laid low in the dust, my heart is stuck to the earth"), or Psalm 118 ("My soul sticks to the floor; make me alive according to your promise").[23]

The Benedictine Rule requires bowing when showing hospitality to arriving and departing guests. The Rule specifies that when a brother comes back from a journey, he should, on the day of his return, lie face down on the floor of the oratory at the conclusion of each of the customary hours of the Work of God. An entering novice prostrates himself at the feet of each monk to ask his prayers. When a monk is excommunicated for serious faults he must bow in full prostration.[24]

The Iconoclasts' Protest: Bowing in Protestant Christianity

European Protestants continue to be troubled by bowing. Leading Protestant reformers in Northern Europe broke from centuries of domination by an all-powerful, hierarchical Roman Catholic establishment that wielded absolute religious and political authority. They protested against the need to show deference on bended knee to mere humans (the various popes, and the Vatican's hierarchy of cardinals and bishops) or to icons and the ever-expanding pantheon of saints and martyrs. Known as "Iconoclasts," the Protestant reformers further rebelled against the ritualization of compulsory respect.

The Reformation's iconoclasm with its antipathy for icons and devotion has shaped Western scholastic discussion of non-Western cultures and Asian religions.[25] Gregory Schopen says that with rare exceptions the scholarship done in the West on devotion in Asian religions projects battle lines, expectations, and categories conditioned by the conflict between Protestant and Catholic issues of papal authority and the source of religious truth. This conflict and resulting interpretive conclusions may have led to ignorance of Buddhist devotional practice and devaluing of bowing.[26]

As we look toward Asia to expand our investigation into comparative bowing practices, we find that obeisance has both secular and sacred significance. In ancient and medieval Chinese society, knowledge of how and when to make ritual prostrations was a requisite skill in civil society's daily etiquette. Buddhism skillfully appropriated the Chinese society's disposition for bowing and adapted it to accord with the principles of Buddhist meditation.

Bowing in Buddhism

Bowing in Buddhism cuts across the lines of traditions and schools. Bowing has been part of Buddhist practice since the Buddha's time in India and continues to this day. Within the Buddhist sangha, or monastic community, the daily liturgical schedule began and ended with dozens if not hundreds of ritual prostrations. On ceremony days, clergy and laity alike might engage in the practice of liturgical repentance and bow up to ten thousand times.[27] Monks and nuns bow to the images of Sages, Awakened Beings, and the Buddhas, to their superiors, and to each other.

In Tibetan Buddhism, prostrations form an important part of the most common foundational practice called *ngondro* ("preliminary practices").[28] Over the course of several months or longer, the beginning practitioner is expected to complete at least 111,000 full-body prostrations along with chanted Refuge Prayers as part of the *ngondro* practices (which include several hundred thousand other prayers, purification mantras, offerings, mandalas, and devotional meditations). Completing these 111,000 prostrations is known as *chak-boom* in Tibetan.

The late Dudjom Rinpoche bowed on a daily basis, even into his eighties. The fourteenth-century Tibetan saint Tsongkhapa is known to have performed over a million prostrations during his four-year meditation retreat in a cave. His Holiness the fourteenth Dalai Lama puts his palms together and bows to whomever he meets, whether person-to-person or before a large audience.

Mahayana Buddhist monastics bow from morning to night. Bowing opens and closes every one of the three daily ceremonies. Each ceremony requires a minimum of nine bows. Interviews and meetings with teachers or superiors, depending on respective rank, require from one to three full prostrations, each set of three prostrations followed by a half-bow (Chinese: *wenxun*). Zen students perform half bows (Japanese: *gassho*) to the altar, to each other, and to the cushion before and after meditation.

Novice monks in training bow hundreds of times each day, to mold the new "habitus" of a monk's deportment and to assist the transition of identity from layperson to sangha member. The canonical texts describe venerable Bodhisattvas of great accomplishment bowing to the ground before the Buddha. The Youth Sudhana, in the *Gandhavyuha* chapter of the *Avatamsaka Sutra,* who is the archetype of the bowing pilgrim, bows to fifty-three teachers. Over and over he prostrates his five limbs (hands, feet, and head) low to the ground to purge arrogance, repent of past offenses, demonstrate respect, and ultimately to realize the highest goals of a Bodhisattva's wisdom and compassion.

Individual monks, historically, took up bowing as an intensive form of practice. For example, Master Xu Yun ("Empty Cloud," 1840–1959), successfully completed an arduous "Three Steps, One Bow" pilgrimage across China, covering a distance of one thousand miles. Years later, after his marathon bowing journey, he bowed one thousand or more bows per day over an extended period of months. Master Xu Yun's mother died in childbirth, and he wished to repay his mother's kindness for bringing him into the world.

The biography of Master Hsuan Hua (1918–95), an accomplished Chinese Bhikshu pioneer in North America, tells how at the outset of his spiritual career he made a practice of bowing 830 times, twice a day, rain or shine, and did so for ten years. His purpose, according to the biography, was to demonstrate his filial regard for his parents as well as to build a foundation for his future cultivation of the Buddha's Way.[29]

What we know about how Buddhist monks bow in India comes in large measure from Chinese Buddhist historians such as Ven. Daoxuan (596–667 C.E.). In his *Shimen Guijingyi* (Buddhist Rule and Breviary), he gives definitions for twelve terms of respect for the Buddhist sangha, or monastic community. Eight of the twelve entail some form of bowing.

Xuanzang (596–664), the famous Buddhist pilgrim and contemporary of Daoxuan, traveled to India during the Tang Dynasty to search out the original teaching and rejuvenate Buddhism in China. In his *Record of the Western Regions in the Great Tang,* Xuanzang discusses the customs of India and lists nine forms of ultimate respect that he witnessed among the Indian sangha. He was aware of the significance of bowing in cultivating the fundamental attitude of humility appropriate to a spiritual seeker. He lists a graded series of bows from a simple nod of the head, raising the hands and bending the waist, placing palms together at chest height, up to genuflecting, kneeling, or touching the head to the ground. Finally, ultimate respect is shown by throwing the entire body to the ground.[30]

As Chinese bowing styles in the *Rites of Zhou* (an account of the rituals of the Zhou Dynasty, 1027–209 B.C.E.) were specific about external form, Buddhism had similar precision in detail and complexity of gesture. The unique quality of Buddhist bowing was that its primary function was internal. Bowing, then as now, helped cultivators "empty out" egotistical impediments that obscure enlightenment. In other words, bowing aimed at restoring the essential nonduality of the Buddha-nature present in all beings.

Thus, bowing in Asian Buddhist practice is real and significant. Given the centrality of bowing in Buddhism, it is a curious anomaly that Westerners who seek the Buddha's Way so seldom encounter bowing. Just as bowing has been largely ignored by academics, so too, has it been overlooked by Buddhist practitioners. What happened to bowing as it was imported to the West?

This writer in the Autumn of 1969 lived as a scholar-practitioner at Antaiji, a tiny Soto Zen temple in the (then suburban) Northwest corner of Kyoto, Japan.[31] I participated in the daily practice of *zazen,* including week-long retreats in total silence, and witnessed the ordination preparation and liturgy in this branch temple of Eiheiji, the headquarters of the Soto School. At Antaiji, under the tutelage of Uchiyama Kosho Roshi (1912–98) and his students, I was taught deportment, which included bowing in every situation. Monks and laity bowed easily and readily. Bowing was as automatic as removing one's shoes before stepping up onto the tatami mats on the temple floor.

I returned to California and began formal study and practice of Mahayana Buddhism with Venerable Chan master Hsuan Hua at Gold Mountain Monastery in 1974. Gold Mountain's schedule included many prostrations during a daily minimum of two and a half hours of liturgical ceremonies. Novice monks and nuns performed an hour each morning of "universal bowing." Optional personal practices included bowing repentances, bowing to each word in a sutra (scripture), or the distinctive "three steps, one bow" practice which requires the practitioner to take three steps and make a full prostration.

In the 1970s in San Francisco many Buddhist traditions were putting down roots and transforming their liturgical heritages.[32] Even so, not all teachers of Buddhism in America presented the practice of bowing in its traditional Asian format. The bias against bowing by Protestants and Iconoclasts clearly influenced Buddhist ritual practice as it developed in the West. Some have decided to restrict, interpret, or Westernize bowing. Others, such as the late Shunryu Suzuki Roshi (1904–71), founder of the San Francisco Zen Center, adapted bowing for Americans who meditated at the Zen Center. Suzuki, according to a story, seeing the "stiff-necked" resistance of Americans, not only did not drop bowing to cater to Americans' likes and dislikes; rather, he increased the required bows before meditation to nine. When asked why, he said that in his view, Americans needed to bow more. Suzuki Roshi, in a *Tricycle* article from 1994,[33] asserts that before reaching liberation, bowing is serious business, an essential tool for the student of Zen.

The Buddhist Churches of America (Jodo Shinshu) represent one of the Japanese Pure Land forms of Buddhism. They were the first to reach San Francisco and establish a temple. The San Francisco Buddhist Temple was established in 1900. The BCA were the first Buddhist denomination in America to replace centuries-old Asian liturgical devotions with a Western style worship. Some would argue that in pruning away Asian devotional elements, Jodo Shinshu has become the most Protestant among American Buddhisms; others give that title to the Vipassana movement. Two founders of Insight Meditation, Joseph Goldstein and Jack Kornfield, were ordained as *Bhikkhus* (monks) in the Thai Theravada Forest Tradition. After returning to America and disrobing, they continued to teach the meditation aspect of Theravada Buddhism to Westerners. They first, however, set aside the bowing, icons, and liturgies of Thai Buddhism's devotional aspect. Thus, for different reasons, Jodo Shinshu and Vipassana have stripped away the icons and the devotional aspects, including bowing, in favor of meditation, psychological *metta* (loving-kindness), and mindfulness.

Given the novelty of Buddhism in America in its second generation, and given our lack of familiarity with Buddhism as practiced by Asians, it is easy to see why Americans need a context for understanding bowing as a legitimate gesture of devotion to the Buddha.

The following story reveals how the contextualization of bowing is evolving in the United States. Norman Fischer, former Roshi of the San Francisco Zen Center, describes in a 1997 article his own initial encounter with bowing, and how he teaches bowing to newcomers.[34] Fischer begins by characterizing the reaction of newcomers to the Zen Center who arrive with mainstream Christian Protestant or Reform Jewish biases against lowering the body in worship. Their typical reaction, according to Fischer, is incredulity, some even being outraged and disturbed by bowing's display of piety and religious fervor.

Fischer explains that during his first visit to the Zendo, he was told by Dainin Katagiri Roshi (d. 1990) to make full prostrations toward the Buddha image on the altar. He asked Katagiri Roshi, "Why do we bow?" Katagiri showed him a tiny image of the Buddha bowing to the ground. "If he can do it, you can do it," he said. Fischer thought that was reasonable. Katagiri explained that "bowing is mutual, just one bow, bowing back and forth."

Fischer goes on to explain to his students that bowing is a mental training method that helps us cultivate an attitude of love and appreciation for the Buddha-nature within our own nature. Piety and devotion are okay as long as one doesn't get hysterical about it; they are tender and splendid states of mind.[35]

He says that by appreciating how the figures are actually symbolic manifestations of oneself, we then become more comfortable with them as "other," and external. The more familiar we get with ourselves as we actually are, the more comfortable we become with the images that are "other."

In their expressions of *upaya,* or expedient means, first Katagiri and then, in turn, Fischer, have homogenized bowing into a democratic, egalitarian exercise. They interpret bowing in psychological language, identifying the images on the altar as capable of bowing back to the bower. By so doing, the exchange is now horizontal, not vertical. Westerners can approach bowing on even turf, and find a symbolic context for the many *gasshos* they will soon encounter in the meditation hall.

The practice of bowing as it enters the West has already begun to be transformed by our logocentric sensibilities and our preference for individual expression.

Later in the article Norman Fischer reports that he observed Katagiri Roshi "mumbling a verse" when he bowed. Fischer asked what it meant, but only partially understood the reply, because Fischer didn't speak Japanese at the time, and the translation came through Katagiri Roshi's impromptu verbal rendering:

> Bower and what is bowed to are empty by nature. The bodies of one's self and others are not two. I bow with all beings to attain liberation, to manifest the unsurpassed mind and return to boundless truth.[36]

I suspect that Katagiri was reciting in Japanese the Chinese bowing contemplation verse that has been recited by monks in both China and Japan since the fifth century. I will amplify Katagiri Roshi's recitation to connect the practice of bowing in Zen, exemplified by Katagiri Roshi, with its Chinese parent, Chan. Below I will offer the Chinese bowing contemplation verse that is likely identical with Katagiri's recitation. The earliest printed appearance of this verse seems to be in a text by Tiantai master Zhanran (b. 711), disciple of the renowned cofounder of the Tiantai School, Master Zhiyi, in a *Lotus Sutra* liturgical text called *Fahua sammei chanyi* (Dharma Flower Samadhi Repentance Liturgy).[37] Dogen Kigen remarked on the line in his *Hokyogi*. Dogen's master Rujing remarks that the line was routinely recited by Chinese monks in daily services during the Song Dynasty (960–1126).[38] Inspiration for mental contemplations performed during bowing as well as while repenting comes from Samantabhadra Bodhisattva, who appears as one of the central exemplars of both the *Avatamsaka* and *Lotus* Teachings of Buddhism.

And nowhere is the nature of the mind—the interpenetration of noumena and phenomena, the unity of Buddha and living beings—more eloquently expressed than in the *samadhi* states of the Bodhisattva of Great Conduct, Samantabhadra.[39] This undoubtedly was the source of Katagiri's recitation, and gets to the heart of my thesis, that bowing in Buddhism, like Chan meditation, is a Dharma-door that opens to *samadhi* and liberation. Let's look at the contemplation verse.

Mahayana Bowing Contemplation Verse

The worshipper and the worshipped, by nature, are empty and still.
The Dao and the response intertwine in ways hard to conceive of.
This *Bodhimanda* of mine is like Indra's pearls,
Shakyamuni Buddha appears within it.
My body appears before the Thus Come One,
With my head at his feet, I return my life in worship and bow down.

Commentary

The worshipper and the worshipped, by nature, are empty and still.

"Worshipper and worshipped" refer to subject and object, the one bowing and the one bowed to. "Nature" is the Buddha-nature, while "empty and still" refers to the doctrine of *anatta,* or "not-self."[40]

The Dao and the response intertwine in ways hard to conceive of.

Dao (Tao) translates variously as "the Way" or "the Path." The same word is used to present the fourth of the Four Noble Truths, *marga.* "Response" refers to changes that take place when one cultivates the *Dao* according to the Buddha's Dharma instructions. "Hard to conceive of" suggests that the transformations of day-to-day, discursive consciousness that occur as one practices go beyond speech and logical thought. This happens because the very functions of conceptualizing and language are affected when one enters *samadhi* via this contemplation.

This Bodhimanda of mine is like Indra's pearls

Bodhimanda refers to the place of cultivation, literally "enlightenment field." In the verse the contemplator analogizes his body first as a *Bodhimanda*, the place where he cultivates, and, second, he likens it to a pearl in Indra's net. Indra's net is said to be an adornment in the Palace of the god Shakra. The net hangs before his "Good Views" Palace. In each interstice of the net hangs a perfectly round, luminous pearl. The many pearls reflect and inter-reflect; through each pearl one can see all the pearls, yet the entire net of pearls is contained within each individual gem. Multiple pearls come forth from each pearl; the entirety can gather back into a single pearl. The cultivator visualizes this pearl inside his purified body/mind.

Shakyamuni Buddha appears within it.

At this point the cultivator, using the power of his mind's eye, visualizes the Sage he or she bows to, in this case, Shakyamuni Buddha, as if he were appearing right within the pearl that he/she visualizes in his body and mind.

My body appears before the Thus Come One

The next step requires an interactive visualization. The cultivator adds an element to his vision: he sees his own body appearing in front of the Buddha.

With my head at his feet, I return my life in worship and bow down.

The interaction continues: the bower visualizes his body in the process of taking refuge. To "return my life in worship" is a literal translation of *namo* or *namah*, the Sanskrit term used to praise a Sage or Worthy. One of *namah*'s meanings is "to return my life back to its sacred source." It can be thought of as recognition that one's life does not belong to one as a possession, that ultimately one does not "own" his or her life. By returning one's life to a higher spiritual identity, one takes refuge with a secure and unchanging presence.

At the end of the visualization the practitioner lets the thought go, and does not attempt to retain or grasp the vision, in accordance with the third of the Buddha's "Four Stations of Mindfulness" (*Brahma Viharas*), which is to realize that all thoughts are transient, and thus not to be grasped at.[41]

It may seem counterproductive to deliberately introduce a thought, no matter how wholesome, into the mind, when the Chan principle is to never allow even a dust-mote's worth of thought to defile the fundamentally pure mind-ground. In Buddhism, however, this is called "fighting poison with poison." It reminds us that all dharmas taught by the Buddha are expedient, not ultimate; yet at the same time, in the process of cultivation, all are necessary. The Chan School has a teaching, "We borrow the false to find the true."

Bowing is a mental yoga, a contemplation used therapeutically for its ability to replace and counteract the view of self, the source of pride and all the other evils that arise from arrogance. Further, to bring the vision of a Buddha or Bodhisattva into one's mind, given that it is technically an illusion that has "marks," is nonetheless a purifying image that increases one's "good roots," and banishes harmful thoughts or instinctual desires, greed, anger, and delusion.

Katagiri Roshi's bowing verse, as witnessed by Norman Fischer, testifies to the continuity of tradition from China of the Song Dynasty through Japan, to meet again in the West. Bowing in Chan and Zen is more than a surrogate for sitting. It has meaning that engages physical, mental, and spiritual aspects of cultivation. Bowing has a psychological function of replacing self-centric delusion. As the view of self drops away, karma has no point on which to gather; the deeper connections of our spiritual nature's interdependence gradually emerge to consciousness.

Contemplations are an aid to *samadhi;* focusing with concentration on a single wholesome and directed thought, one purges the many random, discursive thoughts. Over time, the visualization's sublime aspects can connect with the nature, and the response to the Way can be "hard to conceive of."

The reactions of college students in California who meet bowing for the first time in a monastic environment suggest that bowing appeals to Westerners today as it has historically to people in every culture.

Students' Responses at the City of Ten Thousand Buddhas

Students from Humboldt State University, the University of San Francisco, and the University of California, Berkeley, come regularly to the City of Ten Thousand Buddhas for a Monastic Encounter weekend, as a field trip in their religious studies courses. At the end of the retreat we ask students to evaluate what they enjoyed and what they would improve. One would assume that meditation would be the hallmark experience of a Buddhist retreat, and some students do mention meditation. Others enjoy the vegetarian food, the opportunity to talk with monastics, or the tranquillity and orderliness behind the walls of a Buddhist monastery. To my surprise, every retreat brings the same response: the students liked the bowing most. Here are excerpts from the evaluation forms.

From an eighteen-year-old "atheist," a Caucasian woman in her sophomore year:

> I've never done any religious practice before. The bowing put me off at first, I'd never imagined doing anything at all like that. I felt aversion

but because everybody else was doing it, and because the monks and nuns interpreted the actions in psychological terms, it didn't seem so threatening. When the time came I simply bowed and that was that. Once I tried bowing, it lost its strangeness. By the time I finished the first ceremony, I didn't even notice that I had been bowing for an hour.

From a nineteen-year-old "culturally Jewish" man:

I realized that I had never before taken part in a religious ceremony of any kind. My parents never introduced me to religion. Joining the bowing and the chanting felt like water touching a thirsty plant. A part of my heart opened that hadn't been touched before.

From a nineteen-year-old male Baptist junior:

When I left the ceremony hall I felt lighter in spirit, as if I had left cares and years behind on that bowing bench. I went back and bowed by myself for an hour in the darkened Buddha Hall. I wanted to clean out while I had the chance.

Conclusion

We have seen how the world's religious traditions, from Asia to the Middle East, with exceptions,[42] value bowing. An impressive list of world religions practice bowing, teach about it in texts and liturgies, and hand down stories of the paragons of vigorous bowing. A summary of research into the various purposes of bowing among religions suggests the following typology: (1) secular bowing as a social courtesy; (2) bowing in repentance and reform; (3) bowing to establish a worshipful relationship to deities and sacred presences; (4) bowing to praise a deity's majesty; (5) bowing as a liturgical ritual; (6) bowing to reduce pride and increase humility and goodness; (7) bowing as mortification and punishment.

In all the traditions I have examined, bowing has largely an exterior focus, consistent with the supporting "theology." In Buddhism we see the practice of bowing applied in ways that parallel and overlap with the other traditions, yet a significant difference also emerges. In Buddhism, the focus of bowing turns back to the mind of the bower, instead of moving outward toward a wholly transcendent Other.

Buddha Dharma's approach to bowing invites the practitioner to contemplate the nature of his or her heart/mind. In Buddhism, we discover two more purposes for bowing: first as a complement to seated meditation and second, bowing as a Dharma method that opens directly to *samadhi* and to *prajna,* wisdom.

Bowing in the various traditions looks the same externally, but the internal experiential aspect of Buddhist bowing, it would seem, is different. In

Buddhism, the myriad practices relate back to a central theme, the mind and its nature. The mind and its nature are fundamentally Buddha. The "goal" or the end of the spiritual path, then, is to gradually remove all aspects of the view of self, until one rediscovers his or her nondual nature. Bowing, as a road to the nondual, helps empty out and purify false concepts within. The false, illusory self is being erased as one bows. When the illusion of self yields to a larger context of Dharma, one can bow in empty space. This "true emptiness," as the texts describe, is genuine "wonderful existence." Buddhist bowing, then, aims to reveal the unsubstantial nature of both self and phenomena.

Buddhist bowing, like its quietistic counterpart of seated meditation, also supports and reflects the larger "theology" from which they emerge. The unique aspect of Buddha Dharma is to awaken to the self nature—Buddha. Thus in Buddhism, bowing is neither symbolic icon worship nor penitential mortification; it returns all Dharmas to the mind, where movement and stillness unite.

> Going and returning with no border,
> Movement and stillness have one source.
> Opening and disclosing the mysterious and the subtle,
> Understanding the mind and all its states;
> Deep and wide and interfused,
> Vast and great and totally complete.... [43]

Buddhist devotional practice in general, and bowing in particular, represent another dimension of practice awaiting exploration by cultivators of purity and contemplation.

6

The Historical Hui-neng, the Sixth Patriarch of Chan (Zen) Buddhism, in Dialogue with the Unknown Author of *The Cloud of Unknowing*

NICHOLAS KOSS, O.S.B.

Holy men and women have at times written of their experiences of the Transcendent, thus making these religious men and women also writers of texts to be submitted to literary analysis. But such analysis is problematic because of the additions made to the original texts by redactors. While scholars have carefully traced the practice of interpolation for biblical texts, students of classical Chinese religious texts have rarely accounted for these textual difficulties.

This essay is then, first of all, an investigation of the autobiographical section of *The Platform Sutra of the Sixth Patriarch,* a fundamental text for Chan (or Zen) Buddhism, in search of the "historical" Hui-neng, the purported giver of the long sermon forming the basis of this text. In particular, I will use a literary analysis that can shed light on the process of compilation and redaction. Although I am not a trained biblical scholar, as a Benedictine monk I have delighted in reading biblical scholarship, and have spent much time in analyzing both Western and Chinese works of literature as a student of comparative literature.

Since this essay is also part of a collection of essays dealing with purity of heart in Christian and Asian religious traditions, once a theoretical "historical" Hui-neng has been identified, I will seek to ascertain the appropriateness of the concept of "purity of heart" for him, especially in terms of Psalm 73, which treats, in part, of the "pure of heart." Furthermore, since the essays in this collection are a dialogue between Asian and Christian monastic traditions, I intend to examine *The Cloud of Unknowing* as commentary on Hui-neng and his autobiography. In my understanding, "purity of heart" has to do with certain qualities of a person who has a special relationship with the Transcendent. A cognate expression, "pure of heart," appears in the opening couplet of Psalm 73: "How good God is...to those who are pure of heart." This verse suggests that God will treat in a special manner those who are pure in heart. No description immediately follows as to the essential qualities of the "pure in heart," but the persona of the psalm seems to include himself among them, and concludes this psalm with a good description of purity of heart. First the psalmist notes, "Yet I was always in your presence; you were holding me by my right hand." The pure of heart are constantly before immanent transcendence, and are led by the divine. He then adds, "Apart from you [God] I want nothing on earth." The pure of heart find ultimate fulfillment in being present to the divine. Keeping this psalm in mind, let us now turn to one of the most famous texts of Chinese Buddhism.

The Platform Sutra of the Sixth Patriarch

The Platform Sutra of the Sixth Patriarch was written in the Tang Dynasty (618–907), the first half of which saw the flourishing of Buddhism in China and the founding of the Chan (Zen) school of Buddhism. The Sixth Patriarch in the title of this sutra is the Chinese monk Hui-neng. This work is in the form of a long sermon supposedly given by Hui-neng many years after he had become the Sixth Patriarch. The text does not give a date for the sermon but it does say that Hui-neng was seventy-six years old when he died, which is usually said to be in 713.[1] The sermon presumably would then have been given thirty or forty years before his death. The earliest extant version of *The Platform Sutra* is the text discovered at Tunhuang, China, in the early years of the twentieth century. It was probably written between 830 and 860 and was most likely a copy of a text from around 820,[2] which would have been nearly a hundred and fifty years after the purported presentation of the original sermon.

The Platform Sutra has a complex literary structure and combines the genres of autobiography, biography, sermon, disciple-master dialogue, and doctrinal exposition. In the opening autobiographical section, the structural high point is Hui-neng's enlightenment and assumption of the role of the Sixth Patriarch:[3]

> At midnight the Fifth Patriarch called me into the hall and expounded the Diamond Sutra to me. Hearing it but once, I was immediately awakened, and that night I received the Dharma. None of the others knew anything about it. Then he transmitted to me the Dharma of Sudden Enlightenment and the robe, saying: "I make you the Sixth Patriarch. The robe is the proof and is to be handed down from generation to generation. My Dharma must be transmitted from mind to mind. You must make people awaken to themselves."[4]

Four important things happen in this scene: (1) Hui-neng is "awakened." (2) He "received the Dharma." (3) He is given the robe that makes him the

Sixth Patriarch. (4) And he is commissioned to "awaken" others through the Dharma he has received. It is the first occurrence that allows the other three to follow, so it can be seen as primary. Furthermore, Hui-neng's becoming the Sixth Patriarch and his commission to "awaken" others appear not to be directly related to the experience of being "awakened" and thus do not owe their existence directly to Hui-neng's experience of enlightenment. Moreover, for Hui-neng, the commission to "awaken" others, that is, to teach others, seems to be the occasion that requires revelation of his own personal experience of being "awakened." Hui-neng therefore has two roles: one who has been "awakened" and one who teaches others how to be "awakened." If he had not assumed the role of teacher, there would probably be no need to relate his personal experience of being "awakened." And, he also has a third role: He is the one selected to assume the mantle from the Fifth Patriarch in the Chan tradition.[5]

This autobiographical section of Hui-neng's sermon also has another feature that would attract the attention of a textual scholar: It not only ends with his being "awakened" but also begins with it. At the beginning of his autobiographical narrative, Hui-neng relates what had happened to him while he was still in the world:

> I happened to see another man who was reciting the Diamond Sutra.
> Upon hearing it my mind became clear and I was awakened.[6]

This experience of being "awakened" is purely on the personal level and has no explicit relation yet to his becoming a teacher of others or the Patriarch. But it does make us notice a literary structure to this narrative: It begins and ends with enlightenment. My Buddhist friends have told me that it is not uncommon for Buddhists to have many enlightenments and suggested that this could be the reason why Hui-neng underwent two such experiences in this account.[7] But as a student of textual criticism, I am intrigued that whereas with the awakening at the end of the autobiographical section there are three roles given to Hui-neng (one who is awakened, a Patriarch, and a teacher), at the beginning section there is only one role (one who is awakened). Might not these two awakenings be a doublet, with the second occurrence being written for "theological" reasons? Replicated accounts of the same event are also of great interest to biblical textual scholars. For instance, in the Gospel of Matthew, Jesus feeds thousands twice[8] but, originally, there was probably only a single feeding. The repetition was apparently done for theological reasons: to have a second feeding for the Gentiles.

The opening passage on Hui-neng's enlightenment has a simplicity of expression that suggests it was based on actual experience and could be close to something the historical Hui-neng might have said. It is only concerned with the experience of being "awakened." The second passage at the end of the autobiographical section has an account of being "awakened" too but, as just noted, it also is about the teaching of sudden enlightenment. Moreover, the primary purpose of this passage is to establish that Hui-neng is the Sixth Patriarch and is to devote himself to the teaching of others. Furthermore, a late night setting is given to the moment of enlightenment; and the event is described as unknown to others. Clearly the narrator of this passage has much more than just a description of enlightenment to present. We may therefore take these two very different accounts of enlightenment as being the first hint that the text we are dealing with might not be of single authorship but rather a redacted work, much like some of the books of the Bible. Perhaps the first account of enlightenment can be related to the historical Hui-neng whereas the second might be the work of those who see Hui-neng in a particular light, much as there are some Gospel passages related to the historical Jesus and others that present a pre-Resurrected Jesus in light of the Resurrection.

The complex nature of the text before us becomes clearer if we look at the introductory material before the sermon itself. A setting is given which presents a situation that cannot be taken literally. In attendance are "over ten thousand monks, nuns, and lay followers."[9] This number cannot be taken at face value, since it seems to be physically impossible for so many to hear the voice of one monk at one time. The prefect of Shao-chou, "local officials," and "Confucian scholars" are also numbered among the listeners, so the audience included both the devout and, presumably, at least some Confucian skeptics in matters of religion. But, could one have really gotten Confucian scholars to attend such a discourse? Rather, it is probably polemical reasons that call for their supposed presence. It is also noted that the monk Fa-hai took down what was said. This, given the length of the sermon as we now have it—approximately twenty-nine pages in its English translation— seems to be another physical impossibility. These impossibilities, or at least highly unlikely situations, however, should draw our attention to the fact that we are dealing with a text that is indeed a literary creation written with definite theological purposes in mind. Nonetheless, we should not rule out the possibility of Hui-neng himself at one time preaching a sermon in Shao-chou. Let us simply consider that the text as we now have it could be one that was significantly redacted yet still containing traces of an earlier, actual sermon.

In studying various medieval texts, I have learned that one sign of an interpolation is that the interpolated passage can be removed without harming the narrative logic. Hui-neng begins his sermon:

Good friends, purify your minds and concentrate on the Dharma of the Great Perfection of Wisdom. The Master stopped speaking and quieted his own mind. Then after a good while he said: Good friends, listen quietly.[10]

These lines would fit very well the beginning of the section after the auto-biographical narrative, which is the main part of the sermon that expounds the Dharma. Furthermore, the silence that is described is appropriate for the start of an exposition of Dharma but seems less appropriate as a preface for an autobiographical story. Moreover, the expression "good friends" is not used again by the sermon giver until after the autobiographical section. Had both sections been written by the same person, one would have expected this phrase to have been used at least once or twice in the autobiographical part.

Therefore, the autobiographical section can be removed from the sermon without destroying the narrative flow from the introductory section to the doctrinal part. The introduction and much of the exposition of Dharma are written in a highly literary style of Chinese, whereas the autobiographical section is generally more colloquial in style. This difference in style suggests that the introduction and doctrinal part are from the hand of a redactor whereas the autobiographical part derives from an original transcription of a sermon.

Further literary analysis of the autobiographical section will lead us to a possible historical Hui-neng embedded in the text. As text, it is clear that this autobiographical part is a carefully structured narrative, having plot, characterization, settings, and a time structure. To begin our analysis, let us look at its time structure. In the doctrinal portion of the sermon, the narrative time, that is, the time it would take to say the sermon, and "fic-tional" time, that is, the time structure of the content of the sermon, are basically the same. But in the autobiographical section, the narrative time, which might be one hour or so if recited at a lively pace, is much shorter than the "fictional" time, which is the thirty-some years the narrator has lived before giving this sermon.

Any narrative has realized and unrealized scenes, the former being those in which a detailed description of the event or events of the scene is given. In this autobiographical account of Hui-neng, there are nine realized scenes, each of which has dialogue:

- Selling of firewood as a child and becoming "awakened" (pp. 126–27)
- Obeisance to the Fifth Patriarch (127–28)
- The Fifth Patriarch preaches to his disciples (128)
- Reaction of monks to this sermon (128)
- Reaction of the head monk Shen-hsiu (129–30)
- The Fifth Patriarch sees the verse of Shen-hsiu and reacts (130–31)
- Hui-neng hears the verse and composes his own (131–32)
- Hui-neng is called to meet with the Fifth Patriarch, is "immediately awakened," and departs for the south (133)

- Arrival at mountain where he is now preaching (134)

Even though the "fictional" time of this section is over thirty years, the realized scenes all occur within a year, the year in which Hui-neng achieved enlightenment. Very little information is given in the text related to the time during this year when these events occurred. The first realized scene begins with Hui-neng selling firewood at Nan-hai.[11] Previously it was stated that he and his mother had moved there when he was "still a child." Is he now selling firewood as a child or is he now in his adolescence or young adulthood? The text does not say. Selling firewood, however, seems to be a work that would require one to be older than just a child, as does his later work in a "threshing room . . . treading the pestle."[12] Perhaps we can say that this year is when Hui-neng was either a strong, vigorous adolescent or a young man, rather than a child.

In scene 2 of this autobiographical section it is noted that Hui-neng worked in the threshing room "for over eight months,"[13] a period of time which invites speculation that all the realized scenes took place within approximately one year. In scene 9 it is said that it took Hui-neng "two months" to reach his final destination.[14] Scene 6 mentions "several days" passed.

Although the spans of time passed are only mentioned rarely, a number of the realized scenes indicate or suggest the time of day or night the scene occurred.

Scene 1: After selling firewood to "a certain man," the future Hui-neng is paid and then sees a man "reciting the Diamond sutra." Presumably, then, this scene takes place still during daylight. The selling of firewood, too, is an activity that can easily be associated with the morning market.

Scene 5: Shen-hsiu writes his verse at midnight. The word "midnight" appears twice in this scene. (The literal meaning of the Chinese expression translated as "midnight" is "in the middle of the night.")

Scene 6: The Fifth Patriarch sees Shen-hsiu's verse at dawn.

Scene 8: The Patriarch meets with Hui-neng at "midnight" and Hui-neng departs at "midnight."

The overall temporal structure of this autobiographical section, therefore, is as follows. Scenes 7–9 all occur on the same day, with scene 7 beginning "one day." This day is after the "several days" that Shen-hsiu has had to write a new verse. Scenes 3–6 begin "one day,"[15] and cover a "midnight,"[16] and "dawn."[17] Scene 1 encompasses one day and the traveling time to see Hung-jen; scene 2 is one day. It is eight months from scene 2 to scenes 3–6, and several days to scenes 7–9.

The Structure and Plots of the Autobiographical Section

This time structure allows us to divide the autobiographical section into three discrete narratives:

Narrative One: Enlightenment and visit to Hung-jen (scenes 1–2)

Narrative Two: The failure of Shen-hsiu to write an acceptable verse (scenes 3–6)

Narrative Three: The success of Hui-neng's verse, his enlightenment, and his going south (scenes 7–9).

Narrative One is about enlightenment, as is Narrative Three. Narrative Two is about one who cannot reach enlightenment. Narratives One and Three are clearly autobiographical. Both have a first-person narrator who is present at the events described. Narrative Two, however, while supposedly told by the narrator of Narratives One and Three, contains scenes and events to which this first-person narrator would not have been privy. Consequently one wonders how this part could be attributed to the historical Hui-neng.

Narrative One

The following brief outline considers Narrative One from the point of view of the actions of the narrator in each scene.

I once sold firewood, heard the Diamond Sutra, and became awakened (pp. 126–27)

I make obeisance to the Fifth Patriarch (127–28)

My dialogue with the Fifth Patriarch (128)

Another narrative structure in Narrative One is that of explicit and implicit complications and their resolutions: Complication One (death of father); Resolution One (hard work of mother and son). Complication Two [implicit] (continued suffering); Resolution Two (enlightenment). The banishment and death of the father are the difficulties that Hui-neng and his mother successfully overcome. Implicitly, however, this success does not render Hui-neng fully happy and leaves a void in him that is then fulfilled by enlightenment. Furthermore, enlightenment accounts for the visit to the Fifth Patriarch that will then lead, in Narrative Two, to a new set of difficulties. As a personal story of enlightenment, however, Narrative One can stand on its own with the experience of enlightenment as the conclusion and high point.

As for the characterization of Hui-neng, in the first and second stages of this narrative, he is a filial, energetic worker. His energy is first seen is his carrying the firewood to wherever it is needed. At this point, the narrative sets up a contrast by describing Hui-neng's attention to the recital of the Diamond Sutra, an event that occurred through no causation of his own, and which shows that the cause for enlightenment is from a force outside of him.

In my reading of Narrative One, the first part of scene 1 can be related to words from the historical Hui-neng. However, at the end of this scene, there is a dialogue in which Hui-neng questions the one whom he has just heard recite the Diamond Sutra:

> I asked him "Where do you come from that you have brought this sutra with you?"[18]

There is no polite prelude to this dialogue in which Hui-neng might have respectfully asked the name of his interlocutor. Rather he abruptly requests personal factual information, hardly what is to be expected from one who was just enlightened. This question seems to represent the curiosity of the unenlightened. Its presence here in the narrative suggests the presence of a redactor with the purpose of making Hui-neng the Sixth Patriarch. For Hui-neng to become the Sixth Patriarch he must have contact with the Fifth Patriarch, and this question begins a line of development that will lead to this event. The response given both answers the question and also provides information necessary for Hui-neng to become the Sixth Patriarch:

> He answered: "I have made obeisance to the Fifth Patriarch, Hung-jen, at the East Mountain, Feng-mu-shan, in Huang-mei hsien in Ch'i-chou. At present there are over a thousand disciples there. While I was there I heard the Master encourage the monks and lay followers, saying that if they recited just the one volume, the Diamond Sutra, they could see into their own natures and with direct apprehension become Buddhas."[19]

Narrative Two

Narrative Two is plot-centered. The plot includes the following elements:

1. One day the Fifth Patriarch gives a sermon to his monks in which he presents a challenge: the one who writes a verse showing he is "awakened" will become the Sixth Patriarch. (p. 128)

2. No one, however, is willing to compete with Shen-hsiu, the "head monk": "they all then gave up trying and did not have the courage to present a verse." (128)

   Flashback: The artist Lu Chen had been commissioned to paint pictures in a corridor in the Master's hall, including a picture of the succession of the Sixth Patriarch.

3. Switch of scene to Shen-hsiu late at night:

   A. Thoughts of Shen-hsiu: reasons for and against his writing a verse. (129)

   B. His decision is seen only in his action of writing his verse. Further, he is willing to accept failure. (129–30)

4. Switch of scene to the Fifth Patriarch at dawn:

   A. The Fifth Patriarch discovers the verse of Shen-hsiu, informs the painter to desist, and urges the disciples to recite it so that they will "not fall into the three evil ways." (130)

   B. The Fifth Patriarch speaks privately to Shen-hsiu and tells him he has "only arrived at the front gate [of true understanding]" (131).

The narrative line of Narrative Two continually changes course, but each course has a particular function in the overall narrative. In the first and second scenes, the fact that no monks accept the Fifth Patriarch's challenge out of respect for Shen-hsiu functions to introduce Shen-hsiu as one who is held in the highest respect as well as to set the first step in the plot. The flashback to the painter Lu Chen, who had been commissioned by the Fifth Patriarch, sets the second step in the plot, providing a reason for the Fifth Patriarch to be at the place in the morning where Shen-hsiu has written his verse. The third scene showing a Hamlet-like Shen-hsiu weighing the pros and cons of writing a verse presents his confused internal mental state that is in opposition to the great respect he has within the community. The narrator, moreover, does not give the exact reason for Shen-hsiu's decision to write a verse, and thus forces the reader to review the self-argument Shen-hsiu has had and to try to find the reason for this decision. This scene functions, therefore, to bring the reader more into the narrative. The fourth scene presents a double conclusion, with Shen-hsiu's verse being praised to the monks by the Fifth Patriarch but privately criticized. This conclusion then prepares for Narrative Three in which Hui-neng's verse will reveal his enlightenment. The intricate plot line of Narrative Two reveals a plot structure much different from the basically linear plot development in Narrative One. Such a complex plot suggests the work of a literary redactor, rather than that of a holy, uneducated sermon giver.

Furthermore, Narrative Two is not really first-person narrative, but a good example of a third-person omniscient narrator. We even enter the mind of Shen-hsiu. Though incorporated into an autobiographical account, this narrative does not fit a first-person narrative. The supposed narrator Hui-neng was not present at any of the scenes described, so there is no way that he would have access to the information presented. Nor would he have known the thoughts of Shen-hsiu. Therefore, this narrative can be safely assumed not to be closely related to the historical Hui-neng. That this narrative might be an interpolation into an earlier autobiographical account is further suggested by the fact that its removal would not destroy the narrative line between Narrative One and Narrative Three. Narrative One ends: "Later a lay disciple had me go to the threshing room where I spent over eight months treading the pestle."[20] Narrative Three begins: "One day an acolyte passed by the threshing room."[21] The concluding phrase of this opening line to Narrative Three, however, has this acolyte "reciting this verse," referring to the verse of Shen-hsiu shown in Narrative Two. This statement implies that the verse has already been presented in the text, so the start of Narrative Three would have been revised slightly to accord with the content of the interpolation. The purported earlier version would have had the text presented only when Hui-neng was taken to the corridor to see it for himself.

Nonetheless, Narrative Two has important overall functions within this sequenced, autobiographical section. Its main function is to show the high quality of the person who could not become the Sixth Patriarch: this person was still too much involved with rational thought. Further, it allows the reader to ponder on unsuccessful attempts at enlightenment.

Another structure of Narrative Two is based on three negations or denials. The monks decide not to respond to the challenge given by the Fifth Patriarch. The painter is told by the Fifth Patriarch not to paint what he had originally been told to do. And Shen-hsiu is told by the Fifth Patriarch that he "has not reached true understanding." The Fifth Patriarch is involved with each of these negations and their original premise: He presents the challenge that the monks do not accept; he dismisses the painter he had commissioned; and he privately rebukes Shen-hsiu after publicly praising him.

Clearly then this narrative at one level is about the Fifth Patriarch, who very much determines what the others in this narrative do. Moreover, what these actions will be are foregone conclusions: The monks will not compete; the painter will not paint; and Shen-hsiu will not manifest enlightenment. These results are demanded by the conclusion to the overall narrative: Hui-neng becoming the Six Patriarch. Therefore, the Fifth Patriarch is simply a vehicle controlled by the redactor to reach this conclusion. We are not seeing real decisions being made here. The only one who ever really decides anything is Hui-neng.

Nonetheless, a character is given to the Fifth Patriarch by what he does. Especially interesting is the reversal of what he does in regard to the monks and Shen-hsiu. He praises Shen-hsiu's verse in front of all the monks and tells them to recite it. When alone with Shen-hsiu, however, he points out the inadequacy of the verse. Yet another variation on this pattern will be used after he sees Hui-neng's verse.

The character of Shen-hsiu is appealing. He is respected by the monks, who not only consider him their teacher but also are confident he will help them once he "obtains the Dharma." Shen-hsiu is insightful, knowing that the other monks will not compete with him. He is humble in not wanting, at first, to offend the Fifth Patriarch by offering a verse to get the Fifth Patriarch's position. He is able to suffer "perplexion." He is willing to accept defeat: "If the Fifth Patriarch sees my verse and says that it . . . [text corrupt here] and there is a weighty obstacle in my past karma, then I cannot gain the Dharma and shall have to give up."[22] Yet, he is not the one to obtain enlightenment.

Narrative Two also functions then as the redactor's commentary on Hui-neng and his gaining of enlightenment. Unlike the persons shown in Narrative Two, he is not a monk, thus a surprising candidate for enlightenment. Also, he has no desire to be enlightened. By presenting Shen-hsiu as one who does not gain enlightenment, the redactor is commenting on how special Hui-neng is. Hui-neng has the respect of no one; he understands little of monastic life; his humility is not a conscious stance in relationship to others; he suffers from no perplexing thoughts.

This narrative also allows a comparison between the Fifth Patriarch and Hui-neng. The Fifth Patriarch is cunning and manipulative, though not in an evil way. He must produce a successor and that he does. But he arranges for a successor who outshines him.

Most of the direct speech in Narrative Two is in the form of a monologue: the sermon of Hung-jen, the group response of the monks to the sermon; the thoughts of Shen-hsiu (twice); Hung-jen's injunction to the painter; and Hung-jen's command to monks. The only dialogue is between Hung-jen and Shen-hsiu. That Hung-jen and Shen-hsiu have most of the dialogue emphasizes their importance in Narrative Two, setting up a contrast with Narrative Three in which Hung-jen and Hui-neng dominate the dialogue.

Narrative Three

Narrative Three returns to first-person narrative with the narrator almost always present in the scenes described. The main actions in each scene are as follows:

Scene 7: I hear the verse and compose my own (pp. 131–32)

Scene 8: I meet with the Fifth Patriarch, am awakened, receive the robe, and depart for the south (133)

Scene 9: I arrive at the mountain where I now am (134)

Scene 7 shows signs of being redacted because Hui-neng twice hears the verse of Shen-hsiu and twice comments on its meaning, each time making basically the same comment. The first instance occurs when he hears an acolyte reciting the verse; and the second when he is taken to see the verse and someone reads it to him. The second occurrence I would take to be the earlier textually, for it seems closer to an oral tradition. It fits well a context of preaching or instruction from the historical Hui-neng. The narrator is recounting his experience while at the same time commenting on it for the sake of his audience. The text reads:

> The boy took me to the south corridor and I made obeisance before the verse. Because I was uneducated I asked someone to read it to me. As soon as I heard it I understood the cardinal meaning. I made a verse and asked someone who was able to write to put it on the wall of the west corridor, so that I might offer my own original mind. If you do not know the original mind, studying the Dharma is to no avail. If you know the mind and see its true nature, you then awaken to the cardinal meaning.[23]

This simple yet stately description is premised on the narrator being enlightened. It is his enlightenment that allows him to describe the situation as he does. There is also an admirable humility and simplicity, when he accepts his lowly exterior situation of being illiterate even though he is already enlightened. That he asks "someone" rather than a particular person to write his verse also suggests this passage being closer to an oral account. I am also intrigued and puzzled about the significance of his verse being written "on the wall of the west corridor" rather than on that of the south corridor where Shen-hsiu's verse was written.

That two verses are then given suggests that this text derives from two distinct sources and that the final redactor of the present version felt required to include both versions of Hui-neng's verse that he had before him.

In the first part of scene 7 Hui-neng hears the verse of Shen-hsiu being recited and makes a comment similar to that quoted above. He says: "As soon as I heard it I knew that the person who had written it had yet to know his own nature and to discern the cardinal meaning."[24] The opening of Narrative Three, however, is mainly a precise summary of Narrative Two. As with any summary in a text with a complex origin, we must ask if this summary is really a summary or itself the basis for what appears to be summarized. If it were the basis of Narrative Two, it would suggest that this section belongs to an earlier stratum of this narrative, just the opposite of what I have just suggested. But, the vocabulary of this summary frequently accords verbatim with the vocabulary of Narrative Two. If this summary were the basis for the account in Narrative Two, it would be difficult for the redactor to incorporate intentionally the vocabulary of the summary so carefully into a longer narrative. Therefore I would argue that this summary, too, is from the hand of the redactor/editor who is responsible for Narrative Two. The purpose of this summary is of course related to the overall first-person narrative form.

With this summary Hui-neng learns what has happened during scenes where he was not present. Had this entire section been biography rather than auto-biography, this summary would not have been necessary. Accordingly, the redactor seems aware of the problem of having third-person material in a first-person narrative; this apparent awareness makes us treat this redactor with even more respect.

Scene 8 I take to be from the redactor whose purpose it was to present Hui-neng as the Sixth Patriarch. Here Hui-neng is again enlightened, this time in the presence of the Fifth Patriarch after hearing the Diamond Sutra in its entirety. With this scene we are far from the historical Hui-neng. Scene 9 seems to have purposes related to the propagation of the teachings of the Six Patriarch in the north of China and would therefore also be part of the redactor's work.

Who then is the historical Hui-neng? I would suggest that he exists in Narrative One where his experience of enlightenment is described; in Narrative Two where his work at the threshing pestle is mentioned; and in Narrative Three where he composes his verse. This is the core account that the historical Hui-neng could have given in a sermon in which he told of his own experiences.

Finally, can this historical Hui-neng be among the "pure of heart" described in Psalm 73? In some ways it seems that he can. Like the psalmist for Psalm 73, Hui-neng is led by the Transcendent, in his case, to hear The Diamond Sutra. Once hearing it and having his mind "cleared," he lives, like the Psalmist, continually in the presence of the Transcendent and wants no more than this. Hui-neng is not depressed by doing manual labor for months without any recognition. Nor is he elated when he composes a poem aptly responding to the Patriarch's question. None of this is of much importance to him, for he seems to be one with the "pure of heart" for whom there is a Reality that transcends all else and to be one with that Reality is all that is of any importance.

The Cloud of Unknowing

The Cloud of Unknowing[25] was composed anonymously in the second half of the fourteenth century.[26] In the twentieth century, Christians have looked to this work for instructions on contemplation and mystical union. One cannot help thinking that there may be some similarities between mystical union and Buddhist enlightenment.

In searching for the historical Hui-neng, we found not more than a couple of hundred words that might be directly related to him. But, if there are similarities between mystical union and enlightenment, perhaps *The Cloud of Unknowing* can assist by offering commentary on various aspects of the experiences of the historical Hui-neng. What follows are selected quotations from *The Cloud* that seem to be as fitting for Hui-neng as for a Christian contemplative.[27]

Three passages from *The Cloud* are appropriate to describe general qualities that Hui-neng appears to have possessed. The first one is in chapter 24, where it is said that one who has experienced contemplation has a special relationship with others:

> For the perfect contemplative holds no man as such in special regard, be he kinsman, stranger, friend, or foe. For all men alike are his brothers, and none strangers. He considers all men his friends, and none his foes.[28]

This passage aptly describes Hui-neng's apparent relationship with all of the persons he encountered, whether it be the one reciting the Diamond Sutra, the Fifth Patriarch, the monk Shen-hsiu, or the other monks with whom he lived. None were held "in special regard"; all were his "brothers."

Second, chapter 54 has a description of how a contemplative affects others:

> All who engage in this work of contemplation find that it has a good effect on the body as well as on the soul, for it makes them attractive in the eyes of all who see them. So much so that the ugliest person alive who becomes, by grace, a contemplative, finds that he suddenly (and again by grace) is different, and that every good man he sees is glad and happy to have his friendship, and is spiritually refreshed, and helped nearer God by his company.[29]

The historical Hui-neng, as presented in his sermon, seems to be one "attractive in the eyes of all" who saw him. And this characteristic might have made him eligible to be the Six Patriarch, a position for which he himself, unlike others, had no ambition.

A third passage that could characterize Hui-neng as well is in chapter 71. Here, we are told how a contemplative acts:

> On the other hand there are some who by grace are so sensitive spiritually and so at home with God in this grace of contemplation that they may have it when they like and under normal spiritual working conditions, whether they are sitting, walking, standing, kneeling. And at these times they are in full control of their faculties, both physical and spiritual, and can use them if they wish, admittedly not without some difficulty, yet without great difficulty.[30]

This passage describes especially well how Hui-neng could have lived during his eight months of treading the threshing pestle as well as on his travels from one monastery to another.

As to Hui-neng's sudden awakening when he hears the Diamond Sutra, the author of *The Cloud* seems to have an appreciation for this type of experience when he writes the following in chapter 4:

> This work [of contemplation] does not need a long time for its completion. Indeed, it is the shortest work that can be imagined! It is no longer, no shorter than one atom.... It is so small that it cannot be analysed: it is almost beyond our grasp.... So pay great attention to this marvelous work of grace within your soul. It is always a sudden impulse and comes without warning, springing up to God like some spark from the fire.[31]

Hui-neng did not overtly seek enlightenment; it simply happened to him with his being awakened from a source outside of himself.[32] The author of *The Cloud,* like the narrator of Psalm 73, understands too that contemplation first of all comes from God, from completely outside of the one who contemplates:

> In that most gracious way of his, he [God] kindled your desire for himself, and bound you to him by the chain of such longing, and thus led you to that more Special life, a servant among his own special servants.[33]
>
> Indeed, it is good for you to realize that I cannot teach you. It is not to be wondered at. For this [the work of contemplation] is the work of God alone, deliberately wrought in whatever soul he chooses, irrespective of the merits of that particular soul.[34]

Hui-neng is "uneducated" and not able to read or write. Such a lack of education is also not a hindrance for contemplation from the perspective of *The Cloud,* for it is God who is the teacher:

> There has been no prior help from reading or sermons, no special meditation on anything whatever. This sudden perception and awareness is better learned from God than man.[35]

The author of *The Cloud* also appears to understand the essential nature of the experience of transcendence in a way similar to Hui-neng. In the Tun-huang text of the Platform Sutra, as already mentioned, there are two verses on enlightenment said to be composed by Hui-neng. The first one reads:

> Bodhi originally has no tree,
> The mirror also has no stand.
> Buddha nature is always clean and pure;
> Where is there room for dust?[36]

This poem seems to be suggesting that "bodhi" (knowledge of enlightenment) is not related to anything material, such as trees, mirror stands, or dust. It is precisely this point of the immateriality of the contemplative experience that the author of *The Cloud* often makes. For example, in chapter 45, he explains:

> A young man or woman just starting in the school of devotion hears someone read or speak about this sorrow and longing: how a man shall lift up his heart to God, and continually long to feel his love. And immediately in their silly minds they understand these words not in the intended spiritual sense, but in a physical and material, and they strain their natural hearts outrageously in their breasts![37]

In chapter 47, *The Cloud* author further develops this point:

> You know well that God is a spirit, and that whoever would be made one with him must in truth and in depth of spirit be far removed from any misleading bodily thing.[38]

He reiterates it in chapter 57:

> But I am saying that the work of our spirit does not go up or down, sideways, forward, or backward, like some physical thing. Because our work is a spiritual work, and not physical; nor is it achieved in a physical fashion.[39]

Similar comments are found in chapter 59 and chapter 61.[40] The strongest statement of this sort, however, comes in chapter 68:

> See that in no sense you withdraw into yourself. And, briefly, I do not want you to be outside or above, behind or beside yourself either! "Well," you will say, "where am I to be? Nowhere, according to you!" And you will be quite right! "Nowhere" is where I want you! Why, when you are "nowhere" physically, you are "everywhere" spiritually.[41]

All of these passages function very effectively as a commentary on Hui-neng's verse. Had the Buddhist monk Hui-neng been able to speak with the author of *The Cloud,* I suspect that there is much that they could have shared in their quiet ways. As religious men and women from Asian and Western religious traditions learn more about each other in the twenty-first century, we may allow Hui-neng and the author of *The Cloud* to meet "spiritually."

7

Zen and the Impurity of Purity

FRANCIS H. COOK

It is my modest hope that this paper will contribute a little to interreligious dialogue and understanding. As a century of violence and bloodshed nears its end, I also hope that people who are seriously committed to their religion and practice will be kinder and gentler in their public pronouncements as well as in daily transactions with followers of other paths. Interreligious dialogue is difficult in the most favorable circumstances. Christians struggle to understand an atheistic religion that rejects the notion of selfhood or soul and which has a strong ethic that functions without reference to a deity. Buddhists cannot for the life of us grasp how humans inherit sin from a primordial ancestor or how one person can suffer for another's crimes. Where is the justice? What happened to karma?

But what makes the dialogue particularly difficult is the spoiler lurking in the background—Christian claims to exclusiveness and finality and a missionary aggressiveness that Buddhists see as being a form of violence. It is therefore hard to carry on an interreligious conversation—all very civil and urbane—while all the time knowing that the guys across the table deny your legitimacy and at the same time lust after your scalp. It is my understanding that claims of exclusiveness and evangelical enthusiasm are part and parcel of Christianity and nonnegotiable. Consequently the dialogue continues, but the Buddhist fears for his scalp.

I must say that equally detrimental to full and fruitful dialogue are the demeaning comments made by spokesmen for the Vatican, and here I am referring to Cardinal Ratzinger, who recently spoke of Buddhism as *un autoérotisme spirituel*,[1] thus linking Buddhism with Onan's solitary vice and hinting in the strongest terms that both are wasting their time, to say the least. Such a comment displays a serious misunderstanding of the practices and objectives of Buddhism, as well as a measure of malice. I should also mention that Pope John Paul himself has also made negative remarks about Buddhist meditation.[2] This is strange in the light of the atmosphere of the Second Vatican Council and its stated hopes for more respect and understanding, as well as for more dialogue. Which Vatican are we to believe?

Thus, there are some serious obstacles to progress in these dialogues between Buddhists and Christians. However, those who participate in dialogue agree that there must be dialogue, just as there must be dialogue in interpersonal, political, and international areas of life. The alternative is ignorance, suspicion, antagonism, and even violence. So, in the spirit of friendship and dialogue, I present below some remarks concerning spiritual purity and how it is approached practically by many in the Zen tradition.

Purity in one form or another is a prominent aspect in a number of the world's religions. For instance, Japanese Shinto is primarily concerned with maintaining ritual purity. A believer is very much concerned that he or she will become defiled or polluted through contact with such things as corpses and menstruation that pollute and offend the *kami* (spiritual powers), which will bring calamity to the individual or the whole village. If purity is not quickly restored via ablutions, whole villages can suffer the wrath of the resident *kami*. In fact, the only thing functionally approaching sin in Shinto is loss of purity.

Hindus seem to be obsessed with purity. It can be lost in a number of ways. Traditionally, if a member of one of the social classes was touched by even the shadow of an outcaste, he became impure and had to undergo ritual purification. At one time (not too long ago) the offending outcaste would be killed. So great is the concern for purity in Hindu society that I have come to believe that one of the keys to understanding Indic religions is this pervasive concern with purity, which certainly influenced the beginnings of Buddhism in India.

It is not surprising that the Jewish-Christian Bible, which says somewhere that we must become like little children to know God, places a great amount of weight on the pure heart. The Bible has Jesus saying, in the famous Sermon on the Mount, "Blessed are the pure in heart, for they shall see God" (Mt 5:8). Such a strong statement! Being pure in heart must be like being a child, trusting, guileless, without calculation, and innocent. How interesting that it is such a one who will see God and not the theologian, scholar, enlightened person, or (certainly) the punctilious observer of the law. Such purity differs from that of the Hindu or follower of Shinto.

Purity of the kind mentioned in Matthew 5 is without doubt an excellent quality, and one that can be appreciated by anyone of any religion. At the same time, some religions handle the problem of purity in a most original and unorthodox manner. In the following pages, I will discuss how a Zen Buddhist might talk about purity and how meditation is related. I can, at this moment, hear the voice of my deceased teacher saying to me, "You should have your mouth washed out with soap for talking about purity." Lucky for me that I like the taste of soap.

Purity of heart was an important spiritual quality in the Buddhism of the early centuries and continues to be in some contemporary schools of

Buddhism. The *Dhammapada,* one of the earliest texts in the canon, has a whole chapter devoted to purity and impurity.[3] There, we find the Buddha teaching,

As a smith removes impurity from silver, even so,
Let a wise man remove impurities from himself, one by one,
Little by little, moment by moment. (XVIII, 5 adapted)

Earlier, the Buddha says,

Be a lamp for yourself, strive quietly, be wise.
When your impurities are purged, and you are free of sin,
You will reach the celestial realm, the stage of the saint. (XVII, 2
    adapted)

In this chapter we find mentioned as sources of impurity such things as violence, thoughtlessness, stinginess, theft, adultery, and others. What makes this catalogue of impurities a particularly Buddhist one is the following statement:

But there is an impurity greater than all impurities.
Ignorance is the greatest impurity. O mendicant,
Having cast away that impurity, be free from all impurities. (XVIII, 9)

It is true that impurity results from actions we perform, as well as from thoughts, impulses, desires, ambitions, and so on, in the mental realm. But, according to Buddhism, these mental and physical acts (karma) occur because the individual is fundamentally and massively ignorant, so that impurities such as craving, hatred, and pride, for instance, have their causal source in the mind in the form of massive ignorance. This locating the source of impurity in the mind, with the unspoken corollary that impurity is eliminated and purity is achieved by rectifying one's own mind, is particularly Buddhist. Let us recall the well-known response of the Buddha to the question, "What does a Buddha teach?" The Buddha replied,

Committing no evil;
Doing good deeds;
Purifying your own mind;
This is the teaching of all the Buddhas. (XIV, 5 adapted)

Given this situation in which impurity arises from primordial ignorance and delusion, the solution to the problem of impurity is clear. What is called for is not, as in Christianity, fasting, prayer, self-mortification, or prevenient grace, but something we might call "mind work," which in the West is called "meditation."

This tendency to claim that meditation is the solution for impurity is nowhere more clearly spelled out than in the vast text named the *Visuddhimagga,* by the fourth-century monk-scholar Buddhaghosha.[4] The *Visuddhimagga* portrays the monk's task as being one of purifying himself via the traditional "triple learning" (*trishiksha*), which consists of moral rectification (*sila*), mental development (*bhavana*), and pristine knowing (*panna*). What is interesting to us is that Buddhaghosha understood this spiritual path as being essentially a process of purification. Mind, or consciousness, is seen as being contaminated by a vast array of defilements (*kilesa*) that cloud, distort, and corrupt the mind and sense organs, resulting in ignorance of reality and later suffering in an endless cycle of death and rebirth. The religious path, then, is a process of gradually, bit by bit, over perhaps tens of thousands of lifetimes, uprooting these impurities, permitting the cleansed consciousness to know the true state of things, and in the end becoming liberated and enlightened.

A Chinese Zen work composed many centuries later refers to this approach as "mirror-wiping Zen," which is meditation based on the assumption that the mind is like a mirror that has collected dust on its face and needs to be cleaned so that it will again reflect what is in front of it. Once polished, the mirror reflects clearly and without distortion. Thus, meditation is a practice that purifies the mind and permits pristine knowing. If you seek purity, meditate.

The title of Buddhaghosha's great systematization of the Buddhist path, *Visuddhimagga,* is usually translated as "The Path of Purification," reflecting the commonly held assumption that Buddhist praxis is self-purification. In this matter, the text shows its debt to the larger Hindu socioreligious world, with its obsessive concern for purity and the commonly held assumption that a religious life necessarily involves self-purification. Most Hindus shared the belief that one of the best ways to do this was through grueling feats of self-mortification. The Buddha rejected that assumption and prescribed meditation. A comparison of Buddhaghosha's work with Patanjali's *Yoga Sutra*[5] will show how much the two texts share, including the understanding of the path as one of purification, meditation devices, the importance of *samadhi* (defined as unification of subject and object), the need to cleanse the mind and senses, and many other points of agreement. This approach to the spiritual path may be thought of as that of the realist. The realist sees the defilements or impurity as really existing. These defilements—lust, rage, arrogance, pride, ill will, etc.—infest the individual and block spiritual progress. Because there are so many of these defilements, and because they are so tenacious, the path of purification is a very long one, extending over tens of thousands of lifetimes. The path is not for cowards or the impatient, and to walk the path is an act of heroism. This realist view of the defilements was held by most or all early schools of Buddhism such as the Sarvastivadins and is still held by the Theravada tradition of Southeast Asia.[6]

A new approach to liberation arose in India shortly before the beginning of the Common Era.[7] This new form of Buddhism referred to itself as the "Mahayana," in order to distinguish itself from the realists mentioned above. Later Chinese, Korean, and Japanese schools of Buddhism such as Zen, Hua-yen, T'ien-t'ai, Yogacara, and Pure Land Buddhism are all forms of Mahayana and share many of the doctrinal innovations of Mahayana. The Zen way of regarding purity and its characteristic method of dealing with the problem are rooted in these doctrinal changes. I will discuss four of them here.

The first innovation was to say that compassion is equal in value to enlightened insight. Several texts claim that it is more important, while yet other texts claim that compassion and enlightened insight are identical, compassion being simply any action grounded in enlightened insight. The object of the religious life is not to become enlightened but rather to equip oneself with the knowledge that will enable one to work selflessly for the liberation of all others.

The second change was the rejection of the earlier teaching that only male monastics could achieve the ultimate goal of the religion and the extension of the possibility for all beings to achieve the full fruits, including monastics and laypeople, men and women. Mahayana was and remains a lay movement, although still revering the monastic lifestyle. Mahayana, the Great Vehicle, is a commodious vehicle with room for all, including animals and even grass and trees, on the way to nirvana.

The third innovation was the redefining of what the perfect human being is. The older ideal person was the celibate monastic who strove for liberation from the cycle of death and rebirth. He was replaced by the bodhisattva, who deliberately retains some defilements so that he can be reborn in the realms of pain and suffering in order to work for the liberation of all sentient beings. He or she vows to never enter nirvana until all others enter first, and since for practical purposes there will never be an end to the number of deluded and suffering beings, the bodhisattva will forever be reborn in the human world, the purgatories, among animals, and so on, wherever he or she is needed. The bodhisattva is the one being who will never achieve nirvana, even though it would be possible.

The fourth change is the foundational teaching of Mahayana Buddhism, emptiness (*sunyata*). The other three changes in doctrine can only really be understood in the light of emptiness. To say that something is "empty" is to make the claim that that object does not exist independently but rather exists in dependence on a vast number of supporting conditions. It thus exists in only the most ephemeral and contingent manner. All things without exception are empty, including the very concept of emptiness itself. Seen in this way, any entity, whether psychic or material, enjoys only a shadowy, quasi-existence and is completely lacking in ultimacy. To mistakenly impute any real existence or reality to something is to grasp it falsely, and such a cognitive error will have consequences for the deluded individual. Especially harmful is the naive belief that the world is really composed of dualisms such as self and other, good and bad, ignorance and enlightenment, Buddhas and ordinary people, and—what is germane to this paper—purity and impurity. The awakened mind knows that all dualisms are superimposed upon a raw experience which itself does not exhibit these dualisms and, consequently, are false.

In terms of how we respond to experience and conduct ourselves in the world, it matters whether something exists in its own right or has only a borrowed, contingent existence. One has only to compare the Christian doctrine of the aseity of God to notice the feeling tone of "contingent." God has "aseity," which means that He or She enjoys self-existence. God's creatures—us—have only a contingent, reflected existence, which means contingent on God. There is a great difference here between being contingent and not being contingent. God IS; we depend on God for our shadowy existence. God's aseity is what Buddhists would call "own-being" or "self-existence" (*svabhava*). In Buddhism, nothing possesses self-existence or aseity, even God. I will come back to this point further on.

In Mahayana Buddhism, including Zen, the issue of purity is dealt with in a manner quite different from what I have characterized as "realistic," and this is because of the teaching of emptiness. The Mahayana approach to purity and impurity has been seen by some Buddhologists as being "idealistic" rather than "realistic." Instead of confronting the defilements and impurity as really existing things that constitute one's nature and which must be painfully and patiently exterminated over a very long time, one learns to see all things as empty and insubstantial and, by so doing, eliminates the whole problem at one blow at the very root of the problem—deluded understanding. By doing this, Mahayana Buddhists use what might be called a "shortcut" method. However, the "shortcut" path occurs within the framework of the more traditional path that extends over many lifetimes. That is, one may have been reborn ten thousand times before one has a grasp of emptiness and suddenly eliminates the problem of impurity.

One of Buddhism's favorite exemplars of this approach to purity and impurity is the elderly layman, Vimalakirti, whose name is translated as "He of Immaculate Reputation" in the sutra Teachings of Vimalakirti.[8] Vimalakirti has a family, he is a physician, and he is wealthy, thus exemplifying the Mahayana idea that one may be enlightened and occupy the highest rungs of bodhisattvahood without separating oneself from home, occupation, and material comfort. In the chapter of the sutra named "The Family of the Tathagata," we find this description of a bodhisattva like Vimalakirti:

The bodhisattva commits the five sins that are subject to immediate retribution,[9] but he is free from wickedness, harm, and ill will. He goes among the damned in the purgatories, but he is free of all the contamination of the defilements. He goes among animals, but he is free of darkness and ignorance. He goes among asuras [evil spirits], but he is free of pride, arrogance, and conceit. He goes about in the world of the lord of death, but he accumulates all the equipment of merit and knowledge. He goes about in the trance states (*dhyana*) but does not enjoy being there. He follows the path of love, but he is detached from the pleasures of love. He follows the path of hate, but he has neither hate nor aversion for anyone. He follows the path of delusion, but he has the clairvoyance of keen insight into all things. He follows the path of avarice but, without care for his body or life, he abandons internal and external goods. He follows the path of immorality but, seeing the dangers that are found in the smallest fault, he establishes himself in strict observances and complete austerities and is content with little.... He follows the path of all the defilements of the whole world, but he is without defilements and naturally pure (*svabhavena parishuddhah*). He follows the path of Mara, but in that which concerns the Buddha's teaching, he understands them and knows them personally and does not depend on others. He goes about in the re-birth realms of the whole world, but he escapes all rebirth realms. He follows the path of nirvana, but he does not abandon the stream of death and rebirth.[10]

Vimalakirti is able to shrug off defilement while entering all sorts of terrible and depraved places and engaging in all sorts of disreputable activities because he understands that the defilements are empty and all dualisms are false. He is also able to retain his intrinsic purity of heart because he understands that the only real impurity is the belief that the world corresponds to our ideas of it. In short, his heart is pure because he has no conception of purity. Living and acting in this way, he is able to enter any place, engage in any activity, break any precept, and assume any identity, without becoming contaminated. His knowledge that all things are empty forms a suit of armor that he wears in often terrible places while pursuing his task of freeing all sentient beings from suffering and delusion.

The actions of the bodhisattva are probably best exemplified by the figure of Avalokiteshvara (Chinese: Kuan yin), whose appearance in the world in any of thirty-three forms, some less than respectable, is all done to help people to spiritual maturity and lead them to the other shore of nirvana. Avalokiteshvara appears wherever he is needed, even in the horrible purgatories. He personifies not only the compassion that is so important to Mahayana, but also the knowledge of emptiness, without which he could not be compassionate and liberate countless beings. It is clear that at the heart of the bodhisattva life there is a huge paradox. If we avidly chase after purity as if it really exists and we may possess it, we perpetually miss purity. Instead of replacing impurity with purity, we become infected with the worst kind of impurity. When, on the other hand, we free ourselves from the dualism of pure and impure, we find ourselves abiding in our own intrinsic purity. Nowhere in the Buddhist canon is this paradox enunciated more clearly than in the *Diamond Sutra*:

> The Lord said, "Here, Subhuti, someone who has set out in the vehicle of a Bodhisattva should produce a thought in this manner: 'As many beings as there are in the universe of beings comprehended under the term "beings," as far as any conceivable form of being is conceived; all these I must lead to Nirvana, into that realm of Nirvana [without remainder]. And yet, although numerous beings have been led to Nirvana, no being at all has been led to Nirvana.' And why? If in a Bodhisattva the notion of a 'being' should take place, he would not be called a 'Bodhi-being.' And why? He is not to be called a Bodhi-being in whom the notion of a self or a being should take place, or the notion of a living soul or of a person."[11]

This passage can serve as a kind of paradigm, in the sense that any term—defilement, nirvana, God, liberation, holy, ad infinitum—can be substituted for the term "beings" and the same paradox is found. If a bodhisattva thinks that purity exists, he is not a real "bodhi-being" because a bodhisattva—one whose being is bodhi or awakening—does not operate in a framework of purity and impurity, or any dualism, in fact. To do so would be a blatant contradiction with bodhi. Yet, just as countless beings are led to nirvana by the bodhisattva even though—or because—he or she has no concept of beings, so is the heart of the bodhisattva pure even though—or because—he or she does not conceive of purity.

Even very early non-Mahayana Buddhism knew that the problem of purity and impurity originates in the way ordinary deluded minds deal with experience. Recall the passage from the *Dhammapada* that speaks of the source of impurity in the mind:

> A greater impurity than all other impurities—ignorance.
> Free from that impurity, one is free of all impurities. (XVIII, 243)

Here, in a text from primitive Buddhism, the "shortcut" approach to the path is clearly articulated. The same text says,

> All dharmas are without self (anatta). Realizing this,
> One of wisdom extinguishes sorrow. This is the path of purity. (XX
>   279, adapted)

A much later text, the Chinese *Ch'eng wei-shih lun* (Demonstration of Conscious Only) says,

> Because mind is impure, beings are impure.
> Because mind is pure, sentient beings are pure.[12]

These and many other texts make the same basic point, one which is characteristic of almost all of Mahayana thought; whether one believes that defilements really exist or whether one thinks that they are simply the result of delusion, the source of the religious problem is nothing but a deluded grasp of the world by a deluded mind.

I should emphasize again: The Buddhist critique of things as being empty should not be construed as meaning that they do not exist; there is a world "out there" beyond our minds that we interact with. It exists, but how it exists for us is a far different matter. Thus, things have a kind of reality, vague and shadowing. In the ultimate sense, seen from the perspective of higher truth, they are unreal and only quasi-existent. Inasmuch as they exist and exert an influence on people, they are real enough and engage the bodhisattva seriously. At the same time, they are phantasmagorical and insubstantial enough to free the believer of guilt, obsession, and despair. Richard Robinson, in *The Buddhist Religion,* says, "The Mahayana advocates of emptiness (Sunyavadins) insisted on emptiness in order to summon the hearer to reevaluate transmigration and achieve release within it rather than fleeing it while still considering it real and important."[13]

It will be quite clear to the reader why meditation is the spiritual tool par excellence for seeking the religious goal. The religious quandary is not sin, lack of faith, or disobedience, it is what the Germans call *Urdummheit,* a kind of primordial stupidity, a kind of congenital blindness. Prayer cannot erase this delusion (there being no one to pray to), nor can fasting and other penances, which is why the Buddha rejected them as a viable tool for liberation and taught the Middle Way. And proper morals aid in the search for liberation. However, the saintliest seeker of the Way cannot, by proper behavior alone, advance one foot toward the goal. Only those practices that we in the West call "meditation" perform the task of removing the veil of blindness and giving us a glimpse of the truth.

Later developments in Buddhist thought and practice continued this conviction that the key to the removal of character traits that are inimical to spiritual progress is the practice of meditation. All schools of Buddhism, with the exception of Pure Land Buddhism, agreed on the need for meditation. Different lineages of Zen likewise taught meditation as the sole practice, although there were some radical groups (extreme "idealists" as I have used the term earlier) who said that meditation was not necessary.[14] Most Zen masters, however, taught meditation as the best, or only, form of practice. Indeed, the name of their school is Zen, which presumably translates the

Sanskrit *dhyana,* which means "meditation." These groups, in naming themselves the Meditation School, announced to the world that their business was meditation, not scholarship, ritual, intoning the name of the Buddha, lecturing on the sutras, or attending conferences, in contradistinction with their Chinese contemporaries whose Buddhist practice was precisely those activities. The Zen movement may have been a reaction to this other Buddhism of scholarship, reading the sacred texts, and so on, and a "return to the fundamentals" movement. Zen texts say that to be a practicing Buddhist means to meditate, and one meditates because of the role it plays in the goals of Buddhism.

While there are a number of Zen traditions or schools, and a variety of teaching methods and interpretations of Zen, most would agree that all beings possess an original nature or Buddha nature, or true nature, which means enlightened nature.[15] This original nature is pure and good, and the purpose of meditation is to actualize this nature in one's life. It is this attempt to realize one's own Buddha nature through the practice of meditation that bears on the problem of purity.

As I mentioned earlier, Mahayana Buddhism, including the Zen tradition, does not take a realistic position on such matters as purity and impurity but rather approaches the issue in a much more radical fashion that adopts the teachings of the *Vimalakirti Sutra, Diamond Sutra,* and, indeed, that whole class of scriptures named *Prajnaparamita,* those scriptural works that loudly proclaim the emptiness and vanity of all things and offer true liberation. For that reason, Zen teachers from earliest times tended not to employ the realistic method in their practice but instead insisted that if a Zen student could have a sudden glimpse of his own Buddha nature, even though the student had no previous preparation, such as removing impurity from his mind/heart or traversing the ten bodhisattva stages and perfecting qualities such as generosity, observance of the precepts, patience, vigor, etc.,[16] then the problem of purity would be taken care of at a single blow, immediately and decisively, by using the so-called "shortcut" method mentioned earlier. This approach was widely used in Chinese Buddhist circles, and a famous debate in Tibet between Indian exponents of the realistic, step-by-step path and Chinese advocates of the idealistic, shortcut method focused the arguments on the question of whether a person had to prepare himself or herself by first purifying the mind and heart. The Chinese, representing a new approach, said "no." A person who is deeply sincere can attain the goal just as he or she is, defilements and all.

It is not that Zen masters had no interest at all in purity; the real concern was with the question of the status or nature of purity and how best to confront the problem. One may, as the Jains in India or the Theravada Buddhists do, adopt a common-sense attitude and begin to patiently exterminate each defilement over one's lifetime. Purity simply means the absence of any defilement from one's mind, heart, soul, self, character, and so on. This can be an effective religious practice for a serious, committed person.

However, many a Zen master would laugh and accuse the individual of being rather naive about the matter. "You don't realize," he would say, "that defilements are like desert mirages, and purity resembles a dream." Purity is not the removal of real defilements, but rather the manifestation of the primordial purity of Buddha nature or true self uncontaminated by the illusory dualism of pure and impure.[17] Besides, looked at in the light of the *Vimalakirti Sutra* or *Diamond Sutra,* we need to ask who it is who becomes pure or impure, and just exactly what is this so-called "purity." In the same way, when we repent sincerely in an act of self-confession for our actions and thoughts, the act of repentance is simply the self-expression of this same original purity.

Thus, the purity we seek is already ours in the form of original nature or Buddha nature, and because it is also original purity, it itself negates the dualism of pure and impure. I wonder what the Christian position is concerning essential purity. The original family in the Garden of Eden, Adam and spouse, were created pure of heart, and after their great crime we, their descendants, now dwell in a corrupt state, having inherited the crime from them. I understand that there is some disagreement in theological circles as to whether human beings are essentially pure, albeit having adventitious defilement, or whether their nature became completely and essentially impure or corrupt *in esse.* Most Buddhists would agree that humans are essentially pure because their true nature or Buddha nature is pure. Therefore, defilement is merely adventitious and just obscures intrinsic purity, or, if it does not really exist, it is nothing but a word or concept that vanishes with the appearance of Buddha nature. If it really exists, then it must be dealt with over a very long time; if it is unreal and does not really exist, then there are shortcut techniques that dispel our confusion and radically shorten the path to liberation.

In Buddha nature, which is prior to all dualisms, there is no impure or pure, so in the instant when Buddha nature is manifested, so also is the essential purity of Buddha nature manifested. Now, this may sound too paradoxical at best, or very confused at worst, but what I am saying is that when one's essential nature or Buddha nature is manifested and the ordinary, conceptual, conventional dualism of "impurity" and "purity" is overcome by the knowledge of emptiness, the restored consciousness is truly pure. At least in theory. The spectacle in recent years of American Buddhist leaders committing adultery, having improper sexual relations with students, engaging in power struggles, and worse, raises very serious questions about training and about the very nature of the *kensho* (realizing one's essential nature).

Purity of heart for the Zen tradition is said to be the fruit of meditation, *zazen,* because only in *zazen* does one find that enlightened "self." As I remarked earlier, most Buddhists over a span of twenty-five hundred years have agreed that the key to spiritual liberation is meditation. A sutra from the earliest period, the *Anapana-sati Sutra* (Scripture on Mindfulness of Breathing), has the Buddha saying that this practice, simply observing one's inhalations and exhalations, is the royal road to liberation.[18] Hardly any spokesman for Buddhism in the last twenty-five centuries has argued with that statement, although other methods were employed.

One of the attractive features of Zen meditation is its simplicity. Most meditators either count their breaths from one to ten repeatedly for a certain length of time, simply sit in full mindfulness of breathing, or just sit in a kind of global, unfocused mindfulness, without counting breaths, chanting, muttering (what Hindus call *japa*), or focusing attention on some item. Some attention is given to proper posture and breathing, and the rest is as described above. Unlike the *contemplatio* or *meditatio* of the medieval Catholic manuals, *zazen* is not a discursive practice. It does not involve thinking or pondering a theme such as God's love, the Holy Trinity, and so on. This *contemplatio* may very well have its own result and may be quite effective, but it is not like *zazen.*

The Zen method is based on the idea that a mode of consciousness that is nondualistic, unconfused, and pure lies at the roots of the ordinary, everyday consciousness that we believe to be normal and in full contact with "reality." This dualistic consciousness is the result of a split in consciousness that results in one part of consciousness that acts as an observer, or subject, and a counterpart half that contains memories, desires, projects, fears, and so on, and that the subjective part believes is one's self. Looking outward, the subject part sees a world composed of dualisms: good and bad, sacred and profane, saint and sinner, self and other, success and failure, life and death—the list is staggeringly long. The fundamental consciousness that generated this bifurcated consciousness remains beneath. It is our true self, our intrinsic nature, and our Buddha nature. The function of meditation is to pierce (so to speak) beneath the surface consciousness, abandon its dualisms, its delusions, hatreds, fears, and the like, and recover the enlightened nature that has always been there. Hopefully, we then begin to engage the world with this new consciousness.

I believe that this meditation is Asia's and Buddhism's great gift to the world, free for the taking, and coming with a full guarantee. It is something that a Christian can do without fear of being unfaithful or unchristian, and, in fact, many Christians and Jews do practice it in the belief that it does not compromise one's own Christian or Jewish faith. Benedictines in Vermont do *zazen,* I know of a Catholic priest who is also a Zen master, and I know of one or two rabbis who are also Zen masters. There is at least one nun who is recognized as being highly accomplished. None will ever abandon their original religions, but *zazen* has altered their lives decisively. The pope has, in recent years, tried to discourage this kind of practice among Catholics, and recently the Dalai Lama has said, "Let everybody stick with his own religion," but I'll leave it to the reader to decide, in the light of what I have said about purity and meditation, whether *zazen* can be valuable for a non-Buddhist. Cardinal Ratzinger, that indefatigable protector of the faith, is really correct in his observation that Zen practice is carried out without reference to a supreme being of any sort, though the disparaging way of referring to it was not necessary. Meditation—the whole religious life, really—enlightenment, and the life of compassionate commitment are realized within an atheistic framework. No second party is involved. The Buddhist's basic problem is a cognitive or epistemological one and does not require, and cannot require, a second party. Like Onan, we go it alone.

8

Zazen

A Path from Judgment to Love

WILLIAM SKUDLAREK, O.S.B.

I doubt that there is a Catholic practicing *zazen* in Japan who has not heard of Father Hugo M. Enomiya-Lassalle, a German Jesuit who lived in Japan, practiced Zen meditation for over fifty years, and spent the last twenty years of his life conducting meditation courses in Japan and Europe. Father Lassalle died in 1990, four years before I moved to Japan, so I never had a chance to meet him. However, my first teacher was Ryôun Yamada Roshi, to whose father, Kôun Yamada Roshi, Father Lassalle would refer people who asked him to recommend a Zen master. In addition, I have participated in *sesshins* at Shinmeikutsu, the Christian Zen Center that Father Lassalle founded in the hilly outskirts of Tokyo. Thus, even though I never met Father Lassalle and in fact had not even heard about him before I came to Japan, I know that I am one of the many beneficiaries of his dedication to the practice of *zazen* and to his fostering of the dialogue between Zen Buddhism and Christianity.

In fact, it was something Father Lassalle wrote that persuaded me to accept Father Joseph Wong's invitation to participate in this conference, even though I am but a novice in both the practice of *zazen* and interreligious dialogue:

> As we slowly get deeper into meditation, we all have our own experiences and are always learning something new. When my first book on Zen, *Zen Way to Enlightenment,* was translated into Japanese many years ago, I asked [Kôun Yamada Roshi,] the successor to the late Harada Roshi, my first Zen master, to write an introduction for the Japanese edition. At the end of his introduction he wrote, "When the author has attained enlightenment, he should write another book."[1]

Rather than being chagrined by that comment, Father Lassalle welcomed it, noting, "It is only through constant practice that our experiences grow." In some sense, of course, no matter how much we have discovered, or think we have discovered, we are all seekers. Benedict says that the novice master's

137

main responsibility is to determine whether or not the novice is truly seeking God.[2] But the search for God is not limited to the novitiate; it is the work and the goal of a lifetime. Whenever we sense that we have found God—or that God has found us—is not this awareness coupled with the conviction that we must keep searching, because the true God is beyond all human knowledge or experience? At the same time our experiences, no matter how trivial they may seem—or in fact be!—can help others to remain faithful to their search, to their practice, and to come to a deeper awareness of their true self.

As for the topic of this paper, "*Zazen:* A Path from Judgment to Love," that also came from something I read. This time it was Thomas Merton's *Zen and the Birds of Appetite.* Commenting on the Zenkei Shibayama's comparison of Zen consciousness to a mirror, Merton wrote:

> Zen consciousness does not distinguish and categorize what it sees in terms of social and cultural standards. It does not try to fit things into artificially preconceived structures....If it seems to judge and distinguish, it does so only enough to point beyond judgment to the pure void....
>
> Here we can fruitfully reflect on the deep meaning of Jesus' saying: "Judge not, and you will not be judged." Beyond its moral implications, familiar to all, there is a Zen dimension to this word of the Gospel. Only when this Zen dimension is grasped will the moral bearing of it be fully clear![3]

One of the reasons that observation of Merton struck me with such force was that it was by reading and hearing the Gospels in Japanese that I finally appreciated the force of Jesus' insistence that his disciples refrain from judging others. I suspect that my experience was not all that different from the experience of other Christians who have lived abroad, learned a new language, and then began reading and hearing familiar biblical passages in that new language. Words we have often heard and think we understand can, when heard in a new language and a new cultural setting, suddenly come alive and reveal a richness of meaning that is altogether fresh and provocative.

Jesus' words, "Judge not, and you will not be judged" (Mt 7:1),[4] when I heard them in Japanese, were a case in point for me. In the ecumenical translation of the Scriptures now generally in use by Christians throughout Japan,[5] that saying of Jesus is rendered *Hito wo sabakuna. Anatagata mo sabakarenai tame de aru.*

In Japanese, when you ask another person not to do something, you normally form the imperative by adding ...*naide kudasai* to the verb. The result is more or less equivalent to the English, "Please don't...." Thus, to ask someone not to judge other people, you might say, *Hito wo sabakanaide kudasai*—though it might sound a bit strange to say to someone, "Please don't judge others." A more direct form of the imperative would be *Hito wo sabakanai yôni nasai. Hito wo sabakukoto wa ikenai* or *Hito wo sabaite wa naranai* are other ways to express the negative imperative. But when you really want to be forceful and insistent about something, you simply use what is called the dictionary form of the verb and add *na*. It was precisely this form of the negative imperative that the Japanese translators chose to render Jesus' command, *mē krinete: Hito wo sabakuna!*[6]

The question, of course, is whether or not the Japanese translation of *mē krinete* by *Hito wo sabakuna* is an instance of the well-known Italian dictum *Traduttore traditore* (translation is betrayal). I do not think it is. In fact I would venture to say that *sabakuna* comes much closer to conveying the tone of the Greek present imperative than the somewhat bland "Do not judge" or "Judge not" that are fairly common English translations of Jesus' words. The use of the present imperative in Greek is a way of indicating a general rule, of indicating what should always or never be done.[7] "Stop judging others" or "Don't even think of judging somebody else" might be more precise ways of rendering into English the particular nuance of Jesus' command, at least as it was rendered into Greek by the Evangelists.

Not judging others is, I would propose, a particularly clear and forceful expression of purity of heart. What I propose to do, therefore, is to reflect on the meaning and importance of the command not to judge in the teaching of Jesus and in the teaching and practice of early Christian monasticism. I will then show how I understand this teaching of Jesus in the light of the nondualistic worldview of Buddhism. Finally, I will reflect on how my own practice of *zazen* has helped me to recognize the fundamental importance of not judging others, to recognize, in fact, the impossibility of judging others, and to appreciate the possibility of attaining that purity of heart, which is expressed in a nonjudgmental attitude toward others and toward oneself.

Jesus' Words on Not Judging

Jesus' command not to judge others, as it is recorded in Matthew's collection of sayings known as the Sermon on the Mount, is accompanied by the observation that the way we judge others is the way we will be judged, the amount we give to others is the amount we will receive in turn. Jesus then continues by pointing out how ludicrous it is to be concerned about a splinter in the eye of another while ignoring the plank that is lodged in your own eye (7:1–5).

In Luke's Gospel Jesus' admonition against judgment is preceded by the words, "Be merciful, just as your Father is merciful" (6:36). Like Matthew, Luke also includes in this context Jesus' observation that what we give others is what we can expect to receive, as well as the saying about not being concerned about that splinter in your neighbor's eye while ignoring the plank in your own. In this passage Luke also includes Jesus' observation that if one blind person tries to guide another who is blind, both will end up falling into a pit (6:37–42).

Mark's Gospel does not contain Jesus' prohibition against judgment, but does include the words, "The measure you give will be the measure you get" (4:24).

The command not to judge others is also absent from John's Gospel, but judgment is one of the major themes of Jesus' discourses. However, what he says in one place seems to contradict what he says in another. For example, in chapter five Jesus says, "The Father judges no one but has given all judgment to the Son. . . . I can do nothing on my own. As I hear, I judge; and my judgment is just, because I seek to do not my own will but the will of him who sent me" (5:22, 30), and then later, in chapter eight, he proclaims, "You judge by human standards; I judge no one. Yet even if I do judge, my judgment is valid; for it is not I alone who judge, but I and the Father who sent me" (8:15–16). And still further, in chapter twelve, he cries out, "I do not judge anyone who hears my words and does not keep them, for I came not to judge the world, but to save the world. The one who rejects me and does not receive my word has a judge; on the last day the word that I have spoken will serve as judge" (12:47–48).

The theme of judgment is obviously central to John's presentation of Jesus' person and mission. John is concerned to show in what sense Jesus judges or does not judge us, and to emphasize that in the end it is really we who judge ourselves by our response to Jesus and his word. As mentioned above, John does not include in his Gospel Jesus' categorical command to his followers not to judge one another. When Jesus says, "Do not judge by appearances, but judge with right judgment" (7:24), he is referring to the blindness of the crowd that had passed judgment on him by accusing him of being possessed by a demon. In the story of the woman taken in adultery, Jesus' words to the accusing scribes and Pharisees, "Let anyone among you who is without sin be the first to throw a stone at her" (8:7), are a powerful expression in narrative form of the absurdity of thinking that one person can sit in judgment over another. However this passage may, in fact, be a later addition to the Gospel.[8]

A quick glance at a few English commentaries shows how common it is for exegetes—at least Western exegetes—to tone down Jesus' command not to judge others. Expressions like "He obviously didn't mean . . . " or "What he really meant to say . . . " appear frequently in their interpretations of his words. What may lie behind these attempts to soften Jesus' words is the belief that judging others is simply part and parcel of what it means to be human. One author makes his point by arguing as follows:

Matthew abbreviates and transforms the original Semitic parataxis "judge not and . . . " into the better Greek and clearer logic of "judge not that you may not be judged." This verse liberates us from the need to be everyone's conscience or censor, but it does not free us from all need for judgment. Every simple sentence such as "This cow is brown" is a judgment, and in adult life we cannot escape the obligation to make some judgments even on the moral character of others. Parents, fiancés, employers, civil judges, church administrators, etc., all have this duty. Jesus' teaching warns against usurping the definitive judgment of God, who alone sees the hearts. By contrast, our judging must be tentative, partial, and inadequate (see 1 Sam 16:7; Jer 17:10). But wherever possible, we should mind our own business and not meddle in others'.[9]

Given the conviction that passing judgment is an essential element of being human, Jesus' categorical command not to judge is often interpreted as a form of "Semitic exaggeration," that all-too-convenient escape hatch we resort to when Jesus says something that challenges our assumptions. While it may very well be true that the word "judge" should be understood to mean "condemn," or that "The context would suggest that it is the attitude which fails to show mercy to the guilty which is here being attacked. It is not the use of discernment and discrimination which is forbidden, but the attitude of censoriousness,"[10] I continue to be intrigued by Merton's suggestion that there is a "Zen dimension" to this saying of Jesus. Without going so far as to say that interpreting this command of Jesus from a Zen perspective is the only legitimate way to understand it, I would like to suggest that a Zen approach can help us appreciate and appropriate Jesus' command not to judge at a level deeper than that of moral precept.

Before doing that, however, I would like to look briefly at the teachings of the Egyptian Desert Fathers to show that, at least at one time and place, the word of Jesus not to judge others was interpreted unconditionally.

Not Judging in the Sayings of the Desert Fathers

Admonitions not to judge others occur frequently in the Sayings of the Desert Fathers. One of the reasons for this, I suspect, is that their passionate commitment to a rigorous ascetical regime of fasting, unceasing prayer, sleep deprivation, and solitude very easily tempted them to look down on "worldly" Christians as well as on their fellow denizens of the desert who were not as observant as they. However, as Benedicta Ward, who translated and edited the "Alphabetical Collection" of these sayings, rightly observes, the aim of the monk's life was not asceticism but God, and the way to God was charity. "One of the marks of this charity," she writes, "was that the fathers did not judge."[11]

One of the most categorical sayings regarding the necessity of avoiding judgment comes from Abba Moses: "The monk must die to his neighbour and never judge him at all, in any way whatever."[12] This apophthegm is all the more striking in that it is the first in a list of seven instructions that Abba Moses sent to Abba Poemen with the observation that "he who puts them into practice will escape all punishment and will live in peace, whether he dwells in the desert or in the midst of brethren."[13] Not judging, in other words, is equally applicable to hermits and to cenobites.

The last of Abba Moses' seven instructions expands on what it means to die to one's neighbor:

> To die to one's neighbour is this: To bear your own faults and not to pay attention to anyone else wondering whether they are good or bad. Do no harm to anyone, do not think anything bad in your heart toward anyone, do not scorn the man who does evil, do not put confidence in him who does wrong to his neighbour, do not rejoice with him who injures his neighbour. This is what dying to one's neighbour means. Do not rail against anyone, but rather say, "God knows each one." Do not agree with him who slanders, do not rejoice at his slander and do not hate him who slanders his neighbour. This is what it means not to judge. Do not have hostile feelings toward anyone and do not let dislike dominate your heart; do not hate him who hates his neighbour. This is what peace is: Encourage yourself with this thought, "Affliction lasts but a short time, while peace is for ever, by the grace of God the Word. Amen."[14]

In the end, not judging means "dying to the neighbor," that is, letting go of every attempt to evaluate others and even oneself in relation to some abstract, external norm or rule. For the Fathers of the Desert, not judging others goes beyond looking down on or condemning them. It includes any kind of comparison between self and the other. Such an attitude does not imply that there is no need for conversion and transformation, or perhaps even, at times, the forceful restraint of behavior that is harmful or destructive. The Desert Fathers might not agree with, but I think they would understand, the Buddhist sage who said, "There is no right and no wrong, but right is right and wrong is wrong."[15] Their absolute rejection of any attempt to judge others, however, points to their conviction that interior and lasting change does not come about by trying to make others or oneself conform to some external norm. True conversion is only brought about through the transforming power of the Holy Spirit of God (this is how I, as a Christian, would name the power), and that power can only operate in us when we let go of all pretensions and accept ourselves and others as we and they are. Such truthful acceptance is what the Christian monastic tradition refers to as "humility." As our becoming quiet and centered gradually enables us to let go of every thought of judging others or ourselves, we will, as Abba Paphnutius was told by the old men to whom he went for counsel, be at peace.[16]

Not Judging in Literature of and about Zen

In my limited acquaintance with the writings of and about Zen, I have found very little that speaks directly to the issue of judging. But I believe that even though the word may appear only rarely, not judging is at the very heart of the Zen approach to authentic human existence.[17]

Absolutely fundamental to Zen is a nondualistic conception of reality. Zen's insistence on the unity of all that exists may be a particularly intense expression of the perception of reality that is much more common in the East than in the West.

On one occasion I asked Sister Kathleen Reilly, an American Maryknoll sister who is a Zen Roshi, to explain to me the meaning and purpose of doubt in the practice of *zazen*. I was thinking of the teaching that holds that enlightenment will only come if one practices *zazen* with great faith, great doubt, and great dedication. She said that according to Rôun Yamada Roshi, the most important and basic of the three elements of Zen is faith, the faith that I have my true self, am my true self. Then comes doubt, in the sense that although I am my true self, I still do not "taste" it. My true self, she said, is like something I have lost in my room; I know it's there, but I just can't see it yet. And finally, there must be dedication to the practice of *zazen*.

Sister Kathleen went on to say that, according to a German Zen teacher, the reason some Asian Zen masters emphasize doubt so much is that the Asian has a deep sense of oneness with all that is. For this reason, knowing that people can become complacent, Asian Zen masters use doubt as a way of urging their disciples to strive for the *experience* of this unity. We in the West, however, are much more conscious of our dividedness, of our unworthiness. And therefore we may need to emphasize faith more than doubt.[18]

In the literature of and about Zen one finds numerous references to a nondualistic approach to reality. Kôun Yamada Roshi would often speak about this fundamental insight of Zen in his *teishôs*[19] by contrasting Buddhist teaching with the presumption of ordinary people that subject and object are in opposition, that the objective world is standing before our consciousness as the completely different outer world. For this reason, he says, these "ordinary people" suffer pain and agony because the outer world does not obey their will, and circumstances do not go as they wish. In one of his *teishôs* he insisted that the most fundamental point of Buddhist teaching, the true *satori* of Zen, is that subject and object are intrinsically one. To intuit, experience, and realize this fact is the main reason for doing *zazen*. "In the world of the essential nature, is there anything, after all, to be called gain or loss, good or bad? As I tell you so often, in the world of Mu there are no such dualistic oppositions."[20]

One does find occasional comments in Zen literature that are, in effect, admonitions not to judge. Shunryu Suzuki, for example, once said, "When you listen to someone, you should give up all your preconceived ideas and your subjective opinion; you should just listen to him, just observe what his way is. We put very little emphasis on right and wrong or good and bad. We just see things as they are with him, and accept them."[21] Or, when talking about the necessity of obeying the rules of Zen, he insisted, "It is not a matter of good or bad, convenient or inconvenient. You just do it without question. That way your mind is free.... The important thing is to obey your rules *without discrimination*."[22]

As a Westerner and a Christian I have to say that Buddhism's fundamental perception of reality is so different from mine that my first reaction is simply to reject it out of hand as erroneous, or at least purely subjective. I have been shaped and formed by a culture that esteems individuality, that promotes competition and creativity, that constantly wants to separate (soul from body; active from contemplative; black from white; and on and on and on), that simply assumes as a given that the world is ultimately composed of, or explicable in terms of, two basic entities, as mind and matter. Because I have been shaped and formed by a dualistic *Weltanschauung* I sometimes feel I simply do not have the ability even to begin to understand what Yamada Roshi is getting at when he says "subject and object are intrinsically one." I don't know if I can understand it; but, for reasons that are more intuitive than rational, I am fascinated by it and attracted to it.

What I can understand, however, is that if one operates out of a non-dualistic worldview and strives to come to an experiential realization of this way of conceiving reality, then there is very little reason to insist on the necessity of not judging. That one should not, that one fundamentally is radically unable to judge because there is nothing "out there" to judge, is simply taken for granted. Thus, as I see it, it is precisely because Buddhist teaching is grounded in and built on the affirmation of the intrinsic oneness of subject and object that references to not judging are so rare in the literature of Zen.

Although I have not come across any references in Buddhist literature to the teaching of Jesus on not judging others,[23] I suspect that Buddhists would be especially drawn to the Lucan transmission of Jesus' words, since Luke associates the command not to judge with the command to be compassionate, and compassion is the natural and spontaneous expression of the experience of solidarity with all of life that the practitioner of *zazen* strives to realize. In a *dokusan,* the individual meeting between a Zen master and disciple, Yasutani Roshi once explained that what creates antagonism, greed, and, inevitably, suffering, is the fact that we falsely see ourselves confronted by a world of separate existences. "The purpose of *zazen,*" he explained, "is to wipe away from the mind these shadows or defilements so that we can intimately experience our solidarity with all life. Love and compassion then naturally and spontaneously flow forth."[24]

If a Buddhist were asked to comment on the meaning of Jesus' command not to judge others, I suspect that he or she would say that the reason Jesus says we *should* not judge others is that, ultimately, we are *unable* to judge anyone. Judging is only possible for one who operates out of a dualistic structure of reality. But if the world "out there" does not exist apart from my knowledge of the world, then how can I pass judgment on anyone or anything that comprises that world? To judge someone or something, that person or thing has to be "other," existing independently of my mind. But that is precisely what Zen denies. Therefore, the reason we cannot judge another person is because the other is really not "other." The other is me and I am the other. There is no "this" and "that" apart from me that I can measure by some norm (that norm usually being myself) and pass judgment on. What is, is. All is one. That is all.

Sitting without Judging

Finally, I would like to reflect on my own experience of the practice of *zazen* and how I have come to think of it as a path from judgment to love. As I indicated at the outset, I consider myself a beginner and realize that had my practice already brought me to an experiential awareness of my true self, I would very likely be saying something quite different—or saying it in a quite different way.

Like so many other people who were young adults in the 1960s, I was affected by the West's growing attraction to Eastern religions. I am sure that my interest was in large part fascination with the exotic, but I also remember that when I read Déchanet's *Christian Yoga*[25] as a seminarian, what most impressed me was the author's insistence on the importance of the body in the spiritual life. The theologians I was studying emphasized the unity of human nature, saying that we are not made up of body and soul, but rather that we are enfleshed spirits, or enspirited matter. However, the spiritual practices that were part of my monastic life, although much more humane than those of some other monasteries or religious orders I knew of, still seemed to imply that the body was something that could only get in the way of spiritual growth. *Christian Yoga* was my introduction to a spiritual discipline that explicitly taught that the body is not to be denied or ignored, and that the way we breathe, the way we sit, the way we stand are all intrinsic to the life of the spirit, and can contribute to or hinder our spiritual growth.

I began to practice yoga as a seminarian, doing so with only books for teachers. I continued to practice off and on—more off than on, if the truth be told—for the next thirty years. When I came to Japan in 1994 I sensed that I had finally arrived at the time and place where I could become more systematic and focused in what, until then, had been very feeble and scattered attempts to achieve some kind of unity and integration in my spiritual life.

After two years in Japan I had the good fortune to be introduced to the San'un Zendô in Kamakura and to begin studying with Ryôun Yamada Roshi. I must say that when I checked my journal I was surprised to find that in my *hôken,* a disciple's first meeting with the master, I said that I hoped my practice of *zazen* would make me less judgmental:

> January 28, 1996, Sunday
> First meeting (*hôken*) with Ryôun Yamada Roshi.
> What do I want?
> What I want is not to want. What I want is simply to listen, to be attentive. But to whom? Not to others, in the sense of always observing, judging, criticizing, but to myself, and ultimately to God. Unless I am still, I will never hear what the small, still voice says.
> To be attentive to myself is to become more deeply, more existentially aware of the nothingness, the "Mu" of myself, the "Mu" of all that is not "Mu."

When I began my formal practice of *zazen* in 1996 my pastoral duties were much more limited than they are at present. Thus I was usually able to participate in the twice-monthly Sunday *zazenkai* at the San'un Zendô, and also take part in the *zazenkai* that Yamada Roshi often held in his home on Saturdays. Within a couple years, however, my pastoral ministry to Brazilians living in Japan expanded to such a point that I no longer had any free Sundays. Furthermore, Yamada Roshi, who is employed by the Mitsubishi Bank, was transferred to the London branch and only returned to Tokyo three or four times a year. In May 1999, my monastic community moved from Tokyo to Fujimi, a small town in the middle of Japan's main island of Honshu, thus making access to an English-speaking Zen master even more difficult—and I still do need a teacher who can speak English. Sometimes I am able to join a small group of Japanese people for an early Sunday morning *zazenkai* in a local temple, Sankôji, and occasionally I am able to participate in a *zazenkai* in Tokyo conducted by Sister Kathleen Reilly, but apart from that, my practice at present is pretty much confined to my own sitting. If possible, I try to make at least one and preferably two *sesshins* a year, but since *sesshins* are almost always scheduled over a weekend, it is very difficult for me to take part in an entire program.

My practice at present is quite simple and modest. I try to sit for an hour each day, usually next to the tabernacle of the oratory of our monastery. In my meditation—which I do repeating the syllable "Mu," not audibly but in my mind—I find that I still easily drift off and lose focus; but I continue in the hope that through regular practice I will be able to concentrate more and more on nothing but Mu. When this concentration finally leads me to ask from my guts—as Yasutani Roshi put it—"*What* is Mu? *What* can it be?," when this questioning reaches the point of gripping me like a vise so that I can think of nothing else, then perhaps I shall be able to grasp my true nature.[26]

The Introductory Lectures given at the San'un Zendô recommend that one select a room that one can regard as sacred, and that is the reason I go to the oratory of our monastery and sit near the tabernacle for my practice. But I sit alongside the tabernacle, not in front of it. My reason for doing this is because I regard my practice of *zazen* in the presence of the sacrament of Christ's body and blood not so much as a way of focusing my attention on the mystery of the Incarnation and its continuation in time and space through the sacramental signs of bread and wine but rather as a way of expressing my desire to participate in the Son's silent adoration of the Father, who is Infinite Eternal Silence. Perhaps a better way to put it would be to say that one of the reasons I, as a Christian, have undertaken the practice of *zazen* is to allow myself to be drawn more deeply and more fully into the Son of God's silent adoration of the Father.

In an article entitled "*Zazen* and Adoration of the Eucharist," Father Franco Sottocornola says that the sacramental silence of the broken bread is an invitation to go beyond all words, all imagination and all images, beyond all that divides or separates, beyond all objects, to the perfect communion of life and love, about which the mystics have spoken to us. Through the Son to the Father in the Spirit, that is, through the Word to Silence in Love.[27] Or, as I might put it, in the Spirit I sit with Jesus, joining him in his silent contemplation of the Father.

I understand my practice of *zazen* to be prayer, but prayer expressed not by conversing with God, but simply by being silent in the divine presence. The Japanese Carmelite priest, Augustine Ichiro Okumura, proposes this way of understanding prayer—or at least one form of prayer—in his book *Awakening to Prayer*. In the introduction to that book he recalls an incident that occurred when he was nine years old. Imitating the example of his Buddhist parents, as he left home on his way to school or play he would pause to pray in front of the Shinto and Buddhist altars that were in his home. One day his father asked him, "What are you praying?" He was a bit taken aback by the question and not knowing what to say, he mumbled,

"Well, . . . nothing." "That's it!" his father replied. "For you to remain a moment before God with a pure heart is enough to please him."[28]

Father Okumura believes that these words of his father are very likely the starting point of his ever-growing realization that we also pray when we simply come before God with empty hands, saying nothing. He speaks of the two sides to prayer, the "obverse" and the "reverse." The "obverse" definition—"conversation with God," "raising one's heart to God," "communicating with God"—has to do with active prayer, in which we take the initiative. But the "reverse" definition—prayer as "remaining silent before God"—he says is an expression of passive or nonactive prayer.[29]

Prayer understood as being silent before God, as participating in the Son's apophatic adoration of the Father, takes on, I believe, an even deeper meaning when we reflect on it in the light of Jesus' self-emptying, his *kenosis,* to which Paul refers in the second chapter of his Letter to the Philippians. Commentators are generally agreed that Paul is quoting an early liturgical hymn when he pleads with the Christians of Philippi to be united in heart and mind by having the same attitude that Christ Jesus had when he emptied himself, becoming obedient unto death.

As a Christian, then, I understand my practice of *zazen* to be a way of sharing in that silent, obedient self-emptying of Christ that allowed the glory of God to completely possess and transform the human *morphē* (form) that he, although equal to God, took upon himself. I might add that this way of understanding the practice of *zazen* was encouraged by Kôun Yamada Roshi. In his book *Zen Spirit, Christian Spirit,* Father Robert E. Kennedy recalls that Yamada Roshi told him several times he did not want to make him a Buddhist but rather he wanted to empty him in imitation of "Christ your Lord," who emptied himself, poured himself out, and clung to nothing. "Whenever Yamada Roshi instructed me in this way," Kennedy whimsically notes, "I thought that this Buddhist might make a Christian of me yet!"[30]

To empty oneself in imitation of Christ our Lord in order to share in his risen life, to suffer the loss of all things, regarding them as rubbish in order to gain Christ and be found in him, not having a righteousness of our own that comes from the law, but one that comes though faith in Christ (see Phil 3:8–9), that is the call of the Gospel. For me, at this time in my life, the practice of *zazen* is one of the ways in which I try to respond to that call.

But is this practice helping me to grow in love and compassion by becoming less judgmental? I have to confess that at times it seems to be producing just the opposite effect. On one occasion when I was participating in a *zazenkai* led by Sister Kathleen, I told her that after I began practicing *zazen* I seemed to be getting even more judgmental than I was before, looking down on people who didn't meditate as "poor slobs." Her reply was that progress in *zazen* means coming to the awareness that those "poor slobs" are me.

A couple of months later I repeated this same concern to Kubota Roshi who was conducting a sesshin at San'un Zendô. His response was that because the practice of *zazen* heightens perception, it does make us more "discriminating." But this does not imply that one is to act in a critical way. When the breakthrough comes, we will recognize our oneness with that which, in this dualistic experience of reality, we see as other and inferior. "Continue to live the life of 'Mu,'" he repeated over and over. "That is all you have to do; that is all you have to be."

Those conversations took place two years ago, and since then there have been no dramatic breakthroughs. But I think there has been some movement, and I continue to meditate in the hope—and the conviction—that my practice of *zazen* will continue to move me in the direction of nonjudgmental compassion. If I continue to sit, continue to try to concentrate on "Mu," letting go of my desires to be someone, to accomplish something, I believe that I will gradually—or maybe even through some sudden and undeserved breakthrough—be brought to an experiential realization that it is not I who live, but that it is Christ who lives in me, the Christ who prayed that all be one as he and the Father are one (Jn 17:21), the Christ in whom all things hold together, and in whom all the fullness was pleased to dwell (Col 1:17, 18). As this truth moves from my lips and mind down into the depths of my heart, purifying it from the need to set itself over and above what it still thinks is outside itself, I believe my heart, my true self, will be set free from its compulsion to judge, be set free for love. At that point, I believe, I will be able to realize that the reason Jesus tells us not to judge—*sabakuna*—is ultimately because there is no one and nothing out there to judge. In him we live and move and have our being (Acts 17:28). In him, who is divine love incarnate, we are all one.

Ultimately, of course, the following of Jesus with a pure and undivided heart goes beyond not judging others; it means loving them with the same love with which God loves us in Jesus. In all three Synoptic Gospels Jesus is asked a question about the greatest of the commandments. Each of the evangelists interprets the reason for asking this question a bit differently. Matthew understands the question as a test (Mt 22:39); in Mark's Gospel the question is put by a scribe who is sincerely impressed with the way Jesus engages with other scribes in debates about the law (Mk 12:31). And in Luke's Gospel the questioner wants to know what he needs to do in order to inherit eternal life (Lk 10:37). But in all three Gospels, Jesus' unequivocal and unambiguous answer is the same: Love the Lord your God with all your heart, all your mind, and all your strength; love your neighbor as yourself.

For the Christian the practice of *zazen* can be, I believe, a way of putting this command into practice. One sits in silence before the One whom one loves above and beyond all else, content simply to be silent in his presence. And in this silence one gradually—or perhaps even suddenly—comes

to the realization that in this all-embracing love, all differences are overcome. There is no need to judge; all that is needed, all that is possible, is to
realize our oneness, to love the other as we love ourselves, to love the other
with the same love with which God loves us. In silence one can come to the
ecstatic recognition that all are one in Christ, and that this awe-inspiring
unity is nothing other than the "one Christ loving himself. For Christ is all
and in all."[31]

9

Sacred Fools and Monastic Rules

Zen Rule–Bending and the Training for Pure Hearts

REV. TAIGEN DAN LEIGHTON

Introduction

This paper is inspired in part by my observation some years ago that the "ancient ones" in my extended spiritual community of the San Francisco Zen Center, those who have twenty-five to thirty-five years of steady practice experience, seem distinctive in that they are most truly "themselves." Sometimes this takes the form of their being eccentric or even peculiar, but somehow also particularly true to themselves in some deep, and often inspiring, way. The fruits of long-term spiritual practice do not seem to be an homogenized uniformity of character, but the uniqueness of each person's sincere expression of that which goes beyond egoistic personality, but might well appear quite quirky and individual.

What are the qualities of the sincere, pure-hearted adept? Does the training in monastic, or semi-monastic, practice communities help develop pure hearts and open minds? And if so, how? I will explore these questions within the context of the East Asian Zen Buddhist tradition.

I will begin by examining how monastic forms in the Zen tradition might serve to grow this pure wholeheartedness, focusing on the writings of the pioneering Japanese Zen master Eihei Dogen (1200–1253), from his *Dogen's Pure Standards for the Zen Community*, in Japanese, *Eihei Shingi*.[1] As well as being a manual for procedures in the monastery, with instructions for everything from how to brush teeth to how to receive and eat food in the meditation hall, this work emphasizes attitudinal instructions and the psychology for taking appropriate responsibility for community well-being. Dogen's choice of illustrative stories and exemplars is often unexpected and startling.

Then I will look at prominent examples of the pure of heart in the Zen tradition through the lens of the archetypal bodhisattva of loving-kindness, the future buddha, Maitreya. Also known for his foolishness, this figure provides one primary pattern for the pure of heart in the Mahayana Buddhist tradition.

One typology of historical figures who in some ways have manifested this Maitreya energy can be seen in the hermit adepts who have "graduated" from Zen monasteries, such as Hotei, Hanshan, and Ryokan. I will discuss these three particularly, but many more of such historical "Zen Fools" might be mentioned. Many of these apparently foolish characters were actually accomplished poets, such as Hanshan and Ryokan, and left us some record of their inner sentiments and deep sincerity. But all of them are cherished in the Zen tradition as exemplars of true, pure heart.

The Role of Monastic Regulations

The Zen monastic regulations (*Qinggui* in Chinese; *Shingi* in Japanese) are an outgrowth of the early Buddhist Vinaya, the ethical injunctions dispensed by the Buddha. The first legendary Zen monastic rules are traditionally attributed to Baizhang Huaihai (749–814; Hyakujo Ekai in Japanese).[2] Baizhang is widely regarded in the tradition as the founder of the Zen work ethic, for example with his famous statement, "A day without working is a day without eating."[3] Dogen cites Baizhang as an inspiration for his own Shingi, which for procedural instructions liberally quotes both the old Vinaya attributed directly to Shakyamuni Buddha, and also passages from the *Chanyuan Qinggui* (*Zen'en Shingi* in Japanese), the most comprehensive Chinese collection of Zen monastic regulations, compiled in 1103.[4]

The communal institution has been an important aspect of Buddhism since Shakyamuni Buddha founded his monastic order twenty-five hundred years ago in Northern India. The monastic enclosure developed during the Indian rainy season, when the monks halted their wandering mendicant practice to reside together for a few months of practice. This fellowship of practitioners, or sangha, has functioned ever since as a radical contrast to existing social conventions and conditioning. The Buddhist monastic community has offered an alternative or counterculture to the status quo of exploitative societies that disregarded individual human potential.

The common designation of Buddhist monks as "home-leavers" implies the physical act of renouncing worldly ambition to join the monastic community, and also the inner work of abandoning ensnarement from the bonds of social and personal psychological conditioning. In accord with this liberative purpose, monastic community life is seen as an opportunity for its participants to develop their capacity for enacting the universal principles of awakening in the concrete aspects of their individual lives. The monastic procedural forms are designed to provide the monks a congenial space conducive to inner contemplation. Each ordinary, daily life function, from cleaning the temple to taking care of personal hygiene, is treated as a tool for enhancing mindfulness of one's moment-to-moment state of awareness and innermost intention. The monastic lifestyle, procedures, and forms act as supports for practitioners' immersion in the process of deepening personal experience of the nonalienated, integrated nature of reality described as the basis for Buddhist awakening. These monastic forms allow the psychic and physical space for self-reflection, a harmonious realm for supportive interaction with fellow contemplatives, and also function as practices with which to enact the fundamental teachings arising naturally out of meditation.

While Dogen does offer in his *Shingi* detailed procedural instructions, often borrowed from the Vinaya or previous monastic regulations, his clear emphasis is attitudinal instruction and the psychology of spiritually beneficial community interaction. Zen monastic regulations function as a latticework for ethical conduct. The rules may be upheld and consequences enforced, but they are seen as guidelines rather than as restrictive regulations or rigid proscriptions.

A major paradigm of Mahayana Buddhist monasticism has been oscillation between periods of training in the monastic container and reentry into the marketplace. Monks test their practice by returning to interact with conventional society, and also help fulfill the developmental function of the Buddhist order by sharing with the ordinary world whatever they have learned of self-awareness, composure, and compassion during their monastic training. In Japan, from Dogen's time to the present, monks finish a period of training and go out to function as temple priests, ministering to the laity. Some later return to the monastery for further development, or to help train younger monks. Traditionally, monks would also leave their monastic community to wander around to other teachers and test their practice and understanding.

The essential insight of Buddhist awakening affirms the fundamental rightness and interconnectedness of the whole of creation, just as it is. But along with its effect on individual trainees, the sangha has also served at times as an historical instrument to perform the long-term work of civilizing and developing human awareness so as eventually to actualize and fulfill for all beings the vision of our world as a pure land, informed by wisdom and compassion. This effect has been accomplished both by the inspiration of exemplary individuals and on a wider societal level. Despite its sometimes compromised relationships and accommodations to the ruling powers throughout Asian history, in fact the Buddhist spiritual institution has had, from time to time, a civilizing effect on Asian societies, moderating the brutal tendencies of various rulers.

Until the twentieth-century popularization of his voluminous philosophical and poetic writings, Eihei Dogen was more important historically for establishing a monastic order that became the basis for the Japanese Soto Zen school. In *Dogen's Pure Standards* (*Eihei Shingi*), written to instruct his monk disciples, he presents exemplary models of Chinese monks who had taken on the responsibility of administrative positions in Chan monastic communities. Dogen emphasizes the importance of these positions, such as the administrative director and the chief cook of the monasteries. People who hold these positions need to be devoted to the well-being of all the practitioners, and at the same time they must be exemplary in their own practice directed toward mastering the teaching, and realizing and expressing full spiritual awakening.

Given the emphasis Dogen places on these administrative positions, it is remarkable how many of Dogen's exemplars are involved in rule-breaking or at least rule-bending, precisely in the example or story that Dogen cites. In the *Chiji Shingi,* "The Pure Standards for the Temple Administrators," the final essay which takes up nearly half of the full text of *Eihei Shingi,* Dogen talks about great historical Zen figures and their conduct in the monastic roles, specifically the roles of Director, Supervisor of Monks (*Ino*), Chief Cook (*Tenzo*), and Work Leader, as well as some of the other supervisory positions.

Of the twenty exemplary anecdotes that Dogen cites, ten of them involve actions by the exemplar in which he does something that would be seen from conventional morality as improper and a violation of monastic regulations. A number of them threaten to beat up their teachers or some other practitioner, and one actually does physically beat his teacher. One sets a fire in the monastery, another throws away the community's food. A few are shunned or even expelled from the community. After each of these stories the protagonist is praised by Dogen for his sincere spirit of inquiry, dedication to practice, or commitment to the monastic community.

A Tenacious *Tenzo*

Dogen especially elaborates the importance of the position of the chief cook or *tenzo,* which he describes as equal in importance to the abbot's role. Dogen dedicates a whole essay, the celebrated "Instructions for the Cook" (*Tenzokyokun*), to the virtues of this position. In "The Pure Standards for the Temple Administrators," of all the *tenzos* he acclaims, Dogen most lavishly praises Fushan Fayuan (991–1067; Fusan Hoen in Japanese). After recounting stories about the virtue of a number of *tenzos,* Dogen says, "Especially, we cannot fail to study the *tenzo* [Fushan] Fayuan's faithful heart, which can be met only once in a thousand years.... If *tenzo* do not experience dedication like Fayuan's, how can their study of the Way penetrate the innermost precincts of the buddhas and ancestors?"[5] And yet in the story told by Dogen, Fayuan committed thievery while *tenzo,* and was expelled from the monastery.

The story begins with a demonstration of the physical and spiritual toughness expected in the monastery in question. Fushan Fayuan and a monk comrade, Tianyi Yihuai, traveled to visit and train with [Shexian] Guisheng, a master with a reputation for being "cold and severe, tough and frugal. Patchrobed monks respected and feared him."[6] Fayuan and his friend "arrived in the middle of a snowy winter," and joined the other traveling monks sitting in the monastery visitors' room while awaiting admittance. Guisheng abusively scolded the monks and poured cold water on them, so that the other monks left. When Guisheng further threatened Fushan Fayuan and his friend, [Tianyi] Yihuai replied, "The two of us have come a thousand miles just to study Zen with you, how could we leave from just one scoop of water dumped on us? Even if you beat us to death, we will not go."[7] Guisheng thereupon laughed and accepted them into the monastery.

After some time Fushan Fayuan was promoted to the position of *tenzo*. But the monastery was poor and the spartan diet coarse, and Fayuan was finally moved by his sympathy for the monks to commit a grave offense. Once Guisheng left for the village and

> Fayuan stole the key [to the storehouse], and took some wheat flour to prepare a special flavorful gruel. Guisheng suddenly returned and went to the hall. After eating, he sat in the outer hall and sent for Fayuan. Guisheng said, "Is it true that you stole flour to cook the gruel?" [Fayuan] admitted it, and implored Guisheng to punish him. Guisheng had him calculate the price [of the flour], and sell his robes and bowls to repay it. Then Guisheng struck Fayuan thirty blows with his staff and expelled him from the temple.[8]

Fayuan's offense was motivated only by concern for the monks' health and comfort. Shexian Guisheng instantly tasted the difference in the gruel, and Fushan was not spared prompt and severe consequences for his actions. However, the story continues that Fayuan remained in the nearby town, repeatedly making efforts to gain readmittance into Shexian Guisheng's monastery, but all were rebuffed by Guisheng. "Fayuan was not bothered, but carried his begging bowl through the city and sent the money he received [to the temple to repay his debt]."

Eventually, one day "Guisheng went to the town and saw Fayuan holding his bowl. Guisheng returned to the assembly and said, 'Fayuan truly has the determination to study Zen.'"[9] So finally Fushan Fayuan was readmitted to the monastery, and later became a Dharma successor of Shexian Guisheng.

Fushan Fayuan's sympathy for the monks' lack of food may have been misplaced, and his unswerving persistence after his expulsion may appear foolish or perhaps even obsessive. But it is precisely this kindness, and selfless dedication, even in the face of disgrace and loss of reputation, that seems especially to endear him to Dogen. Fayuan violated the precepts and monastic rules, but never abandoned his intention to express the Way. His teacher Guisheng seems to have consciously used the rules, not for the sake of moral propriety, but to test and more fully mold Fayuan's commitment. The monastic regulations and precepts are at the service of the dual priorities of total dedication to one's own investigation of spiritual reality, and of commitment to caring for the practice community's well-being.

Another exemplary monk whom Dogen esteems most highly, Wuzu Fayan (1024–1104; Goso Hoen in Japanese), was shunned by his fellow monks for the monastic violations of drinking wine, eating meat, and entertaining women. The story goes that Wuzu Fayan had "settled his investigation of the great matter and deeply penetrated the bones and marrow,"[10] and was manager of the monastery's mill down the mountain. Wuzu Fayan devoted himself to the task of increasing the monastery's resources, but somehow incurred the enmity of some of the monks. As even modern monks can testify, in the cauldron of monastic practice supposedly "worldly" human jealousy and pettiness can still arise. When Wuzu heard about the accusations, "He intentionally bought meat and alcohol and hung them out in front of the mill, and also bought cosmetics and makeup for his women friends. Whenever Zen monks came around the mill, [Wuzu] Fayan would touch the women and laughingly banter and tease them, completely without restraint." When his teacher finally questioned him, Wuzu Fayan made no explanation and accepted expulsion. But when he submitted the mill's accounts, including unusual profits for the monastery, his teacher was impressed, "and understood that petty people had just been jealous [of Wuzu Fayan]."[11]

Dogen praises Wuzu Fayan for his dedication to accomplishing his task of managing the monastery's business so as to best benefit the community and its assets. That he did this without any concern for his own personal reputation and standing in the eyes of his teacher is especially admirable for Dogen. Wuzu was willing to accept the blame and punishment of his teacher, as had Fushan Fayuan, without becoming defensive or trying to protect or explain himself.

I discuss these anecdotes of Zen rule-bending and Zen fools not to support an erroneous and misleading stereotype of Zen iconoclasm. In the initial importation of Zen to America, and its reception by what has been called "Beat Zen," the image of Zen "wild men" was provocative and attractive to many. But the history of Zen throughout East Asia has been very predominantly that of sincere practitioners quietly engaged in devotional rituals and contemplative practices. Both Dogen's rule-bending exemplars of temple administrators and most of the "sacred fools" I describe below were veteran monks steeped in conventional monastic practice and decorum.

However, in considering Dogen's description of Zen training, and its relation to the pure sincere heart as its goal, it is notable that Dogen does not hold to a literal interpretation of the regulations. This is so even though Dogen is noted for his own emphasis on monastic forms. He includes in his *Eihei Shingi* a short essay with sixty-two specific instructions for the manners and etiquette with which monks should defer to their seniors. Dogen never advocates bending the monastic rules just for the sake of iconoclasm, and strongly criticizes those who mistakenly believed that Buddhist liberation means freedom from ethical concern and proper demeanor.[12] Nevertheless, it is clear from his exemplars that Dogen sees the purpose of monastic training not as the rigid alignment with some code of conduct, but as the development of kindly concern for the whole community, and sincere, intent, persistent inquiry into the deep mysteries of awakening.

The Meditations of the Foolish Maitreya

The figure of the archetypal, cosmic Bodhisattva Maitreya was based on a disciple predicted by Shakyamuni, the historical Buddha, to be the next future buddha, or perfected awakened one.[13] Many of the accounts describe Maitreya as a novice, or relatively junior disciple. Buddha's other disciples were perplexed when this monk was predicted as the next future buddha, as he was not particularly distinguished for rigorous practice or insightful wisdom. Indeed he seemed fairly naive, even more than a bit foolish.

But Maitreya, whose name means "Loving One," had a caring and generous character, and was known for his great kindness. So Maitreya is an apt emblem for the pure of heart in Mahayana Buddhism, and also to some extent in pre-Mahayana Buddhism, since he appears in the early Pali suttas (as *Metteya* in Pali). Delineating the central aspects of the Maitreya archetype can serve as one major framework for clarifying the qualities of the pure heart in the Mahayana tradition. Maitreya is also associated with three different strands of Buddhist meditation—loving-kindness, patience, and Yogacara consciousness study—so we can see this figure as demonstrating specific relationships between Buddhist contemplation and kindheartedness.

Maitreya's ambiguous, foolish character is evident in some of the early Mahayana sutras. In the first chapter of the *Lotus Sutra*, for example, Shakyamuni Buddha emits a light from between his eyebrows that puzzles Maitreya, who questions Manjushri, the bodhisattva of wisdom.[14] Manjushri reminds Maitreya that in former lives in a remotely past buddha land, they together had witnessed a similar light emitted by a previous buddha, heralding the teaching of the *Lotus Sutra* on behalf of that buddha by Bodhisattva Fine Luster, who was Manjushri himself in that lifetime. Among Fine Luster's eight hundred disciples was Fame Seeker Bodhisattva, actually Maitreya in that former life, who was named Fame Seeker because he sought after personal profit and advantage. Although he read and memorized numerous sutras, he derived no benefit at all and quickly forgot most of them.

Maitreya, or at least his past life, is thus discredited by Manjushri, but the bodhisattva of wisdom goes on to add that this lazy Fame Seeker also had done many kind deeds. His kindness helped him to be able to train with numerous buddhas over many lifetimes, until now he was finally Maitreya Bodhisattva, destined to be the next buddha. This early, humorous image of Maitreya as a spiritually immature monk with many deficiencies in his practice, if anything, heightens the prime importance of his one strong positive quality, his loving-kindness, which seemingly alone qualified him to be predicted as the next buddha.

Maitreya's loving-kindness relates to a specific, traditional meditation practice still widespread in much of Buddhism. The *metta,* or loving-kindness, after which Maitreya (*Metteya* in Pali) is named is a mindfulness exercise in which the practitioner emanates good wishes and loving thoughts toward particular beings. Although the eventual aim of such practice is to mentally bestow blessings on all beings, beginners are advised to start with family and other intimates, for whom loving thoughts are already present. Gradually these thoughts can then be extended to unknown beings and perhaps finally, after some craft in the practice has developed, even toward one's supposed enemies. As in the case of Western prayer, this *metta* practice is reported to have benefits for both the practitioner and for the objects of the loving thoughts.

Perhaps Maitreya's primary meditative practice, as he faces the unknown future, is patience, which might also be called tolerance or forbearance. The best known images of Maitreya Bodhisattva are the delicate Korean and Japanese statues of Maitreya showing him with fingers to his chin, pondering how to save all sentient beings. Maitreya just sits and waits. Supposedly he currently is inhabiting one of the meditative heavenly realms until he can claim his buddhahood. Based on the sutras and early commentaries, calculations as to the amount of time that will pass between Shakyamuni's prediction of Maitreya's buddhahood and his final arrival at that state vary widely. Current estimates of Maitreya's final enlightenment range from the date 4,456 c.e., to thirty thousand years in the future, to seven billion, five hundred sixty million years after Shakyamuni.

As the predicted next buddha, Maitreya has long been an Asian symbol for the possibility of a future enlightened age. Enduring messianic yearning for Maitreya is still scrawled on Himalayan rocks, pleading, "Come, Maitreya, come." Nobody knows when Maitreya will appear. Throughout the past fifteen hundred years of Chinese history, there have been rulers and rebels alike who claimed to be incarnations of Maitreya, or of avatars preparing the way for this new World-Honored One. And there are persons active in the world today who claim to be Maitreya manifested. It may be so; we just don't know.

This not knowing is a highly beneficial aspect of the practice of patience modeled and encouraged by the Maitreya archetype. Sitting up in his meditation heaven, Maitreya Bodhisattva gazes into the unknown future knowing only that he is destined for buddhahood, and that eventually he will bring into being an awakened buddha land. Envisioning such a future necessarily involves recognizing the unfulfilled aspect of the present situation. Maitreya looks to the future and holds in his heart not only the next seven generations, but beings of future millennia, even though he does not know their names and faces. Simple willingness to include in awareness both the near and distant future is an accessible aspect of Maitreya's practice of patience.

At times of crisis, often the most helpful—and difficult—thing to do is to just sit and wait. This practice of patience is not passivity, but active observation of whatever phenomena face us, ready to respond and act when an opportunity for helpfulness appears. When we don't know how to solve our problems, forbearance and ongoing attention can provide the space and calm to see what is possible and helpful.

Along with his loving-kindness and meditations on patience, the figure of Maitreya is closely associated with the Yogacara branch of Buddhism, and with its meditative study of the phenomenology of consciousness. The Yogacara psychological system describes eight levels of consciousness and presents an elaborate model for understanding the mental workings of karma. Although an extended discussion of this and other Yogacara psychological teachings is beyond the scope of this essay, they can be briefly described as follows. The eight consciousnesses include as the first six consciousnesses the awarenesses of the five sense fields (sights, sounds, smells, tastes, physicalities), with the awareness of mental objects, i.e., thoughts, as the sixth consciousness. Thus our normal mental activity, which we usually tend to identify with and cherish, is defined as simply another conjunction of sense faculty (cognition) with sense objects (thoughts). This understanding can be very helpful in developing nonattachment to our preconceptions and thought habits.

The seventh consciousness, *manas,* is the faculty for imagining the self as separated and alienated from the external "objective" world, existing externally as a dead container. This alienating faculty might be termed the Buddhist "original sin," which can be seen through and transformed with practice. The eighth consciousness, the *alaya-vijnana* or storehouse consciousness, acts metaphorically as a repository for all mental habit energies and predilections, karma in Buddhist terms. Within the parameters of formerly embedded potentialities, an individual is free to act to support and develop, or instead weaken, these psychological tendencies, which may be positive or negative. Sustained awareness of the whole mental process may foster transformation of the storehouse consciousness, and support beneficial conduct.

Yogacara psychology developed from contemplation and promotes meditative self-study, a useful practice for facing difficult situations. Despite his foolishness and simple kindness, Maitreya was a prevalent motif historically for the practitioners of this subtle psychological system and its practices. When it seems that there is nothing to be done, we can actively engage our interest and clearly observe whatever appears before us. Such yogic study of awareness and its interaction with the world supports patience, and may reveal new perspectives and possibilities for responding to immediate problems. The fundamental Maitreyan orientation is forward-looking, both individually and collectively. From this perspective we can see the monastic community or sangha as a training ground for future buddhas, and also in society, as potentially promoting future buddha fields.

Hotei as Jolly Maitreya

In the Zen tradition there is a whole genre of eccentric exemplars of the pure-hearted "fool." One of the best recognized examples of these eccentric Zen fools is the historical tenth-century Chinese Zen monk Budai, whose Japanese name Hotei is more familiar in the West, and who is considered an incarnation of Maitreya Bodhisattva. Known for his divine foolishness, in China Hotei came to be identified with Maitreya to such a degree that Chinese images of him are now simply labeled Maitreya (*Milo-fe* in Chinese), and in popular Chinese awareness they are virtually synonymous.

Hotei is legendary as a wandering sage with supernatural powers who spent his time in village streets rather than in the security of temples. Apparently Hotei had completed his monastic training, and was happy to express his awareness by living as a homeless vagabond. His image is recognizable as the disheveled, fat, jolly "Laughing Buddha" whose statue is seen in many Chinese restaurants and in all Chinese Buddhist temples. Hotei's name means "cloth bag," as he carried a sack full of candy and toys to give to children, with whom he is often depicted in play. This scruffy Buddhist Santa Claus expands our view of Maitreya's warmth and loving-kindness.

The ten ox-herding pictures in the Zen tradition depict stages of deepening practice and awakening in terms of the metaphor of searching for and then taming an ox. The final picture, after the ox has been forgotten and spiritual practice is integrated with caring for the world, is called "Returning to the marketplace with empty, bliss-bestowing hands." Most versions of the tenth picture show fat, jolly Hotei with his sack over his back, greeting a townsman.

In one story about Hotei that attests to his deep wisdom, he was stopped on the street by a monk of more orthodox demeanor (possibly critical of Hotei's flamboyance), who questioned Hotei as to the fundamental meaning of the Buddha's teaching. Hotei immediately dropped his sack. The monk then asked about the actualization of the teaching. Hotei picked up his sack and went on his way.

Other stories describe Hotei as a dependable prognosticator of the weather; precipitation reliably accorded with whether or not he was wearing shoes and head cover. It is said that just before he passed away Hotei recited a poem which expressed his regret that even though Maitreya sometimes appears in the world, he is unrecognized by people of the time. This led to the association of Hotei with Maitreya that has endured ever since.

Hanshan Cooling out on the Mountain

Hanshan ("Cold Mountain") is the quintessential Zen mountain recluse poet. He is equally legendary as Hotei, and apparently was a layman who lived near a monastery high up in the temple-filled Tiantai mountains, probably in the ninth or tenth century. His poems, celebrated in American as well as Asian Zen, set the mold for the foolish, carefree mountain hermit, who lives apart from the world, indulging in immersion in nature, but not without occasional acknowledgments of loneliness. Many of Hanshan's poems sing of the rustic life.

While Hanshan is presented as the icon of the unconventional, liberated recluse, and apparently he was never an official monk trainee, it is significant that the story about him is of someone hanging out near the monastery kitchen with his equally spirited monk friend Shide. Hanshan seems to represent a possibility of clear awareness still related to the monastic forms, even if free of them.

I have experienced in contemporary Zen monasteries, both in America and Asia, persons in proximity, but with similar ambiguous relationships, to the monastic rule. They may support the temple in various ways, or even be ordained members of the order, but such characters also function, often through unconventional behavior, to remind the serious monks of the context of their liberative endeavor. The goal of the monastic training, the true "pure heart," is enacted with nonattachment and freedom from worldly concern and grasping, even if this seems foolish or outrageous from conventional perspectives. This echoes writings by Thomas Merton about the monastic as the marginal person who points to the true heart without concern for social standing.

Ryokan and the Simple Life

Ryokan (1758–1831), the Japanese Zen monk and spiritual poet, was fully trained in a Soto Zen monastery, but instead of becoming a temple priest and teaching formally, he returned to live a hermit's life of meditation in

a hut near his home village, and made his modest livelihood via mendicant practice in nearby towns. Ryokan was consciously inspired in his own
writing by Hanshan's poems. Still a deeply beloved figure in Japan today,
Ryokan chose the spiritual name *Daigu*, or "Great Fool," although he was
well-read, intelligent, a skilled meditator, and an elegant calligrapher, whose
brushwork was already valuable and sought after in his own time.

Perhaps best known for his kindly play with children, like Hotei, Ryokan
always carried balls or other toys in his robe sleeves, and frequently broke
from begging rounds to join in neighborhood children's games. One favorite
of the many stories about him tells how Ryokan once hid in a barn while
playing hide-and-seek. It got late and the children were all called to dinner.
When he entered the barn the next morning, the surprised farmer asked
Ryokan what he was doing. Ryokan said, "Shh!! Be quiet. The children
will hear." Ryokan may have been so absorbed in samadhi that he was unaware of the night's passage, but such utter foolishness expresses a charming
naiveté and innocence.

Ryokan cared for even humble creatures. When he came out to sun himself before his hut in the morning, he would carefully pick the lice out of
his robe and gently place them on a nearby rock. When he was finished
he would just as carefully place them back in his robe. Donald Keene, the
great Western scholar of Japanese literature, after telling this story, stated
that no Westerner could take seriously such a person.[15] However, Ryokan's
loving care even for insects illustrates the full extent of Maitreya's loving-
kindness, as Maitreyan figures have often been associated historically with
vegetarianism and kindness to animals, as well as to members of their own
species.

A more comfortably "human" example of his loving-kindness practice
occurred when a relative asked Ryokan's help in dealing with the relative's
son, who was becoming a delinquent. Ryokan visited the family and stayed
the night without saying anything to the son. The next morning as he prepared to depart, Ryokan asked the boy's help in tying up his sandals. As
the lad looked up from doing so, he saw a tear roll down Ryokan's cheek.
Nothing was said, but from that time the boy completely reformed. The
easy camaraderie with children and attention to young people shown by
Maitreyan figures such as Ryokan and Hotei is another form of Maitreya's
concern for the future, in the next generation.

Ryokan's extraordinary legacy of poetry intimately captures the sincerity
and simplicity of the way of life of the pure-hearted Zen adept. For example:

> Without desire everything is sufficient.
> With seeking myriad things are impoverished.
> Plain vegetables can soothe hunger.
> A patched robe is enough to cover this bent old body.

> Alone I hike with a deer.
> Cheerfully I sing with village children.
> The stream beneath the cliff cleanses my ears.
> The pine on the mountain top fits my heart.[16]

Ryokan's simple lifestyle of voluntary poverty and extensive meditation was obviously grounded in a deep dedication to awakening practice. The integrity of Ryokan's awareness and devotion is also apparent in the following poem.

> Spring wind feels rather soft.
> Ringing a monk's staff I enter the eastern town.
> So green, willows in the garden;
> So restless, floating grass over the pond.
> My bowl is fragrant with rice of a thousand homes.
> My heart has abandoned splendor of ten thousand carriages.
> Yearning for traces of ancient buddhas
> Step by step I walk begging.[17]

In this poem we can hear Ryokan's pure conduct and his clear appreciation for a life of simple, unpretentious devotion. Ryokan unashamedly expresses the joys of his life of foolish simplicity, but in some poems he admits the loneliness and even perhaps regret at the difficulties of such a life.

Foolish Conclusions

My approach to interfaith dialogue is to stand on my own Buddhist side of the discussion, presenting my understanding of issues from my Japanese Soto Zen/Mahayana perspective. At best, when engaging in interfaith dialogue I experience fresh perspectives from the other tradition that help clarify aspects of my own practice tradition. So it is only tentatively that I offer the following suggestion of a Christian figure who correlates with the Maitreyan model of kindheartedness.

St. Francis of Assisi shares with Maitreyan exemplars a number of obvious parallels. He is emblematic of Christian kindness, and even the image of his "foolish" speaking to birds and other animals echoes the Maitreyan motif of extreme kindness to animals. Like Ryokan he accepted a life of simplicity and voluntary poverty, and became an inspiration to many through the ages. St. Francis also turned away from the organized monastic life for a rustic life of personal contemplation like Zen characters such as Hotei, Hanshan, and Ryokan. But unlike the latter, St. Francis was more like Dogen in establishing a new monastic order to help train others in a life of simple, pure-hearted dedication.

The exemplars and stories of pure heart I have mentioned obviously just scratch the surface, and only begin to suggest some aspects of one Zen Buddhist ideal. The qualities of the pure heart implied in the Maitreya archetype and through characters such as Hotei and Ryokan include lack of pretension or worldly ambition, simplicity of means and demeanor, and a kindly engagement with children and humble folk generally. The Maitreya archetype further stresses concern for the future of the world and for the problems of future beings; the cultivation of patience and calm; and careful meditative study of the self, of one's own mental processes.

The Maitreyan model, as well as many of the examples of the pure-hearted spiritual practitioner we might cite in connection with it, also exhibits an intentional kindness to animals. This nonanthropocentric quality expresses the inclusivity and outgoing nature of the open heart that relates to going out of the monastery or training ground into the world of creation.

Such innocence and kindness are often considered innate traits. Yet the effort to cultivate and train practitioners toward such openness and dedication seems to be part of the intention of Dogen's pure standards, and of the Buddhist monastic enterprise generally. Yet Dogen's chosen exemplars clarify that the training of pure hearts cannot proceed simply by following some prescribed routine or program. These monastic procedures rather serve as a cauldron for guiding the practitioner toward actualizing the inner spirit of the pure heart. Nevertheless, specific practices to cultivate such devotion and kindness can be discerned from the Maitreya archetype's meditations on loving-kindness, on patience, and on the obstructions of habitual consciousness and attachment.

These reflections on the meaning and training of the pure heart in the Zen tradition are offered in the spirit of interfaith inquiry into the heart of kindness. I look forward to hearing about further parallels to these spiritual patterns in the Christian traditions.

10

Doubt and Breakthrough
in the Desert Fathers

KEVIN HUNT, O.C.S.O.

There is an ancient saying in Catholic theology that any affirmation about God is a denial of God. It is this radical inability of the human to encompass the absolute that is the root of the *doubt* which Christianity and Buddhism have as a common experience. Both the Christian and Buddhist traditions have developed systems to deal with the problems of doubt that arise in the practice of meditation.

In Zen Buddhism, practitioners begin, soon after they start their practice, to doubt their progress or their experience. Zen talks of two types of doubt, the doubt of the skeptic and the doubt that comes through practice. There is not much that can be done with the doubt of the skeptic. The second doubt emerges from the experience of the practice itself. This often discourages the novice practitioners, and it is used by the teacher to encourage the students to enter more deeply into their practice. The standard method involves using a *"hua-tou"* (lit. "word head"), a phrase that serves like a *koan,* or riddle. "Who?" is a commonly used *hua-tou*. It is designed to interrupt the students' discriminating mind, urging them to go beyond the path of rational thinking. They are told that it is only by sitting with that doubt, called the Great Doubt, that true progress can be made.

Similarly, in the Christian tradition, the practitioner experiences doubt and must overcome it in order to enter into the experience of meditation. In Zen Buddhism, doubt is a state of mind which is systematically cultivated as a stage in the meditator's progress toward disintegration of the illusory self (cf. the expression "the Great Doubt"). I use the word "doubt" here in reference to the Desert Fathers, however, in a more general sense. It denotes any obstacle that one encounters on the spiritual journey, especially during the time of meditation. By overcoming these obstacles a breakthrough to greater depth can be achieved. Thus doubt can manifest itself in a variety of ways. It can arise in the form of multiplicity of thoughts that distract the mind and obscure its lucidity during meditation. In this case the remedy is to cultivate "purity of prayer" by discarding thought or sticking to a single thought through the constant repetition of a short prayer. At other times, doubt may take the form of passionate thoughts, such as anger, lust, avarice, fear, etc. The practitioner then should strive to acquire tranquility of mind through spiritual combat. Such disturbances or doubts can be the signs of a necessary purification of the meditator's desires and preconceived ideas. This spiritual combat is the first step in attaining purity of heart, also called *apatheia,* which was lived and described by the Desert Fathers. What they experienced was an existential rather than an intellectual doubt, expressed in terms of relationship to the absolute, seen in the person of Jesus.

Often the lack of results in meditation is experienced as a failure by Christians and produces a sense of moral guilt, i.e., I must be guilty for God is rejecting me in my inability to meditate. Although the Christian system of prayer and meditation has many traditions that center on God as Absolute, as transcendent, and as ineffable, it is still difficult for the practitioner to abandon this attitude of moral inadequacy. Part of the difficulty lies in the current lack of knowledge concerning the ancient Christian systems of explication that the Desert Fathers, the great exponents of meditation, developed, and the failure to make these teachings known in our times.

To this end, I will comment on four of the major writings that have come down to us from the early days of Christian monasticism. The first is the *Life of Antony,* the biography written by Athanasius, Bishop of Alexandria, of the first Christian monk, Antony of Egypt, the man who served as the model of all those who followed him in the monastic way. Doubt is treated here in terms of the spiritual combat, a fight against the demons. The second is the work of Evagrius Ponticus: *Praktikos* and the *Chapters on Prayer.* Evagrius was the first to describe a method or system of the life of prayer and meditation. He treats the problem of doubt when he writes on the problem of thoughts and also on *apatheia.* The third writing is the *Sayings of the Desert Fathers,* an ancient compilation of teachings and stories, where we will see how doubt or the problem of "thoughts" was experienced in the ordinary life of the early monastics. And finally, in the fourth, the *Conferences* of John Cassian, one of the most influential works in Western monasticism, we will see how this tradition was handed down to us.

The Life of Antony of Egypt: Doubt as Spiritual Combat with Demons

Antony of Egypt, generally considered the father of Christian monasticism,[1] was born about 250 C.E. and died in 356. Anthanasius's *Life of Antony* was written within a year of Antony's death, and is addressed to "the brethren in foreign parts"[2] as a model of the ascetic life. It was quickly circulated throughout the Christian world. Augustine refers to it in his *Confessions* within a couple of decades of its being written, and it is later quoted in the *Sayings of the Desert Fathers*. Jerome, writing in 392 C.E., indicates that he knew it both in the original Greek and in its Latin translation by Evagrius. It was probably composed while Athanasius was in exile in the western part of the Roman empire and was meant to be a guide or "how to" book for those who were attracted to the new way of living the Christian life that was coming from Egypt and Syria, much as the East has attracted young people in our own time.

Antony, much like the Buddha, learned from the ascetics who preceded him, taking from each whatever would be of benefit to his own practice. Athanasius tells us that when Antony first began his ascetical practice, "if he heard of a zealous soul anywhere, like a wise bee he left to search him out, nor did he return home before he had seen him; and only when he had received from him, as it were, provision for his journey to virtue, did he go back [home]."[3]

It is Antony's confrontations with demons that illustrate the problem of doubt. Demonology was not only a reflection of the common worldview of the age, but also an indication of how Antony's life conformed to that of Jesus who was tempted at the beginning of his public life.[4] This was a part of a cosmic combat in which the monk participated with Jesus in the effort to return creation to its proper existence under God, united with Christ in his work of bringing all of humanity to salvation. The life of the Christian monk, like that of his Buddhist counterpart, was a realization of the unity of all humanity. It is a life never lived in isolation, even when lived in solitude. When his struggle with the demons dramatically comes to a close, Antony cries out to the Lord: "Where were you? Why did you not appear at the beginning to stop my pain?" And a voice says to him: "Antony, I was right with you."[5] Again, this doubt, for the Christian ascetic, is not a problem of intellectual skepticism, but an existential crisis in relation to the Absolute.

The cosmic struggle with the demons goes through three phases, each one taking place in a progressively more remote locale. The desert is seen as the haunt of demons and Antony consistently defeats the demons in their own strongholds. Finally, after twenty years of solitary asceticism, Antony is forced from his solitude by his friends. Athanasius tells us that

> Antony came forth as out of a shrine.... His body had kept its former appearance, neither obese from want of exercise, nor emaciated from his fastings and struggles with the demons.... Again, the state of his soul was pure... he was a man completely under control—a man guided by reason and stable in his character.[6]

Here Antony is described as the ideal man perfectly in control of his passions and unmoved by the emotions of those around him. This is the very portrait of a monk who has achieved the ideal state which opens the way to union with the transcendent. When the ascetic has reached this ideal level of purity, he has transcended those passions which had made him more like a beast than a man. A sign of this transcendence is his ability to relate to wild animals, creatures who were in a state of rebellion against man just as man was in a state of rebellion against God. The monk, in the imagery of the Christian Scriptures, has returned to a state of "original innocence," he has become like Adam before the Fall. He has reached this state through doubt, his struggle with the demons.

Antony is seen as the Christian who has already achieved a level of love and knowledge of Christ (or of God) which allows him to have a certain knowledge or vision of God in this present life, prefiguring that total realization of love and knowledge that St. Paul tells us is the reward of those who love God. Athanasius is eager to demonstrate that Anthony presents to the world a way of life superior to that of the philosophers. The Christian monk is the true philosopher who not only lives a higher form of human life but also gains eternal life.

Antony appears also as the protagonist of many of the short stories, much like Zen stories, that have come down to us under the general title of the *Sayings of the Desert Fathers*. One of these stories shows Anthony as the teacher of other monks—an abba, a roshi. In this story the question of interpretation of the Christian Scripture arises. In the desert tradition the ability of person to give a correct interpretation of a passage of Scripture was seen as a sign of the profundity of a monk's insight. This example is taken from the collection of the *Sayings* known as "The Alphabetical Collection."

> One day some old men came to see Abba Antony. In the midst of them was Abba Joseph. Wanting to test them, the old man [Antony] suggested a text from the Scriptures and, beginning with the youngest (so as not to have the deference that the young ought to show to the older interfere), he asked them what it meant. Each gave his opinion as he was able. But to each the old man said: "You have not understood it." Last of all he said to Abba Joseph, "How would you explain this saying?" and he replied, "I don't know." Then Abba Anthony said, "Indeed, Abba Joseph has found the way, for he has said: "I don't know.""[7]

The monk's fundamental "I don't know" can express itself in at least two ways. One form is the monk's admission that he really doesn't know how he stands in relation to the Absolute or God, that he is unsure of God's love for him or feels distanced from God. It can also find expression in an admission of ignorance. This ignorance, another form of doubt—which can be interpreted in terms of a relationship that is existential, or in terms of a knowing that is beyond conceptual knowing—flows from the monk's limited, human way of grasping reality.

Evagrius Ponticus:
Doubt as Experienced in the Multiplicity of Thoughts

Evagrius Ponticus was the first of the early Christian monks to develop a *system* of prayer and meditation. Evagrius is the teacher of early Christian monasticism and it is only within the framework of his teaching on *apatheia* and prayer that many of the incidents in the later *Sayings* will really become understandable. He himself does not deal with doubt as a means of achieving enlightenment, nor do the monks of the Egyptian desert, but that they did experience it is abundantly evidenced in their writings. He certainly recommends a condition of doubt when he counsels a monk to reject all ideas and concepts. Such counsel induces a state of relative doubt toward any ideas that occur during the time of prayer. It is this realization—that none of our ideas, concepts, or reasonings are adequate to the reality toward which all prayer and meditation strives—that will be the foundation of much of the exposition of Christian meditation down through the centuries.

The whole of the teaching of Evagrius is devoted to setting forth a method for attaining purity of heart, *apatheia,* through the right ordering of the passions that are so much a part of being human. Such an ordering of the passions is not an end in itself but the royal path that leads to love of God, *agape.*

> The fear of God strengthens faith, my son, and continence in turn strengthens this fear. Patience and hope make this latter virtue solid beyond all shaking and then also gives birth to *apatheia*. Now this *apatheia* has a child called *agape* who keeps the door to deep knowledge of the created universe. Finally to this knowledge succeeds theology and the supreme beatitude.[8]

The term *apatheia* was first used by the Stoics, whose philosophy was the most popular during the early centuries of the Common Era. Evagrius imported *apatheia* from the realm of philosophy to illumine the road to Christian enlightenment. For him *apatheia* is the immediate aim of the ascetic life; without it, it is impossible to really attain *agape,* or love. *Apatheia* was utilized in Christian circles before Evagrius, and Jesus himself was seen to possess perfect *apatheia* according to Ignatius of Antioch. It was Clement of Alexandria who first employed the term *apatheia* as the keystone of ascetical practice. The term *apatheia* had been used previously by Athanasius to describe Antony when he came out of the tomb after twenty years. So it is very possible that Evagrius was simply publishing a common teaching of the desert tradition. It is significant that *apatheia* was seen as the mother of *agape,* or the love of God. For Evagrius one could not exist without the other; they were aspects of one another. Evagrius calls *agape* "the offspring of *apatheia*."[9] This is why Evagrius tells us that ascesis is the keeping of the commandments, or obedience. The *apatheia* of Evagrius is never fully achieved; it must always be protected or guarded by humility and compunction for sin. Fraternal charity is also one of its safeguards. Evagrius does not demand that we love all equally, but rather that we love enough to live in peace with others.[10]

This "right ordering of our human passions [emotions, desires, drives, etc.]" is for Evagrius the first but necessary step toward a great realization. As he says,

> The effects of keeping the commandments do not heal the powers of the soul completely. They must be complemented by a contemplative activity which is appropriate to these faculties and this activity must penetrate the spirit.[11]

We note, in this text, that the soul (human person) is in need of healing, i.e., the condition that it now finds itself in is not its normal condition of openness to God. The early Christian monastic tradition expressed this understanding in the theme of a return to the condition of Adam in Paradise where he conversed with God and his mind (intellect) was completely ordered toward that goal. Doubt occurs because we are in a state where our passions and thoughts appear to go their own way. This is seen as an illness which can and should be cured or rectified. It is important to note that this realization is, in the Christian tradition, a state that can be achieved by everyone, not just by monks.

Evagrius sees the normalization of the Christian being—the return to Paradise—effected in two stages: one he calls "the contemplation of nature" or *theoria physike;* the other is "contemplation of God" or *gnosis.* In the first or lower stage, the monk still has a multitude of thoughts, and it is here especially where doubts arise. Complete simplicity has not been attained. This multitude of thoughts is perceived as always giving rise to doubt, doubt about one's ability to achieve the desired goal being one of the most basic doubts. Complete simplicity, or singleness of thought, occurs in the second stage, *gnosis,* which is intuitive knowledge of the ultimate reality or God. This is a simple, nonconceptual and experiential knowledge, in which God is known as present. This *gnosis* is beyond thought and the capacity of man to attain. It is beyond form: that is, beyond human concepts or ideas. As it is beyond ideas and forms it can be said to be empty, very similar to the Zen idea.

Toward the end of his life, Evagrius wrote *Chapters on Prayer.* In this work, he asserts clearly that the main drive of the Christian is to fulfill the command of Jesus "to pray always" and "to watch and pray." Much of the emphasis of this work is on *purity* of prayer. Purity, for him, is not just control of one's passions. Rather it is moving beyond all limiting concepts, ideas, and thoughts, to true simplicity, for God is beyond all multiplicity.

This realization demonstrates that all distinct ideas are really ignorance, and that true knowledge is infinite ignorance. He speaks of immateriality[12] (ideas, also, had a certain materiality for Evagrius) and formlessness at the time of prayer.[13] Indeed, he can be quite graphic in his demands, as when he counsels, "Strive to render your mind deaf and dumb at the time of prayer and then you will be able to pray."[14]

The Sayings of the Desert Fathers: Dealing Practically with Doubt

Many of the stories that have come down to us in the *Sayings,* the wisdom passed down to us by a group of early monks, are centered in simple questions about the practice of different virtues such as humility and fraternal charity. If you look closely at these stories you can see that they are about the thoughts that are the root of actions and are concerned with the content of the thoughts more than the existence of the thoughts themselves. The abba's answer to a query, beyond advice on how to solve a particular difficulty, leads the learner to freedom from the particular thought and a movement toward interior peace (*apatheia*).

There is the story of the monk who goes to Abba Arsenius and tells him: "My thoughts trouble me, saying, 'You can neither fast or work (the two traditional ways of calming thoughts), at least go and visit the sick, for that is also charity.' But the old man, recognizing the suggestions of the demons, said to him: 'Go, eat, drink, and sleep, do not work, only do not leave your cell.' " Arsenius goes to the heart of the problem. He does not give an intellectual solution, nor even an easy one. He tells the other simply to go to his cell and stay there. Doubt must be confronted and lived through.

This troubled monk is typical of these stories in his preoccupation with seeking interior peace (*apatheia,* purity of heart, or calm)—whether the afflicting thoughts were about food, sex, security, or something else. The monk who was having difficulty with his thoughts actually proposed a traditional solution for his own problem. The care of the sick has traditionally been understood as one of the great works of compassion for the Christian. In another "saying" of the Fathers it is taught that the work of meditation and caring for the sick, or caring for the pilgrim, are of equal value. Care for the sick and for the traveler are always seen in the light of Jesus' saying, "When you did this for the least of my brothers, you did it for me." Arsenius sees deeper, for he understands the roots of the difficulty, why these thoughts are troubling the younger monk. He was filled with doubt about his call to a life of *apatheia,* a life of quiet. So Arsenius goes to the heart of the problem. It is so important to confront one's doubts that the practices which are normally considered to be essential to the practice of prayer become secondary.

"Just don't leave your cell!" The only way through doubt is to confront it and live through it. As the recorder of this incident remarks at the end: "Steadfastness in the cell keeps the monk in the right way."

Another metaphor used by the early monks for working through the doubts that assail the practitioner of meditation was the "war against thoughts." The story is told that

> Macarius was looking down the road when he saw Satan in the likeness of a man and he passed by his dwelling... (Satan) wore a garment filled with holes and a small flask hung at each. "Where are you going?" asked the old man. "I am going to stir up the memories of the brethren." [When Satan returned up the road] the old man asked: "Did you find any friends down there?" "Yes, I have one monk who is a friend... down there. He at least obeys me and when he sees me he changes like the wind." "Who is he?" "Theopemptus." Abba Macarius got up and went to the desert below.... When he arrived at the cell of Theopemptus, he was received with joy. "How goes it?" he asked. "It goes well" was the reply. "Do not your thoughts war against you?" The junior monk replied: "Up to now it is all right," for he was afraid to admit anything. The old man responded that he still suffered from thoughts that warred against him. Theopemptus then admitted to his own troubling thoughts.[15]

Macarius, having won this opening, advised the other on how to fight against such thoughts; this time fasting was encouraged. And Satan was foiled again. In this tradition of "spiritual combat," the monk (or meditator) is seen as the "hero" who goes out into the desert, considered the abode of demons. Here the demons are at home and chaos prevails—unlike the ordered life of the village and city, where the rule of law reigns. The monk personalizes in his life the confrontation between the forces of chaos (evil) and those of order (good).

We humans are thinking beings. So what are we to do? Does *apatheia* or "purity of heart" mean that we must stop thinking? The *Sayings* confront that issue:[16]

> A brother came to see Abba Poemen[17] and said to him, "Abba, I have many thoughts and they put me in danger." The old man led him outside and said to him, "Expand your chest and do not breathe." He said, "I cannot do that." Then the old man said to him, "If you cannot do that, no more can you prevent thoughts from arising, but you can resist them."

The Desert Fathers were realistic enough to understand that a human being must have thoughts just as one must inhale and exhale. The problem centers not on having thoughts but on dealing with them. The advice to "resist" them does not demand a suppression of thoughts—which is impossible—but an effort to civilize them, to order them, to bring them under control. Monks in the desert confront the demons on their home ground. Yet the real battle does not take place exteriorly, but in the mind or heart of the one who meditates and is primarily centered on the distracting thoughts that ceaselessly run through our minds.

Opinion was divided on whether or not it is possible always to control one's thoughts. "A brother asked Abba Poemen, 'Can a man keep all his thoughts in control, and not surrender one to the enemy?' And the old man said to him, 'There are some who receive ten and give one.' "[18] I interpret this as meaning that although it is possible to control one's thoughts, as we would say, "nine times out of ten," it is impossible to have perfect control of every thought. Yet there were those who believed that it was possible to have perfect control: When the same brother put the identical question to Abba Sisoes, he replied, "It is true that there are some who give nothing to the enemy."[19]

When questioned by another brother, Poemen emphasized the need to order one's thoughts.[20] He said to him: "It is like having a chest full of clothes; if one leaves them in disorder they spoil in the course of time. It is the same with thoughts. If we do not do anything about them, in time they are spoiled, that is to say, they disintegrate." I myself am not too sure whether one ought simply ignore such thoughts and they will go away, or whether one must strive to get rid of them. I tend to think that one ought not confront such thoughts head-on, but simply try to replace them with others.

As mentioned earlier, this effort to bring one's thoughts into some kind of control was simply another, less intellectual, way of expressing the idea of *apatheia*. The Desert Fathers were generally an uneducated and unlettered group of people. They therefore expressed themselves in immediate and down-to-earth terms. They did not have the systematic cosmology or psychology that Evagrius had received in his own schooling. This lack of intellectual training was to cause problems for them a little later than the time we are treating. Most were peasants, and they had a certain suspicion of those who came from a more cosmopolitan background.

John Cassian:
How the Desert Tradition Passed to the West

Monasticism, as a professional way of living the meditative life, did not really begin in Western Europe until generations after the Desert Fathers. It was only when the experience of the first generations of monks both of Egypt and Syria was disseminated in Western Europe that monasticism really became rooted there. The man who did the most to bring the Egyptian tradition to that part of the Roman empire was John Cassian.

Regarding doubt, Cassian offers the traditional desert teaching that it is "impossible for the mind not to be troubled by thoughts"[21] experienced as doubt, but that it falls to us to accept or reject them. He gives the traditional classification of the sources of these thoughts: God, the devil, or ourselves. We must examine our thoughts so that we can distinguish whether we ought to accept them or not. This self-examination will sooner or later teach us discretion.

In his first conference Cassian says that the whole point of the monastic life (for Cassian it is the only life worth living) is purity of heart. We have already seen above that Evagrius had used "purity of heart" as the translation or equivalent of *apatheia*. By the time Cassian wrote, however, the term *apatheia* was already misunderstood by many, or was seen to be part of a system (Origenism) rejected by many Christians. "Purity of heart," on the other hand, was part of one of the most famous and loved passages in the Scriptures, the Beatitudes. "Blessed are the pure of heart, for they shall see God." In this one passage the reader of the *Conferences* immediately recognizes that both the goal (*scopos*) and the end (*telos*) are confirmed by the words of Jesus.

The conference of Abba Moses is actually a compendium of the teachings of Evagrius. In it Cassian has Abba Moses expound on "purity of heart" as the object of all Christian or monastic practices. It is the reason why we perform acts of asceticism and works of mercy. The goal of living is not to do or perform heroic mortifications, or to succor all those who suffer. It is rather that we may "offer God a perfect and utterly clean heart and keep it unsullied by any passion."[22] "These observances do not exist for themselves. . . . It behooves us then, to carry out the things that are secondary . . . for the sake of the principle *scopos,* which is purity of heart or love."[23] Cassian then recounts the story of Martha and Mary[24] to confirm that "the Lord considered the chief good to reside in *theoria* alone—that is in divine contemplation."[25] Note that Cassian is using three terms as synonyms: purity of heart=*agape* (love)=contemplation. He continues to use these words and phrases interchangeably. He then finally tells us that all practices and gifts will pass away but "Love never disappears."[26] Here Cassian brings the words of Paul to confirm the primacy of love which is contemplation. Later in this conference Cassian underlines the tradition that knowledge is limited and cannot grasp the ultimate.

In the *Conferences,* John Cassian follows the generally accepted pattern of the teaching method of his time by first telling us the goal of living, then describing the means toward that goal (discretion), before speaking about prayer and meditation, the fruit of all this work. In Conference 10, he finally shows us how to meditate. His preferred method is that of the *mantra;* the continual repetition of a short phrase or word taken from the Scriptures.

> Let the mind hold ceaselessly to this formula ["O God, incline unto my aid; O Lord, make haste to help me": Psalm 70:1] above all until it has been strengthened by constantly using and continually meditating upon it, and until it renounces and rejects the whole wealth and abundance of thoughts. Thus straitened by the poverty of this verse ("O God, incline unto my aid; O Lord make haste to help me"), it will easily attain to that gospel beatitude which holds first place among the other beatitudes. For, it says "Blessed are the poor in spirit, for theirs is the kingdom of heaven."[27] ... Ascending thus to the manifold knowledge of God, thanks to his illumination, from then on he begins to be filled with more sublime and more sacred mysteries.... So it is that our mind will arrive at that incorruptible prayer to which ... the Lord deigned to grant it.... This is not only not laid hold of by the sight of some image, but cannot be grasped by any word or phrase. Rather, once the mind's attentiveness has been set ablaze, it is called forth in an unspeakable ecstasy of heart and with insatiable gladness of spirit, and the mind, having transcended all feelings and visible matter, pours it out to God with unutterable groans and sighs."[28]

We see that John Cassian in his *Conferences* has been faithful to the traditions that had been handed down from Evagrius and the Desert Fathers. He changes some of the terminology in order to make these traditions more acceptable or understandable to his readers. Primarily he is telling us that our thoughts are inadequate to the reality toward which they strive. Words or concepts can never suffice to encompass the absolute. The constant repetition of a short prayer is an effective means for achieving "pure prayer." Note how Cassian speaks of the poverty of the prayer. Such poverty leads to purity of heart because it leaves no place for doubts or thought to arise.

Conclusion

Modern Christians have found themselves in a dilemma: Mystery does not exist, and faith is simply a series of concepts that ultimately have no meaning. For several centuries we have developed such a rational theology and philosophy that all questions seem to have been answered, or could shortly be answered. When confronted with the existential despair of the modern world, our continued exhortation to "just have faith" (when faith was seen as a system of concepts) appears to beg the question. The difficulty is the feeling that doubt indicates a lack of faith. Often we Christians fail to distinguish between skeptical doubt and "great doubt": between that doubt which attacks the entire belief system and the doubt which precedes a further plunge into the faith reality. The role of the spiritual teacher is to help the student to enter more deeply into "great doubt," just as in Buddhism, so that the student can expand his insight more fully.

What is true of the modern Christian is true for our society in general. Never have so many known so much about so much; yet there is a sense that our knowledge and control lead only to greater uncertainty. Our philosophy generally indicates the realization that much of our former "knowledge" can be deconstructed and shown to be misleading. The existential anxiety so often portrayed in the modern arts, or acted out in society, is a manifestation of our modern inability to abide in mystery. The Buddhist tradition of the "Great Doubt" can certainly teach us how to simply exist in the face of uncertainty, waiting in quiet until insight reveals itself. The traditions of the Desert Fathers also indicate that thoughts and doubts are not necessarily obstacles but rather opportunities. By successfully dealing with thoughts and doubts, one attains a breakthrough into greater depths in the practice of meditation.

Through understanding the Desert Fathers we can see that the teaching on the role of "disinterested" love or *agape* must be renewed in the Christian tradition. We have learned that doubt can lead us to *apatheia* and then to *agape*. We have perceived how the Desert tradition speaks of *agape* as the child of *apatheia* or of "purity of heart." *Agape* exists in doubt and confusion and finds its peace simply resting in its own realization. It has no need of reason, or excuse. It simply is.

Part III

TAOISM AND CONFUCIANISM

Lao Tzu (or Laozi) and Confucius, to whom are attributed the two great philosophical traditions of China, Taoism and Confucianism, are believed to have been contemporaries in the sixth century B.C.E. Confucian teachings became established as the norm for life in the social and political world, while the more mystical and paradoxical teachings of Taoism gave rise to a tradition of interior, contemplative, and often solitary spiritual life.

Liu Xiaogan surveys the historical development and transformation of Taoist meditation from antiquity to modern China, with particular attention to the basic spiritual practice of *keeping the One*—a way of maintaining the harmony of body and mind, or of the totality of the person. Reality is one; through meditation and other practices the person pursues an inward path to union with the Tao and thus realizes the unity of the divine and the human, the transcendent and the secular. Paul Crowe presents the concept of chaos, or *hundun,* in Taoist tradition from the time of the *Tao-te Ching* (or *Daode jing*) and *Chuang Tzu* (or *Zhuangzi*) (where it is of central importance) through the inner alchemy or Golden Elixir tradition reaching into the fourteenth century. Here—in contrast to the biblical and Western tradition—chaos is conceived in a positive way: It is "the state of unity and completeness which precedes and makes possible the creation of the world." Inner alchemy, a system of practices centered in meditation, pursues a path of inner return from complexity to an original state of simplicity and unity, of tranquillity and composure. Finally the inner universe of the person is experienced as one with the larger universe in which it exists.

Joseph Wong examines the affinities between Eckhart and Chuang Tzu, the second patriarch of Taoism. He finds strong parallels in the way that the two masters conceive the relation between emptiness or detachment, on the one hand, and vision or the experience of light, on the other hand—terms comparable to purity of heart and to contemplation. While Eckhart stresses the "vertical" fruit of detachment in the emergence of the divine element in the person, Chuang Tzu points rather to the vision of the Tao immanent in all things and the "horizontal" experience of oneness of the self with all things.

Professor Chung-ying Cheng outlined the ideal of human self-realization in Confucius and Mencius, then the development of the doctrine of self-cultivation in neo-Confucianism. In this process, Heaven, nature, and the human person are to be brought together. (Because of other commitments, it was not possible for Dr. Cheng to prepare his paper for publication.)

Sister Donald Corcoran examines the relationship between Benedictine humility and Confucian "sincerity." While humility is central to the great tradition of monastic spirituality based on the Rule of Benedict, modern Westerners find it very difficult to understand the way of humility in a positive way and to embrace it personally. The Confucian concept of *ch'eng* (sincerity) offers a perspective on true humility which can help to overcome the individualistic and moralistic and dualistic influences of the Western religious tradition. The Confucian teaching of self-cultivation constitutes an education of the heart/mind leading to an integration of all the levels of being.

One image, simple and luminous, emerges from the three studies of Taoism. This is a way of return to the Source, the One, the root which is the Tao, to the undifferentiated original unity, to the primordial state of chaos (Crowe). It involves keeping the One (Liu), seeing the One, and achieving union with the One, and thus becoming one with all things (Wong). The person becomes integrated as he or she is united with the One, with the original Chaos (Crowe). This union is experienced, as in Buddhism, in nondual consciousness. In this Taoist conception of the One, however, we find a more positive and "objective" assertion of the original and all-embracing Reality.

From our two presentations of Confucianism, similarly, there results an overall impression of simplicity and wholeness. Rather than the sharp spiritual tension and cognitive shock of Zen Buddhism, there is set forth before us the prospect of a progressive harmony of soul and body. Such a vision of human balance and integration is characteristic of these two older Chinese traditions, Taoism and Confucianism. The latter, particularly, offers both a positive anthropology and a practical teaching of self-cultivation. Here unity is realized as the harmony and integration of heaven and earth, of spirit and body, rather than as a dramatic awakening, a breakthrough into a radically different unitive consciousness.

11

The Taoist Tradition of Meditation:

History, Transformation, and Comparison

LIU XIAOGAN

In order to reveal the main features of the Taoist tradition of meditation for religious dialogue and comparative studies, this paper attempts to survey the historical development and transformation of Taoist meditation from antiquity to modern China, giving special attention to methods and theories of "keeping the One," a basic spiritual practice of Taoism.

The first part of the paper investigates the conception, formation, and transformation of keeping the One from the fourth century B.C.E. to the fourth century C.E., with a textual analysis of some Taoist texts. The second part continues the history, demonstrating the emergence and divergence of keeping the One and other meditative traditions, especially the *Shangqing* (highest purity) School and inner alchemy tradition. In addition, new forms of Taoist meditation in the modern world are mentioned. Based on this brief but comprehensive historical examination, the third part concludes with five features—reaching from the surface level to the essential level—of Taoist meditations, in comparison with the Christian tradition: (1) continuity and endurance, (2) essence and divergence, (3) introversion and extroversion, (4) the spiritual and the physical, (5) gods and humans.

I. Keeping the One:
Forming and Transforming in Early China

For the purpose of comparison and dialogue, we need to investigate the characteristics of Taoist meditation by surveying its history and transformation comprehensively. I will focus on a special term and theory as a typical example, against the backdrop of the comprehensive picture. Among many terms or methods, "keeping the One" (*shouyi*) is most important and popular in various Taoist texts and practices from ancient to modern China. Thus, we use "keeping the One" as a representative method in the Taoist tradition of meditation in order to present a comprehensive history of Taoist meditation.

The Early Conception of Keeping the One in the Laozi and Zhuangzi

The earliest expression of the importance and significance of the One is found in the *Laozi* or *Daode jing,* the first Taoist classic.[1] Laozi repeatedly emphasizes the crucial role of the One in the world in a parallel structure:

> Heaven obtained the One and became clear, if heaven had not thus become clear, it would soon crack.
> Earth obtained the One and became tranquil, if the earth had not thus become tranquil, it would soon be shaken.
> The spiritual beings obtained the One and became divine, if the spiritual beings had not thus become divine, they would soon wither away.
> The valley obtained the One and became full, if the valley had not thus become full, it would soon become exhausted.
> Kings and barons obtained the One and became rulers of the empire, if kings and barons had not thus become honorable and high in position, they would soon fall. (chapter 39)[2]

Probably this is the first systematic emphasis on the One. The relationship of the One and the Tao is not directly mentioned in the text. However, based on its independent and fundamental role in the world, it is equal to the Tao, the ultimate source and ground of the universe and human societies. Therefore, this One is different from the One in chapter 42 of the work in which the One is derived from the Tao. In chapter 42 we read: "Tao produced the One, the One produced the two, the two produced the three." This kind of ambiguity and divergence has been a characteristic in Chinese cultural and religious traditions, in which the mainstream prefers the analogical and intuitive method to convey wisdom about cosmology and human life, rather than logical reasoning and inference. This partly explains the multiplicity of meditative traditions in China.

Although the *Laozi* does not literally present the term *shouyi* or keeping the One, it does use a similar expression, *baoyi* or "embracing the One." "Can you keep soul and body spirits together as embracing One without detachment? Can you concentrate your vital force (*qi*) and achieve the softness of an infant?" (chapter 10). Some commentaries suggest that the One is the Tao. However, this passage discusses the relationship of soul spirit and body spirit (*hun* and *po*), not cosmological issues. Here, embracing the One is to keep body and soul as one or in totality, which is the predecessor of keeping the One. The *Laozi,* as the fountainhead of the tradition of keeping the One, laid the foundation of the theory and purpose of Taoist meditative traditions.

Zhuangzi (the second founder of the Taoist school) and his followers dramatically developed Taoist method and theories of meditation. In the inner chapters, *xinzhai* (heart-fasting), *zuowang* (sitting and forgetting), and *waiwu* (forgetting the outside world) are typical methods of meditation. In the outer chapters, *shouqiyi* (literally "keeping this One") is very similar to keeping the One. In chapter 11, Guangchengzi, a fabled Taoist master, is asked about the art of longevity by the Yellow Emperor, who is a legendary ancestor of the Chinese peoples. His answer presents the key characteristics of Taoist meditation, such as stillness without hearing, seeing, sensation, and thinking. His answer begins with the mysterious nature of the Tao:

> Come, I will tell you about the perfect Tao. The essence of the perfect Tao is deep and darkly shrouded; the extreme of the perfect Tao is mysterious and hushed in silence.[3]

Tao is formless, invisible, and silent. It is from this point that *Zhuangzi* establishes the model and principle of meditation for the purpose of longevity. The same passage continues:

> Let there be no seeing, no hearing; enfold the spirit in quietude and the body will right itself. Be still, be pure, do not labor your body, do not churn up your essence, and then you can live a long life.
>
> When the eye does not see, the ear does not hear, and the mind does not know, then your spirit will keep the body, and the body will enjoy a long life. Be cautious of what is within you; block off what is outside you, for much knowledge will do you harm.

In these paragraphs, three points about meditation are repeatedly presented. First, one must stop the usual functioning of all the senses, typically of the eyes and ears. Second, he or she has to keep the mind or spirit in stillness without its usual thinking and awareness; this is the essential condition for meditation. Third, the stillness of the mind will keep the body and spirit in the state of totality, which is necessary for longevity. The next paragraph emphasizes the harmony of *yin* and *yang*, the two opposite and complementary fundamentals in the universe and in human bodies. The same passage goes on:

> Then I will lead you up above the great brilliance, to the source of the perfect *yang;* I will guide you through the dark and mysterious gate, to the source of the perfect *yin.* Heaven and earth have their controllers, the *yin* and *yang* their storehouses. You have only to take care and guard your own body; these other things will of themselves grow sturdy.

As part of the conclusion, the last paragraph presents the idea of "keeping that one" (*shouqiyi*), another predecessor of the term "keeping the One":

As for myself, I *keep that One,* abide in this harmony, and therefore
I have kept myself alive for twelve hundred years, and never has my
body suffered any decay.

What is the "One" here? Obviously, it is not specified as gods, light, vital
energy (qi), or as related to certain points in the body. The One denotes only
the harmonious state or totality of spirit and body, yin and yang, as well as
individuals and the universe. According to the author, "keeping that one"
is miraculously effectual.

Early Formation of Keeping the One in the Taiping Jing

The idea of "keeping this One" developed into a regular or idiomatic term
in the *Taiping Jing* or the *Scripture of Great Peace,* which was completed in
the late second century c.e. and is one of the earliest classics of the Taoist
religion. The term *shouyi* or keeping the One was quoted and emphasized
dozens of times in the book. The only extant version of the scripture in
the Taoist canon is incomplete, though there are two selected versions and
some fragments in other scriptures or books.[4] The book was not written by
a single author, and its theories are not in coherence. Thus the meaning of
the term "keeping the One" is vague and divergent.

The book mentions a Taoist disciple who wanted to find three hundred
verses on the art of "keeping the One" and "nurturing nature" (*shouyi
yangxing*). This demonstrates the popularity and importance of the method
of keeping the One. What is the One? The *Scripture* argues:

What should be taken as the beginning? It should be to think about
keeping the One. Why is it? That is because the One is the beginning
of numbers; the One is the way of the birth of life; the One is what
the original energy (*qi*) comes from, and the One is the principle of
Heaven.[5]

While this paragraph appears to present four definitions of the One, we
should not take them seriously as definitions.

Actually, the text just repeatedly emphasizes the importance of the One:
that is, the primordial state of the universe, the principle of the universe and
of life. Although there are numerous understandings or interpretations of the
One in Taoist texts,[6] many of them are not necessarily and directly related to
the method and exercise of keeping the One. In the *Scripture of Great Peace,*
at least, the One in meditation is not so complicated. Its essential meaning
is not any specific thing; rather, it is simply the importance of primordiality
in the universe and in lives. The One represents the original and essential
state and principle of the universe and of human lives. "Keeping the One"
generally means gaining and maintaining harmony of spirit/mind and body
in meditation practice.

In this scripture there is one section named the "Method of Nurturing the One and Eliminating Evil," of which the author contends:

> The fundamental, which is original energy, has been treasured since the beginning of the genesis of heaven and earth. To pursue great peace, you must be mindful of the fundamental. If not, there will be great anxiety; what you want to do cannot be accomplished, and disasters come along. These are not mistakes of human beings. It is because they lost the fundamental.... The One is the fundamental of the Tao, the origin of energy, the mainstay of mass hearts, and what life is rooted in.... The roots of human beings are internal, while the branches and leaves are external. May you keep the One.... Who keeps the One will receive assistance from Heavenly gods....[7]
>
> To keep the three is not as good as to keep the two, and to keep the two is not as good as to keep the One.[8]

Thus, the significance of keeping the One is to gain and keep the fundamentality, and not to lose the center of gravity in the colorful, attractive, and perplexing world. This suggests that the specific content of the One is only of secondary and metaphorical significance.

Fundamentality in meditation means the union of the spiritual and the physical. The scripture says:

> The vital ways, from antiquity to the present, all claim that keeping the One promotes longevity and prevents growing old. That one knows the way of keeping the One is called the infinite way. Man has his body that always combines with its spirit.... Keeping them permanently together indicates fortune, while separation signals ill omens.... Keeping the physical and the spiritual permanently together is the so-called One, which leads to longevity.... Thus sages teach the doctrine of keeping the One, that suggests you should focus on your body. Being always preoccupied with it, spirit comes automatically and corresponds [with body] perfectly. Hence all kinds of diseases and ailments will disappear. This is the very symbol of longevity with good eyes and cars.[9]

This paragraph seems to reveal explicitly the essential meaning of keeping the One. To keep the physical and the spiritual in totality is fundamental in the Taoist arts of longevity, as well as in the traditions of Taoist meditation. This should be the clue for us to understand the varied meditative methods and theories in the Taoist tradition, not to be forgotten when we study specific and divergent methods.

It is noteworthy that the scripture presents another method of meditation that is named literally "keeping the one light" (*shouyiming*).[10] This is confused with keeping the One because it has only one more character, light (*ming*), following the term "keeping the One."[11] Because "keeping the one light" as a term is repeatedly used and an auxiliary word *zhi* is used after the term, we cannot read the last word "light" (*ming*) with the following part of the sentence. Keeping the one light is a method of inducing the experience of the vision of light, like sunshine and the sun's brightness. During meditation, the practitioner feels that a fire is built. As soon as it is perceived as a nascent glow, one must immediately keep the image it presents without losing it for an instant. In the beginning the light is completely red; then it becomes white and ultimately turns completely blue. No matter how far the light reaches, you should return to keeping or nurturing the One. Thus inside your body, nothing is not illuminated, and all kinds of illnesses and ailments will be cured. If you hold on to it persistently, it can be called the art of longevity.[12] Keeping the one light may be an offshoot of the Taoist tradition of keeping the One.

As to the essence of keeping the One, Robinet states that it clearly means unifying the various components of the human person. Human nature, as the *Scripture of Great Peace* understands it, is composed of three principles—essence, vital energy, and spirit—all three of which are modalities of a single energy. It is necessary to "reunite the three into one."[13]

A different interpretation of keeping the One is found in another Taoist classic, *Xiang'er's Commentary on the Laozi*. It sounds much like a sectarian catechism, asserting that the One is not inside man. Rather it is beyond the universe and only passes through the world and man. Thus, keeping the One in this text simply consists in observing the precepts promulgated by Taishang Laojun, the deified Laozi.[14] This is the earliest account of the moral aspect of keeping the One. It was developed in a later Taoist movement.

The Development of Keeping the One in Baopuzi

As demonstrated by Robinet, the *Scripture of Great Peace* attaches great importance to the visualization of the body and the viscera.[15] However, it doesn't integrate this directly into the method of keeping the One. Nevertheless, we find the visualization incorporated into the method of keeping the One in another important scripture of Taoist religion, the *Baopuzi* or *The Master Who Embraces the Simplicity,* which was written by a single author, Ge Hong (283–363).

The contents and concepts of the book are clearer and more coherent than those of the *Scripture of Great Peace*. Chapter 18, particularly, focuses on the method of keeping the One throughout. Carrying on the Taoist tradition, Ge too begins his arguments with the significance of the fundamentality of the One. He says: "Here is what I have learned: He who knows the One has accomplished everything. He who knows the One knows all. For him who does not know the One, there is nothing he can know. The Tao reveals itself in the One. It is therefore of incomparable value."[16] Therefore, according to the immortality classics, "If you wish to enjoy longevity, keeping the One must be learned. Reflect on the One till famine, and the One will provide nourishment. Reflect on the One till drought, and the One will provide the refreshing beverage."[17]

Unlike his predecessors, Ge says that the One indicates interior gods. According to Ge, the One possesses names, shapes, and colors. In the male, the One is 0.9 inch long; in the female, 0.6. Sometimes it is 2.4 inches below the navel, in the lower cinnabar field; at other times, it is below the heart, in the central cinnabar field. In the upper cinnabar field, it is three inches behind the space between the eyebrows. Religious Taoism believes that visualizations of the internal gods may serve to keep the deities within; thus, life is guarded. Such are things stressed by Taoists, who for generations have merely been smearing their lips with blood as a seal of secrecy as they transmitted its names orally. The One can form *yin* and beget *yang,* bring on the cold and the heat. Through the One there is sprouting in spring, growing in summer, harvesting in autumn, and storing in winter. All space is no analogy for its magnitude; nor is a hair or sprout an analogy for its minuteness.[18] Ge also names the One as the True One. According to his account,

> As prescription for longevity there is only golden cinnabar; for preservation of body and driving evils afar there is only the True One. For this reason, the ancients valued these things highly . . . preserve the One and keep the True, and you can communicate with gods. Lessen desire, restrain eating, and the One will abide quietly. . . . The One is not hard to know, persistence is the difficulty. Keep it without loss, and you will never know exhaustion. . . . Ghosts will not dare approach, nor blades strike.[19]

Furthermore, keeping the One is the most effective method among a thousand other ones. "If a single process for keeping the One were known, all these other methods could be rejected."[20] If people can keep the true One, the One will also preserve them. In this way, harmful things find no place in them that will admit entrance to their evil; in defeat it is possible to be victorious, and in positions of peril to feel only security. If, on the other hand, you forget to keep the One for but a single moment, the ghosts will harm you.[21]

Another method, named "keeping the Mysterious One" (*shou-xuan-yi*), is introduced in the same chapter:

> The Way of the Mysterious One is an important method too. It is as effective as the True One . . . Keeping the Mysterious One is much easier than keeping the True One. The latter has names, size, uniforms, and color. The Mysterious One appears itself . . . To begin with, you must purify yourself and fast for a hundred days. Only then may you wait

to perceive it, but then it can be obtained in not more than three or four days; once you possess it you will never lose it provided you take steps to keep it.[22]

In comparison with the *Scripture of Great Peace,* some points in *Baopuzi* presented by Ge should be noticed. First, Ge equates the One with interior gods and names it the True One. Second, he incorporates the inner visualization of gods into the theory of keeping the One. Third, he claims the method of keeping the One is the most effective among various other methods. Fourth, he presents another similar method, namely keeping the Mysterious One. Thus, Ge is a critical person in the development and transformation of the Taoist tradition of meditation.

II. Merging and Diverging: Trends in Medieval and Modern China

Methods of keeping the One and other theories of meditation of *Baopuzi* and *Taiping Jing* merged into later Taoist traditions, especially into the *Shangqing* (highest purity) tradition and the *neidan* (inner alchemy) theories. The term and the method of keeping the One is often recited, reinterpreted, and reformed in later Taoist classics, such as *Huangting Jing* (Scripture of the Yellow Court), *Laozi Xisheng Jing* (Scripture of Western Ascension), *Yannian Yisuan fa* (Method of Extending One's Years and Increasing the Reckoning), and *Zhongjie Wen* (On All Precepts), as demonstrated by Kohn.[23]

In addition to some new methods and terms, such as the Three-ones, Female-one, and the Supreme One, the most important feature of meditation in *Shangqing* or the Highest Purity traditions is visualization of the viscera, represented by the *Huangting Jing,* or the Scripture of the Yellow Court. Here, keeping the One essentially means "preserving spirit" (*cunshen*).[24]

Keeping the One and Shangqing Taoism

Kohn provides a brief example of how the practice of keeping the One changed within Shangqing Taoism, which is found in a description given in the *Yannian Yisuan Fa* (Method of Extending One's Years and Increasing the Reckoning). Here, keeping the One stands for the fundamental ordering of the body and mind before higher levels of meditation practice can be attained. In actual application, however, keeping the One here appears to be mainly a fight against strong emotions.

The foundation of guarding the One is found in a strong sense of humility. Thus, when you feel an evil urge, think of the flying immortals. When you are pestered by jealousy, think of the wonderful gods. When you are driven mad by desire think of the realized ones.[25]

This development of the moral aspects of keeping the One originated in *Xiang'er's Commentary on the Laozi.*

One more Shangqing text, *Zhihui Xiaomo Zhenjing* (The True Scripture of Wisdom to Expel Devils), tentatively dated in the Tang dynasty (618–907 C.E.), describes the practice of keeping the One as an exercise in concentrative meditation based on the observance of moral precepts and leading to the attainment of Taoist wisdom. Kohn renders it:

> Whenever someone has courage and daring, and is able to observe the rules and precepts, when he furthermore wants to order and control his body and mind, so that he will accumulate merit and grow in virtue and ultimately become a great sage, then he must begin with keeping the One. The One is basically shapeless, yet it goes along with everything... Keeping the One is wisdom, while losing it is foolishness. Foolishness leads to death, wisdom helps to preserve life.[26]

Evidently, under Buddhist influence, the content of keeping the One here is totally different from its ancient tradition. It bases longevity on moral correctness and cultivation.

More of a Buddhist influence is found in certain Shangqing materials of the Tang dynasty that emphasize a strong connection between the practice of keeping the One and moral goodness. One example is the *Zhongjie Wen* (On All Precepts), which states categorically that "in the practice of keeping the One the proper observance of the precepts is first. As long as one obeys the moral rules and does not do wrong, evil cannot enter." According to Kohn, the practice described here is simpler and more mind-oriented than earlier Shangqing methods. The flow of thoughts should be interrupted, all evil should be eliminated, and one should right oneself and turn fully to the Tao, the spirit, and the One. Visualization and incantations of specific deities have no part in this way of keeping the One.[27]

Keeping the One and Inner Alchemy

After the late Tang dynasty, the dominant trend of Taoist meditation gradually became *neidan,* or inner alchemy, which grew to be the basic religious training in Quanzhen (completely true) Taoism, one of the two main Taoist traditions after the twelfth century. While the term keeping the One is still emphasized and reformed by authors of inner alchemy, it may indicate the first stage in the complete process of inner alchemy practice, namely, foundation-building (*zhuji*). Further, it could suggest keeping the "mysterious pass and one key" (*xuanguan yiqiao*), the meaning of which is highly secret and never transmitted to outsiders.[28] The feature of inner alchemy is neither visualizing deities nor interrupting the ceaseless flow of thoughts, but rather a refining of the three major components of the body—vitality or essence (*jing*), vital energy (*qi*), and spirit (*shen*)—to higher levels of purity in accordance with the system of operative alchemy.[29]

The practitioners of inner alchemy believe that natural processes resulting in the death of human beings can be reversed by self-cultivation, namely, by concentrating and purifying the life energies within the body. Theories and practices of inner alchemy vary among schools and individual Taoists. Generally speaking, inner alchemy is based on Taoist cosmology. The Tao produced the One, the One produced the two, the two produced the three, and the three produced the myriad things. Conversely, in the practice of inner alchemy, creatures return to the three, to the two, to the One, and thus reach the Tao, and realize the eternal state along with the Tao. In the practice of inner alchemy, the eternal sublimation and combination of vitality or essence, energy, and spirit are brought about by sublimating the processes of thought.[30]

According to Robinet, inner alchemy is a method of finding illumination by returning to the fundamental order of the cosmos. This goes closely together with a regeneration of the individual. Both individual and cosmos are axiomatically understood as connected, as one.[31] One may say that texts belonging to the current of inner alchemy are characterized by the following: (1) a concern for training the mind as much as the body, with the mental aspect usually predominant; (2) a tendency to synthesize various Taoist currents, certain Buddhist speculations, and specific Confucian lines of thought; (3) references to the *Yi Jing* (Book of Changes); and (4) references to chemical practices.[32] It is very impressive that the unceasing activity and the constant creativity of Taoism are manifested in a variety of currents and traditions. It continues to amalgamate and merge poetry, intellectual speculation, and pragmatic training. It embraces the twofold aspect of Taoist life. It integrates the remnants of ancient mythology as well as the philosophy of yin-yang and the five agents, of the *Yi Jing* and Han dynasty thought. To all these it adds the newly developed Chinese form of Buddhism, the ideas of the Chan school, and later on the worldview of neo-Confucianism. Inner alchemy for the first time integrates these two later traditions into Taoism in a reflective, organized, and coherent manner, not merely superficially and formally as had happened earlier.[33]

Here are examples of theories related to keeping the One introduced by Kohn. The *Daoshu* (Pivot of the Tao), in its outline of the ideas of Chongzhenzi, describes the central idea of Taoist practice as consisting of *actualizing the three and keeping the One*. The three are essence, energy, and spirit; keeping the One means that one "uses energy to keep vitality, uses vitality to guard spirit, and uses spirit to guard energy." Another description of keeping the One can be found in the *Xiuzhen Jing* (Scripture on Cultivating the Truth). The section on "keeping the One and preserving the spirit alive" merely presents advice on how to keep the One at rest. In a later paragraph, the text links meditation to morality. This text shows that keeping the One has changed from a technique of assembling, preserving, and nourishing the vital energy of the Tao into a practice of self-examination.[34]

Meditation in Modern China

In the twentieth century, with the diffusion of modern natural scientific knowledge throughout China, Taoist meditation was seriously challenged and transformed. The preeminent Taoist scholar, practitioner, and religious leader Chen Yingning (1880–1969) contributed greatly to promoting Taoist meditation among the masses, in addition to teaching professional disciples. While keeping in the line of the traditional Taoist heritage, especially northern inner alchemy techniques and doctrines, he also took scientific views and modern life into account.

Another new form of Taoist meditation, *Yinshizi Jingzuofa* (Method of Sitting Still by Yinshizi), authored by Jiang Weiqiao, was popular in China (including Hong Kong and Taiwan) from the 1920s through the 1980s.[35] Although his method carries on Taoist traditions,[36] his language is plain, without Taoist jargon and mystery. For example, he uses "center of gravity" (*zhongxin*) to replace the traditional term "lower cinnabar field" (*xiadantian*). The basic theory is in accordance with that of keeping the One in ancient time, emphasizing primarily vitality and the harmony of the spiritual and the physical. In addition to basic instruction, Jiang introduces his personal internal experience, something rare and valuable for the study of meditation.

His method teaches that the meditator should let go of everything and abstain from giving rise to thoughts. He should look within so that all false thoughts cease of themselves. A long practice of meditation usually results in a kind of vibration being felt in the lower belly below the navel; suddenly the lower belly vibrates and the whole body shakes. The meditator should not be scared but should let this state take its natural course. The speed and length of this vibration differs for each individual; it just happens and should neither be sought nor repressed. When this vibration is felt, the meditator should imagine (but without exertion) that the hot force descends and passes through the coccyx and then rises up the spine until it reaches and passes through the top of the head, thence coming down through the face, the chest and the pit of the stomach to return to the belly below the navel. As time passes, this moving heat will go up and down of itself and can, by imagination, be spread to all parts of the body, reaching even the nails and the ends of the hair, with the result that the whole body is warm and unusually comfortable. This may take a few months or even a year after the first vibration. His experience is exactly similar to classical accounts and difficult to explain with modern scientific theory and language. He and some of his students, however, asserted that they had experienced this phenomenon personally and could not deny it.[37] Jiang's method is helpful and successful for many people. While mysterious, however, it is not religious or sacred. It is an early example of modern people taking some elements from religious traditions to respond to pragmatic needs rather than an expression of faith.

The method of keeping the One, merged into later traditions, is still practiced in Taoist societies today. Eva Wong, an active Taoist practitioner and translator, says that in olden times, such as in the Shangqing tradition, keeping the One involved visualizing the various manifestations of Laozi or other deities, which are images of the Tao. These visualizations served to keep the deities or the guardian spirits within the body. In modern practice, however, the method of keeping the One no longer requires visualization. The key to this meditation lies in dissolving the duality between the self and the world so that oneness can be attained. In the early stages, the practitioner first stills the mind and body so that no thoughts, emotions, or sensations arise. Once the stillness is attained, the "mind of the Tao" will emerge. The mind of the Tao is consciousness that is rooted in the Tao and sees all things as one. With continued practice, the experience of oneness will take hold, and union with the Tao is achieved.[38] Wong also introduces eleven other methods practiced today, which are helpful for readers who need further information and knowledge about Taoist meditation.

III. Analysis and Comparison

In response to the orientation of this symposium, "A Monastic Dialogue between Christian and Asian Traditions," I will try to make some comparison between Taoist and Christian traditions of meditation. These are preliminary observations on the similarities and differences between the two traditions. I hope that they may serve at least as proposals for further dialogues and comparative studies.

1. Continuity and Endurance

This may be the most evident surface characteristic of the history of Taoist meditation, especially in comparison with Christian traditions. As mentioned in this paper, Taoist meditation originated in ancient Chinese culture, at least before the fourth century B.C.E., the middle of the Warring States period. In addition to classical documents like the *Laozi, Zhuangzi,* and *Guanzi,*[39] newly unearthed documents also prove that meditation techniques and theories developed and matured long before the movement of institutionalized Taoist religion. *Taiping Jing* and *Baopuzi* collected many methods and doctrines of meditation practiced from the first to fourth centuries. The Shangqing School significantly developed the theories and techniques of meditation from the fourth century and merged with other schools into Zhengyi (Correct One) Taoism in southern China in the fourteenth century. During the same period, inner alchemy took its shape in the ninth century and grew into the mainstream of Taoist meditation until the modern era in China. Since the challenge of the movement of modernization and the pressure from Communist revolution, Taoism, as the only indigenous religion, withered dramatically along with other religions, especially from the 1950s to the 1970s. Nevertheless, the meditation traditions are carried on in some Taoist monasteries. At the same time, Taoist traditions are found in some popular movements and methods of meditation, usually known as "still exercise" (*jinggong*), "inner exercise" (*neigong*), or—a more popular and all-embracing name—"breath work" (*qigong*), which has prevailed since the 1950s. Most of these methods have little relation to religion. It is evident that Taoist traditions of meditation have a long and continuous history. It cannot be a mere coincidence that the Taoist arts of longevity are long lasting. People may prolong life with their techniques even though they do not believe in Taoism.

2. Essence and Divergence

Taoist meditative tradition, however, has undergone transformation and divergence. For example, the concept of the One and the idea of "embracing the One" were created by Laozi. Then Zhuangzi's disciples developed its essential theory in the expression "keeping that One," and laid a great emphasis on the primordiality of human life and the fundamentality of the union of the physical and the spiritual in human life, as well as in the universe. This essential principle runs throughout all methods and theories of Taoist meditation, but is embodied in different forms and directions. The idea of "keeping that One" grew into a technical term, "keeping the One" in *Taiping Jing,* and was presented as the fundamental method of longevity and meditation. During the same time a derivative method, i.e., "Keeping the one light," was introduced. A more divergent version of keeping the One that consisted of observing the precepts promulgated by the deified Laozi was found in the *Xiang'er's Commentary on Laozi.* In *Baopuzi,* the method of keeping the One merged with the theory of visualization of inner viscera in order to keep internal deities within and prevent life vitality from draining. In *Huangting Jing,* keeping the One means preserving the spirit (*cunshen*). Further, in the tradition of inner alchemy, keeping the One could be the first stage of the complete practice named foundation-building (*zhuji*). Sometimes it also refers to keeping the "mysterious pass and one key" (*xuanguan yiqiao*), which is highly esoteric.

As demonstrated above, while the essence of keeping the One is commonly accepted and repeated, its form and concrete content have been varied. The development of keeping the One, or the general tradition of Taoist meditation, is a union of continuity and divergence, of tradition and transformation, and of conservatism and creativity. Both aspects—the consistency of the essential principle of meditation, and the divergence of the methods and theories—are remarkable in comparison with other traditions. Taoism, with its creativity, is never monolithic or dogmatic. Thus Taoist traditions of meditation are plentiful and prosperous. We may find the same phenomenon in the Christian tradition of meditation: that is, consistency and discrepancy. Its varied development, however, cannot be compared with the length and enormous variety of the Taoist tradition of meditation. This multiple creativity may explain the first feature, namely its endurance and continuity.

3. Introversion and Extroversion

In the Christian tradition, meditation usually is an appeal to God; thus it is essentially directed outward, toward the external and absolute God. There may be silent activities of thinking and reasoning within, but the Christian orientation is definitely outward. In contrast, Taoist meditation is essentially inward. Even the final end is the union with the Tao, which is an internal and personal experience. Transcendence must be reached through one's concentration on mind or internal organs to purify one's heart and body. The method of keeping the One emphasizes the importance of the harmony and unity of body and mind, and the center of attention during meditation is usually internal, such as mental activities, points of the body, viscera, or internal deities. Christian meditation means communication with God, and therefore maintaining one's selfhood during the meditation. Taoist meditation pursues unity with the Tao; thus the practitioner has to forget selfhood. This is to be achieved through interior activities—both conscious and subconscious—which include concentration, forgetting, visualization, imagination, reflection, intuition, etc. There is no verbal communication with or appeal to the Tao, because the Tao is not a god and would not give humans any response or instruction. While there are stories that Taoist practitioners met a god or the deified Laozi and received instructions and scriptures in dreams, this has nothing to do with meditation. In short, Taoist meditation attains transcendence of selfhood and union with the Tao mainly by interior practice and transformation. Introversion is an important feature of Taoist spiritual training, and this feature is determined by the next one.

4. The Physical and the Spiritual

In the Christian tradition, theoretically speaking, the goal of meditation is purely spiritual. The purpose of Taoist meditation, however, is always both spiritual and physical. The spiritual aspects include transcendent experience, union with the Tao, purifying mind and heart, promoting morality, improving psychological health, correction of one's thoughts and (indirectly) of one's behavior. The experience of being united with Tao is the highest spiritual attainment of Taoist practice, and the purpose of purification of heart and soul is realized at the same time. All of these goals are to be reached *only* by meditation. In the context of this spiritual pursuit, moral purification is always an important part of Taoist purpose. This is more pronounced in the Quanzhen tradition, which has absorbed elements of Confucianism and Buddhism. The physical aspect of Taoist meditation is more remarkable, perhaps a unique feature. It focuses on eliminating ailments and diseases, improving physical health, promoting vitality, prolonging life, and even pursuing immortality—physically in the early period and spiritually in the later period. This pursuit of physical health and longevity is the underlying reason that Taoist meditation is more inward-oriented than meditation in the Christian tradition. With this physical quality, Taoist meditation is more practical. It is easily incorporated into modern life, as is happening in contemporary China under the popular name "breath work" (*qigong*). Taoist meditation, in thus combining a physical pursuit with a spiritual ideal, may be exceptional among the major world religions.

5. Humans and Gods

As to the relationship between human beings and gods, Taoism is also very remarkable because of its polytheistic system. The longer the ancient Taoist religion developed, the greater were the number of deities that became part of its polytheistic system. As an indigenous religion, Taoism created deities from traditional legendary and folk beliefs. In its early age, Taoist gods were created according to three categories: heavenly gods such as stars, the sun, and the moon; earth deities such as mountains, rivers, and land; human immortals and ghosts, including cultural heroes and characters in legends. In the sixth century when Tao Hungjing (456–536) edited the book on the positions of Taoist deities, there were more than five hundred gods and immortals. Before the tenth century, the highest god worshiped by Taoist believers varied greatly from school to school, or sect to sect. Then appeared the worship of the "Three Purities" (*sanqing*), the three gods on the uppermost level generated and transformed directly from primordial energy (*qi*). The Taoist polytheistic system is consistent with its belief in immortality, whether physical or spiritual. Taoist polytheism contains many kinds of gods; there is no absolute gap between gods and human beings, or between the transcendent and this world. The universe, including the world of deities and that of creatures, is continuous and total, without separation. Thus the relations between gods and human beings are completely different from those in monotheism. The divine will is not as significant and powerful as it is in Christian traditions. Meditation, therefore, is not for the purpose of reporting to the uppermost gods or of receiving instructions from them. Rather, meditation may be a way to visualize deities, and sometimes to retain or to exorcise particular gods according to the interest of humans. Taoist polytheistic belief may be the ultimate ground of all the other features.

The traditions of Taoist meditation, as demonstrated in this paper, have enjoyed a long and varied history. Some of them are significant and helpful for modern people, even for nonreligious people. Among the Taoist doctrines, some principles—such as the unity of the physical and the spiritual, the harmony of the sacred and the human, the primordiality of human vitality, and the belief that human beings may prolong their lives through their own efforts—may provide spiritual nutrition and inspiration for all human beings.

12

Chaos

A Thematic Continuity between Early Taoism
and the Way of the Golden Elixir

PAUL CROWE

Introduction

In his fascinating and wide-ranging study of the chaos theme in early
Taoist texts, Norman Girardot puts forth a compelling argument against
the tendency to erect a dual construct of "philosophical" versus "religious"
Taoism.[1] In *Myth and Meaning in Early Taoism* he looks to mythic themes
as a source of historical momentum which helps to provide a form of continuity, if not consistency, to subsequent expressions of a given worldview.
By "mythic themes" he means

> ...the detectable presence in written texts of recurrent symbolic
> images, or particular paradigmatic clusters of related images that both
> summarize a central mythological idea and condense in an ideal-typical
> way the basic structure or logic of a set of myths, not all of which
> necessarily have the same historical or cultural background.[2]

Thus, for example, while the writers of the *Zhuangzi* or the *Daode jing*
may have been subject, during the Warring States period (476–221), to very
different social and political circumstances from those of the Sung Dynasty
(960–1280) Taoists, it is nevertheless possible to detect some very basic
consistencies in the symbolic repertoire from which they each drew in order
to configure their respective senses of how they fit into the scheme of things,
and the best course of action to take in responding to such a predicament.
Today the argument for continuity between texts such as the *Zhuangzi* and
the *Daode jing* and much of the later corpus of material found in the Taoist
Canon (*Daozang*) hardly needs to be made. After the work of scholars such
as Henri Maspero, Kristofer Schipper, and Isabelle Robinet, the argument
can be considered well and truly laid to rest. The purpose of this paper
is simply to describe one example of this continuity as it is found in the
Golden Elixir (*Jindan*) texts which reached full maturity by the Song and

Yuan (1280–1368) dynasties. Girardot has made the case for the centrality of *chaos* within the texts of early Taoism, and I wish to take up this theme to demonstrate how it is incorporated into the method of the Golden Elixir. Prior to launching into this description, it is worth devoting some space to considering the appropriateness of translating the Chinese term *hundun* as "chaos."

I. Chaos and *Hundun*

Generally, in European and North American cultures, chaos is thought of in decidedly negative terms evoking images of disorder and mayhem which represent a fall from structure, stability, and rationality. This understanding of chaos can be traced back to the ancient Greeks. Under "chaos" the *Oxford English Dictionary* (2d ed.) states that the term is derived from the Greek term *khaos,* meaning a vast chasm, a gaping void or abyss.

In his *Dictionary of Philosophy* Peter Angeles explains that for the Greeks, chaos is what the world was like prior to the imposition of rational principles that brought order to the universe.[3] This is exactly how Plato describes chaos in the *Timaeus*.[4] In his conversation with Socrates, Timaeus provides an explanation concerning the Creator's motivations for bringing the world into existence.[5] The state of affairs prior to the divine act of creation is unacceptable due to its random, disordered nature. Only through the imposition of reason can the world come to exist as it does.[6] In the *Timaeus* Plato describes the inherently rational order and design resulting from the creative act. Plato considered the divine, rational part of the soul to be eternal and, by virtue of its ability to gain access to the world of forms, of primary importance.[7] What Plato describes in the *Timaeus* is the creation, from without, by a craftsman god, of a self-contained cosmos.

In the introduction to his translation of the *Timaeus* Desmond Lee points out that this is a significant departure from earlier cosmogonists who had employed metaphors of human or animal procreation. Previously the focus had been on accounts which described the creation of the world through an inherent and natural process. Thus the earth was *given birth to:* "the Orphic world-egg was laid and hatched."[8] This earlier description of the creation process, as an internal and organic process, is very similar to the account found in many Taoist texts where one frequently finds the language of procreation used to describe the origins of the world. Perhaps the most famous of these references is found in chapter 42 of the *Daode jing* in which the Tao is said to have given birth to the One and the One to the two followed by the birth of the ten thousand things. With Plato's introduction of a craftsman god this kind of cosmic unity, so similar to Taoist notions, is broken and a distance is introduced between the divine or rational world and the material world of pale formal imitation.

Obviously, for Western cultures, one of the most powerful and pervasive images of creation out of chaos is found in Genesis 1:1–2 (RSV). While the term "chaos" is not employed specifically, it is evident that a chaotic state of affairs is being outlined. The imagery used refers to formlessness, darkness, a vast watery expanse,[9] and the void. Subsequent to the creation of the heavens and the earth, God observes that the earth lacked form and was void. In what follows God begins the process of imposing divisions upon the results of the initial phase of his creative act. He separates light from darkness and thus day from night. He then divides the waters by creating the firmament.[10] There is a definite sense of succeeding layers of order and division and the language of governance is applied to the product of creation. God gathers the waters under the heavens in one place so that dry land appears, and then He calls the dry land earth. God continues by creating lights in the heavens which make it possible to give proper sequence to day and night as well as to the seasons and the years; the "two great lights" of the sun and moon are said to rule over day and night.

Over and above the order imposed by God, there is a further sense of restraint and control over the results of the divine act of creation: having completed the earth and the heavens, God elects to give humanity *dominion* over all that has been created. "Dominion" implies the existence of a lord or master who occupies a position of sovereignty and control over all that has been made. In the Genesis account the world comes together when the dark void of chaos is molded into something. Order and structure are imposed through God's efforts and then humankind is given an ongoing role as steward over the results of God's labor. This account is very reminiscent of Plato's creator. External order is brought to bear on primordial chaos and the result, as we are told in Genesis and the *Timaeus,* is good.

Generally, chaos in a Western cultural context is something which must be overcome and then held at bay. The positive results of creative energy are measured in terms of the degree to which order, stability, and predictability can be seen to hold sway. Timaeus's creator imparted a rational structure to the world so that it became amenable to human intelligence. A world without rational underpinnings would be incomprehensible to all but the creator. In Genesis God sets about forming the world through a process of shaping and dividing. In both cases chaos is at best a dumb, raw material which requires the guiding hand of an intelligent creator with design and purpose in mind.

In Taoist texts, chaos (*hundun*) is full of creative potential. It is whole and has its own inner "logic." Within the *Daode jing* and the *Zhuangzi* and the texts of alchemy, chaos is what precedes the series of transformations which yields the world as we know it. Strictly speaking the cosmogonic process is not so much one of creation as it is of internal transformation (*zaohua*). Here chaos does not stand in opposition to order; instead it is like a single cell which, through mitosis, gradually yields an organism of increasing complexity. As in the Genesis account, divisions are part of the process but they arise naturally from within. Rather than being associated with a "subduing" they are an internal development. Chaos, pregnant with possibilities, is the point of origin and the state to which things will eventually return. The place of chaos in Taoist cosmogony appears to bear little resemblance to its place in the thought of Plato or Genesis. These culturally foundational texts are the sources of the Western vocabularies and commonsense ideas that have shaped the contemporary Western concept of chaos. This principally European and North American idea of chaos is far removed from the more positive role of *hundun* found frequently in Taoist texts.

II. Inner Alchemy: An Overview

Inner alchemy is a way of cultivation which combines the cultivation of nature (*xing*) and life (*ming*). Translating these two terms requires the avoidance of absolute dichotomies such as mind and body. It is the *qi*, coursing through and constituting the body, which places life on a continuum with the nature. *Qi* defies the hard categorical distinctions invoked by philosophers such as Locke and Descartes in the speculations of their Anglo-European philosophy of mind.[11] These distinctions made it possible, indeed necessary, to assert the existence of two separate ontological species so that the mind could be associated with the nonspatial and nontemporal while the body could be held to occupy both space and time along with the rest of the "material universe." *Qi,* on the other hand, provides the basis for a pervasive underlying set of assumptions about the integrated nature of the person and the concomitant need to address all dimensions of the individual if a process of cultivation such as inner alchemy is to succeed.

This sense of a continuum on which the poles of nature and life are situated is reflected in a conversation between the founder of the Complete Reality (*Quanzhen*) school, Wang Chongyang (1112–70), and one of his disciples, Ma Danyang (1123–83). Ma enquires about what are designated by the terms "nature" and "life," and his teacher responds by explaining that nature is the original spirit while life is the original *qi*.[12] What this means is that nature, as spirit, is also *qi* and so is only separated from the original *qi* by its relative degree of clarity or purity. It is not different in kind, and, rarefied though it may be, the original spirit is not the final state to be reached as even original spirit can become coextensive with the great void, often referred to as "the limitless" (*Wuji*), which is synonymous with chaos and the Tao. Within the process of inner alchemy one can think of life (*ming*) as the foundational level of *qi* which supports the process of consolidating and strengthening the spirit (*shen*) so that a return to the Tao becomes possible. Life is more closely associated with the *qi* which animates the body, and its abundant presence and free flow throughout the body brings with it good health. Clearly though, this foundational position should not necessarily be taken as implying that life must be cultivated first while attention to the spirit comes later. The two are cultivated together, as is reflected in the phrase which came to be a stock characterization of inner alchemy: "dual cultivation of nature and life" (*xingming shuangxiu*).[13]

Inner alchemy draws upon Confucian, Buddhist, and Taoist strains of thought. By the time of the Southern Song Dynasty, neo-Confucian ideas were also very influential. The cosmological speculations of Zhou Dunyi (1017–73), for example, were taken very seriously by the great Southern Song inner alchemist Li Daochun (fl. 1288–90). The result of this syncretic tendency is a method of training which involves a variety of activities such as performing various exercises and breathing techniques. Included also are an element of moral training (achieved, at least in part, through the practice of good works) and, finally, at the center of the practice, meditation. Through meditation the adept brings about a self-transformation from within. The language used to describe this process of transformation employs terminology taken from the way of outer alchemy (*waidan*), which sought to transform the individual by means of the ritual production of elixirs. These elixirs were compounded through the mixing and heating of various minerals or plants. The tools of the operative alchemist, such as the stove (*lu*), the sealed reaction vessel (*ding*), and the fire, which was carefully regulated through various phases of heating and cooling, were adopted by the inner alchemist as metaphorical representations of processes which occurred within the body of the adept throughout the training. Inner alchemical texts are also full of references to the sixty-four hexagrams of the *Yi jing* (Classic of Changes) and the eight trigrams (*bagua*), as well as to the system of the five phases (*wuxing*) and the dynamic interaction between *yin* and *yang*.

This form of alchemy is often designated "inner" because the raw ingredients of the inner alchemist are found within the body. The primary ingredients are three forms of *qi*: The first is *jing* or "essence," which is associated with various fluids and secretions in the body. In inner alchemy, *jing* is usually related to the reproductive potential of the body, and so is often linked to the fluids associated with sexual reproduction. The second ingredient is simply referred to as *qi*, the animating principle within the body. In this context *qi* must be understood as a subcategory of an anterior or primary *qi* out of which the three ingredients presently being described arise. The final ingredient is *shen* or "spirit," which supports mental processes. One of the most famous practitioners of inner alchemy, Zhang Boduan (d. 1082), describes these three ingredients in the following way:

As for refining the essence it is the original essence [which is refined] not the [kind of] essence which is influenced by lewd and depraved [behavior].

As for refining the *qi* it is the original *qi* [which is refined] not the [kind of] *qi* [which is] exhaled and inhaled [through the] mouth and nose.

As for refining the spirit it is the original spirit [which is refined] not the [kind of] spirit [which is involved in] the anxious thoughts of the mind.[14]

Zhang is very explicit that the student of inner alchemy should not confound the three primary ingredients with the functions that they support. In this way Zhang guards against the possibility of understanding the language of inner alchemy in any literal sense which might lead the adept to conclude that it simply describes a method for prolonging life or even avoiding death altogether, and that this method is one which rests primarily on cultivation of bodily health through focusing exclusively on breathing exercises and various gymnastic techniques.

The process of training is described as a gathering of essence, which constitutes a form of raw "energy"[15] that can be transformed into *qi*. The gathering and strengthening of the *qi* then provides for the transformation of *qi* into spirit. It is through the strengthening of spirit that the adept is finally able to return to emptiness. This process is described by Zhang Boduan in his brief treatise on the Golden Elixir, entitled *Jindan sibai zi* (Four Hundred Words on the Golden Elixir):

Take the [original] essence and transform it into the [original] *qi;*
Take the [original] *qi* and transform it into the [original] spirit;
Take the [original] spirit and transform it into emptiness.[16]

Throughout inner alchemical literature the prevailing themes are those of gathering as opposed to depleting, inversion or reversal, and integration—which might also be described as the reestablishment of unity. It is important to understand these activities as ways of living rather than as static endpoints toward which the adept moves. The sage is one who has shifted his or her mode of being from that of "later heaven" (or, acquired), which is the way of decay, complexity, and attachment, to that of "earlier heaven" (or, innate), which is the way of life or robust health, simplicity, unity, and detachment. The Buddhist metaphor of the lotus—with its roots in the dirt but with its flower in the clear air—is also appropriate in this context. In what follows, some of the continuities which exist between this way of training and the ideas expressed in the *Zhuangzi* and the *Daode jing* will be described.

III. Chaos as Creative Potential, Unity, and Completeness[17]

In the second chapter of the *Yunji qiqian,* under the heading *Hundun,* the chaos which precedes the successive divisions of creation is described as resembling a chicken's egg.[18] In Taoist texts the egg is an important image employed to convey some of the qualities associated with the ineffable primordial state of chaos. The egg is a source of new life, which emerges in all of its complexity out of the egg's simple structure. It is also a unity unto itself, enclosed with no openings to the world outside; the preservation of its creative potential depends on this structural integrity right up to the moment when that potentiality is actualized in the emergence of new life. Both of these features are related in the texts of early Taoism and both are of central importance in the cultivation of the inner elixir.

Within the cosmogonic scheme of the emerging universe, chaos is the state which precedes division. As such it can be identified with the Tao, from which all that is proceeds. This unfolding of creation is described in the *Daode jing:*

> The Way gave birth to the One.
> The One gave birth to the two.
> The two gave birth to the three.
> And the three gave birth to the ten thousand things. (chapter 42)[19]

Earlier in the *Daode jing,* descriptions of this primordial undifferentiated state are offered:

> There was something formed out of chaos,[20]
> That was born before Heaven and Earth.
> Quiet and still! Pure and deep!
> It stands on its own and doesn't change.
> It can be regarded as the mother of Heaven and Earth.
> I do not yet know its name:
> I "style" it "the Way."
> Were I forced to give it a name, I would call it "the Great."
>   (chapter 25)[21]

Earlier, in chapter 21, the Tao is described as shapeless and formless. It is hidden and obscure. Furthermore, the Tao is empty "like an abyss! It seems to be the ancestor of the ten thousand things."[22]

In the texts of inner alchemy these descriptions of the creative potentiality of the chaotic Tao are applied to the human body and to the arising of its constituent forms of *qi,* which emerge out of the pristine original and unified *qi* of earlier heaven. In the foreword to an inner alchemical text, Weng Baoguang (fl. 1173) describes the emergence of the original, unified *qi* as follows:

Prior to the time when chaos had not yet appeared there was [only]
     empty
nonbeing, alone, silent, and nameless.
If forced to give it a name [I] call it Tao.
Tao descends giving birth to the unified *qi.*
Motionless it is not still; neither muddied nor clear,
Abstruse it is impossible to fathom.
The sages, compelled to explain it, call it the *qi* of true unity of the
     chaotic beginning.
The unified *qi* having split then transforms becoming *yin* and *yang.*
As for *yin* and *yang,* they are heaven and earth.
As for male and female, they are also heaven and earth.
Heaven and earth [mix their] generative vapors and the myriad things
     are transformed and purified.
Male and female copulate and the myriad things are transformed and
     created.[23]

In this inner alchemical text, we have an obvious thematic reiteration of division emerging from unity. There is also an intensification of the *Daode jing's* procreative account, as the place given to heaven and earth in this scheme is that of male and female progenitors which engage in a kind of sexual union, thereby occasioning the creative transformations giving rise to the "myriad things," which in turn constitute the world. The text goes on to explain that these events all take place within the body and that they must be comprehended if the elixir of immortality, also described as a fetus moving through the nine moons of gestation, is to take shape. A second passage taken from the *Wuzhen pian* (Chapters on Awakening to the Real) explains the same process of internal creation using phrases which more closely parallel the "One ... two ... three" progression contained in chapter 42 of the *Daode jing:*

From empty nonbeing the Tao produces a single *qi;*
then from this single *qi, yin* and *yang* are given birth.
Yin and *yang* then come together to give birth to the three substances;
these three substances further produce the splendor of the ten thousand
     things.[24]

The "three substances" refer to the three forms of *qi* to which the single *qi* gives rise. They are the essence, *qi,* and spirit mentioned earlier. This internal microcosmic cosmogony is described frequently in inner alchemical literature, and it takes full advantage of the cosmogonic scheme laid out in the *Daode jing.* The sage understands the significance of these events for his own practice and is aware of the need to reverse this process within his own body:

Therefore the sage gathers the unified *qi* of earlier heaven and prepares
    the elixir.
Refining his form he returns to unified *qi*.
Refining the *qi* it returns to spirit. Refining spirit it is joined with the
    Tao returning to the form without form.[25]

Here the sage recognizes the significance of this cosmogonic process recounted in the *Daode jing* and knows that preparation of the Golden Elixir
requires its reversal. The creation, out of chaos, of the inner world is really
only the starting place from which the practice of inner alchemy proceeds.
To the adept, chaos, or the Tao, or the unified *qi* is not merely the starting
place out of which the inner universe emerges, it is also the place of completion. A life reconfigured to emulate the way of "earlier heaven" is a life
which is redirected back toward this origin.

Chapter 40 of the *Daode jing* offers the following comment on the nature
of the Tao:

> "Reversal" is the movement of the Tao;
> "Weakness" is the function of the Tao.
> The things of the world originate in being,
> And being originates in nonbeing.[26]

Hence chaos, equated here with nonbeing, is the place to which all things
return. Again this return is described:

> Take emptiness to the limit;
> Maintain tranquillity in the center.
> The ten thousand things—side-by-side they arise;
> And by this I see their return.
> Things [come forth] in great numbers;
> Each one returns to its root.[27]
> This is called tranquillity. (chapter 16)[28]

Moving back to inner alchemy, *Wuzhen pian* (Chapters on Awakening to
the Real) draws on this theme of reversion:

The ten thousand things flourish and each reverts to the root;
by reverting to the root and restoring life [you will] lengthen [your
    years].[29]
To know the constant and revert to the root, people find difficult to
    understand;
[but] reckless practices which bring misfortune are known to
    everyone.[30]

The challenge for the adept of inner alchemy is to move toward reintegration, re-union. This is envisioned as a shedding by the mind of complexity

and attachment, which leads the thoughts astray and causes one to become lost. It is also a reintegration which depends upon and is interwoven with the cultivation of *qi* within the body. Two descriptions of this process are usually offered. The first, mentioned previously, involves the successive transmutation of the essence, *qi,* and spirit, culminating in the transformation of spirit into emptiness. The second involves a correlation of five different forms of *qi* with the five directions and five of the internal organs.

The *qi* of the north, south, east, and west, which are correlated with the kidneys, heart, liver, and lungs, respectively, are brought together in the center, which is occupied by the spleen, before being circulated throughout the body. The spleen is correlated with the center but is also understood by the alchemist to represent "true intention" or perhaps "true thought" (*zhen yi*) which is established through seated meditation. By means of disciplined practice the adept is able to maintain the center and by doing so is able to reintegrate the four forms of *qi* corresponding to the cardinal directions. This movement of the four forms of *qi* back into the center is often couched in the language of the *Yi jing,* so that this process may also be described in terms of the four signs (*si xiang*) moving back into the *Taiji* (Great Ultimate) and finally into *Wuji* (the limitless). *Wuji,* which can be identified with the original, unified *qi* out of which the universe (macrocosmic and microcosmic) is born, first divides into *yin* and *yang,* also known as the "paired forms" represented in the *Yi jing* by one solid and one broken line. These two "forms" (or lines) then combine to form the "four signs" which are all the possible permutations generated by the combination of the *yin* and *yang* lines. The alchemist employs meditation to reenact this cosmogonic sequence internally and in reverse. Here, too, the narrative employed to give shape to the alchemist's practice draws upon the themes of unity and completeness embodied in chaos.

Another feature of chaos exploited in the formulation of inner alchemical practice is its completeness. The movement toward unity and integration is brought about through seated meditation, during which the adept's body is held perfectly still and all thoughts are let go. The *Daode jing* states, "Take emptiness to the limit; maintain tranquillity in the center." In a deep meditative state, during which the stillness of the center is maintained, the adept becomes self-contained, complete, sealed up. Nothing can enter and nothing can escape. Ye Shibiao (fl. 1202) says, "[You] must be empty both internally and externally and understand that inside and out the luster of gems pervades. If [you] establish [even] a single grain of dust [within your mind] then there will be a complete leaking out."[31] This attention to the potential for leakage is a common concern in the texts of inner alchemy. It refers to the draining of both body and mind which results from a lack of internal stillness and stability. Zhang Boduan urges students to learn from his teachings so that the body's completeness is not compromised:

The words of the ten thousand scrolls and scriptures of the immortals
    are all the same;
the Golden Elixir, only this is the foundational teaching. . . .
Do not blame the intelligence bestowed by heaven for complete
    leaking out and exhaustion.[32]

This notion of internal stability and completeness is another feature of chaos
which is sustained as long as the integrity of its undifferentiated nature remains uncompromised. A chapter in the *Zhuangzi* entitled "Fit for Emperors
and Kings" includes the well-known story of Mr. Hundun ("Mr. Chaos"):

> The emperor of the South Sea was called Shu (Brief), the emperor of
> the North Sea was called Hu (Sudden), and the emperor of the central
> region was called Hun-tun (Chaos). Shu and Hu from time to time
> came together for a meeting in the territory of Hun-tun, and Hun-tun
> treated them very generously. Shu and Hu discussed how they could
> repay his kindness. "All men," they said, "have seven openings so they
> can see, hear, eat, and breathe. But Hun-tun alone doesn't have any.
> Let's try boring him some!"
>
> Every day they bored another hole, and on the seventh day Hun-tun
> died.[33]

The alchemist must avoid the fate of emperor Hundun by preserving his
own internal state of chaos. This is achieved by closing the apertures of the
senses and insulating himself from potentially distracting external influences.
Wang Chongyang, the master of Complete Reality Taoism, describes this
self-contained meditative state in the following passage:

> True meditation requires that within the twelve double hours, while
> standing, walking, sitting or lying down, during every activity, the
> mind neither moves nor flickers, just like Mount T'ai, and it bars the
> four door-ways: the eyes, the ears, the mouth, and the nose do not let
> the external world enter the inner spheres [of the body]. But if there is
> the slightest moving thought, it cannot be called "quiet meditation."[34]

The primordial state of chaos is maintained if the adept is able to follow the
advice of Master Wang, which echoes the admonition in chapters 52 and
56 of the *Daode jing* to "block up the holes" and "close the doors."[35] In
doing so the dust can then settle—"This is called Profound Union."[36] The
Zhuangzi describes this closed, meditative state, somewhat paradoxically, as
"fasting of the mind" (*xinzhai*) and "mind nourishment" (*yangxin*). In the
following passage, taken from "In the World of Men," Confucius provides
instructions on meditation to Cloud General (*Yunjiang*):

> Make your will one. Don't listen with your ears, listen with your mind.
> Don't listen with your mind, listen with your *qi*. Listening stops at the

ear and the mind comes to rest on [what is] agreeable. As for the *qi* it is empty and attends to all things. Only the Tao gathers in emptiness. [And,] it is emptiness [which] is the fasting of the mind.[37]

So, in order to make way for the Tao, there must be emptiness within, and emptiness proceeds from "making the will one." Making the will one is another way of saying, prevent the fragmentation of the will or intention. One must not let it be pulled in many directions by external influences. The adept of the Golden Elixir understands these instructions to preserve unity of intent as extending to everyday life. As Wang Chongyang stated above, the mind does not flicker even while walking, standing, or sitting through the entire day. Thus, the body must not be worn down by seeking for fame and wealth; both of these merely wear down the body, draining it of its valuable inner treasures.

The *Zhuangzi* comments on this link between conventional desires and the health of the individual. At the end of chapter 5 the text frames this connection in terms of the preferences which drive behavior and tax the body. *Zhuangzi* becomes frustrated in a conversation he is having with his friend Huizi about whether a person can remain a person even if they lack emotions (*qing*). *Zhuangzi* tries once to explain that that is not what he means, and restates his point about how a person can be a person while having the kind of detached view of the world he is trying to convey. He describes the realized person in the following way:

> The Way gave him a face; Heaven gave him a form. He doesn't let likes and dislikes get in and do him harm. You, now—you treat your spirit like an outsider. You wear out your energy, leaning on a tree and moaning, slumping at your desk and dozing—Heaven picked out a body for you and you use it to gibber about the "hard" and "white"![38]

This passage explains that being without emotions simply means that one's inner state is not subjected to the destructive force (literally, "injury") of emotional turmoil that arises from an attachment to one's likes and dislikes. The text continues with *Zhuangzi* berating Huizi for exhausting his body by preoccupying himself with futile discussion of various logical conundrums which he refers to here as the "hard and white."

The exhaustion of the body is described as treating the spirit (*shen*) like an outsider; this can be understood as failing to keep the spirit preserved within. Instead it is focused on external interests and so is weakened. *Zhuangzi* also explains that such wrongheaded behavior belabors and wears down the body's reserve of essence (*jing*). *Zhuangzi* appears to see Huizi's interest in logic as leading him away from the more natural course of action which can be followed by listening to the relative state of the body's health. Here one senses a definite anticipation of the more systematic approach to cultivation developed much later in the texts of Golden Elixir alchemy. This kind of observation is reminiscent of Wang Chongyang's advice to "not let the external world enter the inner spheres [of the body]." If due care is not taken the "inner spheres" of the body can be compromised and weakened. Again this concern is voiced by Zhang Boduan in the following verse,

> Simply coveting profit and favor, seeking honor and fame,
> not caring for the body and suffering the distress and decay of
>   ignorance.
> Let me ask, if you piled up gold as high as a mountain peak,
> at the end of your life could you prevent death from coming?

The avoidance of worldly "traps" is a necessary prerequisite to "sealing off" the mind from the myriad distractions which prevent the establishment of true intention.

Once the adept has cultivated a sufficient degree of detachment from the conventional worldly preoccupations with wealth and fame, it is possible to sit quietly and allow reintegration to occur spontaneously, along the Tao's path of return to primordial, undifferentiated chaos:

> Smash your form and body, spit out hearing and eyesight, forget you are a thing among other things, and you may join in great unity with the deep and boundless. Undo the mind, slough off spirit, be blank and soulless, and the ten thousand things one by one will return to the root—return to the root and not know why. Dark and undifferentiated chaos—to the end of life, none will depart from it.[39]

13

Through Detachment to Vision

Chuang Tzu and Meister Eckhart

JOSEPH H. WONG, O.S.B. CAM.

Meister Eckhart's thought has often been compared with Buddhism. My paper is an attempt to compare Eckhart and Chuang Tzu, commonly considered the second patriarch of Taoism. The purpose of the comparison is to illustrate the similarity in their views of the relation between emptiness, or detachment, and true vision. The two terms "detachment" and "vision" in the title stand for "purity of heart" and "contemplation," respectively. While Chuang Tzu is often represented as a hermit, the monastic dimension of Eckhart will be pointed out in the discussion.

Although the texts of the *Lao-tzu* and of the *Chuang-tzu* have inspired different types of Taoist meditation, this paper does not deal with meditation practice but with Chuang Tzu's insight that true light or vision comes from emptying the mind. This insight is expressed in various chapters of the *Chuang-tzu,* but especially in chapter 6, entitled "The Great Teacher" (*ta-chung-shih*). For a similar view in Eckhart I find two of his treatises very pertinent: *On Detachment* and *The Nobleman.* In my presentation I shall develop the following points: (1) vision through emptiness in Chuang Tzu; (2) the manifestation of the divine image in humans through detachment according to Meister Eckhart; (3) A comparison of Chuang Tzu and Eckhart.

I. Vision through Emptiness: Chuang Tzu

True Knowledge of a True Person

In chapter 6, "The Great Teacher," the *Chuang-tzu* describes the image of a "true person" (*chen-jen*) in great detail. For Chuang Tzu, a "true person" means an accomplished person, one who has obtained Tao. Chuang Tzu also employs other terms for the same purpose, such as "perfect person," "spiritual person," or "sage." It is debatable whether the "Great Teacher," the title of this chapter, means Tao or the "true person" who has attained Tao. Probably Chuang Tzu intentionally leaves the meaning open so as to include both interpretations.

The following are some of the descriptions of a "true person" given by Chuang Tzu in this chapter:

What is meant by a true person? The true person of old did not mind having little, did not brag about accomplishments, and did not scheme about things. . . . Being of this character, he could scale heights without fear, enter water without getting wet, and go through fire without feeling hot. . . . The true person of old knew neither to love life nor to hate death. He did not rejoice in birth, nor did he resist death. Without any concern he came and without any concern he went, that was all.[1]

Therefore, a true person is one who is utterly free and unfettered, not attached to or concerned with anything, including even life and death.

Early in the chapter, Chuang Tzu makes a striking statement, connecting the idea of "true person" to that of "true knowledge" (*chen-chi*): "There must be the true person before there can be true knowledge."[2] It is not easy to define what Chuang Tzu means by "true knowledge." The opening reflection of the chapter may shed some light:

He who knows the activities of Heaven and the activities of humans is perfect. He who knows the activities of Heaven lives according to Heaven. He who knows the activities of humans nourishes what he does not know with what he does know, thus completing his natural span of life and will not die prematurely half of the way. This is knowledge at its supreme greatness.[3]

Thus true knowledge here means knowing the activities of heaven and of humans, that is, knowing the Tao as reflected in their activities. Chuang Tzu believes that only a "true person" can acquire "true knowledge." This shows that in his understanding, true knowledge is not merely an intellectual pursuit; rather, it depends on the cultivation of the whole person. This view of the unity between knowledge and the way of life or spirituality is typical of the *Chuang-tzu,* and of Eastern thought in general.[4]

In view of the profound and mysterious character of its object, which is nothing less than Tao itself, true knowledge is described by Chuang Tzu as "not knowing." Thus in chapter 22 No-Beginning says, "Not to know is profound; to know is shallow. Not to know is to be on the inside; to know is to be on the outside."[5] Chuang Tzu distinguishes two different ways of knowing: to know through knowing and to know through unknowing. In a fictitious dialogue, Confucius is reported to say to his disciple Yen Hui: "You have heard of flying with wings, but you have never heard of flying without wings. You have heard of the knowledge through knowing, but you have never heard of the knowledge through unknowing."[6] The true knowledge of a true person is a knowing through unknowing.

The meaning of "knowing through unknowing" is best conveyed in the opening story of chapter 22, in which Knowledge poses some questions about acquiring knowledge of Tao to three different personages. He begins his enquiry with Do-Nothing-Say-Nothing:

> Knowledge said to Do-Nothing-Say-Nothing, "There are some things I'd like to ask you. What sort of pondering, what sort of cogitation does it take to know Tao? What sort of surroundings, what sort of practices does it take to find rest in Tao? What sort of path, what sort of procedure will get me to Tao?" Three questions he asked, but Do-Nothing-Say-Nothing didn't answer. It wasn't that he just didn't answer—he didn't know *how* to answer![7]

Knowledge put the same questions to Wild-and-Witless, who said that he knew the answer. But just as he was about to say something, he forgot what it was he was going to say.

Knowledge, failing to get any answer, returned to the imperial palace, where he was received in audience by the Yellow Emperor, and posed his three questions.

> The Yellow Emperor said: "Only when there is no pondering and no cogitation will you get to know Tao. Only when you have no surroundings and follow no practices will you find rest in Tao. Only when there is no path and no procedure can you get to Tao."
>
> Knowledge said to the Yellow Emperor, "You and I know, but those other two that I asked didn't know. Which of us is right, I wonder?" The Yellow Emperor said, "Do-Nothing-Say-Nothing—he's the one who is truly right. Wild-and-Witless appears to be so. You and I in the end are nowhere near it. Those who know do not speak; those who speak do not know."[8]

The story tells several things. First, only when there is no pondering and no cogitation will one get to know Tao. True knowledge of Tao is not the result of analytical, discursive thinking; rather, it is an intuitive knowledge. Second, he who truly knows does not speak. Third, the knowledge of one who knows that he knows is imperfect. One who truly knows does not even know that he knows.

Sitting in Forgetfulness

In the chapter, "The Great Teacher," where we find the statement that "there must be the true person before there can be true knowledge," Chuang Tzu also presents concrete teaching about how to become a true person and so to acquire true knowledge. His teaching in this regard is given especially through two stories: "sitting in forgetfulness" and "seeing the One in the

brightness of dawn." The theme of "sitting in forgetfulness" is again presented in a fabricated conversation between Confucius and his disciple Yen
Hui. One day Yen Hui told the Master that he had made some progress by
forgetting humanity and righteousness. Confucius said that it was good, but
not enough. On another day Yen Hui said that he had made some progress
by having forgotten ceremonies and music. Still, the Master said that it was
not enough. Finally, Yen Hui saw Confucius again and said:

> "I have made some progress." "What do you mean?" asked Confucius.
> Yen Hui said, "I sit in forgetfulness." Confucius changed countenance
> and said, "What do you mean by sitting in forgetfulness?" "I cast aside
> my limbs," said Yen Hui, "discard my intelligence, detach from both
> body and mind, and become one with the Great Universal (*ta-t'ung*).
> This is what I mean by sitting in forgetfulness."[9]

"Sitting in forgetfulness" is later taken to mean a meditation practice of
sitting quietly and emptying the mind completely. The term "sitting" in the
expression of "sitting in forgetfulness" clearly means a state of quiet and
tranquillity. "Forgetfulness" means casting aside the limbs or the body and
discarding intelligence or knowledge of the mind. On the one hand, it means
keeping the bodily desires under control and not being fettered by them; on
the other, it means abandoning the use of the reasoning mind, putting aside
its conceptual, analytical activities.[10]

However, forgetting is only the negative aspect of "sitting in forgetfulness." "Forgetting" is a preparation or disposition for something positive
which is described as "becoming one with the Great Universal." According
to Ch'eng Hsuan-ying, a seventh-century Buddhist monk who wrote a major
commentary on the *Chuang-tzu*, the "Great Universal" means the "Great
Tao," which gives birth to the myriad things in the universe.[11] Rather than a
speculative, analytical knowledge, the experience of being one with Tao is an
intuitive, experiential knowledge through participation in and identification
with Tao.[12]

Seeing the One in the Brightness of Dawn

In another colloquy of the same chapter, Chuang Tzu teaches how to achieve
enlightenment, or the vision of Tao, through detachment. In this narrative
Nü-yü shows the way toward "seeing the One in the brightness of dawn":

> Nan-po Tzu-k'uei asked Nü-yü, "You are old but have the look of a
> child. How is this?" "I have learned Tao," replied Nü-yü. "Can Tao
> be learned?" Nan-po Tzu-k'uei said.
>   "Ah! How can it?" replied Nü-yü. "You are not the type of man.
> Pu-liang Yi had the ability of the sage but did not know the way. I
> knew the way but did not have his ability. I wanted to teach him so he

could become a sage. But that was not such a simple case. It seemed easy to teach the doctrines of a sage to a man with his ability. But I still had to teach and keep at him. It was three days before he was able to disregard worldly matters. After he disregarded worldly matters, I kept at him for seven days more and then he was able to disregard all material things. After he disregarded all material things, I kept at him for nine days more and then he was able to disregard his own life and death. Having disregarded life and death, he became as clear and bright as the dawn. Having become as clear and bright as the dawn, he was able to see the One. Having seen the One, he was then able to abolish the distinction of past and present. Having abolished the past and present, he was then able to enter the realm of neither life nor death.... This is called tranquillity in disturbance. Tranquillity in disturbance means that it is especially in disturbance that tranquillity becomes perfect."[13]

In this passage Chuang Tzu makes a distinction between the "ability" and the "way" of becoming a sage. According to Ch'eng Hsuan-ying's commentary, the "way" of becoming a sage consists in humility, eagerness, attention, and simplicity, while "ability" means intelligence and cleverness in learning. Comparing the two, Ch'eng believes that possessing "ability" is something less important than knowing the "way."[14] For when someone knows the way to attaining Tao, it means one has already found Tao because real knowledge of the way to Tao can only be experiential knowledge. For this reason, to teach the "way" cannot be limited to a verbal instruction; rather, it has to do with the transmission of personal experience. That is why Nü-yü "kept at," or accompanied, his disciple Pu-liang Yi.

In this episode, Nü-yü gives an account of a journey toward enlightenment and vision of the One, consisting in a progressive exercise of renunciation. I have adopted the word "disregard" for the Chinese character *wai*, which literally means "outside." Here it is used as a verb meaning "putting something outside" of oneself, or "laying aside" something. Both Kuo Hsiang and Ch'eng Hsuan-ying explain *wai* as "forgetting," in the sense of "disregarding," "transcending." The object of forgetting follows a certain gradation: from worldly matters, through material things, to one's own life and existence. In agreement with Kuo Hsiang's interpretation of "material things" as things that meet our daily needs, Ch'eng believes that it is more exacting to forget "material things" than to disregard "worldly matters" or happenings in the world, which, important as they are, remain remote. But, of the three, the most difficult is to disregard one's own existence, to be unconcerned with life and death.[15] The discussion on life and death actually constitutes a major theme of this chapter on "The Great Teacher." A "true person" is one who does not lose equanimity and serenity in the face of his own death or that of his loved ones.

After Pu-liang Yi had accomplished the threefold detachment—that is, from worldly matters, material things, and concern with life and death—all of a sudden, as though the morning sun had risen in his mind, he was able to see the One in the brightness of dawn. Seeing the One is presented as the climax of the entire episode. The Chinese character for the "One" in this passage is *tu,* which means "alone," "single," or "absolute." *Tu* is a major epithet for Tao in the *Chuang-tzu,* as well as in the *Lao-tzu.*[16] The rising of dawn and seeing of the One are actually two sides of the same coin. The point which Chuang Tzu wishes to make is that enlightenment is not a merely subjective phenomenon; rather, it is the result of an encounter with a mysterious, yet concrete, reality.[17] The sudden eruption of light is due to the presence and manifestation of Tao. Thus, enlightenment can be described as a mystical experience of Tao when a person's mind has become empty and clear.[18]

A similar view is presented in another well-known conversation between Confucius and Yen Hui, on "fasting of the mind." Confucius concludes with the following words: "Tao gathers only in emptiness. Emptiness is the fasting of the mind."[19] This means that Tao finds a fitting dwelling place in an empty mind. In a later paragraph of the chapter, we hear Confucius discuss "flying without wings" and "knowing with unknowing." Then the Master utters the mysterious sentence: "Look into that closed room, the empty chamber where brightness is born!"[20] Here the "empty chamber" means an empty mind where brightness arises. According to Ch'eng Hsuan-ying, the "brightness" is Tao.[21] Tao shines forth in a mind that is empty and free, thus rendering the person enlightened. Similarly, the episode of Nü-yü teaches that when a person's mind has become empty and nonattached, Tao shines forth and manifests itself to him.

Compared to Lao Tzu, Chuang Tzu is far more concerned with the meaning of Tao as the subjective state reflected in humans. However, one can also find passages in the *Chuang-tzu* in which the author discusses explicitly the objective, metaphysical significance of Tao. One of the most important passages in this regard is found toward the beginning of the chapter on "The Great Teacher":

Tao has reality and evidence, but no action and form. It may be transmitted, but cannot be received. It may be attained to, but cannot be seen. It is its own source, its own root. Before heaven and earth came into being, Tao existed by itself from all time. It gave spirits and rulers their spiritual powers. It created heaven and earth. It is above the Zenith but it is not high. It is beneath the nadir but it is not low.

It is prior to heaven and earth but it is not old. It is more ancient than the highest antiquity but is not regarded as old.[22]

Here Tao is depicted as the ultimate reality or all-embracing first principle that produces the universe. Tao exists by and through itself: "it is its own source, its own root." Without beginning or end, it is eternal. All things in the universe depend upon it to be constantly brought into being. This passage clearly points to the ontological status of Tao.

By applying the epithet *tu* (the "One") to Tao, Chuang Tzu wants to say that Tao is something absolute, independent, and without peer. It exists by itself and is sufficient unto itself. The term *tu* points to the fact that Tao is absolutely transcendent. Paradoxically, however, Tao is immanent in the world as much as it is transcendent. The idea that Tao is present and inherent in all things is clearly brought forth in a dialogue between Chuang Tzu and Master Tung-kuo:

> Master Tung-kuo asked Chuang Tzu, "This thing called Tao—where does it exist?" Chuang Tzu said, "There's no place it doesn't exist." "Come," said Master Tung-kuo, "you must be more specific!" "It is in the ant." "As low a thing as that?" "It is in the panic grass." "But that's lower still!" "It is in the tiles and shards." "How can it be so low?" "It is in the dung." Master Tung-kuo made no reply.[23]

Thus, the transcendent Tao is present in all things, high and low, great and small.

When Chuang Tzu says, "the sage's mind in stillness is the mirror of heaven and earth, the glass that reflects the myriad things,"[24] he means that a sage's mind, which is empty and clear, is able to perceive the presence of Tao in the myriad things. As a consequence of its presence in all things, "Tao identifies them all as one (*Tao-t'ung-wei-yi*)."[25] In this way, the One, by being present in the many, turns the many into one. The sage is able to perceive this truth and realize that "the universe and I exist together, and all things and I are one."[26] This is true enlightenment. It is the presence of Tao in all things that abolishes distinctions among the myriad things and eliminates humans' clinging to particular objects.

The episode of Nü-yü conveys the same teaching. Through a progressive process of forgetting and self-emptying, a detached person finally achieves enlightenment. He sees the One in the myriad things and perceives the unity of all things. Nü-yü tells of his disciple Pu-liang Yi: "Having seen the One, he was then able to abolish the distinction of past and present. Having abolished the past and present, he was then able to enter the realm of neither life nor death."[27] Thus, Tao not only eliminates distinctions in things, but also abolishes distinction of past and present, death and life, so that an enlightened person may attain immortality.

II. Manifestation of the Divine Image in Humans through Detachment: Meister Eckhart

Detachment as Perfect Likeness to God

The *Chuang-tzu* states: "There must be the true person before there can be true knowledge." The way to becoming a true person, and hence, to attaining true knowledge, is through a process of self-emptying, which can be described as forgetting or renunciation. For Meister Eckhart, the key word in this regard is "detachment." The well-known treatise *On Detachment* is Eckhart's attempt to portray detachment (*Abgeschiedenheit*) as the highest of all the virtues because it brings humans closest to God. John Caputo well sums up the meaning of "detachment" in Eckhart's treatise bearing that title:

> Here *Abgeschiedenheit* means the state of having cut off one's affection from everything created and creaturely, from the "world" and the "self." It is a condition of "purity" from created things, from "attachment" to them. It does not refer to a physical or spatial separation but to a detachment of the "heart" from worldly goods.[28]

Seen in this light, Eckhart's "detachment" clearly belongs to the same monastic tradition as that of Cassian's "purity of heart."[29] Eckhart's monastic dimension is probably mediated through Pseudo-Dionysius, commonly recognized as a sixth-century Syrian monk, whose writings exercised a major influence on Eckhart.[30]

Eckhart extols detachment above love. Many find this position offensive as it seems to contradict the Gospel primacy of love. Eckhart gives the following explanation: "Love constrains me to love God, but detachment compels God to love me."[31] In reality, Eckhart distinguishes between the active and passive aspects of love and considers our actively loving God as the consequence of receiving God's love for us. This latter aspect is precisely the fruit of detachment. Hence, Eckhart's primacy of detachment is in harmony with the primacy of love. According to Eckhart, detachment is not primarily an ethical category but a religious one. This means that by practicing detachment, one is rendered receptive to God. Everything wants to be in its natural place. As God's natural place is unity and purity that comes from detachment, God delights to stay in a detached heart.[32]

The key to Eckhart's claim that detachment is higher than any other virtue, even higher than love, lies in the fact that God himself is pure detachment: "For the reason why God is God is because of His immovable detachment, and from this detachment He has His purity, His simplicity and His immutability."[33] Eckhart points to detachment as the most distinctive mark of God. God is wholly "detached," completely separate from all beings as the *ens separatissimum*. To understand detachment as God's fundamental trait, one must refer to Eckhart's doctrine of God as presented in his other writings. His concept of God is based on the foundational proposition: "Existence is God" (*Esse Deus est*).[34] From this statement two conclusions are drawn: first, creatures are nothing *in themselves*, that is, insofar as they are creatures; God is the existence of things that exist. Second, from this latter statement Eckhart further deduces the paradoxical double aspect of God's immanence and transcendence. God is at once totally immanent in all things as their real existence and, by that very fact, utterly transcendent to—or detached from—them as *esse absolutum* (absolute Being).[35] In other words, God is immanent in all things as the ground of their being. But precisely as such, God exists on an entirely different level: God is not a thing among other things, or a being among other beings. God is not *this* or *that*; he is "nothing," or *no-thing*.

Thus the absolute detachment of God belongs to his metaphysical nature. In the treatise *On Detachment,* however, Eckhart wants to demonstrate that the immovable detachment of God also defines his free dealings with humans and the world. Eckhart points out that creation itself does not affect God's immovable detachment: "and you should know further that when God created heaven and earth and all creatures, this affected His unmoved detachment just as little as if no creature had ever been created."[36] What Eckhart means by this statement is that the act of creation does not change God's will. Eckhart agrees with Isidore who says: "No new *will* ever arose in God, for although a creature did not exist in itself (as it is now), yet it was before all time in God and in His reason."[37] For Eckhart all the creatures were already spoken by God in the one Word, which he uttered from eternity.[38] Eckhart further states that God is not even affected by the prayers and good works performed by humans. This highly controversial statement needs more careful explanation. What Eckhart intends to say is that, as God is above time, he is not affected by the prayers or good works accomplished by humans in time. He has answered our prayers and rewarded our good works from eternity.[39] It is in this sense that God remains unaffected by creatures and is unchangeable from eternity.

Eckhart teaches that it is through the practice of detachment that humans can achieve uniformity with God's nature. As God is "immovable detachment" by nature, humans are brought into the greatest likeness to God by the same quality:

> You should know that true detachment is nothing else but a mind that stands unmoved by all accidents of joy or sorrow, honor, shame or disgrace, as a mountain of lead stands unmoved by a breath of wind. This unmovable detachment brings a man into the greatest likeness to God.[40]

Here Eckhart explains "unmovable detachment" in terms of imperturbability and equanimity in face of the vicissitudes of life. The idea of "unmovable detachment" resembles Evagrius's *apatheia,* which Cassian renders as "purity of heart."[41]

It is clear that detachment as a moral quality in humans has primarily a religious significance. Detachment means emptying oneself of creatures so as to be filled with God: "You must know, too, that to be empty of all creatures is to be full of God, and to be full of creatures is to be empty of God."[42] Detachment conforms a person to God and draws God to oneself. Eckhart holds that, if a person's mind were detached and "able to stand formless and free of all accidentals, it would assume God's proper nature."[43] Detachment also renders a person receptive to nothing but God: "Now detachment is so nearly nothing that there is nothing subtle enough to maintain itself in detachment except God alone. He is so subtle and so simple that He can stay in a detached heart."[44] Just as God is no-thing, the royal way to God is through detachment, or the way of nothing.

Eckhart also employs another word for the idea of detachment: "letting-be" (*Gelassenheit*). It has a twofold meaning, negative as well as positive, that is, letting go of something and letting God work freely.[45] Likewise, the term "detachment" implies a double aspect, negative as well as positive: to be set free from creatures in order to be receptive to God. God only works as he finds readiness and receptivity. In this regard, Eckhart compares the human heart to a wax tablet: "If God is to write the highest on my heart, then everything called 'this and that' must be expunged from my heart, and then my heart stands in detachment. *Then* God can work the highest according to His supreme will."[46] Detachment is the highest virtue because it renders one most receptive to divine influence, which is the most decisive factor in the spiritual life. One's receptivity to God's influence is in proportion to one's uniformity with God; and uniformity with God depends on the practice of detachment.[47]

Whereas Chuang Tzu, in the chapter on "The Great Teacher," deals with the true *knowledge* of the true person, Eckhart, in the treatise *On Detachment,* is mainly concerned with demonstrating that detachment effects the highest degree of uniformity with God. However, the theme of knowledge is implied. It is even made explicit toward the end of the treatise, where Eckhart mentions knowledge of God among the fruits of detachment.[48] This is based on the Aristotelian view, shared by Eckhart and his contemporaries, that "knowledge depends on likeness."[49] Inspired by another Aristotelian axiom that, in the process of knowing, the object known is present in the knower, Eckhart formulates the following statement: "Union presupposes likeness."[50] Since detachment accomplishes the greatest likeness to God in humans, it brings about the highest knowledge of God as well as the most intimate union with him.

Manifestation of the Divine Image
Hidden in Humans

On Detachment and *The Nobleman* can be viewed as twin treatises. Whereas *On Detachment* speaks about the excellence of detachment, which brings about the highest likeness to God, *The Nobleman* depicts, through varied imagery, the realization of the "nobleman" as a result of detachment. Even though the term "detachment" is not used in this treatise, Eckhart employs similar terms, such as "forgetfulness," "removal," and "cutting away," to convey the same concept of renunciation.

The title of the treatise is taken from Eckhart's citation from Luke's Gospel: "A certain nobleman went away to a distant country to gain a kingdom for himself, and returned" (Lk 19:12). Eckhart begins his reflection by distinguishing the twofold nature in humans: body and spirit. Following Paul, he designates the body as an "outer man" or "earthly man," and he calls the spirit an "inner man," "heavenly man," or a "nobleman."[51] Eckhart likens the "inner man" to a field in which God has impressed his own image and sown the seed of divine nature, which is God's Son or God's Word. The "outer man" is compared to the enemy who has sown tares on the field.[52] God's image and God's seed are the chief metaphors used in this treatise, both referring to the same reality.

Citing Origen, Eckhart is convinced that the divine seed or image, sown and impressed by God in humans, "can indeed be covered over and hidden, but never destroyed or extinguished in itself; it glows and gleams, shines and burns and inclines without ceasing toward God."[53] In addition to this twofold metaphor of image and seed, Eckhart also uses other similes to describe the process of appearance of the divine image in the nobleman. Thus, again referring to Origen, God's image is compared to a "living fountain" in the ground of the soul: "If earth is thrown on it (that is, earthly desire) that hinders and covers it up so that it is not recognized or perceived; yet it remains living within, and when the earth that was thrown onto it from without is removed, it appears visibly."[54] The appearance of the "living fountain" hidden in the ground of the soul depends on the removal of earth, which means earthly desire.

Eckhart offers another example: that of an artist wanting to make an image from wood. Eckhart's contention is that the artist does not put the image into the wood, but he cuts away the excess wood that had concealed the image. Eckhart writes: "He [the artist] *gives* nothing to the wood but *takes* from it, cutting away the overlay and removing the dross, and then that which was hidden under it shines forth."[55] Eckhart presents yet another simile. The sun is always shining but, if there is a cloud or fog, we do not perceive its radiance. Likewise, if the eye is weak or sick, or is covered over, it perceives no light.[56]

In all three examples there is a common factor; that is, the reality sought after in each case—the fountain, the image, the sun—is already present but is concealed or veiled. Once the obstacles are removed, the object will shine forth and become visible. The process of removing the obstacles can be better understood by Eckhart's reference to St. Augustine who teaches that when the soul is turned outward or downward, God's image is veiled. But when the soul is turned upward into eternity, into God alone, then the veil is removed and God's image shines forth and glows.[57] So the removal of the veil depends on the soul's turning away from creatures to God, from what is temporal to what is eternal.

Eckhart's main interest in *The Nobleman* is the emergence or manifestation of the divine image hidden in the ground of the soul. As Eckhart understands the divine image impressed in humans to be the Word or the Son of God, the emergence of God's image is also described in terms of "the birth of the Son in the soul."[58] This constitutes a central theme of Eckhart, especially in his vernacular sermons. Eckhart points to detachment as absolutely essential for the birth of the Son in the soul, just as it is indispensable for the appearance of God's image in humans. Regarding the theme of the birth of the Son, Eckhart insists that it is one and the same Son born of the Father from eternity that is born in the detached soul in time.[59] Eckhart gives the following illustration in defense of his view: "It is the same Son without any distinction whom the Father has naturally begotten in the Trinity and whom he generates in us through grace, just as many parchments are marked with one seal and many images born in many mirrors from a single face."[60] Here Eckhart employs the metaphor of "mirror" to explain the fact that one and the same Son is born in each one of us.

Even though Eckhart is less concerned with seeing or knowing the divine image than with its emergence in humans, he does discuss the topic of knowledge toward the end of *The Nobleman*. Eckhart enunciates the basic principle that being implies knowing: a white person knows himself to be white.[61] Elsewhere Eckhart even cites the axiom of identity of being and knowing with approval: "The masters say being and knowing are all one...whatever has the most being is best known."[62] Therefore, with the emergence of God's image in him, the nobleman knows the image without mediation, by becoming it.

Eckhart distinguishes between two kinds of knowledge: "evening knowledge" and "morning knowledge." When one knows creatures in themselves, that is, in distinct and diverse images, it is "evening knowledge." But when one sees creatures in God, "without all distinction, stripped of form and deprived of all 'likeness,' in the One that is God himself," this is called "morning knowledge."[63] For Eckhart, the "One" stands for the "indistinct" that abolishes distinctions in things. Eckhart also raises the question of whether true felicity consists in the fact that one knows that one sees and knows God. Eckhart's answer is negative, for "eternal life is knowing God alone as true God, and not in knowing that one knows God" (cf. Jn 17:3).[64] In the former case, one knows only God; in the second, one has knowledge of both God and oneself, which is less perfect.

Eckhart then asserts that the essential condition of felicity consists in seeing God naked and resting on the bare ground of God, beyond knowing and not knowing: "From that she [the soul] derives all her being and her life, and draws all that she is, from the ground of God, knowing nothing of knowledge, nor of love, nor of anything at all."[65] Drawing one's being from, and resting on, the bare ground of God is more important than the act of knowing. The treatise then concludes by referring to the nobleman's being born from "the innermost ground of divine nature and of his wilderness," into which God intends to lead the nobleman back so that God may speak to his heart (Hos 2:14).[66] Thus the ending opens up to a major theme in Eckhart: "the breaking-through into the divine ground," which constitutes the final stage of our return movement to God, even beyond the birth of the Son in the soul.

A detailed discussion of this theme lies beyond the scope of this paper.[67] However some insight into the relation of this divine ground or wilderness to knowledge and love is offered by *Sermon 52*, entitled "Blessed are the poor in spirit." Here Eckhart poses the question: Wherein does blessedness lie most of all—to know or to love? He gives the following answer: "But we say it lies neither in knowing nor in loving: for there is something in the soul from which both knowledge and love flow: but it does not itself know or love in the way the powers of the soul do."[68] In the "breaking-through" into this bare ground through spiritual poverty, the soul—as the undifferentiated source of the powers of knowing and loving prior to their coming forth— simply rests on the divine ground as its own ground.[69] Analogous to the ground of the soul, the "divine ground" is the ultimate source and origin of God's knowing (i.e., the Word) and loving (i.e., the Spirit). Eckhart calls the "divine ground" either the "Godhead" (*Gottheit*) beyond God, or, in his Latin works, the "Father."[70]

III. Chuang Tzu and Meister Eckhart Compared

Between Chuang Tzu and Meister Eckhart stretches an enormous distance both geographically and chronologically. There is also a great difference between their two philosophical systems. Despite these discrepancies, however, one finds profound resonance in the wisdom teachings of the two masters. In this final section I shall point out the parallels, as well as differences, between Chuang Tzu and Eckhart in their views on attaining true vision through self-emptying and detachment.

We shall begin with a comparison between Chuang Tzu's "true person" and Eckhart's "nobleman." In the chapter entitled, "The Great Teacher," Nü-yü depicts the "sage" or the "true person" as one who is able to forget or disregard worldly matters, material things, and one's own life and death. The same chapter also presents a true person as one who does not mind having little, does not boast of his accomplishments, is not worried about failure or success, and does not concern himself with death or life. In a word, a true person is one who is not attached to anything, and is utterly free. Eckhart, on the other hand, employs the term "nobleman" to indicate the "inner man" or inner self of the human person. One becomes a "nobleman" when one has allowed God's seed or image, hidden deep within oneself, to shine forth and become visible. Since the most distinctive character of God is his "immovable detachment," the emerging divine image in humans must reflect this fundamental trait. Although Chuang Tzu's true person is a concrete person and Eckhart's nobleman stands for the inner self of the human person, they both refer to the same basic quality: total detachment and inner freedom.

A second parallel lies in the way they understand forgetfulness and detachment. Both in Chuang Tzu and Eckhart, forgetfulness has a positive as well as a negative aspect. For Chuang Tzu, forgetting the things of the world and silencing the activities of the mind can be described as the process of removing the veils that cover the mind's eye, so that one may perceive an inner light and become enlightened. Moreover, enlightenment is not the result of speculative thinking; rather, it comes from the encounter with Tao, which shines forth and manifests itself when the mind becomes empty and still. Thus, for example, through "sitting in forgetfulness," the sage is able to experience being one with the Great Universal. Likewise, through disregarding everything, the sage sees the One in the brightness of dawn. For Chuang Tzu, therefore, the positive aspect of forgetfulness and renunciation is the ability to perceive the manifestation of Tao present in all things. Enlightenment is understood as a mystical experience of being one with Tao and with the universe.

In a similar way, Eckhart presents the twofold aspect of detachment. As Eckhart believes the presence of God's image to be deeply engraved in the innermost being of humans, detachment means removal of the dirt or the veil covering this image, so that it may shine forth and become manifest. The positive aspect of detachment consists in the appearance of a divine reality— God's image—hidden in humans. The manifestation of God's image is also expressed by "the birth of the Son in the soul." Following upon this birth is what Eckhart calls the "breaking-through into the divine ground." In this breaking-through, one goes beyond the powers of knowing and loving and returns to the bare ground of the soul, realizing that God's ground and one's own ground of existence are one. Thus, as in Chuang Tzu, so also for

Eckhart, detachment leads to a profound mystical experience. Moreover, the "ground of the soul" as the originating source, from which the powers of knowing and loving derive, represents the deepest unitive center of the person and the point of being at one with the divine reality. It is at this point that Eckhart approaches most closely the unitive experience which is so central to Chuang Tzu.

There exist, however, important differences between these two views. Whereas the chief emphasis of Chuang Tzu is on the vision of Tao enjoyed by an empty mind, Eckhart is mainly concerned with the birth of the "nobleman" through the manifestation of the divine image hidden in humans. As Eckhart adheres to the principle of the identity of being and knowing, for him vision is implicit in the self-luminosity of the emergent being. Nonetheless, the difference between the two views on this point should not be overstressed. While concerned with seeing the One, Chuang Tzu also presents the positive outcome of sitting in forgetfulness as "becoming one with the Great Universal." The idea of a close connection between being and knowing is likewise present in Chuang Tzu's lapidary statement: "There must be the true person before there can be true knowledge."

Perhaps it is more accurate to see the contrast between the views of Chuang Tzu and Eckhart as that of two different perspectives within the same basic form of mysticism. If we adopt the distinction of two basic types of mysticism: "metaphysical mysticism" (*Wesensmystik*) and "nuptial mysticism" (*Brautmystik*), both Chuang Tzu and Eckhart can be classified as representing a "metaphysical mysticism" or "mysticism of being."[71] Whereas in a "nuptial mysticism" the intimate, personal communion between the mystic and God is expressed in terms of "spiritual marriage," "metaphysical mysticism" can be described as aiming specifically, as Oliver Davies puts it, "to transcend images and to enter the 'darkness' and the 'nothingness' of the Godhead itself in a journey which leads the soul to the shedding of all that is superfluous, contrary or unequal to God as he is in his most essential Being."[72] This description becomes more inclusive if one replaces the word "God" with a term such as "ultimate reality,"that can denote either a personal or impersonal Absolute.[73] While the views of both Chuang Tzu and Eckhart correspond to this description of metaphysical mysticism, their differing perspectives can be easily demonstrated.

Chuang Tzu's perspective can be described as horizontal; it is cosmos-oriented and puts emphasis on the true person's perception of the great Tao as present in the myriad things in the universe. The true person experiences oneness with the Great Universal and realizes that "the universe and I exist together and all things and I are one." In Chuang Tzu's poetic descriptions, the true person is one who "mounts upon the clouds and forces of heaven, rides on the sun and the moon, and roams beyond the four seas." Thus the true person expands, merging into and becoming a part of the universe.

Eckhart's metaphysical mysticism, on the other hand, adopts a vertical approach, which moves toward the center and ground of the human person to experience God's presence there. It focuses on the emergence of the divine image hidden in the depths of the individual person or the birth of the Son in the soul. Beyond this birth, Eckhart envisages a further step of return to the divine source, that is, a "breaking-through into the divine ground." Thus the return movement goes deeper and deeper, until one reaches the divine reality present at the core of one's being and there experiences one's own ground to be one with the abysmal divine ground. For this reason, Eckhart's vertical approach is at once anthropological and theocentric, just as Chuang Tzu's horizontal perspective is cosmic.

There remains a major problem to be tackled. With their ruthless emphasis on forgetfulness and detachment, one might wonder what exactly are the attitudes of Chuang Tzu and Eckhart toward people and the things of the world. At first glance, their attitudes seem to be negative. But on closer inspection, their positions appear in a different light. For Chuang Tzu, forgetfulness leads to enlightenment, that is, seeing the great Tao as present in all things. This universal presence of Tao abolishes the apparent distinctions found in things and identifies all things as one. Hence, the fruit of enlightenment is not negation of people and things of the world but a profound sense of unity and equality, which overcomes discrimination, loosens selfish clinging, and nurtures universal love.

While Chuang Tzu's emphasis is on the equality of things by eliminating their distinctions, Eckhart insists on the futility and nothingness of all created things. For this reason, Eckhart's approach seems to be even more radically negative. However, Eckhart's outlook on humans and the world is basically positive. This is clearly true with regard to his anthropology. He sees, indelibly impressed in the depths of every human being, the divine image waiting to be unveiled. This belief in the presence of the divine reality in humans implies a genuine respect, even veneration, for the human person.

Eckhart's view regarding the rest of created things is not very different. In a way he also teaches the equality of things. On one level, as seen *in themselves,* creatures are pure nothing. On another level, all created things participate in the existence of God, being rooted in God as the ground of their being. Eckhart describes this vision as "morning knowledge," which abolishes all distinctions in things by pointing to the contingent character common to all creatures. Such a vision at once affirms and relativizes all created things. What Eckhart intends to transcend through detachment is not created things as such, but the "this and that" of particular objects. For him, detachment consists in going beyond particularity, and overcoming discrimination. Eckhart's view regarding the unity of all created things is further strengthened by his special understanding of creation: even though creation came into concrete existence in time, all things virtually existed in the mind of God from eternity, as they were spoken together in the one eternal Word. This view provides a solid basis for the unity and equality of all created things.

Conclusion

In this paper I have presented the views of Chuang Tzu and Meister Eckhart on the relation between detachment and the rise of inner light or vision. Both highlight the positive result deriving from self-emptying or detachment. While Chuang Tzu emphasizes true vision as the fruit of an emptied mind and points to "true knowledge" as the property of a "true person," Eckhart is more concerned with the birth of the "nobleman," that is, the emergence of God's image in humans as a consequence of detachment. Both represent a metaphysical mysticism, but with different perspectives. Whereas Chuang Tzu's mysticism adopts a horizontal, cosmic approach, by which the true person experiences oneness with Tao present in the universe, the approach of Eckhart's mysticism is vertical, that is, anthropological as well as theocentric, moving deeper and deeper into the core of the self until one realizes the divine ground as one's own ground.

These themes, of intense concern to Chuang Tzu and Eckhart, are also central to Buddhism: enlightenment through emptiness and the manifestation of the innate Buddha nature through renunciation. The intimate connection between Taoism and Chan or Zen Buddhism has been pointed out by the late Chinese scholar, John C. Wu: "If Buddhism is the father, Taoism is the mother of this prodigious child [Chan or Zen Buddhism]. But there can be no denying that the child looks more like the mother than the father."[74] Finally, I would like to invite my discussant, the Rev. Heng Sure, to further develop the topic with Buddhist parallels and initiate a *trialogue* between Chuang Tzu, Meister Eckhart, and Buddhist thought.

14

Benedictine Humility
and Confucian "Sincerity"

DONALD CORCORAN, O.S.B. CAM.

Whenever a great spiritual tradition has provided wisdom regarding "inner work"—rectification of the heart—there has been a resonance with the great masters of monastic asceticism. At the risk of being simplistic or reductionist, one might say that all the great spiritual traditions begin with a diagnosis of the human condition and propose a remedy, a way of progress toward enlightenment, deliverance, redemption, and so on. The past few decades have witnessed an increasing dialogue between the Christian and Buddhist traditions. An interchange on a deep level was held at Gethsemani Abbey in 1996, for example. This meeting was partially devoted to a discussion of passions and virtues—a topic not unrelated to the question of purity of heart treated in this conference at Big Sur.[1] Such dialogue will help Christians, especially monastics, to reappreciate the classic wisdom of their tradition. Whereas the rich heritage of Hinduism and Buddhism has been dealt with rather extensively, the classic spiritual wisdom of China has been less pursued in monastic dialogue. The purpose of this essay is to suggest some links between Benedictinism and the classic Confucian tradition, especially on the question of Benedict's notion of humility.

The notions of *apatheia* in Evagrius Ponticus, purity of heart in John Cassian, and humility in the Rule of Benedict, while not directly parallel or expressly identical, are at least somewhat functionally parallel in the Christian spiritual journey. They are not simply analogous concepts, they are homologous. It is commonly recognized that John Cassian's "purity of heart" is his rendering of Evagrius Ponticus's term *apatheia*. Though the Stoic influence on the notion of *apatheia* is, at best, indirect, the notion of purity of heart clearly has more biblical roots, especially the notion of oneness of heart and simplicity. John Cassian certainly retained Evagrius's emphasis on the need for inner asceticism, a control of the dispositions of the heart. Evagrius's insights passed via John Cassian to the Rule of Benedict. The degree of this influence may well be debated, since Benedict never cites Evagrius as a source. However, Benedictine scholar Aidan Kavanaugh

227

argues that Evagrius's basic notions of ascetical progress are "the key to understanding the core of spirituality represented in Benedict's monastic vision."[2]

Benedict also does not explicitly cite John Cassian's assertion that purity of heart is the immediate goal of monastic life. Benedict was less a theoretician of the spiritual life than either Evagrius or John Cassian. His purpose was to write a practical guide to monastic living. The remote influences on Benedict from the earlier Christian and monastic literature are often subtle and indirect. Yet the centrality of humility for Benedict, and its implicit link to Evagrian *apatheia*, deserve greater study by historical specialists. Kavanaugh claims, for example, that Benedict's twelve degrees of humility can be viewed as a "series of glosses on Evagrius's notion of what constitutes *apatheia*."[3] He is indicating, therefore, a clear link, not simply a functional parallel between Evagrian *apatheia*, John Cassian's purity of heart, and Benedictine humility.

In this essay we will focus on Benedictine humility, not from historical and textual study of the influences on Benedict by Church Fathers such as Evagrius Ponticus and John Cassian, but rather by elaborating some insights from the classic Confucian tradition, particularly by drawing parallels to the Confucian virtue of "sincerity" (*ch'eng*). The methodology of the history of religions can provide insight into Benedict's notion of humility and perhaps give us particular insight we might not find through a study of Benedict and his sources alone.

A renewed understanding of humility as a fundamental element of Christian and Benedictine ascesis is a challenge for the modern mentality. In the words of Terrence Kardong, "It is no use pretending that the concept or the treatise in RB7 is obvious or attractive or easily adapted to the conditions of modern life, monastic or otherwise."[4] Few would contend that there is a virtue more central to St. Benedict than humility, yet humility has tones which the contemporary sensibility finds unattractive if not repulsive. Humility is immediately suspected of being self-deprecating and therefore psychologically unsound. Commentators and interpreters rightfully insist on the exigency of proper self-esteem but a lingering suspicion of "humility" remains, and not without reason. Three centuries of Jansenistically tainted popular spirituality tended to read "humility" as a kind of voluntarist, moral self-posturing. It is an important challenge, therefore, for contemporary Benedictines to take up a serious reclaiming of this important central axis of Benedict's spiritual ethos. The purpose of this essay is to suggest Confucianism as a possible helpful optic through which one can come to a deeper understanding of why humility is so central in Benedictine tradition.

Ultimately, the deepest and most genuine insight into true Christian humility cannot be articulated apart from its Christological foundation. Father

Terrence Kardong's recent work is an important contribution.[5] Undoubtedly, for Benedict as for the whole Christian tradition at its best, humility is connected to one's deepest participation in the Paschal Mystery; it is a Christological reality. True Christian humility does not exist apart from the mystical reliving of Christ's total giving of self. Kardong points out that humility was not a value in classical pagan culture. The way of Christ may be "counter-cultural" in all cultures to some extent. But many traditions speak of a passage from a false self to a more genuine self which happens only through a kind of surrender of one's personal identity.[6] Benedict's chapter in the Rule "On Humility" might best be retitled "Have that Mind in You," which points explicitly to the kenotic model of Christ's self-emptying.[7] Yet, as central and foundational as the Scriptural/Christological meaning of genuine humility must be, there are a variety of perspectives which might also be helpful. Is humility merely an attitude of "Christ-likeness"—a moral virtue, a voluntarist, moral, exterior imitation—or is there something deeper which is certainly not only spiritual, but perhaps even ontological? In the context of such a question, the insights from other major religious and spiritual traditions may prove very helpful.

In suggesting that Benedictines may find the Confucian virtue of sincerity (*ch'eng*) an enlightening parallel to their founder's central virtue of humility, we are obviously not implying identity. We must be cautious not to read classic Confucian notions of interiority from too much of a modern Western perspective.

I. General Confucian and Benedictine Parallels

The classic Confucian word for spirituality is "self-cultivation." Though Confucianism is *not* monastic, the parallel to Western monastic, especially Benedictine, life is significant. Classical Chinese Taoism, Confucianism's counterpole, is apparently more "monastic," with its emphasis on marginality, hermits, contemplative intuitive practice, and a kind of spontaneous naturalism. Confucianism generated no monasticism of any variety—eremitic, cenobitic, or in between; it sees the whole world, practical affairs and daily life, as the arena for spiritual work and responsibility. It is non-monastic rather than anti-monastic. Chan Buddhism, however, would create a significant Chinese monasticism.

For Confucianism, as Herbert Fingarette so aptly puts it, the secular is sacred and a certain moral/spiritual cultivation necessarily creates *a way of life,* as it did for Benedict. Both Benedict and Confucius lived in times of profound social and political upheaval. Though Benedict did not concern himself with the broad human community or human affairs in general, his wisdom is shown precisely in his wise governance of the monastic community. His monasteries were to have a tremendous impact on Western

Christian civilization. It might be argued that civility is one of the most significant Benedictine contributions not only to the early Middle Ages but to the larger Western tradition. For this reason, philosopher Alasdair MacIntyre, when calling for a moral reinvigoration of the West in our time, suggests that possibly we need a new "yet doubtless very different St. Benedict."[8]

In this connection I might mention a parallel insight from sociologist Robert Bellah. His book *The Good Society*[9] is a study of the increasing failure of primary American social institutions such as education, the professions, and even the churches. We are in a time of intense cultural change and even disintegration. Interestingly, stepping beyond the "objectivity" of a social scientist, Bellah suggests that the answer to this crisis is what he calls "self-cultivation." Bellah's early work was in eastern Asia and his term "self-cultivation" comes directly out of the Confucian stream of the Asian cultural heritage. So it is noteworthy that both Benedictine and Confucian wisdom are pointed to as sources of wisdom in our current cultural search for spiritual grounding and inspiration. Is there something in both the wisdom of Benedict and the wisdom of Confucianism that has particular relevance to civilizational wisdom?

Confucianism has often been described as a kind of ethical humanism but recent scholarship has increasingly stressed that it is also a spiritual way.[10] The Confucian and neo-Confucian ways are both ascetical and contemplative. They demand a rigorous praxis of self-examination, rectification of the heart, and a deepening of interiority. Confucianism also shares with Benedictinism a sense of the absolute priority of worship, a sense of the Sacred found everywhere, though contemporary Confucianism often lacks the sense of a personal god. The very genius of Confucianism is its sense that life in society is based on "holy rite" or "holy ritual." This was called the Confucian principle of *li* ("rite"). True humanness came through learning the reverent disposition connected to *li*. Herbert Fingarette describes the pervasiveness of the Confucian sense of *li* in words with which Benedictines could easily identify:

> The image of Holy Rite as a metaphor of human existence brings foremost to our attention the dimension of the holy in [human] existence.
> ... Rite brings out forcefully not only the harmony and beauty of social forms, the inherent and ultimate dignity of human intercourse; it brings out also the moral perfection implicit in achieving one's ends by dealing with others as beings of equal dignity, as free coparticipants in *li*. ... To act by ceremony is to be completely open to the other, for ceremony is public, shared, transparent; to act otherwise is to be secret, obscure and devious, or merely tyrannically coercive. It is in this beautiful and dignified, shared and open participation with others who are

ultimately like oneself that [human beings] realize [themselves]. Thus perfect community of [persons] . . . becomes an inextricable part, the chief aspect of Divine worship. . . .[11]

It is not difficult to see life in a Benedictine monastery—from the small rituals of respect at table to the grand beauty of liturgical recitation in choir—as a language and grammar of respect, reverence for Mystery. Reverence is the inescapable foundation and necessary consequence of a profound liturgical sensibility.[12] Benedict's description of "the good zeal that monks are to have" equates it with mutual respect.[13] For the Confucian tradition, the principle of *li* or rite is lived out in the mutually influencing virtues of "sincerity" (*ch'eng*) and "reverence" (*ching*). *Ching* may also be rendered as "seriousness, reverence, mindfulness." It is not unlike Benedict's notion of *gravitas* and the Benedictine characteristic of sobriety of spirit; *ching* is expressed in personal modesty and self-restraint, a "deep humility which gives rise to self-correction."[14] The Chinese sage was characterized by such reverent piety, something one could easily also ascribe to what might be called a truly Benedictine character.[15]

The wisdom of Confucius and the wisdom of Benedict are, therefore, quite remarkably parallel and their ways of life are deeply resonant. Confucians would easily see St. Benedict as a sage personality, one whose spiritual depth translated into wise governance and the creation of a whole way of life (*politeia*). This is what the Jewish tradition would call *halakah*. Benedict was a prime example of a sage personality, even in his own Greco-Roman world. Sage personalities are widely found in the great religious traditions. They are often agents of cultural invention and revitalization. To see a resonance with the classic Chinese sage personality is therefore not surprising. Rodney Taylor describes the Chinese sage thus:

> The Confucian sage lives his life within the framework of the Way of Heaven or the Principle of Heaven. The sage is he who is aware of the relations of his own nature with that of Heaven, and it is the concreteness of the life lived that serves as the exemplification of the sage's understanding and religious depth. Such a figure serves as a model or example, and his life itself is the measure of his understanding. The sage is both imitable and inimitable: imitable as a model and inimitable in terms of the depth of his understanding. The biographies of sages and worthies found in the *Chin-ssu-lu* serve to illustrate the importance placed upon the imitability of the sage, yet there is always the recognition of an inimitable dimension. . . . The sage is quiet, at ease, serene, compassionate, and committed to serving fellow beings. The degree to which such features are prominent in the saint is the degree to which the sage and the saint share common ground.[16]

St. Benedict's humanity, moderation, and discretion are qualities of a spiritual balance that the classic Chinese would also share. All the virtues are displayed in a wise governance and an ability to work with human nature in all its dimensions. St. Benedict is unquestionably a kind of Western sage personality and one of the principal archetypal wisdom figures of the West. Even in the East, eight centuries after the division of the Christian East and West, Gregory Palamas would point to St. Benedict as the great model of the hesychast.[17] It seems to be Benedict's vision of the "Taboric" light which, in Palamas's mind, links Benedict to the hesychast tradition. This tradition, in turn, is related to the Evagrian tradition of *apatheia* and to John Cassian's purity of heart. Though neither Evagrius, John Cassian, nor Benedict taught what later became the formal practice of hesychastic prayer, the tradition of incessant prayer is clearly present in John Cassian.[18] In a way, we can speak of a Western or Latin hesychasm.[19]

Benedict's spirituality is a way of the ordinary and the everyday. The genuine Confucian strives to cultivate "mind-heart." The Chinese notion of mind-heart is somewhat parallel to the Greek *nous* and the Hebrew *lebh*. The "mind-heart" cultivation is seen to be directly related to service in society, to everydayness. Contrast this with Plotinus's sense of ascent of the alone to the Alone and one sees a fundamental dispositional difference between the Greek sense of contemplation and the Confucian sense. Confucian "contemplation" or "enlightenment" was never a question of private bliss or escape from the reality of life in society. The document called *The Great Learning,* a major Confucian classic, teaches what is called *ming-ming-te* ("illustrious virtue in the world") shown in loving the people and resting in the supreme goodness. The practice of sincerity (*ch'eng*) is the basic means to such realization. Sincerity will lead to *jen*—a real and practical love. William Theodore de Bary calls *jen* "a sense of an affinity and organic unity among all things."[20] The Confucian sense of *jen*, "human heartedness," is so significant that Hans Küng proposes it be considered as a foundational concept for world ecumenicity.[21] Just as John Cassian would equate purity of heart with charity, the Confucian tradition knew that sincerity (*ch'eng*) was immediately related to *jen* or deep human heartedness. For both the Benedictine and the Confucian tradition, the right relationship with persons, places, and things stems from a "rectification of the heart," from a humility or centeredness rooted in profound reverence. Benedict's ladder of humility begins with a strong sense of "fear of the Lord"—the biblical sense of reverence—an awesome sense of the reality and exigencies of the Sacred. This is something a Confucian would understand, even without a sense of a personal god. Contact with the Sacred Principle transforms all dimensions of life.

II. Confucian Sincerity as Ontological Humility

The foundational and essential virtue of Confucianism is called "sincerity" or *ch'eng*. Sincerity is the key to sagehood. Its classic formulation is the great document known as *The Doctrine of the Mean,* also simply referred to as *The Mean.*[22] *The Mean* is a superb spiritual classic, unfortunately little known in the West. It ought to be required for reading, study, and internalization in every monastic novitiate. In China it served as a bridge between the Confucian tradition and the two other principal traditions—the Taoist and Buddhist. Both *The Mean* and the Taoist classic, the *Tao Te Ching,* are excellent commentaries on the virtue of humility. The Confucian virtue of sincerity (*ch'eng*) is a kind of meta-virtue and is the presupposition of all listings of the Confucian virtues. *The Mean* calls the ontological ultimate *chung;* the Chinese title of *The Mean* is *Chung-yung. Chung* is translated by the great Confucian scholar, Tu Wei-Ming, as "centrality." It is the axis of all truth, the center of all spiritual reality, the "center which is everywhere."[23] Rodney Taylor calls *The Mean* "a vivid image of the centering process and a suggestion of the subtle point of the Confucian religious dimension."[24] Thus *The Mean* counsels, "to follow our nature is called the Way (*Tao*). Cultivating the Way is called education."[25] Education involves a spiritual reordering. It is to realign oneself with Nature, Reality, Cosmic Harmony. This is impossible without "sincerity" (*ch'eng*), just as Benedict's ascent to spiritual realization presupposes a "ladder of humility." Benedict's ladder paradoxically ascends by descending—realization is founded on lowliness. This is also a very Confucian and Taoist perception. *The Mean* says:

> Sincerity is the Way of Heaven. To think how to be sincere is the way of man. He who is sincere is one who hits upon what is right without effort and apprehends without thinking. He is naturally and easily in harmony with the Way. Such a man is a sage. He who tries to be sincere is one who chooses the good and holds fast to it.
>
> Study it [the way to be sincere] extensively, inquire into it accurately, think it over carefully, sift it clearly, and practice it earnestly.[26]

It is not possible to live in harmony with truth, with ultimate reality, unless one has "sincerity" (*ch'eng*). Sincerity is the center, within which one relates to the Center which is everywhere. If the *chung* of *The Mean* can be rendered "centrality" as Tu Wei-Ming suggests, we might, in turn, suggest that *ch'eng* (sincerity) can be understood as "centering"—a continuous return to a point of truth and integration. This continuous return is by contemplative apprehension, sacred study, and a contemplative harmony of life. The goal is also the means. *Chung* has the sense of a noun, a substantive; *ch'eng* has a more active sense, indicating a process.

The Chinese character *ch'eng* can also mean completion, actualization, perfection, honesty, genuineness, truth. The frequent translation of *ch'eng* into the English "sincerity" is not entirely satisfactory. Sincerity in common English may be seen as a quality of character, ethical and moral perhaps, but often unhinged from a broader, and we would maintain, spiritual, viewpoint. Therefore, one must be cautious of the translation of *ch'eng* as "sincerity," since it can easily miss the religious, even mystical aspects of the term, unless it is understood in terms of the whole Confucian spiritual universe. The translation of *ch'eng* as sincerity has become standard, whatever its inadequacies. Suffice it to say that the common English notion of sincerity or authenticity needs to be qualified when used in the Confucian context. It is not merely psychological—a goal of good character—it is ontological and deeply spiritual. Tu Wei-Ming cites Mencius to substantiate the spiritual ramifications of "sincerity," *ch'eng*. *Ch'eng* in the following passage in Mencius is translated as "true"; one might also translate it as "to be centered":

> The desirable is called "good." To have it in oneself is called "true." To possess it fully in oneself is called "beautiful," but to shine forth with this full possession is called "great." To be great and be transformed by this greatness is called "sage": to be sage and to transcend the understanding is called "divine" (spiritual).[27]

This is an important point for our purposes. The Chinese sense of sincerity (*ch'eng*) takes on a deeper and deeper significance as one studies it within the whole Confucian worldview and its sense of spiritual attainment. The Evagrian notion of *apatheia* implies a spiritual reordering of the self which is an opening of the heart leading to *theoria physike* and *theoria theologike*—a vision of all things and the Mysteries of God. The ordinary modern Benedictine understanding of humility has no such magnitude and profundity; it is here that the insights of the Confucian tradition may help Benedictines to reappreciate humility with greater depth.

Sincerity is a characteristic of the enlightened person but it is also a dynamic way of progress. Sincerity is the *sine qua non* of all self-cultivation. It is the key to integration, right order, clarity, truth. In a similar way, "the mind of Christ" (participation in the kenotic mystery) opens the door to reality for the Christian. The doctrine of *The Mean* says of sincerity:

> Only those who are absolutely sincere can fully develop their nature. If they can fully develop their nature, they can fully develop the nature of others. If they can fully develop the nature of others, then they can fully develop the nature of things. If they can fully develop the nature of things, they can assist in the transforming and nourishing process of Heaven and Earth. If they can assist in the transforming and nourishing

process of Heaven and Earth, they can form a trinity of Heaven and Earth.[28]

It is important to remember Tu Wei-Ming's emphasis on *ch'eng* as "centrality"—a point which is also an axis of connection—the way to harmony and integration. "Forming the 'sacred third' is a Confucian way of understanding spiritual completion."[29] The wise person lives in harmony, creating a sacred bond with heaven, earth, and the human.

III. Confucian Praxis: A Spirituality

There are other parallels between Confucianism and Benedictine spirituality. Both stress interiority, *nepsis* or interior vigilance, emphasis on disposition rather than technique or method, and the practice of *lectio* or internalization of values through sacred study. Finally, both point toward consummation through harmony, integration, or cosmic vision (what Father Bruno Barnhart refers to as unitive vision).[30]

For Benedict the door to spiritual growth is humility; for Confucius it is "sincerity" (*ch'eng*). Sincerity is attained by profound self-reflection, therefore interiority is a way that is directly available. *The Mean* says, "The way is not far from man."[31] In our nature, we can have immediate access to the way. One must be cautious of easy comparisons, but there is a resonance here to the whole *imago Dei* tradition of early Christianity. Though not self-consciously developed by Benedict, one may understand that all the practices of the monastic life are meant to deepen one's interiority and, therefore, true identity. This vision becomes highly refined, for example, in the spiritual anthropology of the Cistercians some six centuries after Benedict. Interestingly, this happened in the twelfth century when a kind of premodern sense of the individual was strongly emerging. The twelfth century in China was also when classic Confucianism underwent a deepening sense of interiority in response to the Taoist and Buddhist challenge, and emerged as so-called neo-Confucianism.

Inner rectification of the heart, both for the early Christian monastic tradition and for Confucianism, required a kind of "watchfulness." The Christian monastic tradition called this *nepsis*. Both *The Mean* and its companion classic, *The Great Learning,* assert that "the noble person is watchful over himself when alone." Gregory the Great, when describing Benedict's early monastic life at Subiaco, says that Benedict "lived with himself" (*habitare secum*).[32] Humility/sincerity is necessarily linked to true self-knowledge, vigilance over one's thoughts and emotions.

Early and classic Confucianism did not teach specific "techniques." After the twelfth century, neo-Confucianism would be more specifically concerned to lay out a systematic "learning of mind/heart," a true system of interior-

ity with regard to the concrete, the practical, the social, the political—the
so-called "things at hand." Thus the neo-Confucian tradition avoided a di-
chotomy between action and contemplation and was not touched by the
dangers of anti-intellectualism and quietism of some Buddhist and Taoist
authors.

Relationships are as crucial for the Confucian ideal as they are for Benedict. In chapter seventy-two of the Rule of Benedict—probably its original
ending before chapter seventy-three was added—Benedict defines the goal
of monastic life as precisely the living out of the Christian life in terms of a
web of relationships. Reverence—a fundamental attitude shaping one's way
of relating—is evidenced in the Benedictine monastic attitude toward God,
other persons, and to all things. Commenting on Confucius's saying "the
noble man is ever reverent," William Theodore de Bary explains that this
"conveys the sense that one should deal with all persons as if they had a
high dignity and all things as if they had an infinite value."[33] Such profound
and expansive reverence is the spirit which suffuses the whole of Benedict's
Rule. For Benedict, even the tools of the monastery are to be treated as if
they were the vessels of the altar. His exquisite care for the sick, his delicacy
in dealing with the alienated, his sensitivity for the multiplicity of personality
types and the variety of personal gifts, his recognition of special needs of the
old and the young, etc., witness to the reverence which becomes innate in
the Benedictine disposition. It is not without significance that all these traits
are listed in regard to the duties of the cellarer, the monastery manager—the
person who is certainly concerned with "the things at hand"—and that the
qualities of the cellarer are a summary of the essentials of humility.[34]

Benedictinism and Confucianism both emphasize a spiritual way that is
concrete and daily—a "way of the ordinary." The Confucian sense of cultivating "mind-heart" is seen to be directly related to service in society,
everydayness, and ordinary relating in the human community. It is not a
question of just recharging one's spiritual batteries and then returning to
the fray, so to speak. I think that St. Benedict would instinctively appreciate the Confucian virtues and qualities of reverence, reciprocal respect,
loyalty, and good faith. Sincerity (*ch'eng*) is expressed in personal modesty,
self-restraint, courtesy, polite manners. Confucian *ching*—reverent seriousness—is expressed in being "sedately gracious, mindful." These qualities
are not just a stilted mannerism, the Hollywood caricature of the Confucian
mandarin. Confucianism would never see becoming a profound person as
a private or individualistic project. Spiritual wisdom is necessarily related
to ongoing service of the wider community. But the living out of the ideal
is hardly a mere realization of an ethical ideal. Confucianism has been described as a moral metaphysic. It teaches that restoration of human nature
necessarily realigns one with heaven and earth and the human, and that
inner work is the way to all truth. Harmony and integration are both the

means and the end. Benedict's depth of contemplation in the tower (the cosmic vision described by Gregory the Great) was both a vision of God and all things in God. More will be said of this in my conclusion.

IV. The Spiritual Culture of Study

To pursue the Confucian ideal was not possible without serious, disciplined study of the great classics. The study of the great classics, no doubt, eventually became for many routine, a bureaucratic formalism. But at best it was a kind of *lectio* (sacred study), the internalization of a "scripture" or a classic textual tradition that formed character and spiritual sensibility. Just as the devout rabbi would pore over the Torah, or the Christian monk would thoroughly absorb or internalize sacred Scripture, so the Confucian sage would be formed by study and memorization of the great Chinese spiritual classics. That these great classics formed a kind of baseline of the culture is without question. They form the underlying culture of today's Pacific rim in a secularized fashion perhaps, just as Judeo-Christian values have formed the West.

The way of "sincerity" (ch'eng) brings a sense of connectedness with all things. Again, this is certainly akin to the experience of Benedict described by Gregory the Great. Nowhere is this more poetically described in the Confucian tradition than in the so-called "Western Inscription" of Chang Tsai:

> Heaven is my father and Earth is my mother, and even such a small creature as I finds an intimate place in their midst. Therefore, that which directs the universe I consider as nature. All people are my brothers and sisters, and all things are my companions.[35]

There is an inseparable connection in Confucianism and Benedictine spiritualities between moral progress and deep spiritual attainment. To advance on the spiritual ladder for Benedict means a passage from servile fear and sheer "observance" to ease and delight in virtue. Does this not correspond to the Eastern notion of *wu-wei*? After his description of the twelve steps of humility in chapter seven of his Rule, Benedict adds a little coda describing, in sum at least, what monastic holiness will look like.

> Due to this love, he can now begin to accomplish effortlessly, as if spontaneously, everything that he previously did out of fear. He will do this no longer out of fear of hell but out of love for Christ, good habit itself and a delight in virtue. Once his worker has been cleansed of vices and sins, the Lord will graciously make all this shine forth in him by the power of the Holy Spirit.[36]

Benedictine praxis leads to a restored human nature, an effortless effort (*wu-wei*) or delight in virtue acquired through good habit and deep interior transformation. The true monk becomes a *pneumatikos,* a spirit-filled "workman" whose whole life overflows into love. Cassian says that purity of heart simply *is* love.

For Confucius too there is a transformation which is arrived at through constant practice; it too manifests in a spontaneity of goodness. Spontaneity is perhaps a surprising virtue to find in Confucianism, which we are apt to associate with a kind of encrusted formalism. As Fingarette puts it, however, "only the sage is able to walk the Way in a completely stable and spontaneous way."[37] That combination of stability and flexibility, old and new, tradition and innovation is a quality of the Confucian sage and also Benedict's ideal abbot. In the chapter on the abbot Benedict quotes the Gospel of Matthew which describes the kingdom of God as "like the wise person who takes from their cellar things both old and new."[38] This is what C. G. Jung called the senex/puer archetype—a two-part archetype which is an expression of the Self archetype. The meaning is that great and living wisdom integrates new and old together.

V. Centeredness and Benedict's Cosmic Vision

Benedict is not alone among early Christian monastic writers in emphasizing the excellence of humility. The Eastern Fathers, Greek and Syriac, have always viewed humility as the mother of all the virtues. Benedictine humility has an undoubtedly Christological and eschatological formulation obviously lacking in the Confucian treatment of "sincerity," yet there are clear parallels. Humility might be called the door to true Christian *gnosis*—to a vision of all things consummated in Christ the Center. Through humility one attains a felt unity with all of creation, all of reality, symbolized by Gregory the Great's account of Benedict's cosmic vision. The humble and purified heart is in harmony with all of creation. Humility is the way to a true unitive vision, an aligning of the heart with Reality that opens one to greater and greater mysteries. St. Gregory the Great explains St. Benedict's vision of all reality in God in this way: "the light of holy contemplation enlarges and expands the mind in God ... in His light all its inner powers unfold."[39]

The event known as "Benedict's cosmic vision" is reported by Gregory in the second of his *Dialogues.*[40] Historians warn of pious elaboration in such hagiography but perhaps the lesson of this event exists on another level than literal history. Benedict, shortly before he died, went into a tower to pray. He saw the whole cosmos gathered before him as if in a ray of sun. Gregory comments: "It was not that the world grew small, but that his heart was enlarged." This event might appear from the outside as too apparently "ecstatic" to relate to the ordinariness of the Confucian spiritual way. Yet,

in some sense, perhaps allegorical and archetypal, Benedict's experience in
the tower is paradigmatic both for the Confucian "profound person" (*shun
tzu*) and for Benedict's ideal of the monk. The Confucian tradition's deepest spiritual conviction is the teaching of *The Mean* that rectification of the
heart will bring one to "centrality"—the sacred center uniting the three basic
realms of heaven, earth, and the human. This journey of integration begins
with the discovery of the sacred point within our heart. Benedict's turn inward in the tower, as he prayed, was a return to his own deepest center,
but also that Center which is the center of all centers and which also has no
circumference. The monastic journey is about enlarging the heart—*dilatatio
cordis*. The "mean" (*chung*) of *The Doctrine of the Mean (Chung-yung)*
is both a point of integration and an axis uniting those three basic ontological realms: heaven, earth, and the human. The noted poet Ezra Pound
translated *The Mean* as "The Unwobbling Pivot." He also translated it as
"standing fast in the middle."[41] Aidan Kavanaugh interestingly attempts to
explain Evagrian *apatheia* by calling it a kind of "dynamic equilibrium."[42]
We will now venture some poetic amplification, as it were.

The noble person, the sage, the truly humble monk, is con-centrated.
Truth, sincerity, authenticity puts one "on center"—not in a frozen stability,
but in a creative and true opening. The person who has found the inner
truth in the depths of his or her own being has an immediate link with
heaven and earth. The sacred center is not confining but opens to universality. Thus, when medieval Christian spiritual writers spoke of God as "that
reality whose center is everywhere and whose circumference is nowhere"—a
phrase taken up from classical paganism—they are asserting not only that
there is nowhere where God is not, but also that the center which is everywhere opens to totality, total inclusion. The symbol of the center may be
one of the greatest symbols of the Sacred, just as the symbol of the spiral is
keenly appropriate for the spiritual journey or spiritual progress. The spiral moves to and from the center, and also extends itself on an axis as the
dialectic of inner and outer play on each other. The dynamic of a spiral is inward, outward, and forward or progressive. The heightening of the dialectic
creates an "ever-widening gyre," in the words of Irish poet William Butler
Yeats.[43] Noted Chinese scholar Tu Wei-Ming comments, "self-cultivation is
an unceasing process of gradual *inclusion*" (italics mine).[44] One of the most
creative monastic spiritual theologians of our time, Father Bruno Barnhart,
has been striving to articulate a true sense of *gnosis*, integrative or unitive
vision. To see it only as a rare or passing moment of ecstasy is to not see its
link to the whole of Benedictine and monastic ascesis. Dom Odo Casel in a
brilliant essay on Benedict as the classic *pneumatikos*[45] explicitly links the
injunction in the Rule's Prologue "to open one's eyes to the deifying light"
with the cosmic vision reported by Gregory. The cosmic vision is why Gre-

gory Palamas in the fourteenth century points to Benedict as the true model of the hesychast.

A number of years ago one of my students, a Korean Benedictine monk, commented on a Chinese character on an invitation card on my desk, an invitation to the installation of a Zen master. He exclaimed: "Ah! It is our vocation!" I asked, "What do you mean?" He said, "In Chinese this character means two things—purity of heart and to see the 10,000 things clearly." Surely St. Benedict saw the 10,000 things clearly. Would Evagrius not recognize in this experience of Benedict a living out of the *theoria physike* and *theoria theologike* to which a life of *apatheia* and purity of heart lead? This is the contemplative vision Father Bruno calls "unitive" knowledge—implying integration, holism.

VI. Conclusion: the Vessel of the Heart

An appreciation of classic Confucian wisdom would help Western monastics to recover a sense of purity of heart and humility as a reverent openness. This is the meaning of St. Benedict's phrase "to incline the ear of the heart." It demands that we stand honestly and reverently in reference to a transcending Ultimate as the foundational and pervasive spirit of our whole life. Such a stance is the first of Benedict's steps on his ladder of humility.

Evagrius Ponticus, when describing purity of heart, uses the image of the "vessel." In his *Ad Monachos*, Evagrius writes that the "vessel of election (is) the pure soul."[46] Evagrius here is pointing to purity of heart as foundational to spiritual enlightenment—as did early Christianity, especially monasticism. Purity of heart is a fundamental receptivity of our being. Similarly, the way of sincerity for a Confucian leads to *jen* (human heartedness, love, compassion). For Evagrius the work on the heart is an opening to love "in front of love, passionlessness (*apatheia*) marches, in front of knowledge, love."[47] John Cassian was the primary influence on the Rule of Benedict. Cassian specifies purity of heart as the proximate or immediate goal of monastic life, and equates it with charity. I think he means by this the opening of the heart, making a vessel of the heart, creating an ever-widening capacity for the spirit. We have already mentioned the great monastic theme of *dilatatio cordis*. Benedict, in his Prologue to the Rule, writes, "as we run the way of God's commandments, our hearts *expand*."[48] He referred to the same process earlier in the Prologue when he enjoined his followers to "open our eyes to the deifying light."[49] Purity of heart, then, leads directly to illumination and to a cumulative unitive vision—the *theoria physike* and *theoria theologike* of Evagrius.[50] Far from being a privatized experience of bliss, the widening of the heart to the spirit is universalizing, grounding compassion for what the Chinese would call "the myriad, ten thousand things." Benedict's cosmic vision thus understood is paradigmatic of the whole Christian spiritual journey. The opening of the heart through humility, *apatheia*, *hesychia*, brings illumination and harmony with all of creation. Genuine spiritual illumination is universalizing, not private; it is progressively inclusive, grounding one in the concrete, the human, the particular. The Chinese, historically, have a great instinct for the spirit in the marketplace, the common, familiar, political, earthly reality.

Spiritual illumination necessarily results in greater and greater wisdom— a whole way of living in the particularities of one's *actual* existence. To be progressively filled with the Spirit, to be a *pneumatikos*, is to become a fountain of light, love and wisdom, healing and compassion. "If anyone thirst let that person come to me and from the person's center will flow a fountain of living water" (Jn 7:37). The human journey is a matter of becoming a soul-full vessel, empty and lowly, in order to be a spirit-filled fountain. Confucius in the *Analects* tells the story of Tzu-Kung who asked, "What would you say about me as a person?" The Master replied, "You are a utensil." "What sort of utensil?" "A sacrificial vase of jade."[51] How Benedictine! The "descending ascent" of Benedict's ladder refines the vessel of the heart. It is the liturgy of one's life that becomes a cosmic liturgy.[52] It is a life of centering that is ever empowered at the Center to progressively return to an ever-widening circumference of inclusiveness.

Part IV

CHRISTIAN AND WESTERN PERSPECTIVES

Our contributions from Western perspectives are marked by a sensitivity to personal experience, to subjectivity. Laurence Freeman's graceful essay ranges freely through a wide and varied terrain of human experience. He presents the journey to purity of heart as a way of the transformation of desire. The human person is "an animal of desire, a wanting being." Here we may sense a strong, existential contrast with an Asian conception of the true self as *Atman* or absolute consciousness. Father Laurence introduces us to four teachers in this way of desire: William Shakespeare, the eleventh-century Tibetan master Langri Thangpa, the fifth-century Greek bishop Diadochos of Photiki, and the twentieth-century writer Simone Weil. The key to the transformation of desire, and the thread which joins these four writers, is *attention*.

Bede Healey explores the same subject—desire—from the viewpoint of a professional psychologist as well as a Christian monk. Here it is the *re-creation* of distorted desire that is proposed as a path toward the attainment of purity of heart. Following the Benedictine spiritual writer Sebastian Moore, Bede Healey examines the central role of *fear* in the distortion of desire. He uses an Object Relations model of human development, which understands human experience as based on relationship. A false self is constructed through the distortion of desires, largely through fear. God is the "Desiring One"; "recognition that we are desired by the Desiring one can lead us to the surrender of our falseness." A model for the re-creation of desire is outlined, based on the potentially transforming experience of crisis moments.

Mary Margaret Funk's presentation takes the form of a dramatized fictional dialogue between herself and Thomas Merton, centering in the phrase *le point vierge* which Merton had appropriated from the Sufi tradition. What is the relationship of *le point vierge* to purity of heart? The phrase is explored in the light of Merton's celebrated account of his enlightenment experience in Louisville, and then of two moments of profound crisis in Sister Meg's own life.

Bruno Barnhart proposes that dialogue with the Asian traditions, centered in nonduality, can open Christianity to a rediscovery of the simple fullness of its beginnings. Conversation with the Asian traditions draws Christianity back toward its own internal "East." Here is discovered the original unity and apophatic transparency of the Christ-event. Here is the wilderness, the symbolic place of Christian baptism or "illumination." This baptismal birth of the "new person" is the pivotal point of contact with the Asian spiritual traditions. Eastern nonduality catalyzes the reawakening of the pole of *unitive identity* in Christianity. This, in turn, is the core of a new "Christian wisdom." Purity of heart appears as a characterization of this "new self" of the baptized person, under the particular aspect of interiority. Baptismal rebirth and illumination is the primordial Christian contemplative experience, as an experience of nonduality, the awakening of the nondual divine-human self. Subsequent contemplative experience is to be understood in the same way. Nonduality in the Christian context, however, pursues a distinctive course which may be summed up in the word "incarnation."

While each of the three great religions of the Word found some expression in the symposium presentations, only Christianity was amply represented. *Islam* appeared only in the Sufi perspectives brought forth by Thomas Merton in his dialogue with Sister Mary Margaret, as he unfolded the context of *le point vierge.* This "virgin point" itself relates easily both to the Western "purity of heart" and to the Asian nondual self.

While there was little direct reference to *Judaism,* the religion of Israel, during the symposium, Norman Fischer boldly confronted the problem which biblical religion presents from the point of view of an Asian nonduality. He quoted the words of a friend to the effect that the strength of Buddhism is in its "making sense," while the strength of Judaism, in contrast, is precisely in its "*not* making sense." Fischer senses in this "irrationality" of Judaism a resonance with much of the experience of humanity in the twentieth century: spiritual darkness, meaninglessness, the absence of God. Here we may see the revelation to Israel taking up once again its historical role of theological criticism: demolishing premature sufficiencies, perfect closures and enclosures—even those of the spirit. This mystery, at once intimate and alien, resonates with the mystery of the cross in Christianity.

The specific strengths of *Christianity* appeared only indirectly and obliquely. Perhaps this is because they are largely to be found outside the perimeter of the dialogue's common ground—in the sphere of acceptance of a divine event and participation in Christ through faith and love. Christianity is not primarily a "monastic" religion. Enlightenment, nondual consciousness, and transformation tend to disappear into faith and love in a movement of incarnation and of a divinization of ordinary humanity and ordinary life. The ultimate mystery reappears in the difficult language which is the human person: in the "ordinary" human experiences, decisions, actions, and relationships. Some qualities expressive of this movement do appear in the papers from the Christian perspective—as well as in Norman Fischer's presentation. We may sense a broad humanism and a respect for subjectivity and for personal experience—whether from a psychological, a literary, or a spiritual perspective. Here, perhaps with surprise, one may also detect a "feminine" dimension. This is evident in the attention given to *desire,* to relationality, and perhaps in the more-than-rational hope invested in dialogue itself.

15

Purity of Heart

Discovering What You Really Want

LAURENCE FREEMAN, O.S.B.

It is generally agreed among the religious traditions that the human being is an animal of desire, a wanting being. At times it even seems we define ourselves by what we are wanting and explain meaning in terms of our desires. This may be as true of our grosser desires such as for food, sex, fame, or possessions as of our nobler aspirations. But even when we desire peace, justice, or holiness it is not unusual that less altruistic desires should mix with these goals. So we may desire another's well-being but want to be acclaimed by others for our altruism. When desires become mixed in this way, as they do much of the time, we can speak of desire becoming distorted. Other ways in which desire gets distorted include, of course, not getting what you want and seeking for it in some compensatory form. We lack the emotional security we need and try to fill the inner emptiness by overeating, or we replace our spiritual practice with addiction to alcohol or overwork. Distorted desire is the problem. Fulfilling our natural human desires does not impede our spiritual development. Quite the reverse. But blocked or diverted desires can make purity of heart seem a remote or fantastic ideal. We are all to some degree subject to this distortion. It is the law of the "flesh" that St. Paul linked to sin. It is the problem of "negative afflictions" or the Buddha's *dukkha,* the inherent unsatisfactoriness of life.

It is also generally agreed among religious traditions that human suffering is bound up with wanting and, equally, that peace, fulfillment, and happiness result from not wanting. But if being actually desireless seems incompatible with human existence we may speak of a transformation of desire. In the vocabulary of some Christian schools the "desire for God" is the final transformation. But we need to remember Aquinas's warning that we use words in relation to God with a very different sense than we use the same words about ourselves.

One way to end desire is, of course, to get what you want. But it is a temporary cessation and before long the ache of desire starts again. This is true of biological desire that is tied to bodily rhythms such as those which control our need for food, sleep, and sex. It is no less true perhaps for our psychological desires, for affection, recognition, or emotional security. We need to be reminded fairly frequently that we are loved. Whether desire in the spiritual realm is tied to this pattern of recurrence is something that should become obvious by the end of this paper. When we think of desire we usually think first of our individual wants. My desires set me apart from others and even if I may deeply sympathize with the desires of others and try to fulfill them even at the expense of my own happiness, it remains an interesting question whether desires can ever really be shared. Does desire, so tied to the consciousness of the isolated ego, condemn us to fail in what may be our deepest longing of all, to be one in communion with all? This is why desire is at the heart of all religious thinking. It characterizes us; and the way we deal with it is, however narrow and painful, the path to the ultimate goal.

But desire is also culturally conditioned. We can see this in the case of a recently "developed society" like Ladakh. Within thirty years it passed from a state of economic self-sufficiency in which money was unnecessary, and which was characterized by stability, harmony, and a remarkably high level of happiness. Desires were moderate and limited to what was available. Modernization, as a result partly of militarization, has distorted the cultural pattern of desire. Western images of happiness, consumer goods, and money itself have complicated and distorted both what people want and how they deal with desire. Even so the Westernization of desire in Ladakh meets inherent resistance. One Indian official complaining of his frustration in convincing the Ladakhis to embrace his government's idea of progress put it succinctly: "the problem is they are not greedy enough."[1] Irish society has similarly undergone a rapid and extensive increase in prosperity within the past decade. But the fulfillment of material desires has, as elsewhere, pointedly raised new forms of unhappiness and suffering in the forms of stress, social fragmentation, and moral and spiritual confusion. Getting what we want does not make for the happiness that we really want. But what do we *really* want?

Desire, then, serves as a link between understanding ourselves as spiritual and social beings. The way we deal with desire will affect our personal spiritual development as well as the balance of health in society. Dealing with desire is the work of purifying the heart.

The Desert Fathers saw purity of heart as the immediate goal of their life, while remaining focused on the Kingdom of God as their ultimate goal. Such purity of being, according to one of Jesus' Beatitudes, makes for the happiness we *do* really want: the vision of God. It is a state of high human development but best described by childlike simplicity, clarity of purpose, and fine moral discrimination. It is a difficult state to attain but merely realizes our essential good nature which includes generosity, compassion, and detachment. It is achieved by a judicious balance of will and surrender of will, personal effort and grace. The Desert Fathers shrewdly saw the dangers of this path and understood both the discipline of self-control necessary for the transformation of desire and the moderation and humility necessary to avoid the demon of pride or the perils of psychological imbalance. Kierkegaard saw purity of heart as the desire for one thing. This might mean the "desire for God" that we shall explore later. But it could also describe a state of obsessive fixation. Perhaps because they struggled continuously with these distinctions and existential dangers the Desert Fathers became experts in the mental states that produce images both of reality and fantasy. Their greatest watchfulness was against the dangers of fantasy, the daydreaming that, as we shall see later, Simone Weil called the root of all evil.

Desire and its transformation is an education of the heart, a human universal, but like other basic human skills it requires teachers. The most useful teachers will be those who have mastered the skill and know from experience the nature of desire and the process of transformation. Such masters will not be found only in religious circles. Art, science, and daily family life will bring us into contact with people who, famous or unsung, will have learned from their own experience and observation how desire works and unfolds, how it damages and how its transformation can heal. The common characteristic of such teachers will be that it is very difficult to define what they have in common because their wisdom is the fruit of high individuation. In this paper we will listen to a number of such masters speaking through specific texts, from different cultures and traditions. So we will move through what they can teach us toward an understanding of what it is the human being really wants.

William Shakespeare

Shakespeare is one of the universally acknowledged teachers of humanity. He is a rather Christlike figure in the relative obscurity of his personal history. What we do know of his personal life, as a theatrical impresario and Warwickshire man of property, hardly prepares us for his exceptional development of mind. His perception of the world has the quality of an infinite comprehensiveness. Not his technical perfection but his perception gives his plays a sense of divine multilocality: We see the same situation from many personal points of view simultaneously as well as, at times, from a transcendental perspective.

Shakespeare is not a moralist, as the Victorians liked to see him, but his vision of the world is inescapably moral. As author he seems egoless, empty of self-interest or partiality. He has by gift the ability to do what the Buddhists call an "exchange of self" and this, as one might expect, produces a nonjudgmental discrimination and compassion. It is a state of purity of heart, colored by a Zen-like mundaneness, that could be compared with what Keats called the poet's "negative capability":

> A poet is the most unpoetical of anything in existence because he has no identity—he is continually informing and filling some other body— the sun, the moon, the sea and Man and Woman who are creatures of impulse and are poetical and have about them an unchangeable attribute. The poet has none: no identity—he is certainly the most unpoetical of all God's creatures.[2]

Shakespeare teaches us much about desire because of this capability to inform and fill his characters, those bodies of his imagination that have entered the realm of the immortals. At times he is absorbed by the desire for power, wealth, and fame as in *Macbeth*. But it is dealing with the most basic and universal desire for love that he has imparted the greatest wisdom.

What we all most deeply and originally want is love. There are many forms of this desire conditioned by our age and social context, sexual orientation, and psychological history. An infant needs love in a mainly passive way, to be cared for and held in emotional security. An adolescent begins to desire reciprocity in love, and for the rest of our lives we remain preoccupied with "relationships." The process of educating the heart thus begins in earnest in adolescence when powerful new desires arise, some driven by the needs for socialization, others by hormones. Shakespeare most famously explores this tempestuous time of life and these passionate states of desire in *Romeo and Juliet*.

The play could be called *Romeo and Rosalind* because when we first meet Romeo on stage he is infatuated with her. We never see her and don't need to. What we need to learn about this kind of desire and about the character of Romeo is given us in Romeo's lovesick complaints. "In sadness, cousin, I do love a woman." "Sad hours seem long," he bewails, and indulges his feelings in purple poetry. His friend Benvolio healthily laughs at him and tries to get him to look for another object of his desire if this one is rejecting him. He tells him to give "liberty unto thine eyes; examine other beauties." Objects of desire are replaceable especially at this stage of life. He and we know that Romeo's suffering is partly theatrical. It is adolescent posturing but behind the pain is another deeper unfolding of identity. Shakespeare's genius is, however, to suggest even more than this. The language Romeo uses about Rosalind is inflated and melodramatic but it evokes the imagery and vocabulary of the mystics.

Romeo's sense of time, as we saw, has been distorted. Language also strains toward the hyperbolic and paradoxical: "she is too fair, too wise, wisely too fair." He seeks out solitude to be "his own affection's counsellor." He struggles to know who he is: "I have lost myself, I am not here, This is not Romeo, he's some other where." When he uses such language under the sway of his desire for Juliet after the Capulet ball it has greater seriousness and poetic beauty because the intensity is more genuine. But the anticipatory echo of the mystic's poetry of love for God is even stronger when he addresses Juliet. His language—and his desire—is coming closer to its ultimate goal. His desire has become a religion and the object of his desire has become his God. There is a passionate fundamentalism about this, a terrible certainty: "there is no other God," she is the "only beautiful." This is loving God with your whole strength and whole mind; but what God? There is the mystic's terrible sense of desolation and abandonment: "under love's heavy burden do I sink, I have a soul of lead." But what kind of dark night?

The significance of this connection between Romeo's immature romantic passion and the erotic language of the love for God will become clearer. What it suggests is that the emergence of one's true, deeper identity occurs through the processes of human development by which the heart is educated and desire is painfully transformed. This purification of the heart, because it involves the death of desire and its regeneration in a higher form, will inevitably involve feelings of emptiness, dread, and the fear of death. *Romeo and Juliet* is a play about youthful love but it is also, very seriously, about the meaning of death.

The instant he sees Juliet, Rosalind is history. "Now old desire doth in his deathbed lie / And young affection gapes to be his heir." Romeo's poetry continues to evoke the cry of the mystic: "the more I give to thee the more I have." His desire now intoxicates and delights him just as it had earlier tortured and depressed him. Very quickly, however, he faces the dilemma of the real world. Juliet, although blissfully reciprocating his passion, is inaccessible because of the feud between their families. Now, instead of moping around, he seeks advice from his mentor Friar Laurence and we are introduced to one of the central concerns of the play. How does the heart of the young learn to deal with the waves and storms of desire? Who are their educators? Friar Laurence is the only elder in the play who fulfills the responsibilities of his role in this respect. The parents of Juliet betray her by trying to force her desire into a lust for their proposed marriage candidate for her. Even her devoted nurse fails her at the crucial moment. These young "star-cross'd lovers" are victims of the feud between two families but also suffer from the dereliction of duty by those who should be teaching them how to move from one level of desire to another with the minimum damage to the heart.

Friar Laurence, when we first meet him, is collecting medicinal herbs in the morning dew and praising the healing properties and bountiful beauty of Gaia, mother earth. He knows nature and respects and loves its ways. His wisdom allows him to listen to the passionate anxieties of his "pupil" with calm compassion even when Romeo dismisses him as too old to understand what he is feeling. The priest does not try to repress or distort this burst of erotic energy but to channel it. He recognizes the dangers inherent in such passion and counsels moderation:

> These violent delights have violent ends,
> And in their triumphs die like fire and powder,
> Which as they kiss, consume. The sweetest honey
> Is loathsome in his own deliciousness,
> And in the taste confounds the appetite.
> Therefore love moderately; long love doth so;
> To swift arrives as tardy as to slow.[3]

St. Benedict and the Buddha would have applauded.

Friar Laurence steers Romeo through his flirtation with suicidal longings toward further self-knowledge and we see the youth take further steps in his maturing. He is learning to handle desire without distorting it. However, the plot, their fate, gathers speed as well. When Juliet comes to the priest to ask him "out of thy long experience'd time give me some present counsel" he declares that a "thing like death" is needed. The stratagem of Juliet's counterfeit death tragically fails because of the accident of the messenger not reaching Romeo, and the play ends in the exposure of the heavy blame carried by the now broken and despairing parents.

A Christian writer like Shakespeare cannot describe the tomb without evoking the hope of resurrection. Although the play ends with tragedy its theme and symbolism offer redemptive insights. Desire leads inevitably to death because its nature is cyclical. But although whatever is born must die, whatever dies is reborn. In the short tragic course of Romeo and Juliet's love we have glimpsed that human growth is the transformation of desire. Although there is pain in this, there is also the joy of knowing we are moving in the right direction. We have seen that the role of the religious tradition, in the benevolent form of Friar Laurence, is to educate, guide, console, and counsel the purification of the heart and to maintain a perspective focused on the ultimate goal. If this can be described as the desire for God we must be careful how we explain the meaning of that well-worn phrase. A last desperate cry of Romeo before he is forced to kill Paris in Juliet's tomb ironically suggests what it does mean. "O be gone! By Heaven I love thee better than myself." As with his earlier language of erotico-mystical passion, Romeo does not fully grasp the meaning of what he is saying. But he and the play point us toward a form of desire very different from that which he had felt, a self away, for Rosalind.

The tragedy of the young lovers is that of all desire. The successive phases of life incorporate the essentially human process by which the heart is educated about desire, about what to desire and how to desire. Like all growth it is not linear but cyclical and it incorporates the cycle of death and rebirth.

After passion we die and are laid in the tomb. *Post coitum omnis animal tristis est.* But after three days in the heart of the earth we are reborn. This education of desire comes with the computer, software already loaded. But who does not need to have it explained to them at least once, however simple it is? The tragedy of the play is the tragedy that Jesus identified when he complained that the people were like sheep without a shepherd—the shortage of teachers. Friar Laurence symbolizes the ideal role of the church in Western society, a role that Jung accused it of betraying and a role that most of the young today see as having become the repression rather than education of desire.

Perhaps part of the Western church's tragedy is its having been confronted so early with the cult of desire in the romantic tradition of the troubadours. A culture that so exclusively identified love with the passion of erotic desire finds it particularly difficult to hear about the goal of elimination of desire or its transformation into the desire for God. The role of the church as a teacher of this wisdom developed very differently from that of the monastic wisdom applied to human life in Buddhist cultures.

Langri Thangpa

In Tibetan *lo-jong* is a tradition of spiritual wisdom that concerns the education of the heart or literally the "training (or transformation) of the mind." Our next teacher will be the eleventh-century Tibetan master Langri Thangpa and his short text "The Eight Verses on Transforming the Mind," which is a favorite of the Dalai Lama.[4] His commentary on this text illuminates and analyzes further aspects of the interior process of purifying the heart by regulating and redirecting the forces of desire.

In his introduction to this beautiful text, the Dalai Lama emphasizes the basic distinction between physical and mental experience. If we are concerned with the basic desire for happiness, the mental realm, he says, is of greater importance to us. We can, for example, be wealthy, healthy, and surrounded by friends and yet be miserable. On the other hand, we can be sick, impoverished, and alone and yet be at peace provided our mind is clear and centered in truth. *Romeo and Juliet* also shows that happiness is conditioned by the mind's patterns of thinking and feeling. Before we can attain what we *really* want—the happiness that is not dependent on the cycle of desire and gratification—we will need to develop both awareness and control of these patterns. The longer they are repeated unconsciously, the more deeply set and intractable they become.

So the transformation of desire demands a certain degree of conscious introspection and self-criticism. We must examine our mental activity as it arises and then identify and deal with negative or destructive feelings and thoughts such as anger or lust or pride. Like Friar Laurence we need to know what remedies and antidotes to apply. There will be appropriate spiritual practices and symbols that will soothe and heal the mind and thus purify the heart. Jesus called this repentance. When he began his teaching mission this was his message: "The Kingdom of Heaven is upon you. Repent and believe the good news." For some, the announcement of the Kingdom's imminent presence was felt as a threat of judgment rather than the revelation of an inner reality. A Christian spirituality of a like spirit often understood repentance as the cultivation of sin-centeredness and guilt, whereas it is actually the elimination of the corrosive and paralyzing demon of guilt from the psyche. Similarly, believing in the good news was felt to mean merely conforming to certain expressions of dogma rather than acting on the revelation just made about the Kingdom, acting *as if* it were really true.

Deep parallels between Christian and Buddhist thinking emerge when we reread the words of Jesus in this way. Reading the texts of other traditions frequently has this effect of making us reread our own familiar texts in clearer ways. The Buddhist text is understood in traditional commentaries as referring to the practice of meditation that allows the mind to be transformed. Just as the body can develop bad posture that causes pain, so the mind can slip into habits that prolong suffering. As yoga or tai-chi might help straighten out the body, meditation gives right posture to the mind. It strengthens the ability of the mind to place its attention where it *really* wants to be placed: not on anxieties, anger, or pride but on harmony with others in compassion and wisdom. Several complementary forms of meditation are practiced, just as Christian spiritual practice employs many forms of prayer. There is *shamatha,* tranquil abiding, and *vipassana,* a more analytical form of insight.

Monastic wisdom, whether Buddhist or that of the Desert tradition, developed a systematic analysis of the content and methods of stabilizing the mind. It may call this stability *apatheia* or *samadhi* but the underlying experience is the same. Nothing more clearly shows that at an experiential level all human beings share common ground than a comparative study of the transforming of the mind or purification of the heart. How this primary experience of change or conversion is then understood, what it is seen to say about the nature of ultimate reality or the nature of the experience itself, will differ. This understanding does not need to be merely philosophical or theological. When there is real understanding and insight, a further dimension of experience is itself opened up, a higher consciousness attained. But this does not mean that even in this higher experience the practitioners of different traditions are actually diverging. The experience is the same, but the language used to describe this level will be untranslatable into the terms of the Other. At the more primary level of experience, however—when we are talking about purity of heart rather than God, about *samadhi* rather than *nirvana*—the language is remarkably similar.

The Desert Fathers would have no trouble, for example, concurring with the Buddhist list of the four obstacles or their mode of operation. Distraction, dullness, mental laxity and mental agitation describe states and tendencies that any meditator is familiar with. Mental distraction "arises at the coarse level of mind" and is simply the layer of trivial or superficial concerns that flit into consciousness in rapidly passing images or thoughts. For the Desert Fathers this was the terrible discovery of one's instinctive inclination to spiritual adultery. Dullness is the tendency to fall asleep; controlling this requires discipline of body as much as of mind and the regulation of a daily schedule consistent with the amount of practice one is doing. Desert Fathers' stories often deal with this problem with an amused wisdom. Mental laxity is the state of a mind that has lost sharpness and clarity, and so tends toward a de-energized condition such as Cassian referred to as the *pax pericolosa* or the *sopor letalis*. Mental agitation operates at a more subtle level of mind, as it recalls or anticipates pleasant experiences. Dealing with this would introduce one to the first "night of sense" described by St. John of the Cross.

Dealing with these obstacles to transformation demands mindfulness, vigilance. Once we begin to practice this we cannot help noticing that we—or at least our mind—are in a state of constant change. Romeo's helter-skelter of emotion mirrors our own continuous mental flux. A deeper consideration of this awareness inevitably leads us to the primal question, "who am I?" As Buddhism in particular shows, this question of all questions leads into extremely subtle levels of thought. The Dalai Lama's commentary, however, is practical rather than philosophical at this point. He refers to basic Buddhist belief in the nonexistence of a permanent self, however, in order to explain later the full significance of what egotistical desire is transformed into. The person I think and feel I am, he says, is merely the function of psycho-physical constituents. The aggregates are in constant flux but underlying them is Mind, the luminous nature of which should not be interpreted as denoting a permanent or real self.

> Persons do not exist in and of themselves but in the context of language and of the understanding that prevails in the transactional world.[5]

We are, then, as Shakespeare said, merely players, and the world is our stage.

As made by the Buddha, this assertion can be deeply disturbing to the Western mind and to Christian religious thought with its twin assumptions of individual integrity and divine origination. But the Buddhist doctrine of emptiness has necessary parallels in Christian belief as well. It helps to be reminded by the Dalai Lama that "there is a great difference between emptiness and mere nothingness."[6]

Insight into emptiness is the essential Buddhist contribution to the universal wisdom about purity of heart. It frees us from mental afflictions and the karmic actions they give rise to. We feel better and so we act better. This insight is an experiential event, not a notion we entertain and reflect on—another characteristic of monastic culture in all traditions. Emptiness, as experience, according to Nagarjuna is what really dispels ignorance or misperception of the world and opens awareness into the inherent emptiness of all things. Many of the negative thoughts and emotions are simply eliminated by the power of this insight. This experience has been called "natural nirvana" which forms the basis of the three remaining levels of nirvana in Buddhist scriptures.[7] It also corrects the four great "Misperceptions" about reality that underlie so much suffering. The question of who remains to enjoy nirvana after emptiness has disproved the permanent self need not detain us as it entertains the Buddhist mind endlessly.

What might concern us more immediately is the notion of being so pure of heart, so potentially desireless. The disturbing doctrine of emptiness, like the injunction of Jesus to "leave self behind," threatens our very identity and existence. Is this what we *really* want? Probably not, unless the masters also remind us of the connection between emptiness, selflessness, and joy. In the Buddha's own words, "Through the samathic practice joy arises and from the joy insight arises."[8] As Jesus looked deep into his own emptiness on the eve of his death and communicated what he felt to his disciples, it was joy, even in face of the suffering he felt and anticipated, that he passed to them: "I have spoken these words to you so that my joy may be in you and your joy may be complete."[9]

It is a strange idea, but also a widely held one, that the insight into emptiness (even before it has been perfected in direct realization) releases us from suffering, purifies the heart, unties the knots of the heart, straightens out disordered desire, and unleashes boundless joy. Desire however has still not found its final form even with this insight into emptiness. If we are still desiring happiness primarily for ourselves we will inevitably relapse into disordered states of desire and old patterns of unhappiness. The skillful means here, according to Tibetan Buddhism, is that of the bodhisattva, the transformation of self-centered desire into altruism, desire for the happiness of others.

Bodhicitta is developed under two aspects: first, the desire to be of help to others and, second, the aspiration to attain enlightenment. The Tibetan term for enlightenment is *chang-chub*. The first syllable means "purified" in the sense that all mental pollutants have been overcome. The second means "having realized" all knowledge. Enlightenment therefore means the overcoming of negative qualities and the fulfillment of positive ones. Insight into emptiness frees one sufficiently from attachment to oneself to be able to combine these two aspects within the intention of serving others, even with our own personal spiritual practice:

The highest form of spiritual practice is the cultivation of the altruistic intention to attain enlightenment for the benefit of all sentient beings, known as *bodhicitta*.[10]

Insight into emptiness and *bodhicitta* combined are the winning ticket for the spiritual race. Other means are secondary, such as the seven-point cause and effect method, the cultivation of equanimity toward all, or thinking of others as someone especially dear, or an exchanging and equalizing oneself with others which affirms the fundamental equality of all beings. Shantideva expressed this with universal simplicity:

> The source of all misery in the world
> Lies in thinking of oneself
> The source of all happiness
> Lies in thinking of others[11]

This wisdom is universal. The teachings of Jesus and the letters of St. Paul testify to the bodhisattva ideal and see the transcendence of self as the means of fulfilling this ideal in daily practice. We need now to turn to the Christian teacher to see how this practice of transformation of desire and purification of heart can be understood as realizing the desire for God, which, St. Augustine said, is the "whole life of the Christian."

Diadochos of Photiki

Diadochos of Photiki was a fifth-century bishop in Northern Greece teaching in the generation after Cassian but strongly influenced by Evagrius and the desert tradition. We will follow his teaching in his text of a hundred chapters, *On Spiritual Knowledge and Discrimination*.[12] Like his monastic forebears he saw contemplation as the goal of life although he stressed the role of sacramental life more than they did and gave more theological weight to the primacy of love. Like them, too, he saw prayer—for him this meant particularly the Jesus prayer, the prayer of the heart which he called "continual remembrance"—as the foundational practice of purifying the heart. The human being is thus an active player in the work of its own creation and salvation. While the initial creation is purely the work of God, the development of the human person through life continues this work and requires the cooperation and conscious effort of the creature to become what he or she is called to be. This occurs through a process that can be seen as realization or transformation, as it contains elements of both. Its driving force is joy and its goal is *theosis,* divinization or complete union with God.

> [Man] transforms himself into what he is not when his soul by devoting itself to its true delight, unites itself to God, in so far as its energized power desires this.[13]

His starting point for understanding this transformation is human nature seen in the light of the account of creation in Genesis. The human person is created in God's image and likeness. Baptism reveals the human being as the image of God by a kind of ontological purification. But the "infinitely superior" grace that comes next requires our cooperation. As the mind perceives "with full consciousness" the action of the Holy Spirit, it sees that grace is painting the likeness over the foundational image. When God sees us longing with all our heart for the beauty of this likeness and as we stand humbly naked in the divine workshop, then step by step the realization of humankind that is also our divinization unfolds as "one virtue after another comes into flower." This is not altogether a hidden or passive action. It requires both our awakened perception of the action of grace and our active cooperation.

The painting of the divine likeness is compared with the work of a portrait painter creating the truest possible image of the subject—expressing his true identity. This is perfected in the smile that the painter adds last but which symbolizes the "luminosity of love" and declares that the "image has been fully transformed into the beauty of the likeness." For Diadochos the inner person is renewed day by day above all "through the experience of love and in the perfection of love it finds its own fulfillment."

Love, beauty, conscious awareness, the energized power of the Holy Spirit, and the fervent desire for holiness are the cooperative elements of the transformation of the human person into its true being. Such an affirmative conception of human nature provides a confident foundation for exploring the nature of evil and the self-dividedness that causes humanity so much suffering. As for Simone Weil, for Diadochos the origin of evil is not explained by a gnostic struggle between the powers of light and darkness but by the power of human imagination. The human being, like every part of creation, is essentially good. It is by understanding the genesis of desire in the human mind that we can understand the origin of evil.

> When in the desire of his heart someone conceives and gives form to what in reality has no existence, then what he desires begins to exist.[14]

Desire can enable us to create. But disordered desire starts the chain of events that leads to evil when in its pain and ignorance it imagines the unreal and attaches itself to these images. In this understanding of evil, illusion cannot be lightly explained or dismissed. Responsibility for it sits squarely with human beings. Until its unreality has been exposed and it destroys itself (as it does by competing with the real), illusion can wreak destruction both in the soul and on the earth. Even though the "good that exists by nature is more powerful than our inclination to evil," we are powerfully attracted to the images of our own desire—and not always so charmingly as in young romantic love.

The powers of desire and imagination together explain the conflict of inner division that tears the human heart apart and robs it of its natural purity. We thus experience the alienation that St. Paul describes poignantly in Romans:

> I do not even acknowledge my own actions as mine, for what I do is not what I want to do but what I detest. It is no longer I that perform the action but sin that dwells in me. And if what I do is against my will, clearly it is no longer I who am the agent, but sin that has its dwelling in me.[15]

The easy explanation for this—that the human soul is the battleground of two opposing armies of good and evil—has been popularly established in Christian thinking but it is not the explanation that either St. Paul or Diadochos proposes.

> The reason why we have both good and wicked thoughts together is not as some suppose because the Holy Spirit and the devil together dwell in our mind, but because we have not yet consciously experienced the goodness of the Lord.[16]

Consciousness, the focusing of attention, rather than mere emphasis on the will, is therefore the main key to transformation of desire and the purification of the heart. The Buddhist might remark that "experiencing the goodness of the Lord" means realization of emptiness, but he would agree with Diadochos that human motivation and determination is indispensable. It is up to us which direction we turn. Having turned, though, grace "reveals its presence ineffably" and the transformation of the whole person has now passed the point of no return. It is at this point that Diadochos reveals the importance of personal practice, the prayer of the heart that has of course accompanied the process from the beginning. By "calling ceaselessly upon the Lord Jesus" in his heart the Christian undergoes a remarkable physical and mental transfiguration.

> The fire of God's grace spreads even to the heart's more external organs of perception, consciously burning up the tares in the field of the soul.[17]

Purity of heart is the result of the action of the fire of grace. It begins in the heart, which is the unified organ of human perception and therefore the medium of nondualistic consciousness that allows us to see God. But once purity has begun here, its effect is felt progressively in the physical and mental realms as well. Disordered desires and negative afflictions are, as with all forms of evil, gradually exposed as being essentially unreal. As disordered desires fall away, what is left it what we really want. In the breakthrough to self-knowledge we recognize and simultaneously attain what our heart most profoundly longs for.

The desire to love God, according to St. Augustine, *is* the love of God. We cannot desire God in the way we desire sex, fame, possessions, or even emotional fulfillment. It is a desire that has ceased to be desire in the ordinary sense of the term because it has already been fulfilled. This is not exactly how Diadochos puts it, but he says that by loving God consciously in our heart we know that we are known by God, and to the degree that we consciously receive the love of God we enter into God's love. From this moment, when the desire for God becomes a conscious act, we are stricken with an "intense longing for the illumination of spiritual knowledge" which never leaves us. We have fallen into the hands of the living God. The strength of this desire penetrates the bones. We no longer know ourselves. We are "completely transformed by the love of God" with the full richness of the ambiguity of this phrase. Romeo and Juliet were heading for this. "Happy is the person whose desire for God has become like the lover's passion for his beloved."[18] Importantly too, however, this consummation devoutly to be wished is not the satisfaction of the ego but the ego's final transcendence. "He has once and for all transcended self-love in his love for God."[19]

How do we know this? We know it in a way that echoes the Buddhist concept of *bodhicitta* but expresses it in different terms. As transformation gradually unfolds we notice a reduction in the level of anger and hatred or at least in their power to master us. These demons were particularly of concern to the desert tradition whose masters often saw them as the root of sin. At first we experience anger whenever our own desires have been thwarted. The child's foot-stamping tantrum at being denied what it wants becomes the terrorists' revenge or the politician's threat of war or sanctions. With time we learn to cover up the self-centeredness of our anger. We rarely feel genuine anger when the rights of others have been transgressed provided our own well-being remains unaffected. "Preoccupied with its own desires, (the soul) pays no attention to the justice of God."

The justice of God, here in the thought of Diadochos, means specifically the rights of others. The sign, therefore, that we have been transformed in desire and purified in heart is that we cannot bear "even in our dreams" to see justice set at naught. Diadochos's reference to the unconscious here illustrates the depth of the transformation, its absolutely genuine and spontaneous nature. Anger becomes a passion for the restitution of justice to the oppressed, not a desire for revenge or self-promotion. Like the bodhisattva, the transformed Christian is more concerned about the well-being of others than about his own.

Simone Weil

Erotic love, *samatha, vipassana,* examination of conscience, prayer of the heart: These are stages and means employed by the pilgrim soul on the journey to purity of heart. Simone Weil, who is the last teacher we will turn to, explored this journey when she wrote her own great spiritual autobiography, *Waiting for God*. It is in a short essay in that volume, "Reflections on the Right Use of School Studies with a View to the Love of God,"[20] that her central spiritual and philosophical theme is most succinctly displayed.

Elsewhere she has said that "attention purifies." In this essay she applies this far-reaching insight to the role of the educators in the training of the young. We saw in the case of Romeo and Juliet how tragic were the consequences of their parents' dereliction of duty. (Shakespeare's own daughter was about the age of Juliet at the time of his writing the play.) It is difficult not to read Weil's essay on education without being reminded of the guilty sense of betrayal of the young that is uncomfortably growing in our culture today.

Weil's nonconformity, as in the case of the other teachers we have learned from, is a prophetic challenge.

> A time is coming when people will go mad and when they meet someone who is not mad they will turn to him and say "you are out of your mind" just because he is not like them.[21]

Certainly Weil's conception of the purpose of education collides violently with the social engineering policies of departments of education today. For her, school studies serve primarily to train the power of attention. Although it is the lower end of the spectrum of attention with which academic study is concerned, the development of this range of consciousness is essential to realizing the potential of the higher part which is concerned with conscious contact with God. Because study is for the development of the faculty of attention, one can say that it is about developing the spirit of prayer. Developing attention is equivalent to the transformation of desire and the purification of heart we have seen described by our other teachers on desire and purity of heart.

> [School children] should learn to like all these subjects because all of them develop that faculty of attention which, directed toward God, is the very substance of prayer.[22]

Desire—both what is desired and how it is pursued—is directly affected because the first thing the child learns is that the purpose of study is not good grades. Desire is in fact purified (that is, it is directed toward reality rather than imagination) by the simple work of attention: "There is a real desire when there is an effort of attention."[23]

No such effort is wasted even if it produces failure in the short term. Progress is made "in another more mysterious dimension" and the fruits of this progress will be enjoyed at another time, and perhaps on a quite different level of experience. Not only must the students be taught right motivation for study, but they must also learn how to analyze their failures or second-ratedness. The first of these generates altruism and the second humility. Characteristically, Weil insists that a sense of mediocrity is more beneficial to humility than a sense of sinfulness.

Study, for her, is an anticipation of pure prayer; she explains this when she says that twenty minutes of concentrated, untiring attention is infinitely better than three hours of the kind of "frowning application" that merely fulfills a sense of duty. These terms are readily translated into the language of prayer and forms of prayer.

Romeo and Juliet could not take their eyes off each other or tear their thoughts away from their love. They were learning the first lessons of whole-hearted attention. Langri Thangpa explains the need to direct attention from self to others after appropriate self-examination. Diadochos shows how attention to one's true nature is both attention to God and love of neighbor. Simone Weil can conclude our brief survey of this theme in words that any of the other teachers we have turned to would have understood:

> Attention consists of suspending our thought, leaving it detached empty and ready to be penetrated by the object; it means holding in our minds, within reach of this thought, but on a lower level and not in contact with it, the diverse knowledge we have acquired which we are forced to make use of. Our thought should be in relation to all particular and already formulated thoughts, as a man on a mountain who, as he looks forward, sees also below him, without actually looking at them, a great many forests and plains. Above all our thought should be empty, waiting, not seeking anything, but ready to receive in its naked truth the object that is to penetrate it.[24]

This remarkable description of spiritual consciousness illustrates how much more there is to the transformation of desire than ascetical discipline. The intelligence, Simone Weil says, can only be led by desire, but for desire to be truly the desire for God there "must be pleasure and joy in the work."

We return in the end, then, to the symptom of joy as the sign that transformation and purification of heart are truly in progress. Buddhist or Christian, joy is always recognizable and infectious. Furthermore, "the intelligence only grows and bears fruit in joy."[25] The ground of joy is desire that has been transformed wholly into the desire for God and that is indistinguishable from the desire for the well-being of others.

Romeo and Juliet had just begun to see this.

16

On the Re-creating of Desire and Purity of Heart

An Exploration

BEDE HEALEY, O.S.B. CAM.

Sebastian Moore, in his book *The Crucified Jesus Is No Stranger,*[1] writes:

> Gautama, who became the Buddha, came to think that desire is the cause of all suffering. Therefore, eliminate desire and you will come to peace.
>
> This analysis does not go to the root of the matter. The cause of our unpeace and unfreedom is not desire, but desire mixed with fear.... Desire as we experience it is clandestinely married to fear, very often even directed by fear. I spoke of fear as a *spur* to desire. Desire is the horse; fear the rider that has gotten onto its back. The horse is a good horse, and, liberated from this dark rider, will bound for the heart of the sun.[2]

This may be a limited and simplistic understanding of the Buddhist position, yet Moore's words have led me to reflect on the role of desire in the Christian Way.

Dom Benedetto Calati, prior general of the Camaldolese Benedictine Congregation for many years, loved to say that first we are human beings, then we are Christians, and then we are monks. According to him there is work to be done and there are lessons to be learned at each level. A different arrangement of these three elements would suggest that first we are human, then monks, then Christians, recalling Panikkar's concept of the monk as universal archetype. In any event, each of these provides a perspective from which to view aspects of ourselves.

In the human condition I am a psychoanalytically oriented clinical psychologist with a strong affinity for the British School of Object Relations'[3] approach to understanding the curious inner life of the human person. I have worked with many people, some in great turmoil seeking help in understanding themselves—their thoughts, feelings, behaviors, and, ultimately, their

263

desires. The traditional psychoanalytical approach would focus on the sexual and aggressive drives and their derivatives, on the developing structure of the ego and the manifold defenses erected to assist the person in the assimilation of the disparate aspects of self with the demands of the culture and society. Following the Object Relations approach, I am keenly interested in the relational world, both real and imagined, and the vicissitudes of these relationships in the individual's life. Many have sought therapy for a wide array of clinical issues, to work through real pain and suffering or for personal growth. A significant portion of my clinical work has involved religious professionals (ordained clergy of various denominations, monastics, members of religious orders) in crisis, often involved in boundary violations, and these were often of a sexual/genital nature. In almost every instance, the sexual acting out of the boundary violation, such as a married minister having a sexual relationship with a member of the congregation, reflected a more complicated inner dynamic, and at its root was distorted desire.

I am a Christian, a "cradle Catholic," born and formed in my early years in the pre–Vatican Council II tradition, living and growing through the Council and its continuing reverberations to this day. I have experienced Jesus, the Crucified-and-Risen-One, and have known the working of God in me. God has been present deeply within me and also present to me very powerfully through others.

As a Camaldolese Benedictine monk, I am seeking God in that rich tradition, fueled by the centuries of monastic experience available to me down through the ages, and in the living monastic traditions of today. When I became involved in the formation of others in the monastic way and in guiding other Christians on their path to God, our work would often focus on the individual's deep desires, and the myriad ways individuals would seek to simultaneously attain and subvert these desires. Reflecting on my own ongoing journey, on my clinical work, and on my current work in spiritual formation, the role of desire has increasingly come to the forefront of my thinking.

Desire is a complex word, not simply defined. Desire[4] means to crave, to wish or long for, to want, to yearn for. It is the feeling that impels a person to the attainment or possession of something. It is associated with enduring, deep, imperative, intense, wistful wishes. It is an eager energy for life. A common psychological approach to elucidating the inner, unconscious workings of the individual is to use the word association technique. The pattern of responses offers insight into one's inner life. Commonly responses to the word "desire" have sexual connotations, powerful feelings that are certainly part of the landscape of desire, but not the only flower in the field. Also people will often perceive desire as referring to something out of their control, something powerful, something simultaneously attractive and frightening. It is both a part of themselves and yet not truly themselves either. They can discuss their desires as something they actively seek to fulfill or as something to be passively waited for. There is often an unsettled, alien quality to the experience of desire.

In talking about desire, we are attempting to define something that is, at least in some respects, indefinable. We come close at times, but fall short of capturing its true meaning. For instance, desire is both associated with unfulfillment (we desire something we lack or are missing) and paradoxically with complete fulfillment (we search for our heart's desire). How can this be? How are we, in the midst of recognizing our utter unfulfillment, somehow fulfilled, complete? What is being fulfilled? These are interesting and important questions.

Desire is often misunderstood. Often associating it only with craving, with an addictive seeking for something, it seems to me that we are, in these instances, mistaking deformed desire for true desire. Yet there is something of the forbidden fruit associated with desire, and this speaks to the key issue—distorted desire. Indeed, I would go so far as to state that our typical understanding of desire is only of a deformed or distorted aspect of desire. As Moore states, the root of the distorted desire is fear.

What is this fear? It is variously defined as an unpleasant emotional state in anticipation of pain or danger or great distress, agitated foreboding, dread, fright, horror, a condition somewhere between anxiety and terror. Fear may be well grounded or unreasoned and blind. It is associated with visceral reactions. We experience fear in our bodies. Interestingly, it also means reverence and awe. More about this part of the definition later.

Let us first look at fear from a modern, psychologically informed viewpoint. It is a pervasive, overt and yet subtle questioning of our own worth, goodness, abilities, motivation, and desirability. Over time, it undermines our basic sense of selfhood and self-worth, ultimately deforming our desires, and leaving us with the sense that what we want is not good or right, and we are not deserving of it anyway. It fosters shame and guilt. It is the insidious process of dampening our life force and creativity. Over time we become inured to this process and accept it as the ordinary way of being. We become less free and are unaware of the impingement on our freedom by fear. Interestingly, acting on our deformed desires can make us feel freer, though actually we may be binding ourselves more tightly. This fear impinges upon us at many levels. It limits our creative, potent, full self from coming to be; it inhibits our ability to act. Simultaneously, this fear undermines our capacity to be, to rest, to be receptive, to surrender, to be transformed. This paralysis of our potent, active aspect, as well as our receptive aspect, can effectively inhibit us from changing ourselves or being open to the possibility of change from the outside. It can also paralyze our relationships with others.

The early Christian writers perceived fear differently. "Fear of the Lord is the first stage of wisdom."[5] They write time and time again on the theme that fear leads to love and that perfect love casts out all fear.[6] They distinguish a slavish fear associated with punishment from a fear associated with being a child of God, a fear of offending or damaging love. For them, this fear of the child of God is really a sign of the beginning of the right relationship between the creature and the Creator. It is awe, reverence for God. It leads to rest, contemplative rest, wordless rest in God. Their use of fear is essentially positive, in that it brings us to love. In a sense, then, fear itself has become distorted. We respond more often to an awe associated with judgment and power than to an awe that is primarily reverential. We need a deeper, clearer vision of the possibility of growth inherent in the right understanding of fear. A certain tension or anticipation is healthy and can challenge us, while too little may not encourage us to strive, and too much can paralyze us. Perhaps from this classical perspective fear will make a better rider for the horse of desire.

To have our desires limited or shaped is an excellent way to be controlled. We surrender our capacity for change and transformation when we accept our deformed and distorted desires as our true desires, as reflections of our true self, when they are in fact layers and layers of false aspects of ourselves. Others, such as parents, spiritual guides, and friends, can help or hinder us in the process of re-creating our desires. We need to look honestly not only at ourselves, but at the important people in our life, and more particularly, at our relationship with them. This includes the real possibility, even likelihood, that we, in some way, may be hindering others.

We are often many levels removed from our true desires. We cannot even consciously admit some of them to ourselves. We dread being in touch with what we, because of the operation of fear in our lives, believe we can never possibly have. So we repress our consciousness of these desires.

Becoming aware of our deepest and truest desires is an integral part of becoming who we truly are. In a sense we need to "uncover" ourselves. And this is no small or unimportant task for monastic men and women. I believe that an essential aspect of attaining purity of heart,[7] the proximate goal of monastic life according to John Cassian, is the "re-creation" of desire. I choose this word intentionally and purposefully. I do not see it as a process of *restoring* our true desire, as if we had it, and then lost it, or put it aside. It is not even a process of *returning* to a state of true undistorted desire, as though we could, or somehow should, go back and undo aspects of our lives. This desire we yearn and long for is not some pure, unsullied, pristine experience or even gift that we can somehow *regain*. Rather, in the human condition as seen through the eyes of Christian belief, the movement I call the re-creation of desire is our participation in the divine, transcendent, creative energies through which we all "live and move and have our being,"[8] our participation in the process of "making all things new."[9] Desire, true, undistorted desire, is ultimately good, a "good horse," as Sebastian Moore puts it. It is essentially an aspect of the Divine, the Godhead, God the Desiring One, wanting us, desiring us to be with God and in God. Again from Moore, desire is the allure of God. In Christian thought, the Paraclete, or Spirit, can be considered the personal endowment of Divine Desiring. In this light, the interesting discrepancy or division we often feel about our desires makes sense. It can be said that our desires are simultaneously aspects of our deepest selves and yet seemingly so far from our grasp. The Spirit, too, is both utterly "other" but also most ourselves, our truest self. As Sebastian Moore says, original sin is not growing psychologically,[10] and the key point here is the idea of growth, the growth that leads to the divinization of humanity.

This divinization, in the Christian tradition, has as its anchor the sacrament of baptism. This sacrament is a singularly important moment in the re-creation of desire, the beginning of our growth into union with the Divine. Building on natural desire, it is through this sacrament that the fullness of Desire[11] is given to us. The fullness of the expression of this Desire is yet to be actualized, however. The Paraclete is divine Desire as well as the gift by which we participate in divine Desire. We draw closer to this fullness as we cooperate in the re-creation of desire. Desire, in its re-creation, needs to be claimed, and made our own. This desire must be a part of our personal and ontological identity.[12] The process begins universally in concert with our development; at the time of baptism, the Divine, in a special way, enfolds us and awaits our movements toward growth. From this point forward, there is a dynamic flow of Desire and our desire.

God the Desiring One is constantly true but always changing: revealing, adapting to us to call us to true desire, to true humanity, depending on our development. This development, viewed from an Object Relations perspective has its own course; this is set forth, for example, in the work of the British pediatrician and psychoanalyst[13] D. W. Winnicott, a major figure in the Object Relations school. He highlights the inevitability of imperfect human development and goes on to make the point that perfect development is not necessary. In his discussion of the concept of the "good-enough mother,"[14] Winnicott states that there are some basic needs that must be met to provide a facilitating environment. But we, as a matter of course, come up against limits, failures, wrongs, sins of omission and commission. This leads to the development of what he calls a false self. The term "false self" as commonly used, however, is really a misnomer. Over the course of our development, in response to the many shortcomings of this world and those who inhabit it, we develop many false aspects of ourselves, efforts we use to protect that which is our truest essence. It is not just that some aspects of us develop falsely, but rather that we develop layer upon layer of falseness, of false aspects of many facets of ourselves. We frequently think that we have encountered our true self when we have, in fact, only arrived at another layer of falseness. Inherent in the development of the false self is the distortion of desire.

Consider someone who for a number of reasons has developed a false aspect that idolizes, craves, and "desires" power. Consider further that at some point this individual comes to understand this as a false aspect, covering over a sense of self that is weak, ineffectual, pitiable, and unlovable. In reality, this level of powerlessness is not the true self, but yet another layer of the many false selves developed over time. This layer is likely developed in response to an experience of perceived attack and denigration to expressed potency and self-assertion. Falsely believing oneself to be powerless, one forms the next level as compensation for this. Now multiply this process by the whole host of assaults that we all experience to get a sense of the complexity of false self development.

According to Winnicott and other Object Relations theorists, these false aspects of ourselves develop to protect us, to enhance our capacity to live safely in this world and with those who people it. It is an effort of adaptation and self-preservation. It is an effort to adjust to the demands placed upon us. Early in our lives we do not have a wide repertoire of approaches to use to respond to the demands, so we end up changing ourselves instead. The changes we make are often the best we can come up with under the circumstances. Unfortunately, even when new capacities have emerged we tend to respond according to the pattern learned earlier. Since much of this process remains outside of our awareness, we do not awaken to the possibility of a fresh response. Under these circumstances, even when a new response does come forth it will very likely be a further expression of the false self.

Dynamically, it takes a significant experience to influence the inner world that houses, metaphorically speaking, the representations of the highly charged relationships that were developed in response to the perceived demand or threat. That is, we perceive our relationships with others in the "real world" colored by these earlier experiences, now uniquely rarified in our inner world. It is important to note that for us, the so-called real world is not the real world at all. Insofar as our experience and evaluation of it are filtered through the inner world, the inner world is more real. So, something significant must occur to effect a change in our inner world of guiding perceptions and appraisals. These significant events can either reinforce the continuing development of the false aspects of ourselves or break through these, to varying degrees, to bring us closer to our true self.

In the preceding summary of false self development, a process that is endemic to the human condition, we see the subtle and not-so-subtle energies at work, thwarting our awareness of our true self. Much of this happens outside our awareness, resulting in an accumulation of disowned and unacknowledged aspects of ourselves, which in their own way contribute to the development of the false self. This concept of the false self is very important in psychoanalytically informed clinical practice, but it is also useful in explaining many other aspects of the human condition besides the purely psychological.

Inherent in the development of this false self is the distortion and deformation of desire. Our desires are an integral part of our identity. When John of the Cross was asked what was the most important thing he discovered in his spiritual quest, he responded, "my desires."[15] To know one's desires is to know oneself. From our perspective developed so far, we can say that to know one's (distorted) desires is to know one's (distorted) self. However, the mistake most often made is to equate our distorted desires with our true self. This belief limits our growth and diminishes our freedom. An awakening to this misconception allows us to work on change; to remain unaware is to remain prisoners of our false self.

Yet there is a "thread"[16] of Desire, constant and true, that is always in relationship with our desires, no matter how distorted and deformed. We, and our desires, are always in relationship with Desire. This is an important point to consider, because we often believe, in the throes of our deformed desires, that we are far removed from God. It may be a time of tension, perhaps estrangement, but not removal from God. This Desire is equivalent to, in many ways, our deepest life force; we can never be removed from it.

Interestingly, we become attached to those false aspects of ourselves that develop over time. This is part of the struggle. We are not really all that willing and eager to find our true selves. As illustration recall the example of the individual with distorted desire for power mentioned earlier. If the next level of false self that we come to understand more fully is believed to be the true self, it is not surprising that we do not rush to embrace this, especially since distorted desires will continue to pull us further away from our true self.

As I stated earlier in this paper, the word desire is often associated with sexual desire. While our desires are more varied than this, our sexual desires provide a unique lens through which to view aspects of ourselves. And nowhere are we more prisoners of our distorted desires than in the area of our sexual desires. I have found in my clinical work with others, and in my spiritual direction and monastic formation work, an interesting trend. Our introduction as children to our sexuality and our ongoing experiences of sexuality have, more often than not, led to the development of crucial false aspects of us. If we are to more completely understand ourselves, we must attend to the false self build-up and the distortions of desire associated with our sexual learning, our sexual history, and with the shame and guilt so often associated with it.

From an Object Relations perspective, I view sexuality not as being primarily a drive that needs to be discharged, with the object of the discharge being secondary, as classical drive theory would have it. Rather, sexuality can be understood as contributing to our essential aliveness—our sexuality heightens our aliveness. It helps us know more about ourselves. In this way it is first and foremost relational, helping us relate to ourselves. It is also one of a number of ways we seek relationships, the sustaining force of our lives. Sexual feelings are powerful feelings indeed, and although present in some way from birth onward, come to the fore most forcefully during puberty. Sexual fantasies develop with great intensity during this time, and are preparatory for the later genital sexual behavior that develops. They are also preparatory for the further development and enhancement of all aspects of our relationships with others.

Our desires include our sexual desires but are, of course, much more than that. However, many people often equate the word "desire" with their sexual desires. Perhaps because these aspects of our desires are intimately associated with physical feelings as well as the whole host of inner reactions, we can most completely experience the intensity, transcendence, and otherness of these aspects of these desires. Understanding our sexual selves is important to a fuller understanding of ourselves. What is sexually arousing to us, under what conditions, with whom, at what times—these are important questions. Our reflection on our erotic life can tell us much more; it can shed light on our relationships more generally, outside of the genital arena. Genital sexual desiring is multiply determined—it is always more than it seems to be. What do our sexual attractions tell us about our sense of ourselves, of our sense of others? What do we seek? What do we avoid? What do we fear? Why do we engage in genital sexual activity? Why do we choose not to? What many and varied purposes does it serve? Why do we choose whom we choose? Are we attracted to others because of certain physical characteristics? Are these characteristics more important than the person? All these questions, and more, help flesh out the larger picture of our inner world of object representations, thus giving us a greater sense of who we are and how we see others in relation to us.

Now at times the answer to these questions can be disconcerting. Our genital sexual feelings can seem to be beyond us, beyond our understanding, beyond our control. Some aspects of our sexual fantasies may be disturbing to us, body parts may be more important than the whole person. Fear of our own sexuality can develop. Some people, in the face of this, repress their genital and larger sexual selves, in the unconscious hope of restraining that which seems wrong, alien, or too much for them. All our desires are connected, so to repress our sexual desires is to effectively diminish the whole range of our desiring selves. This distances us to a greater or lesser degree from our life force, and from our experience of Desire.

In essence, then, the power of our sexuality is determined not so much by our sex "drive," but from the whole host of relational issues (with ourselves, others, God) in all our aspects. All of these experiences are expressed, to some degree, in our sexuality. This, in turn, is expressed and experienced bodily.

Embodiment is a much discussed topic these days.[17] Why is embodiment such an important concept, especially from a Christian perspective? Fundamentally, Christianity is an incarnational religion. As Christians we see in Jesus Christ the whole expression of humanity: body, mind, and spirit. There is physical energy, heat, associated with this embodied Christian life. Recalling Moore's earlier quotation, desire "will bound for the heart of the sun," calls up many images of God as light, fire, intense burning, but not necessarily all-consuming love. Christianity has had a love-hate relationship with desire, and very mixed views on the place of embodiment in theological thinking. Historically, there has been the continuing struggle between two opposing conceptions of God: as immanent and incarnational or as disembodied and transcendent.

To own and claim our physicality, and the desires associated with it, is an essential part of the Christian approach to the uncovering of the true self and the re-creation of desire. Our embodiment is not something to be tolerated in this life, but to be celebrated. If nothing else, Jesus gives us the permission to celebrate our bodies, and to understand them as integral parts of our total self. Indeed, I believe that in our bodies we have a useful key to the work of accessing our true self and carrying forward the re-creation process. Remember, however, that we are still operating to a greater or lesser degree under the pressure of distorted desires. Embodiment, certainly a potential corrective to the split inherent in false self development and the distortion of desire, is also subject to deformation. What some would call celebrating their bodies may not be a true celebration at all, but a distorted attempt to experience freedom by denying the distortions that drive their thoughts, feelings, and actions. Being "sexually free," for example, can either be an acting out of distorted genital sexuality, or it can be an integrated, unitive, truly freeing experience of love.

How does all this fit into the schema I am proposing for the re-creation of desire? We never totally lose our connection with Desire, from the time of our nascent development onward. The road to Desire is the path to the true self; our sexual desires can be a map for this journey and embodiment, especially seen in the light of the Incarnation, can be the vehicle we use in the process of re-creation.

If I had to choose one word to give a sense of the process of re-creating desire, it would be *uncovering*. We need to uncover ourselves. What does it mean to uncover? It means to expose, reveal, discover, to become naked, nude, stripped, undressed, unclothed, undisguised, to be bare, unprotected, unadorned, undecorated, stark, simple, and empty. Like desiring, uncovering is not neatly defined. Like the building up of our false self, the uncovering process is also multifaceted.

What are some aspects of this process? Although it is unique for each person, there are some common elements:

- Experiencing crisis moments calling for a realignment of our identity, of us-in-relationship
- Awakening to the awareness of
    - the distance between where we are and who we are; the sense of being strangers to ourselves
    - the constraints on our current way of living
    - the gentle voice of Love, of Desire, calling out to us
    - the power of our desires, especially our sexual desires
    - fear, and often an intensification of fear
    - our true self, the true desiring self, wishing to surrender
- Surrendering to the risk of uncovering
- Abiding in the disorganization that usually follows
- Embracing this altered, more embodied self

Note that although the process of the re-creation of desire has a strong psychological component to it, it is not just a psychological process. We can use psychological constructs to help us understand the process, but we must always bear in mind that the movement is toward a deeper and deeper relationship with the Divine. It is awkward to speak of levels, but in an effort to convey the difference between this process and a psychological process, we can say that in the process of re-creating desire we are working on multiple levels simultaneously. Ultimately, this process of re-creation is our life's work.

Still, we are developing beings, and there are any number of key moments or occasions that offer us the opportunity to attend to who we really are. Crises can be either developmentally related or the result of external or internal incursions. What is common to all crises is the unbalancing and disorganization associated with them. We will, as humans, experience many crises. What marks these crisis opportunities as special is that they allow us to have a deeper, clear, and radically truthful awareness of our current state of affairs. These occasions can include such things as falling in love, recognizing that someone loves us, losing someone important to us or losing a highly cherished ideal or ability, entering or ending a committed relationship, rites of passage, and other experiences associated with moving from one developmental period to the next. They also include tragedies such as "hitting bottom," as is discussed in the Twelve-Step literature, acting out our distorted desires including, but not limited to, sexual acting out, and the helping processes that we often seek in response to these opportunities. These opportunities can also come about in very powerful ways as a result of prayer, spiritual direction, and other activities that draw us deeper into our hearts. Some writers talk about the vast impact that spiritual emergencies and spiritual emergence can have on individuals. There are many other key moments. What is common to them all is the potential to see ourselves in a new light, the potential to look deeper, as it were, to get a glimpse of the Truly Good in us. We can say that these moments are ubiquitous in the human situation.

Something further is needed, and that is awareness. To develop this awareness, we need to pause, to see what richness awaits us in this moment. The richness is not always pleasant or enjoyable; indeed, there is always the confrontation with fear that must take place. I outlined earlier some of the various aspects of this period of awareness. To be aware of our essentially divided self, of our being chained and bound by what we originally thought to be freeing, aware of our being controlled by our distorted desires (this is especially painful when we have believed that we had our desires "in control") is a humbling experience, one that we might prefer to avoid. Fear will drive us away from this necessarily humbling experience. Interestingly, we will usually not even know it is fear that holds us back; rather we end up believing it is someone else's problem, that it really isn't so bad, that it will all blow over. And many times it will! The opportunities for experiencing a self-crisis, if you will, are legion. More often than not we do not see these experiences as the opportunities that they truly are for us. We let them pass by. This is a victory for fear, which, beyond our awareness, has yet again held us hostage. We must name fear, to see it for what it is, to see its workings in our lives. Naming fear, realizing its hold on us, can often be extraordinarily painful, but necessary.

Are there some forces, some aspects of this drama that work to counter the vise-grip of fear? Yes, there are. First, there is the gentle but insistent call of God, of Desire, deep within us, in our heart, residing in our truest self, reaching out to us. Second, there is the experience of the reality of our true self, and the glimmer of what we can eventually be. If we can pause and open ourselves to ourselves, we can experience these two almost silent realities, unobtrusive yet most real.

It is the belief in these two realities that allows the next step, that of surrendering to uncovering. Taking advantage of the moment, pausing and allowing ourselves to become aware of both the pain and the promise, we surrender to that first, primary urge. Sebastian Moore says that "we desire to be desired by the one we desire." Recognizing that we are truly desired by Desire, in our falseness and brokenness, allows and encourages our surrender. Surrendering to uncovering has multiple nuances. Reflecting on the many words that help us understand uncovering, we perceive a number of them as having a sensual or sexual sense; to become *naked, nude, undressed*. This recalls the Garden of Eden story in Genesis. However, we are not returning to an original innocence; we are embracing a new, developing desiring self. Our stripping removes the layers of falseness—we experience a new freedom, the freedom of ever less distorted desires. This work of surrender is not our work alone—far from it. Like all of this process it is relational, with an underlying mutuality in that center where we are so entirely with God. Time collapses in this process; simultaneously we experience "in an instant, in a twinkling of an eye" the transformative process of the shattering of the false self; yet we will, in the temporal cycle, continue to work through this shattering change.

Other words convey a different sense: *undisguised, unadorned, undecorated, stark, simple, empty.* Here the meaning seems more related to fundamental approaches to life. Simplicity and emptiness are crucial words. As Christians, the paradox is that only by experiencing our emptiness are we full. Again, everything is relational. Ordinarily, when we experience being "full," it is a false fullness; we are usually "full-of" ourselves. We then become empty, but it is a becoming "empty-for"—in this case for God, for Desire. This emptiness allows the creative power inherent both in God and in ourselves to flourish. We become transparent to truth and experience the loss of pretence. So we continually strive to be less full-of and more empty-for. This uncovering is an ongoing process, really a way of being. We are engaged in a process of continually allowing ourselves to become more undressed, simple, and empty. In the face of an ever-increasing awareness of our many layers of falseness, we simultaneously experience a deep freedom and greater clarity of our desires.

In many ways this is a process of reorganization, and this involves disorganization. We need to abide in this disorganization as the transforming power of this process—our process—continues to work. We abide in the disorganization because we abide in God. John's Gospel highlights the importance of abiding, of remaining. Jesus speaks here in intimate relational terms. To abide in and during this disorganization is to abide in God in faith. This abiding dynamically relates us to Jesus and to the Godhead by the power of the Paraclete. This remaining, this abiding, is an ever-increasing experience of the divine Desiring penetrating us and uniting us with God: Creator, Son, and Spirit. Nevertheless, it is an uncomfortable and often painful process. This abiding can be experienced as standing in a deeper place, having the sense of being grounded in God in the midst of swirling torrents. The sense of our trueness and the clarity of our desire comes at a price, especially in those moments that call forth a more radical change.

What is the experience of this developing self, becoming ever more true, with clarity of desire? Does it mean that we no longer have distorted desires, desires for power, lustful desires, or are no longer troubled by the seven capital sins, hallmarks of distorted desire? No. Rather there is a clearer sense of the inherent falseness in these attractions and behaviors. We are slowly able to see the role of fear in our distorted desires, and we can choose to address these fears head-on rather than acting in such a way that fear continues to control us. In addition, we are more and more drawn to that which is good and true in us, and the characteristic associated with this is a sense of increased freedom.

A fundamental outcome of this process of re-creating desire is a greater sense of unity, and especially a lessening of the artificial dualism between our bodies and our minds and spirits. This unity is signified by our embracing our changed, more embodied self. Ever more true, uncovered, simple, and empty, we are ever more truly incarnated. We abide in the unity of our body, mind, and spirit and in doing this we are abiding in God who is that unity for each of us in a unique way.

How do these ideas about the process of the re-creation of desire relate to the ancient concept of purity of heart? I believe that this process is a way of attaining purity of heart. Simply put, the process of re-creation of desire brings us to that essential unique and unified relationship, of God in us and us in God. Terrence Kardong, in his commentary on the Rule of Benedict, repeatedly refers to Cassian and his concept of purity of heart. He understands Cassian to mean here the transformation of the human person, the movement from fear of punishment to love of virtue itself, and quotes Michael Casey's lively expression "aiming the heart at the target," which is God.[18] Esther de Waal relates purity of heart to a stripping process.[19] Transformation, movement from fear, being heart-linked with God, stripping, are all part of the re-creation of desire. Teilhard de Chardin has observed that union differentiates. William Johnston comments on this affirmation:

> If this Teilhardian principle is taken seriously, it could revolutionize mystical theology East and West, changing our approach to the self. In union with the other, in becoming the other, in dwelling in the other, in intimacy with the other I find my true self.... Union differentiates.[20]

In many ways, this is truly a revolution, calling for further exploration. Uncovering ourselves in the transcendent sense we are discussing here is done for others and with the help of others: of God and of those close to us. The transformation associated with the re-creation of desire and with purity of heart can and should be seen in our relation with others and the created world. We experience a joining, a connection with others that allows for a clearer sense of who we are and what we are made for. I am reminded of Merton's experience on the street corner as an example of this. Everything around us is seen in a different perspective. But how can we characterize the inner transformation? Perhaps the notion of *unitive participation* can help. Here too union differentiates. This unitive participation with God is a nondualistic relationship, based on our participation in the creative transforming energies of Desire, the Desire of which all other desires are aspects. This union brings about true self-realization, the emergence of the new person (St. Paul), the coming into being of our true individuality. Indeed it is only in this divine participation that these things can come about. This differentiating union exemplifies the paradox that characterizes spiritual experience.

Earlier I mentioned another paradox, the simultaneous awareness of Desire and the Spirit being totally other and yet our most real self. Here at the ground of our being, at our still point, inside God, things are different. Here again words fail us. Desire and relationship, in this place, inside God, have a certain otherness. Again picking up on Moore, the desire and relationship we experience are only aspects of desire and relationship inside God. Finally, quoting Merton, in a conference he gave (quoted in de Waal),[21] "if you penetrate by detachment and purity of heart to the inner secret ground of your ordinary experience, you will attain to a liberty that nobody can touch." Liberty, freedom, the loving fearful (in its undistorted sense) freedom of the child of God that we are, allows us to bound for the sun, to aim our heart toward the heart of God and to reach the target.

I began by quoting Sebastian Moore regarding Buddhism and desire. Let us return to this for a moment. What do those who bring together Buddhism and psychology have to say, and especially about this falseness of self that I believe underlies distorted desire? I will comment on a few of the Buddhist approaches that have appeared in recent books.

In his thoughtful book *Thoughts without a Thinker: Psychotherapy from a Buddhist Perspective,* Mark Epstein, M.D., a Buddhist practitioner and psychiatrist, discusses the Buddhist approach to self, informed by his understanding of the Buddhist perspective on the true and false self. For example,

> People always come to therapy seeking their "true selves," demanding of the therapist in much the same way as Vacchagotta demanded of the Buddha. Much of the identity confusion that propels a person into therapy or that arises as a result of therapy can be understood from this perspective. People often bring the sense of falseness about themselves to therapy with the expectation of somehow shedding it.[22]

Epstein goes on to make the point that if the therapist accepts the notion of having a false self that needs to be shed, important opportunities, from a Buddhist perspective, will be lost. He argues against giving form to the self, whether true or false. He quotes Winnicott: "There is but little point in formulating a True Self idea except for the purposes of understanding the False Self." He then quotes Object Relations psychoanalyst Christopher Bollas: "The true self [is that which is able to be spontaneous].... The true self listens to a Beethoven sonata, goes for a walk, reads the sports section of a newspaper, plays basketball and dreams about a holiday."[23] He then goes on to say that "in the Buddhist view a realized being has realized her own *lack* of a true self." And later he says "The true self experience that has come to preoccupy Western analysts is achievable most directly through the appreciation of what the Buddhists would call emptiness of self."[24]

I would say that people often do bring this "sense of falseness" to therapy, and to other situations that offer the possibility of chance. But because of their distorted desires, about which they are usually pretty much unaware, they seek to shed an aspect of their falseness for another false aspect. At a purely psychological level, Winnicott makes an important point: The true self may be best known by what it is not. Similarly, Bollas, in describing the deep processes at work in the human condition, refers to the "unthought known." In this, and in the previous quotation, I think Bollas is attempting to put words to mystery, to the mystery of the human person. In addition, the concepts of true self, false self, and ego, id, and superego, for that matter, are constructs, poor attempts, a shorthand as it were, to convey some of the mysterious aspects of humanity. And I would agree that the true self experience is approached through emptiness, the emptiness-for that I mentioned earlier. Whether the approach Epstein describes is the best or the most direct approach is open to debate.

Another helpful book is the edited volume *Beyond Therapy: The Impact of Eastern Religions on Psychological Theory and Practice.*[25] Colette Ray's chapter on "Western Psychology and Buddhist Teachings: Convergences and Differences"[26] is balanced and helpful, but here again I found something lacking in the comparison, because of the way a Buddhist-informed psychology is compared to "psychology." Earlier, when I discussed Epstein's ideas, I used the term "purely psychological." I use it advisedly. I do not believe such a state of abstraction is possible. As Epstein himself notes, he did not set out to integrate therapy and Buddhism—it just happened. We bring more to our understanding of the human situation, to the therapeutic encounter, and to all those moments that offer the possibility of change than just our learned body of psychological knowledge. Just as Buddhists bring a perspective, so do Christians. I would make the point that in using the psychological ideas of Object Relations theory to understand the human situation from a Christian point of view, the relational component makes a good fit with the essential Incarnational element of Christianity. And, for me, the play of language associated with the musings of Bollas and Winnicott helps convey the mystery of Christian experience. Psychologists try to understand the religion of Christians with the Object Relations modes—it is a way to make sense of the "god-representation," as they refer to it. Christians can use the same principles in an attempt to understand and put into words what cannot be named or explained but what is still surely experienced and known. This is a subtle but important difference.

In discussing the goal or end of Christian monastic life, Cassian writes in his first Conference, "The end of our profession is the reign of God or the reign of heaven; but the nearer goal, or aim, is purity of heart, without which it is impossible for anyone to arrive at that end."[27] This process of re-creation of desire brings us to Desire, to God. I believe that the radical uncovering I have been describing—the removing of the layers of falseness— is a purifying process, bringing us to our truest self: to that which is and has always been true. There, empty at last, our hearts "overflow with the inexpressible delights of love."[28] In the Christian monastic tradition, Benedict offers the ladder of the degrees of humility as a way to God. Bernard writes similarly of a progression through the degrees of truth: the truth of ourselves, of our neighbor, and of God. Both of these processes have at their center, as does the process of re-creation of desire, the movement away from alienation and disidentification and a movement toward awareness and acceptance. We are, paradoxically, most ourselves when we are one with God; we are our most unique self when encompassed by Desire; we are one when we are two. John McDargh[29] talks of the Christian contemplative union as "one-but-two." Further, as Christians, the Incarnate Lord calls each of us to personally and uniquely participate in the *creative energy* that is God. This too is a movement into enlightenment, but enlightenment of a kind that has been even less commonly recognized. Again: As we become fully human, we become Divine.

17

Purity of Heart

A Dialogue

MARY MARGARET FUNK, O.S.B.

Purity of Heart: easy to say, quick to write but hard to define and harder yet to achieve. In our times of East-West exchange, spiritual traditions bring us closer to each other and to ourselves. In this context of dialogue, poets and scholars emerge who have the ability to articulate things which, for the most part, we have only been able to glimpse wordlessly in the depths of our hearts. Among these in the Christian tradition, Thomas Merton, a Trappist monk of the Abbey of Gethsemani, has been foremost. Not only has he left a literary legacy of many books, articles, and letters, he has also set in motion a sustained dialogue with spiritual traditions of the East: Zen and Tibetan Buddhism, Hinduism, Taoism, and Sufism. In this extended exchange, Christian terms, such as "purity of heart" are often reclaimed and explored through the insights of other traditions.

This paper will continue the exchange. In an imaginary dialogue between myself and Thomas Merton, I hope to reveal both his understanding of the term "purity of heart," and the process by which he arrived at his understanding. My part of the dialogue consists in asking him to speak the relevant insights that he has expressed in his writings as well as in reflecting, in the light of these ideas, on some related experiences of my own. I've made an effort to remain close to the content of his actual written words, while fitting these ideas into the context of the imaginary dialogue. Direct quotes and sources are documented in the endnotes.

I have focused our discussion on the relation between purity of heart and *le point vierge*—that phrase that held such deep meaning for Thomas Merton. Two other themes will appear: "dread" and "final integration." In Merton's explorations of purity of heart, these three concepts are interwoven; together they reveal the beauty and depth of his thought.

The Dialogue: Father Louis (Thomas) Merton (TM)
and Sister Mary Margaret Funk (MMF)

MMF: Greetings, Father Louis. Thank you for agreeing to talk with me about purity of heart for this conference at Big Sur.

TM: I am happy to reflect on this with you. Purity of heart is a deep and engaging question.

MMF: I heartily agree. And ever since I read *Merton and Sufism: The Untold Story*,[1] I've wanted to ask you about *le point vierge*. Do you find "purity of heart" in the Christian tradition to be the same as *le point vierge* in the Sufi tradition?

TM: Now that you mention it, *le point vierge* does hold something like the same place in Sufi mysticism as does purity of heart in John Cassian's teaching. It reminds me also of Evagrius's concept of *apatheia*, and the fountainhead of peace that appears at the conclusion of Benedict's Prologue: "hearts overflowing with the inexpressible delight of love."[2] The goal of the monastic life is understood in that tradition as a heart prepared for the enjoyment of divine contemplation.

MMF: It was Louis Massignon, the French scholar and advocate of Christian-Muslim dialogue,[3] who introduced you to the expression *le point vierge*.[4] What do you understand by that phrase?

TM: I'll have to confess that I don't understand it. It fascinates me, and I keep searching around its edges: "the 'point vierge' of the spirit, the center of our nothingness where, in apparent despair, one meets God and is found completely in His mercy."[5]

MMF: You used that term—*le point vierge*—to describe your experience at Fourth and Walnut Street in Louisville in 1958.[6] Can you tell me about that experience?

TM: We were in town, on routine errands. "Then it was as if I suddenly saw the secret beauty of their hearts where neither sin nor desire nor self-knowledge can reach, the core of their reality, the person that each one is in God's eyes." "If only they could all see themselves as they really are."[7]

MMF: What a wonderful gift! What did you understand from seeing into the hearts of others?

TM: The realization was that I was one particular man, yet united center to center with all other particular men and women. We were one.

MMF: And you related that experience immediately to *le point vierge*?

TM: "Again that expression . . . comes in here. At the center of our being is a point of nothingness, which is untouched by sin and illusion, a point of pure truth . . . from which God disposes of our lives, which is inaccessible to the fantasies of our own mind or the brutalities of our own will. This little point of nothingness . . . is the pure glory of God in us. . . . It is like a pure diamond, blazing with the invisible light of heaven."[8]

MMF: For you, then, this sense of profound interconnectedness was experienced at an untouchable center of our being that belongs to God?

TM: Exactly. "It is in everybody, and if we could see it we would see these billions of points of light coming together in the face and blaze of a sun that would make all the darkness and cruelty of life vanish completely.... I have no program for this seeing. It is only given. But the gate of heaven is everywhere."[9]

MMF: Why do you relate this experience to *le point vierge*? And what is the background of that expression?

TM: As I thought about that experience, the phrase kept coming to consciousness. Louis Massignon, who introduced it to me, quoted a saying of al-Hallaj to the effect that "our hearts are a virgin that God's truth alone opens."[10]

MMF: I like that—"our hearts are a virgin that God's truth alone opens." Is it something like the mysticism of Gertrude, Lutgarde, or Margaret Mary?

TM: It doesn't feel like it to me. Those Christian saints describe the experience of spousal mysticism. This Sufi conception is more apophatic or metaphysical, if I may say so.

MMF: And what is the difference between apophatic and spousal mysticism, for you?

TM: These seem to be the two main doors to union with God. Spousal mysticism is experienced through images and creation, mediated by love and devotion. Apophatic mysticism is through the mystery of nothingness, that ineffable experience beyond experience. I find that the term *le point vierge* belongs to that apophatic kind of mysticism.

MMF: How does Hallaj relate this apophatic mysticism to the heart?

TM: "Hallaj retains and expands the Quranic notion that the heart is the organ prepared by God for contemplation. The function cannot be exercised without the organ ... he declares mystical union to be real; far from being the total disappearance of the heart ... it is its sanctifying resurrection.... The final covering of the heart ... is the *sirr,* the latent personality, the implicit consciousness, the deep subconscious, the secret cell walled up (and hidden) to every creature, the 'inviolate virgin.' The latent personality of man remains unformed until God visits the *sirr,* and as long as neither angel nor man divines it."[11]

MMF: *Sirr:* would we call that our heart of hearts?

TM: "It's clear that 'the virgin' is the innermost, secret heart—the deep subconscious of a person. It is to this heart that the saying of al-Hallaj applies: 'Our hearts, in their secrecy, are a virgin alone, where no dreamer's dream penetrates ... the heart where the presence of the Lord alone penetrates, there to be conceived.'"[12]

MMF: Let's stop here for a moment. This place in the heart—is it something physical? symbolic? mystical?

TM: The place is both physical and mystical. Much like the Eastern Christian teaching about "the heart." It's a physical spot in our anatomy and it's the place were there's an intensely centered pulsation and bundles of energy. This is very deep. People can live their whole lives and not find this place, though each of us has it. It's all there in each of us.

MMF: So, if this is the place where God is in our heart, that virgin place, then each of us already has purity of heart, right?

TM: Yes, we have it. We only need to realize it consciously.

MMF: So, we have to feel that place in the heart?

TM: Yes, and no. I used *le point vierge* to express my felt experience, but I couldn't *try* to have that experience and then have it. Though it would certainly make life in the Gethsemani community easier if I could feel that way all the time. Nor was it an intellectual bond; we were *one,* heart to heart! I did nothing to arouse such love for everyone. It just happened by the grace of God. It was a routine trip to the printer. Suddenly I was almost giddy with the delight of a solidarity with all people." "This sense of liberation from an illusory difference" [between Merton the monk and everybody else] "was such a relief and such a joy to me that I almost laughed out loud. I suppose my happiness could have taken form in the words: Thank God, thank God that I am like other men, that I am only a man among others."[13]

MMF: So, a transcendent experience of being an ordinary human being?

TM: What I realized that day in Louisville was that "It is a glorious destiny to be a member of the human race, though it is a race dedicated to many absurdities and one which makes many terrible mistakes; yet, with all that, God Himself gloried in becoming a member of the human race. A member of the human race! To think that such a commonplace realization should suddenly seem like news that one holds the winning ticket in a cosmic sweepstake."[14]

MMF: You go on speaking of an immense joy of being human, of being a member of a race in which God became incarnate. "As if the sorrows and stupidities of the human condition could overwhelm me, now I realize that we all are one."[15] Do you remember writing that?

TM: Yes... I stand by that statement; "if only everybody could realize this! But it cannot be explained. There is no way of telling people that they are all walking around shining like the sun."[16]

MMF: How did the experience affect you? Did your consciousness change?

TM: It sharpened my desire and purified my motivation for solitude, "for it is, in fact, the function of solitude to make one realize such things with a clarity that would be impossible to anyone completely immersed in the other cares, the other illusions, and all the automatisms of a tightly collective existence."[17] It increased the intensity of my desire for the hermit life, but at the same time made me realize that "my solitude ... is not my own, for I see now how much it belongs to them—and that I have a responsibility for it in their regard, not just in my own. It is because I am one with them that I owe it to them to be alone—and when I am alone they are not 'they' but my own self. There are no strangers!"[18]

MMF: So your solitude seems like a way for you to dwell in that place—your heart of hearts—and experience intimacy with God and others, in a place of unshakable truth. What you are saying brings to mind an experience I had when I was about to take my doctoral exams.

TM: What was it?

MMF: Right before the exams I was going through a great deal of conflict—anxiety not so much about the study as about what the Ph.D. would mean in my life. I remember standing before a window in my room at Catholic University which overlooked the Shrine of the Immaculate Conception, asking over and over, "to be a scholar, not to be a scholar." Then at one moment I suddenly became aware of a place in my heart that nothing had touched yet, a place in my heart that "knew." God's place. I realized that everything was complete. All the study and preparation and training was irrelevant, unnecessary. All was done, finished, settled, and at peace. I reached a place in which no more knowledge could be added, and nothing could be taken away. I was already there. Just there, in the knowing. It seems to me now that I didn't need to know more, I needed to be more knowing.

TM: Your realization of *le point vierge!* So, did you drop out of your studies?

MMF: Unfortunately, when I came back to ordinary awareness, I did not follow up and change my life to fit that experience. A few weeks later I failed comprehensive exams. I left dejected, misunderstood, and confused.

TM: I understand. Reaching that point is not easy and not expected, but coming back from it is harder, and life becomes more challenging because of what we realized.

MMF: Indeed. Although I reached that place in my heart, and knew all was well and right and complete, and that I did not need to become a scholar, I still suffered from failing my exams. Why can't we stay in that awareness? It seemed to evaporate so quickly for me.

TM: It does seem that we are raised to that level of consciousness and then slip back again. What gives us hope is that the point, *le point vierge*, never leaves. You experienced that one-pointed place in the sincere questioning of your direction, and I imagine that it nourishes and guides you still. My experience in Louisville opened my heart and that realization of connectedness and being a member of the human race has never really left.

MMF: Through the description of your realization at Fourth and Walnut, as well as through my own experience, I get a sense of what *le point vierge* might be. Could you explain how it is understood in Sufism, and how it is related to purity of heart?

TM: As I said, in the Sufi tradition, the innermost heart is referred to as "the virgin." The "point" is that primordial place of knowing God within, of which al-Hallaj and other Islamic mystics often speak. "So the 'virgin point,' *le point vierge*, in Massignon's parlance is, by analogy, the last, irreducible, secret center of the heart."[19] Massignon described this further when he wrote to a friend: "The return to our origin, to the beginning of our adoption— by reentering our Mother's womb, as our Lord told Nicodemus, to be born again—by finding again at the bottom of our heart, the virgin point (*le point vierge*) of our election to Christianity and the action of God's will in us."[20]

MMF: So for the Sufis, the experience of *le point vierge* is a return to our origins, a reentering of the womb, a rebirth, in the secret and hidden bottom of the heart. What about the sin, the evil inclinations that are so much a part of us?

TM: I understand *le point vierge* as the place of God, the deepest part of ourselves beyond sin.[21] Nothing reaches this part of God's creation. Sin is real, but in that place forgiveness is always already given.

MMF: Can you say more about *le point vierge* and its relation to purity of heart?

TM: Perhaps Massignon's most relevant passage is from 1957, when he was comparing Muslim and Christian mysticism in the Middle Ages:

> The "science of hearts," the early nucleus of the methodological traits of mysticism in Islam, began with the identifying of anomalies in the spiritual life of the believer who prays, who must be simple and naked; the early technical terms served to designate the errors of judgment, the mental pretences, the hypocrisies.... The "heart" designates the incessant oscillation of the human will which beats like the pulse under the impulse of various passions, an impulse which must be stabilized by the Essential Desire, one single God.[22]

MMF: This reminds me of Kierkegaard's classic book, *Purity of Heart Is to Will One Thing*.[23]

TM: Yes, it's the same principle: To will the good, which is God, one must be single-hearted. No double-minded intentions penetrate beyond these veils protecting our *sirr* (innermost heart).

MMF: I interrupted you. Do continue with what you learned from the Sufis.

TM: The Sufi tradition goes on to teach that "introspection must guide us to tear through the concentric 'veils' which ensheathe the heart, and hide from us the virginal point...the secret (*sirr*), wherein God manifests Himself."[24] Massignon used the expression often in other contexts. For example, he spoke of the faith of Abraham as the very axis of Islamic teaching, the "true virgin point that is found at its center, that makes it live and by which all the rest is sustained invisibly and mysteriously."[25]

MMF: Our impulses are stabilized by Essential Desire, by our one single God. But my experience has been more on the negative side.

TM: That's the way it seems, sometimes positive and sometimes negative. The Desire runs into "apparent despair" of penetrating all these veils that cover the soul. Is that what you mean by negative experience?

MMF: I know the place of despair. You said earlier that *le point vierge* is "the center of our nothingness where, in apparent despair, one meets God— and is found completely in His mercy."[26] Until now, I had not seen despair as the door to *le point vierge,* but it is.

TM: Tell we more about the place of apparent despair and *le point vierge.* When did you come to know that place of apparent despair?

MMF: Right after final vows in 1968. At age twenty-five, I sank into a major depression. During the school year I was a fourth-grade teacher at St. Barnabas. A mass of details won't convey the picture, so I'll just paint one moment that stands out in my memory. I was hospitalized at St. Vincent's Psychiatric Hospital in St. Louis for over seven weeks that summer. One afternoon I walked out front all the way to the end of the property, and down some old cement steps. There I sat that whole afternoon, dejected. A train went by at a moderate speed. There was no inclination to take my life; even that seemed useless. The train signaled my life going by. Death didn't seem to offer an escape from this existence that was my burden. I had no way of knowing if there was a way to get free of this suffering to which even death wasn't the answer. I stopped crying; there was no one to cry to. Somewhere was God, I thought, but not available. I was utterly alone. I was thinking that none of the psychoanalytic theories, drugs, group therapy, or activities seemed to relieve the burden of being human during those weeks.

TM: So you just sat there?

MMF: Yes, I sat still and sank into my misery. There was no relief from this despair until several months later.

TM: You went back to teach fourth grade in Indianapolis?

MMF: Yes, but during Holy Week and Easter break in 1969 I asked to return to St. Louis and get off the medication, as it was interfering with my teaching. So I returned to St. Vincent's Hospital in St. Louis. On Holy Saturday evening we had a short form of the services for the long-term patients. I joined the line to follow the Easter Candle and Father McIntyre into the shapeless institutional chapel. I shared a pew with a bent, toothless woman. I was thinking how shameful it was for me, a professed Benedictine nun, to be having my Vigil Service in a psych ward. Then, as I mindlessly followed the leading of the ritual, I felt her hand in mine. "Well, here I am," I thought to myself. This intimacy with folks who were just "being there" scattered the darkness.

TM: Tell me, why did this dark experience relieve your despair?

MMF: My despair was real, not an illusion. I was "in truth" sitting on that concrete step in August and watching that train go by. That was real. There is a tug to "nonbeing." This Vigil moment was another moment of truth, and it was a profound experience of *le point vierge*. I was with the old woman. Also, the moment had a presence unto itself, a freestanding sense of well-being that just is because it *is*. Or I could echo your words at Fourth and Walnut and say, "Thank God, I am like all the other folks."

TM: So, rather than seeing each other person radiant like the sun, you had the experience of yourself being "creature."

MMF: I don't think I can relate even to you how satisfying it was to be "in the truth." When I read chapter seven of Benedict's Rule after that, I was no stranger to its degrees of humility.

TM: So you reached your own *point vierge* through emptiness.

MMF: Despair empties all that isn't real. The result is a peace-filled "right feeling" in the face of nothingness. But why can't we sustain these insights so that they can change our lives? I got out of despair, but I don't think it changed me much.

TM: It was the same for me; after profound experiences I returned to my ordinary, unreliable self in my day-to-day life. And that may have been behind my own dark experience—of *dread*.

MMF: We all know the feeling of living in "dread." And we've also felt the ambiguity that lurks within our own monastic institutions. What is an *authentic* monastic life? You've written about monasticism as—ideally—the place for "final integration." What would that be like?

TM: "Final integration is a state of transcultural maturity far beyond mere social adjustment, which always implies partiality and compromise. The man who is 'fully born' has an entirely 'inner experience of life.' He apprehends his life fully and wholly from an inner ground that is at once more universal than the empirical ego and yet entirely his own. He is in a certain sense 'cosmic' and 'universal man.' He has attained a deeper, fuller identity than that of the limited ego self, which is only a fragment of one's being."[27]

MMF: This vision of openness and solidarity recalls our experience of *le point vierge,* doesn't it?

TM: Yes, "He is in a certain sense identified with everybody: or in the familiar language of the New Testament...he is 'all things to all men.' He is able to experience their joys and sufferings as their own, without however becoming dominated by them."[28]

MMF: One with everyone and yet not confined within their limits?

TM: "He has attained a deep inner freedom—the freedom of the Spirit we read of in the New Testament. He is guided not just by will and reason, but by 'spontaneous behavior subject to dynamic insight'... Again, the state of insight which is final integration implies an openness, an 'emptiness,' a 'poverty' similar to those described in such detail not only by the Rhenish mystics, by St. John of the Cross, by the early Franciscans, but also by the Sufis, the early Taoist masters, and Zen Buddhists. Final integration implies the void, poverty, and nonaction which leave one entirely docile to the 'Spirit' and hence a potential instrument for unusual creativity."[29]

MMF: But what about one's past experience, one's own culture?

TM: "The man who has attained final integration is no longer limited by the culture in which he has grown up. He has embraced *all of life* ... he has experienced qualities of every type of life: ordinary human existence, intellectual life, artistic creation, human love, and religious life. He passes beyond all these limiting forms, while retaining all that is best and most universal in them, 'finally giving birth to a fully comprehensive self.' He accepts not only his own community, his own society, his own friends, his own culture, but all humankind. He does not remain bound to one limited set of values in such a way that he opposes them aggressively or defensively to others."[30]

MMF: This sounds ideal—especially in our world of today.

TM: The vision is in the spirit of our tradition. "He is fully 'catholic' in the best sense of the word. He has a unified vision and experience of the one truth shining out in all its various manifestations, some clearer than others. He does not set these partial views in opposition to each other, but unites them in a dialectic or an insight of complementarity. With this view of life, he is able to bring perspective, liberty, and spontaneity to the lives of others. The finally integrated man is a peacemaker, and that is why there is such a desperate need for our leaders to become such people of insight."[31]

MMF: I'm beginning to see the relation between *le point vierge* and this final integration. It is one thing to have a glimpse of our universality as you did in Louisville that day, but it is another thing to live the life consciously: working collaboratively, and promoting social interaction where differences are celebrated.

TM: As we both know, moments come and moments go. It's daily life that holds the promise.

MMF: I've heard you say that this kind of maturity is exactly what the monastic life should produce.

TM: "The monastic ideal is precisely this sort of freedom in the spirit, this liberation from the limits of all that is merely partial and fragmentary in a given culture. Monasticism calls for a breadth and universality of vision that sees everything in the light of One Truth, as St. Benedict beheld all creation embraced 'in one ray of the sun.' This too is suggested at the end of chapter seven of the Rule where St. Benedict speaks of the new identity, the new mode of being of the monk who no longer practices the various degrees of humility with concentrated and studied effort, but with dynamic spontaneity 'in the Spirit.' It is suggested also in the 'Degrees of Truth' and the 'Degrees of Love' in St. Bernard's tracts on humility and on the love of God."[32]

MMF: Would you say then that *humility* is the final integration, and that to experience humility is to experience purity of heart?

TM: Yes, I think so; it has to be where Truth and Love meet. We are free, liberated and totally immersed in God's love. At some point in our monastic life, we should feel the peace promised by Cassian's vision of purity of heart. Even that dread should ease up if we are doing what we feel is our best. What others see in us ought to be truthful. What is truth if it can't be detected either by us, living the monastic way of life, or by those who observe it from the outside?

MMF: Without truth and the striving for it, we are all living a lie, and that seems a double waste. As you experienced at Fourth and Walnut Street, we are all the same, lay and monastic. To be religious is pretentious if there is not some "way of living" that makes living authentic. This was my experience, too, at St. Vincent's. We were all creatures. And *le point vierge* isn't attainable since we already have it—only we don't experience it?

TM: What we experience is the cross. Suffering is our way. And purity of heart isn't "achieved," either. We do sense truth, though. That seems to be the fruit of living a life toward purity of heart.

MMF: Can we say that we experience *le point vierge* when we undergo an apparent despair in this center of our nothingness? Apparent despair creates the truth that sets us free, right?

TM: Notice the expression you used, "apparent" despair. When I look back on the low points of my life, I see that all those afflictions brought me to apparent despair. Despair was my experience, but *le point vierge* in my heart of hearts remained pure and nothing touched it except God and God alone.

MMF: You pointed out "an important distinction between mere neurotic anxiety which comes from a commitment to defeat and existential anxiety which is the healthy pain caused by the blocking of vital energies that still remain available for radical change."[33]

TM: Yes. Dr. Arasteh has something good to say about this. He takes Viktor Frankl's existential psychotherapy to a deeper level in the light of the tradition of Persian Sufism.[34] "The importance of existential anxiety is to be seen not as a symptom of something wrong, but as a summons to growth and to painful development. Carefully distinguishing existential anxiety from the petulant self-defeating sorrows of the neurotic, Dr. Arasteh shows how this anxiety is a sign of health and generates the necessary strength for psychic rebirth into a new transcultural identity. This new being is entirely personal, original, creative, unique, and it transcends the limits imposed by social convention and prejudice. Birth on this higher level is an imperative necessity for man."[35]

MMF: But to get there we must go through a loss of self, right? I am thinking of my painful experience at St. Louis.

TM: "The consecrated term in Sufism is *fana,* annihilation or disintegration, a loss of self, a real spiritual death. But mere annihilation and death are not enough: they must be followed by reintegration and new life on a totally different level. This reintegration is what the Sufis call *baqa.* The process of disintegration and reintegration is one that involves a terrible interior solitude and an 'existential moratorium,' a crisis and an anguish, which cannot be analyzed or intellectualized. It also requires a solitary fortitude far beyond the ordinary, 'an act of courage related to the root of all existence.' It would be utterly futile to try to 'cure' this anguish by bringing the 'patient' as quickly and as completely as possible into the warm bosom of togetherness."[36]

MMF: I find this quite comforting. And if we live the monastic life, we can expect to experience this final integration?

TM: "Seen from the viewpoint of monastic tradition, the pattern of disintegration, moratorium and reintegration on a higher, universal level, is precisely what the monastic life is meant to provide."[37] This is what we need to call our fellow monastics, and our institutions, to nurture. I also think final integration is one of the personal benefits of East-West Dialogue. We need to transcend cultural boundaries for our own inner work.

MMF: Can we return once more to our starting point, *le point vierge?* I understand that this is the inviolate place where evil has no trace, where we are one with the truth of our being, one with God.

TM: Sometimes we know it as pure mystery, nothingness, a nonplace, and sometimes with the fullness of heart that I found at Fourth and Walnut Street in Louisville.

MMF: It can be comforting—also in pastoral situations—to remember that *le point vierge* is always there, no matter how far we have strayed from Grace.

TM: Herbert Mason wrote this in a letter to me: "More and more I understand the visiting of prisons; for once the soul has been dragged out to its virginal point by the sharpest sin, as a friend here said, 'grace may enter in.' "[38] Father George Anwarti, O.P., "spoke of Massignon's own personal ability to discern the problems of other people, 'to touch within them,' he said, 'the virgin point where the conscience is affected and disarmed before the living God.' "[39]

MMF: The truth is always good, even when it is about the evil in our midst. You are being quite clear that the point of truth itself is inviolably good. In my experience, as awful as it was, the truth was comforting and freeing. I was literally disarmed by that old woman. God then became the living God for me.

TM: You know the truth of darkness and the truth of light. In my experience of universal one-ness I realized that point in others and in myself at once. It's real, not just an idea. Once in a while you see it in yourself, or in others—as I did that day in Louisville and my friend did at the prison.

MMF: Then is *le point vierge* still at work in you and in me?

TM: I don't think it's something "at work" in us. It just is.

MMF: That moment of truth at Catholic University was so pervasive that it gave me a perspective beyond all my studies. I suppose it could have pointed me to continuing with my academic work, but in that moment of truth, it was a clear indication to shift and go a different direction. All my studies wouldn't get me there. Truth was really calling me away from those studies at that time. It was my pride that distanced me from that moment of truth. To fail the exams was a humiliation that taught me more than passing them would have done. So it always returns to truth!

TM: It really wasn't about the exams, was it? It was the realization that you couldn't *achieve* truth. Right?

MMF: Yes. My *point vierge* experience was already a dwelling with truth. I needed to accept my nothingness rather than proceed full steam into self-achievement. I've since had other experiences that hold the same message. I have to lift veil after veil to find my heart of hearts.

TM: We already have our heart's desire. And at this point there is an existential harmony not only with God but with the whole created universe. I tried to get the feeling of this into words. "The first chirps of the waking day birds mark the *point vierge* of the dawn under a sky as yet without real light, a moment of awe and inexpressible innocence, when the Father in perfect silence opens their eyes. They begin to speak to Him, not with fluent song, but with an awakening question that is their down state, their state at the *point vierge*. Their condition asks if it is time for them to 'be.' He answers 'yes.' Then, they one by one wake up, and become birds."[40]

MMF: Purity of heart seems like our continuous presence at this *point vierge*, our continuing consent to our nothingness there and to our coming into being.

TM: Yes. All is given, even our consent. We are like those birds chirping at dawn.

MMF: Mystery again. Thank you for this conversation about purity of heart. Thank you for bringing us into your own rich dialogue with so many traditions. Thanks especially for *le point vierge*.

18

Christian Self-Understanding in the Light of the East

New Birth and Unitive Consciousness

BRUNO BARNHART, O.S.B. CAM.

In the dialogue between Christianity and the Asian traditions today, the principle of "nonduality"—with its corollary, the nondual self—emerges as a central point both of resonance and of contrast. This paper is an exploration of nonduality as the theological principle of a rebirth of sapiential (or "wisdom") Christianity in our time. For this purpose we shall be looking at the earliest Christian tradition, as expressed in the New Testament.

Christianity as It Encounters the East Today

As Western Christianity—and I am thinking first of all of Roman Catholicism—encounters the Asian religious traditions today, it does so from a very unbalanced position. Often, therefore, we find a shallow and brittle version of Christianity brought forward to confront a deep and powerful Hindu or Buddhist spiritual tradition. Roughly speaking, we can say that the West—and Western Christianity within it—has been living, since the Renaissance and Enlightenment, in a sapiential vacuum. The epistemology of Western consciousness has been contracted largely to the rational-empirical level, and this has had a withering effect upon Christian theology. It is a commonplace to observe that the perfecting of analytical rational methods—of "science"—has been at the expense of a diminishment on the other levels of human knowledge and experience. It must quickly be added, however, that this rational development—if not the resulting imbalance—has been absolutely necessary.

To put it very simply, the dominant rational-analytical consciousness of the past few centuries in the West has largely extinguished the participative and unitive modes of consciousness in the mainstream of Western thought—whether theological or secular.

We need not enlarge upon the human and spiritual costs of these developments, which have been amply catalogued already. We can hope that this time of sapiential desert is only a stage on the way to a new and deeper integration.

The Interior East of Christianity

Christianity has its own "East," and that East is connected with its origins. Eastern and Western Christianity have been divided for the whole of this second millennium. They have grown further apart through the centuries. The two great streams of Christian tradition seem to me to be represented already in the Gospel of John by the beloved disciple (or John) who, in the words of Jesus, is to "remain here until I come," and by Peter, who is to "follow me." Eastern Christianity remains at the place of the origin—theologically and spiritually as well as geographically. It is Western Christianity that moves forward, away from its beginnings and away from its original center—and this in many ways. This is true both in Protestantism and in Roman Catholicism.

The words "East" and "West" have more than a historical meaning, however. They have an archetypal or theological meaning as well. East connotes mystery, wisdom, origins, a primordial tradition and primordial revelation. East, also within Christianity, suggests a deeper kind of knowing, a vision of all things in one single light, a unitive life and experience, a luminous innocence. West suggests movement, a voyage, an eclipse of the first light, exile, alienation, journeying in the common light of day, by the everyday way of knowing. East suggests nonduality and West duality.

I believe that today's encounter with the East—with the Asian traditions—attracts Western Christianity back to its own forgotten and repressed East, its "internal East": a spiritual East, psychic East, theological East. During recent centuries the Western church (globally speaking) has moved farther and farther from this East of its origins. The more Christianity has adapted itself to the modern West, the further it has moved away from the sacramental fullness and organic simplicity which have always characterized the Eastern Christian traditions of Syria, Egypt, the Middle East, Greece, and Russia.

"East" for contemporary Christianity also connotes *monasticism*. Monastic life remains at the center of the Eastern Christian churches, while this has not been true in the West since the twelfth century. This means a spirituality of interiority, of separation from the world, of asceticism and the quest for continual prayer. It is typified by the continual practice of the Jesus Prayer, which has also come to the West in our time. Within Christian monasticism itself, East and West are different. While Eastern monasticism continues to cherish the solitary life of contemplation at its center, Western monasticism became institutionalized almost universally in the Benedictine cenobitical form. The solitary life has remained only as a marginal exception. Solitude, silence, and contemplative prayer have seldom remained the central concerns in a Roman Catholic monasticism which has become engaged very largely in pastoral, cultural, and educational activities.

East, Orient, is beginning (Greek *arche*), and at the beginning there is light. In the New Testament this *arche,* or first principle, has multiple levels of meaning. It is God, Father, ultimate Source. It is the moment of first creation (Gen 1:1ff.). It is the second creation which happens in the coming of Jesus Christ. The beginning is the written Gospel. And it is "initiation," baptism. This will be important for our study. Fullness is present at the beginning, at this "eastern pole," this orient and origin of Christianity. Our journey eastward into the Christian mystery will lead us ultimately to the Jordan, the place of baptism. We shall return to this central subject of Christian initiation.

Our conceptions of purity of heart and of contemplation, in Christian tradition, originate in the East: with the desert monks and the early Greek mystical writers who created the first Christian spiritual theology.[1]

Christianity as Wisdom

"Wisdom," as I am using the term, is a participative consciousness and knowing which surmounts the duality of subject and object. It is experiential, holistic rather than differentiating, and inseparable from personal life. As the Western world continues its journey through a postsapiential age, however, everyday consciousness tends to move largely on the multiplex surface of reality, with little awareness of a vertical or unitive dimension. Meanwhile we find ourselves surrounded today—especially in California, I suppose—by "wisdoms," by claims of other and deeper levels of consciousness and experience. Our long Western sapiential parenthesis—which has reached its fullness since the eighteenth-century Enlightenment—may be nearing its end.

Today it is in the Asian traditions, particularly, that we find ancient wisdom expressed profoundly, simply, gently, luminously. An Eastern light awakens the sleeping seeds of wisdom within Christianity. A new Christian sapiential literature begins to appear along the Eastern frontier: We see this in Thomas Merton, in Abhishiktananda, in Raimon Panikkar, in Bede Griffiths. This "new wisdom" is sometimes clearly rooted in the classical Christian sapiential tradition. More often, it expresses a fresh experience which will find integration with the tradition of the Word only in a second moment.

Our search for the roots of a Christian wisdom within the tradition is a journey back into the "theological East" of Christianity. It is a journey from a more differentiated to a less differentiated consciousness; from an objectified to a participative theology and spirituality. In the earliest literature of Christianity, we find the traces of an experience of undivided oneness.[2]

A movement toward the archetypal Christian "East" today, however, must be at once a return from a predominantly scientific to an overall sapiential worldview, and an integration of the empirical-rational level of knowledge into the full spectrum of ways of knowing. Mainstream Christian tradition, before the sudden ascendancy of Western science, had striven to achieve such an integration; it was both sapiential and rational. In the latter half of the twentieth century, a renewed contact with the Christian East has stimulated a desire for such a balance once again in the West.

The foundations of Christian wisdom are in the letters of Paul[3] and in the Gospel and First Letter of John. The *Logos,* or Word, of John's prologue (Jn 1:1–18) has been the cornerstone of this sapiential tradition. "In the beginning was the Word...and the Word became flesh, and dwelt among us...and of his fullness we have all received." It is the Johannine literature which most continually expresses the sapiential perspective. Contact with Hinduism, Buddhism, and Taoism draws Christianity toward its Johannine pole.[4]

The Unitive Principle

Wisdom knows reality as mystery, and mystery involves ways of knowing that transcend everyday consciousness and ordinary thought. Central to the Asian traditions is the *apophatic* way: a knowing through unknowing. This way of knowing is most fully characteristic of Buddhism, and the encounter with Buddhist traditions draws Christianity toward its apophatic pole. This too belongs to the "East" of Christian tradition.

On the level of practice, this apophatic attraction is expressed in the widespread interest in Eastern meditation methods among Christians. In silent meditation (*zazen, shikantaza, mahamudra, dzogchen*) one descends beyond the conscious mind and its processes into the depths of the person, where unitive spirit is encountered. The two major contemporary schools of Christian meditation, Centering Prayer and Christian Meditation, have originated under the inspiration of the Asian traditions.

If the Asian traditions attract Christian spirituality toward its own Eastern pole, or apophatic and contemplative side, it is here that we find the principle which most deeply characterizes the three great traditions of Hinduism, Buddhism, and Taoism. At the heart of each of these religions is *nonduality.*[5]

At this point, let us attempt a very simple overall scheme of the great world religions. I shall denote as the "West" the family of three great religions of the biblical Word: Israel, Christianity, and Islam. As counterpole, or "East," I propose that we have an analogous but very different constellation of three great traditions: Hinduism, Buddhism, and Taoism. Taoism does not appear to share a common root with Hinduism and Buddhism, however, which would correspond to the biblical and historical root of the three Western traditions. These three Asian traditions do have at their core the principle of *nonduality,* or identity. We may, therefore, think of them as the traditions or religions of the *unitive Absolute*—that is, of nondual reality, of the ineffable One, which is at once transcendent and immanent. While the three traditions of the West have prioritized *relationship,* the three Eastern traditions have developed the dimension of *identity.*[6]

This unitive Absolute, or principle of identity (not to be equated with the Western philosophical term), is the supreme metaphysical and spiritual archetype which appears today from the East to confront the divine Word,[7] exercising a profound tidal attraction upon Christian spirituality and thought. This unitive Absolute is the heart of what has been called the "perennial philosophy."[8] Philosophically, indeed, it is the supreme idea which becomes the solar principle of a metaphysic which has never been surpassed in its profundity. For this is the ultimate Absolute. It is also the unthinkable thought, the vanishing point and convergent zenith of all conceptual reason—and indeed of all human experience. The influence of this Principle—as it comes to us from the Asian traditions—upon Christian thought and spirituality today could be illustrated from the writings of a number of contemporary Christian writers, including Thomas Merton, Abhishiktananda, and Bede Griffiths. A brief passage from the late work of Griffiths gives an idea of its synthetic and magnetic power.

> This reality which has no proper name, since it transcends the mind
> and cannot be expressed in words, was called Brahman and Atman
> (the Spirit) in Hinduism, Nirvana and Sunyata (the Void) in Buddhism,
> Tao (the Way) in China, Being (*to ōn*) in Greece, and Yahweh ("I am")
> in Israel, but all these are but words which point to an inexpressible
> mystery, in which the ultimate meaning of the universe is to be found,
> but which no human word or thought can express. It is this which is the
> goal of all human striving, the truth which all science and philosophy
> seeks to fathom, the bliss in which all human love is fulfilled.[9]

While the Principle has never been entirely absent from Christian thought, it has seldom been expressed in its purity and autonomy within the Christian tradition. This strange suppression is parallel to the ambivalence of mainstream Christianity toward mysticism. It is related to the extreme emphasis upon *mediation* in Christian tradition: mediation through the biblical word, mediation through church authority, mediation through sacrament and ritual. The "Western" traditions of Judaism, Christianity, and Islam have evolved chiefly in the direction of person, relationship and authoritative mediation.

The unitive Principle emerges powerfully in the New Testament, but neither with the metaphysical clarity with which we find it in the Upanishads nor with the rigorous apophatism with which it is present in the Buddhist tradition. The unitive Principle appears now as incarnate in a human person: in the Christ who, on the cross, joins humanity with God and Jews with Gentiles.[10] The Principle is present everywhere in the letters of Paul, where he speaks of the disciples' being in Christ, "in him." The unitive Principle is expressed here in terms of a participation in the One through the mediation of a participation in the "body of Christ": the new reality which comes to birth in Jesus' resurrection.

The unitive Principle emerges in the New Testament both in the "vertical" dimension of identity and in the "horizontal" dimension of human relationship. It is present in the "I and the Father are one" and the "I AM" of Jesus in John's Gospel. It is present in the *koinonia,* or communion, of the baptized believers, which is a participation in the One which is God.

> I do not pray for these only, but also for those who believe in me through their word, that they may all be one; even as you, Father, are in me and I in you, that they also may be in us, so that the world may believe that you have sent me. The glory that you have given me I have given to them, that they may be one even as we are one, I in them and you in me, that they may become perfectly one, so that the world may know that you have sent me and have loved them even as you have loved me. (Jn 17:20–23)

Here in the New Testament, unitive participation in the divine One, the nondual Absolute, is opened up to those who believe in Christ and who, through him, receive the divine Spirit. The unitive Principle itself corresponds, fundamentally, to Yahweh, the God of the Old Testament, and to the God and Father of the New Testament. What is new, in the Christ-event, is the explicit participation in the One through the Word and Spirit of God which have come newly into the world—though they have been present in the world from its beginning.

The projective or "extrovert" character of the Christian revelation and Christian God—the Divinity coming forth in the act of creation, in the missions of Word and Spirit, in incarnation and apostolic mission, in a moral law of active love—generates a continual outward movement within Christian tradition, a continual movement "westward," away from that East which is beginning, source, nondual origin, and forward into the world. Dimensions of relationship, activity, and historical dynamism dominate, and the interiority and metaphysical depth of the unitive dimension become recessive. "Identity" is eclipsed by relationship.

It is in the contemplative monastics and mystics of the Christian tradition that we find the countermovement to this mainstream flow. It is these who attempt to swim upstream and inward, in a "Johannine" movement into the unitive Source. Despite a constant mediatory insistence, the nondual Source asserts itself strongly in the patristic tradition: in such writers as Gregory of Nyssa, Evagrius Ponticus, and even in Augustine. In this current a Platonic or Neoplatonic influence is always evident.

What is new as Christian spirituality rediscovers the nondual center *to-day,* under the influence of the Asian traditions, is the purity and autonomy with which the Principle emerges. This is a very significant development for the self-understanding of the Christian. The unitive Principle, standing free in its purity—detached from the second principle which is the Word, and then illumining the Word from within—becomes a hermeneutic eye which opens up each sector of Christian theology (long divided into nearly distinct kingdoms) to the central Mystery, itself newly open and luminous. In the light of this Principle, the dissociated members of the Christian mystery once again become a single organism. Trinitarian theology, anthropology, christology, pneumatology, ecclesiology, and cosmology begin to shed their partitioning academic suffix and to appear once again in their inner unity. The Christian contemplative tradition, particularly, opens up from its own center in this light, and itself illuminates the inner identity of the person. From the God "up there" and "out there" of a dualistic Western Christian tradition, we move to a conception of God become one with humanity in Christ: the central theological principle of *divinization* reemerges.

So powerful is the liberating influence of the nondual Principle upon a Christian tradition that has become encumbered with the baggage of twenty centuries that it is tempting to make this the sole principle of Christian theology. Some Christian spiritual writers, ecstatic in the discovery of an "Ultimate Reality" with its simple, luminous depth, have leaned far in this direction. In the Christ-event, however, the nondual Absolute becomes present in humanity in a new way. While the gift of Asian spiritualities to Christianity in our time is centered in the unitive realization, a unilateral exaltation of this Principle can eclipse *that which has happened.*[11]

This unitive Principle, which we find so strongly and purely expressed in the Asian traditions, generates the further developments in Christian self-understanding that we shall explore.

Toward the Fullness

Let us bring this unitive Principle of the East to bear upon the Judeo-Christian revelation at its root. Fundamental to the biblical revelation—and to the whole of this tradition, and to the consciousness of the West—is the *distinction* between God and the world. God is the absolute Person who creates the world, who speaks his Word in the world. God is not the world or anything in it; God remains emphatically transcendent. His sacred Name becomes unspeakable in Israel, and no images of God are permitted. From the perspective of Asian nonduality, on the other hand, God and the universe are not distinct. The Divinity is immanent everywhere in the universe—if even that degree of distinction can be allowed. In Christianity, the one God appears as Father, Word or Son, and Spirit—still radically and absolutely distinct from the world, but present in the world, gathering the world into God in Christ. Divine Trinity and world remain ontologically distinct, and must not be confounded. Within Christian theology, Trinity and Incarnation stand as the two great central pillars, remaining strangely separate through the centuries.[12]

What happens when we look at Trinity and world together, unfocusing our Western eyes through Eastern lenses? It is then, I believe, that we may suddenly glimpse (as if in some theological particle accelerator) *what happened* in Jesus Christ, in his cross and resurrection. In this "fusion" which takes place in the body of the crucified Christ is the symbolic power of the figure of the cross.[13] The nonduality here, comprehending heaven and earth, God and the universe, God and all humanity, is not the nonduality of the *beginning* (focus of the Asian traditions), but the nonduality of the *end*.[14] In the "cross" of Jesus—his death and resurrection—God (or Trinity) and the Cosmos become one. This new unity is the "body of Christ."[15]

At this point, the Asian traditions bring forward today a further contribution: the *mandala*—a quasi-universal symbol of wholeness, and of the unity of all reality. The "mystery of the cross"[16]—Trinity and creation become one—can be represented by a mandalic figure. The mandala which emerges from the representation of this mystery in the Pauline letters, however, is not the mandala of the beginning but the dynamic mandala of the end. In contrast to an ontological figure of wholeness corresponding to the perennial philosophy, this figure visually symbolizes an *event* that has become the center and pivot of history, and represents the progressive consummation of history as an integration—or "recapitulation"—of all reality around that center.[17]

The Christian mandala does, however, have an ontological level of significance as well. The ultimate quaternity, as we find it in the New Testament and in theologians of the second century, is that of God, Word, Spirit, and World. The Word is that divine Word or Son which has become a human person in Jesus Christ.

I God

II Word   +   III Holy Spirit

IV Cosmos

This quaternary vision, as we find it already in Irenaeus,[18] offers itself today as the structural framework of one possible "new Christian wisdom."[19] Christian tradition has been, until now, very largely confined to the dimension of the Word (II). The pluralistic paradigm, which sees all reality gathered together at its center (which is at once the risen Christ and the individual person and the "new heart" of the person), opens up from the perspective of the East, that is from the viewpoint of the absolute unitive Principle (I).

Dialogue with the Asian traditions tends to open Christianity to potential dimensions of development which have been largely excluded, suppressed, or forgotten through the centuries. In a chronic climate of ecclesial over-mediation, Christian consciousness has often remained confined within the security of a "logos-container" (II). Hinduism confronts this one-sided Christianity with its full spectrum of "paths"—margas or yogas. Four main "yogas," or Hindu spiritual paths,[20] correspond to the four poles of this Christian mandala and suggest how these dimensions may be opened further within Christian spirituality and spiritual theology. I—*Dhyana* or meditation yoga, or less strictly, the *Raja* yoga of Patanjali, corresponds to our first pole of nonduality. II—*Jnana* yoga is the way of abstract thought, discriminating phenomena from reality. III—*Bhakti* yoga is the way of devotion. At this third pole we might place also *kundalini* yoga and other paths which are centered in the ascent or sublimation of human energy. IV—*Karma* yoga, the path of selfless action, corresponds to the main path of Christian moral teaching. *Hatha* yoga, the integrative discipline of the body, hardly finds a counterpart in a Christian tradition which has emphasized a domination and disciplining of the body through renunciation and asceticism. In Christian tradition, each of these four paths has been cultivated in some way, but several of them—notably the contemplative path and the integrative discipline of body and energy—only to a very limited extent.

The "mystery of the cross," essentially participative, was very soon eclipsed as Christian theology became objectified and the trinitarian Divinity was sealed within itself by successive conceptual schemes.[21] Contact with the East invites Christians today to rediscover the fullness of the mystery within themselves rather than merely projecting it into a transcendent divine world or into the mediating institutional structure of the church.

Each of the great Asian traditions invites Christians to rediscover the fullness of potentialities within their gift—the many-faceted plenitude disclosed in the New Testament. Hindu Vedanta, Zen Buddhism, and Taoism, further, invite the individual Christian to realize the simple immediacy of this fullness present within herself or himself. The mystery of the cross, the germinal Christ-event, dwells within the person, ready as always to unfold its unlimited potential.

Unitive Self and Baptism

Now let us narrow the focus of our discussion to its central point: the human person, the "self." Here, particularly, the Asian traditions call Christian spiritual theology today to a more integral perspective. Hinduism, Buddhism, and Taoism are not merely theologies or philosophies but ways of life, spiritual paths for the individual person. Eastern spiritualities have had great influence upon the Christian West in the form of methods of meditation, yogic practices, ways toward the integration of body, soul, and spirit. At the center of these multiple "wisdoms" lies a unitary conception of the person, and it is this which I would like to explore. From the Hindu Vedanta, in particular, the West awakens to an inner Self beyond the ordinary self or functional ego. The West becomes aware of the *Atman*. Until recently, both the spiritual theology and the psychology of the West had regarded the human person almost entirely from an analytical rather than a unitary perspective. Through Carl Jung, this Asian notion of the "transpersonal" Self has influenced Western psychology.[22]

The New Testament points to a transformation of the *person as a whole*.[23] It is not surprising, when a unitive metaphysical view of the person has been lost for many centuries, that Christians have discovered the Eastern anthropology with something like a cry of "eureka!"

> The whole question is, what is the true Self? What is the true Center of man's being? Is it the ego, making itself independent, seeking to be master of the world, or is there an "I" beyond this, a deeper Center of personal being, which is grounded in the Truth, which is one with the universal Self, the Law of the universe? This is the great discovery of Indian thought, the discovery of the Self, the Atman, the Ground of personal being, which is one with the Brahman, the Ground of universal being. It is not reached by thought; on the contrary, it is only reached by transcending thought.[24]

Awakening to the Self introduces a duality and tension between this deep center of the person and the practical center of the personality which is the ego. Sometimes the duality has been radicalized into a relation of opposition between the true or interior Self and a "false" or purely exterior self. There is, however, already in the New Testament, a contrast between the exterior person and the interior person.[25]

In the New Testament, the interior person is the *new* person, born into Christ. The tension between "spirit" and "flesh,"[26] on the other hand, represents not an ontological distinction within the person (as in Greek philosophical anthropology) but the contrast of two orientations of the whole person: toward the "old world" which is centered in the unredeemed self (in the "flesh"), or toward the "new world" which is participated through self-giving in faith and love (in the "spirit").

The Christ-event, then, brings about a unification of the person. The Greek Christian theological tradition, however, adopting a dualistic Platonic anthropology, developed a conception of the human person as "image of God" which practically excluded the body—and even the psyche—from this divine image, or essential humanity. The Augustinian view of the person, which dominated Western thought until recently, conceived the image of the Trinity to be present in the human person in the faculties of memory, intellect, and will. As in the earlier Greek anthropology, body and psyche hardly appeared in this scheme.

Adopting an Asian "nondual" perspective, we regard the person as a whole; this whole person is often called the *Self*. To contemplate the human person in this unitive way in a Christian context—the new person—leads us immediately to *baptismal initiation*. It is here that the total person is reborn in the Holy Spirit, according to the New Testament revelation. The "new person" is a newly unitive person, participating in the divine One.[27] The tension between flesh and spirit, between individual and community, is overcome through a new participation in the divine Spirit itself.

Equivalent to the awakening or enlightenment event in Buddhism is the initiatory event in Christianity: a personal appropriation and experience of the Christ-event.[28] The baptismal experience, in early Christianity, was known as *photismos*, illumination. It was a unitive awakening to the divine light, a new awareness of oneself as light participating in the uncreated light. This initiatory unitive experience becomes the foundation of a person's subsequent mystical and contemplative experiences.

Implicit in this initial experience of fullness is a double *revolution*. First, the fullness—contemplation, unitive experience, realization—is not the fruit of long ascetical efforts and of a long development of meditative practice, but is received at the beginning as a pure gift, a *grace*.[29] This basic truth of the New Testament has for a long time hardly been present to Christian consciousness. The history of Christian spirituality has been largely a record of the construction of paths and ladders toward spiritual realization or perfection. It is obvious that growth in the spirit is necessary, that the mature spiritual person is not born all at once. Yet it becomes equally obvious that the mediation of these imposing schemes of spiritual ascent has obscured the essential simplicity, fullness, and gratuity of the gift of Christ.

Second, the revolution initiated by the Christ-event, according to the New Testament writings,[30] involves a restructuring which embraces all created reality. The coming of Christ into the world recenters the world. The coming of the grace of Christ into the individual recenters the human person, and recenters the world in the human person, which comes at this point into its destined place in creation. The person is newly centered, but not in the *nous* (spiritual intellect), or in the "spirit," or in the unitive spiritual self or *Atman*. The person, in Christ, is centered in the *heart*.[31] It is the bodily human person—indivisibly body, soul/mind, and spirit—which enters into this divine participation. This is an essential point. The extremes of God and matter become indivisibly joined in Jesus Christ and then in the baptized person. It is in the human heart, finally, that these metaphysical antipodes are experienced as one.

This mystery cannot be understood "objectively"; the theological object disappears immediately into participation, into the subject, into myself. It is here that we discover a "one-pointed Christianity": the entire mystery, the unitive fullness, has become identical with my own bodily being. No interior hierarchy, no ladder of spiritual ascent, remains in this unitive kingdom of God. The spiritual nonduality of the perennial philosophy has become, in the event of Christ, an *incarnate* nonduality. The "center" becomes the human person who is Christ. At the same time, in the baptismal event, this center becomes the new human person who is myself. This, finally, is the "one point" at which all the lines converge, the place where unitive fullness is to be realized.

Encounter with the East, in drawing Christianity back to its own East, brings it finally to the sunrise at the Jordan which is baptismal initiation. The "interreligious dialogue" leads us deeper than practices, spiritual ways, to the core of the person, to the new "unitive identity" which is born in baptism. The deepest encounter of Christianity and the East is here, at the heart of the Christ-event itself, in the birth of a new self. It is in the event of this new divine-human birth in Christ—as historical event and as personal experience—that Christianity also begins to differentiate itself from the Eastern tradition. At the very point at which Christianity most deeply resonates with the unitive perennial philosophy, "center-to-center," a decisive difference emerges.

Purity of Heart

Purity of heart, from our interpretive perspective, is a characterization of the "new self" of the baptized Christian,[32] under the aspect of interiority. We have proposed that baptismal rebirth and illumination is the primordial Christian contemplative experience, as an experience of nonduality, of the "nondual self." Purity of heart, as it appears in Cassian's first Conference, is practically equivalent to the integral state of this same unitive self. Purity of heart is an expression for the self-awareness of the person as unified at its center, as participating in the unity which is God.[33]

In the discourse of Abba Moses, purity of heart and contemplation—our two themes—appear as two aspects of the same inner state.[34] Indeed, purity of heart appears as the inner person's comprehensive well-being, as the consummate perfection of the spiritual person. Purity of heart, according to Moses/Cassian, is synonymous with "sanctification" (n. 5), with love (n. 6ff.), with the tranquillity of a "heart free from disturbance" (n. 6), with "peace of heart" (n. 6), with "the simple and unified contemplation" of the Lord (n. 8), with the "knowledge of God" (n. 10) or "spiritual knowledge" (n. 14), with knowledge of the truth and love of virtue (n. 13), and probably (as an anticipation of the kingdom of God) with joy in the Holy Spirit (n. 13).[35]

In the contemporary encounter with Asian traditions, purity of heart is a natural meeting place. The most nearly corresponding terms in Hindu and Buddhist traditions have already been brought into comparison—into "dialogue" with the purity of heart of Christian monastic tradition.[36] This confrontation brings to light the difference in orientation between non-Christian East and Christian West at this point. We have already seen the "recentering" of spirituality which takes place in the Christ-event; a re-centering which can be envisioned in a series of concentric circles. As the cosmos becomes newly centered in Christ, the Divine-human person, the world is also newly centered in humanity, in the human person, the "new person." The human person, in this new infusion of the divine Spirit, is newly centered in the heart. There occurs, as it were, a descent of the center of spirituality from "pure spirit," equivalent to *Atman* (or to *nous* in the Greek Christian tradition), to the heart. *Heart,* here, is conceived as the central point or axis of the person, where body, psyche, mind, and spirit are present together. The heart is both the center of human awareness, experience, and decision in this world, and the place of unitive realization.[37] *Purity* is an inadequate term—little more than a metaphor—for the condition of this recentered, indeed reborn, person. We shall soon consider some further dimensions of this new self.

Contemplation

The word "contemplation" connotes that area in which the Eastern influence upon Christian spirituality is most visible. This is true even when the word itself is not heard. The influence is evident in the greatly increased popularity of various forms of meditation, and of Asian meditation methods. We have found *nonduality* at the core of the Eastern traditions. Contemplation, understood as nondual consciousness and experience, is the deep pivotal point at which the Asian influence is most decisive. This point generates the central viewpoint from which the unity of other currents of Eastern influence may be seen.

The understanding of contemplation has changed in the Christian West during the past half century, under the influence of the Asian traditions. Fifty years ago, a standard Roman Catholic guide to the spiritual life might define contemplation as "gazing with love upon God," or "the experience of union with God." Today we are more likely to understand contemplation not so "objectively," but as unitive experience or, in Eastern terms, nondual experience. Similarly, "meditation" half a century ago was still considered, in the West, as a deliberate reflection upon revealed truths. Today most people understand meditation not as discursive thought but as a practice of silent deepening which transcends thought. Here I shall consider contemplation in the latter sense, as we have come to regard it under the influence of the Asian traditions: as unitive experience, nondual experience. Further, we can understand contemplation not as exclusively "supernatural," but also as the natural realization of a human potential, and therefore as essentially universal in human spirituality as is life or consciousness or love.

Nonduality, we have seen, is a key which opens Christian theology and spirituality at its center, making possible a new emergence which is free of the inherited "container," the shell built up of the accretions of twenty centuries. Contemplation in the Christian context will be related to this center, that is, to the core of the Christ-mystery which is the new union of Divinity and humanity in Jesus Christ.

The interpretation of Christian contemplation as nondual experience demands that we understand this phenomenon in terms of the whole person rather than as a fulfillment of one human faculty—be it even the contemplative intellect, the *nous* of Plato and Plotinus. Our understanding of contemplation is thus drawn toward the archetypal Christian "East," toward the beginning, toward initiation. We have already proposed that the basic contemplative experience, in the earliest Christian tradition, is the baptismal experience of *photismos,* illumination, rebirth: the birth of the "new person" in Christ. Furthermore, subsequent contemplative experience is to be understood in the light of this primordial enlightenment: that is, as an experience of the "new self" which is born in baptism.

An equivalent in the Hindu tradition is the interpretation of unitive experience as the emergence into consciousness of the preexistent *Atman* or unitive self. In Mahayana Buddhism, nondual awakening has been understood as experience of original nature or buddha-nature. In Taoist tradition one may speak of realizing the Tao as returning to the origin or the "uncarved block," or to the One.[38]

Contemplative experience in the New Testament can be understood basically as the experience of the new, unitive self. Since "contemplation" is not explicitly spoken of, however, we must infer its presence within a context in which other concerns predominate. Contemplative experience is implicit in references to baptism, to illumination, to new birth, to receiving and experiencing the Holy Spirit.[39] The purest references to contemplative experience (nondual experience) in the New Testament letters, I believe, are implicit in statements about the new identity, the new person who is in Christ, who is one with Christ, one with God, who has awakened to a new depth of identity in God.[40]

Paul refers repeatedly to his own experience of Christ. In these passages, while Paul's accent is often upon the "objective content" of his interior experience of the *gnosis* or *epignosis,* it is evident that the experience is saturated with unitive light.[41] Sometimes Paul speaks of the union itself.[42] If New Testament allusions to contemplative experience often seem imprecise, ambiguous, or inconclusive, it is usually not because we are dealing with a diminished, weak, or diffuse unitive experience. The "contemplative" dimension is only one component of a more global experience. This outpouring of light and life refuses to be confined within a particular category such as the "intellectualist" concept of contemplation.[43]

Let us summarize this conception of contemplation—in the Christian context but from our Eastern perspective. Contemplation is a direct, "nondual" experience of the inner self. It is, therefore, not merely an isolated phenomenon, but the momentary awareness of something that is present at every moment of our life. Contemplation is a direct experience of the ground of consciousness, of a depth from which we may live continually. Contemplation is the illumination of faith; faith may thus be experienced either as darkness or as light. Faith is a dark unitive knowledge, the beginning of contemplation. Qualities of the contemplative experience include interiority, unity (or nonduality), luminosity, and freedom. Contemplation is inseparable not only from faith but from love. Love and contemplation generate one another, and appear as the two faces or modalities of the same interior development. Contemplation and love originate from a common source, a "nondual center" of the person which is sometimes identified with the heart. This constellation, as the Western Christian tradition recognizes, is an image and participation of the divine Trinity of persons in the human person.

Pure contemplative experience—an imageless "nondual" illumination at the center of the person—is related to a variety of mixed or participatory experiences, some of them colored by a context of relationship or of aesthetic perception. Contemplation is the beginning of a dynamic process which moves toward expression in action, which fulfills itself in embodiment. The contemplative experience, further, is qualified by its concrete historical context, by the movement of the divine Spirit in history.

As in our discussion of purity of heart, we have found ourselves, in considering Christian contemplation, drawn eastward to the self, and thus to the "Jordan" of baptismal initiation. We have seen that purity of heart and contemplative experience have, from the early Christian centuries, been understood as closely related: purity of heart is the doorway to contemplation. Traditionally, the purified heart has been understood as the organ of contemplation. From our comparative perspective of the non-Christian East of nonduality and the Christian East of baptismal initiation, however, purity of heart and contemplation appear as complementary aspects of the same new identity, the same new "nondual self" in God.

It is here, at the unitive "new person," that the two lines intersect: the nondual axis of the *perennial philosophy,* or cosmic revelation, and the "historical" axis of the divine self-communication to humanity in Christ and the Holy Spirit. This is the meeting point of the two axes of "identity" and of "relationship."[44] Further, the "Eastern light" of nonduality opens up our understanding of the contemplative experience to its full unitive depth and universal scope. Here we seem to step onto a ground on which all spiritual traditions—indeed all human beings—can meet. Standing upon this consensual ground, however, the Christian may experience a restless stirring. An energy, an inner dynamic, pushes outward to realize itself. A breath, a Spirit within the heart presses outward and forward—and downward—from the contemplative experience. Rather than remaining the otherworldly goal of the human journey, contemplation becomes the starting point from which the human person—and humanity as a whole—grows into a "new creation," in which this material world finds its own transformation and fulfillment.[45]

A Second Principle?

As we have seen, encounter with the Asian traditions today draws Christianity back toward its own center and beginning, in the New Testament event of baptismal initiation. There Christianity—and Christian spirituality—find their unity, simplicity, and fullness. The fullness of the beginning, however—of baptism and of the New Testament as a whole—is not yet the *final* fullness, not yet the conclusive point of arrival. It is at this beginning—at the point of closest affinity to the Asian traditions centered in nonduality—that Christianity discovers both its distinctness and its peculiar dynamism. We have spoken of an archetypal movement from "East to West," a movement forward into history, a movement from the divine Ground into the material world.

In baptism the person is immersed, sacramentally, in Divinity and reborn at its center. From this point a movement begins: forward and outward. This personal dynamic is reflected in the forward movement of history itself—particularly in the Western world—since the time of Christ. I suggest that we conceive this "second movement" from the nondual center outward as the progressive emergence of *the person*—who is now participating in a divine incarnation. The person gradually emerges into its place in the world both individually and collectively (communally). It is obvious today, however, that the individual and collective progressions are not yet integrated. In the extreme individualism of the West—and the many-sided fragmentation of the modern Western world—we see an emergence of the individual person which has not yet been balanced by a growth of the collective person.[46]

We might call this a predominance of the masculine differentiating principle over the feminine participative principle of growth. We may, at present, have reached the peak of imbalance and may be starting down the farther slope.

Participating in the energy of the Christ-event, the person is actualized not only by a rooting in the unitive divine Ground, but by *a creative movement into the world*. Something new has been planted in the heart of the human person, a seed of fire which begins to transform the world around it. Purity of heart becomes more actively the root of love. Contemplation becomes the beginning of transformative and incarnational action. Neither purity of heart nor contemplation is complete or fulfilled without this further movement.

The simplicity of the unitive Absolute, of Nondual experience, of contemplative interiority, seems to be lost in this incarnational movement. The unity reappears, I believe, at the level of the heart, the center of the whole person. Nonduality is to be realized in the whole, embodied person and in the larger body which is humanity as a whole. Meanwhile a "one-pointed Christianity" is to be experienced in living from the awakened heart. The interior unity of the contemplative experience at the center of the person, the unity of the heart, the unity of the person, the unity of humanity and of creation, are all participations in the supreme Unity which is God. This supreme Unity is realized alternately—and concurrently—in a rhythmical movement between interior light and exterior embodiment.

The life of *faith* has often been presented dualistically, as an alienating heteronomy: belief and obedience exacted by a God "up there" and "out there." From the moment of "identity," however—Christ-event and baptism—faith means a living *from within,* from the divine-human person which one has become. This living from within is a living *outward:* that is, in fontality.[47] This is an essentially creative life. Identity and fontality are the two poles of the new life in Christ, corresponding roughly to baptism and eucharist.

The faith that—in contrast to an "Eastern" unitive enlightenment—is seen to characterize Christianity may be interpreted in unitive terms, according to the inner dynamic of the Christ-event. Christian faith corresponds to incarnation. In a first phase it is an affirmation of the union of God and humanity in Jesus Christ. In a second phase it is an affirmation of—and rooting of one's life in—the same unity in oneself, as one's true identity. The unitive illumination of baptism disappears into this life of faith as the seed disappears into the ground. The implanted grace, the new identity veiled within the ordinariness of bodily being, then brings forth its fruit in fontality.

Conclusion

The Asian contemplative traditions attract Christians today by their depth, simplicity, and experiential power, and in doing so invite Christianity back to the unity and fullness of its own "East." Here is monasticism, "blessed simplicity" and contemplative interiority. Here is rediscovered the original unity and apophatic transparency of the Christ-event. This "East" is also the place of solitude and emptiness, the wilderness of Exodus and the burning bush and the revelation of the burning Name, "I am." This is the place of Jesus' baptism, where the words are heard over the waters, "You are." It is the place of Christian baptism or "illumination," the birth of the new person in God. Asian "nonduality" catalyzes the rediscovery of the pole of unitive identity in Christianity. This, in turn, is the core of a new Christian wisdom.

The ways and practices of classical Christian spirituality—especially within the Eastern monastic tradition—are both expressions of this new self and means toward establishing one more deeply and continuously in the new self. It is at the place of this beginning—orient, sunrise—that Christianity finds its original charism. At the same time there emerges a dynamic within the heart which drives the person toward an individual and communal growth and realization that moves away from the Eastern beginning. The essential "newness" of the person does not cease to unfold. The move "from East to West" is an emergence of the person in this world. First comes the differentiating ascent of the individual person, and then a descent in which the individual rejoins the community, the body. From the baptismal dawn, the person grows toward an individual zenith and then declines toward the sunset which is eucharist. Today Christianity, in the West, is experiencing this change of direction at the point of maximal differentiation of the individual and the nearly complete eclipse of the sense of communal participation. Contemplative experience is relative to the movement of the Spirit in history. This history itself is centered in the development of the person: of the individual person in its multiplicity and of the one "Cosmic Person."

It is urgent in our time for Christian faith to become conscious of itself with the new depth, spaciousness, and vitality that the Asian traditions call forth. Through new clarities, confrontations, and integrations, this can only bring new vigor to the dialogue itself.

Notes

Introduction: Bruno Barnhart and Joseph H. Wong

1. Ewert Cousins has written of the present time as the dawn of a "second Axial period" of global consciousness corresponding to the Axial period which Karl Jaspers had characterized as the historical moment of the unfolding of personal or individual consciousness. See E. Cousins, *Christ of the Twenty-First Century* (Rockport, Mass.: Element, 1992), 4–10; Karl Jaspers, *The Origin and Goal of History* (New Haven: Yale University Press, 1953), 1–21.

2. The word "monk" will be used often in this book to denote both men and women in monastic life.

3. Articulate representatives of Hinduism and Buddhism had already been present in Europe and North America since the nineteenth century.

4. See *The Journey* in this Introduction, p. 8.

5. See Donald W. Mitchell and James A. Wiseman, O.S.B., eds., *The Gethsemani Encounter* (New York: Continuum, 1998), 5. See also the *Monastic Interreligious Dialogue Bulletin* (formerly the *Bulletin of Monastic Interreligious Dialogue*), where church documents relevant to interreligious dialogue and monastic participation in the dialogue have regularly been noted and often published.

6. Sister Pascaline Coff gives a concise account of the history of this monastic dialogue in *The Gethsemani Encounter,* 4–9.

7. Early participants in the contemporary Hindu-Christian dialogue included Jules Monchanin, Henri Le Saux (Abhishiktananda), and Bede Griffiths. See Judson B. Trapnell, *Bede Griffiths: A Life in Dialogue* (Albany: State University of New York Press, 2001); *Hindu-Christian Dialogue: Perspectives and Encounters,* ed. Harold Coward (Maryknoll, N.Y.: Orbis, 1989); and the *Hindu-Christian Studies Bulletin* published annually by Harold Coward at the Centre for Studies in Religion and Society, University of Victoria, Victoria, British Columbia.

8. See *The Gethsemani Encounter*, and the journal *Buddhist-Christian Studies*, published annually by the University of Hawaii Press.

9. Short biographical accounts of those who presented papers will be found on pp. 345–50; the discussants are listed on p. 350.

10. See "The Heart of Dialogue" by Thomas Hand, and "The Dialogue in its Monastic Setting" by David Steindl-Rast, above.

11. Cf. "Meditation," in *The Encyclopedia of Religion,* ed. Mircea Eliade (New York: Macmillan, 1995), 9:325.

12. Harriet Luckman and Linda Kulzer, eds., *Purity of Heart in Early Ascetic and Monastic Literature: Essays in Honor of Juana Raasch, O.S.B.* (Collegeville, Minn.: Liturgical Press, 1999). A reading of these essays will be helpful for a better understanding of the present book. The pioneering study of Juana Raasch is "The Monastic Concept of Purity of Heart and Its Sources," *Studia Monastica* 8, no. 1

(1966): 7–33; 8, no. 2 (1966): 183–213; 10, no. 1 (1968): 7–55; 11, no. 2 (1969): 269–314; 12, no. 1 (1970): 7–41.

13. Cf. Bernard McGinn, *The Presence of God: A History of Western Christian Mysticism,* vol. 1, *The Foundations of Mysticism* (New York: Crossroad, 1994), 105–7. McGinn points out the influence of Greek philosophy on Clement's idea.

14. Origen calls the three stages ethics, physics, and enoptics, which correspond to three wisdom books respectively: Proverbs, Ecclesiastes, and Song of Songs. See Origen, *The Song of Songs: Commentary and Homilies,* trans. R. P. Lawson (New York: Newman, 1956), 39–40; cf. Andrew Louth, *The Origins of the Christian Mystical Tradition: From Plato to Denys* (New York: Oxford University Press, 1981), 58–59.

15. Evagrius Ponticus, *The Praktikos* 86, 89, in *The Praktikos and Chapters on Prayer,* trans. John Bamberger (Kalamazoo, Mich.: Cistercian Publications, 1981), 38. Cf. Jeremy Driscoll, *The "Ad Monachos" of Evagrius Ponticus: Its Structure and a Select Commentary* (Rome: S. Anselmo, 1991), 10–11.

16. For Evagrius's penetrating treatment of the eight evil "thoughts" (*logismoi*) see *The Praktikos* nn. 6–39, in *Praktikos and Chapters on Prayer,* 16–26.

17. *Praktikos* Prologue; ibid., 14.

18. Cf. Evagrius Ponticus, *In Prov.* 19:17: "Here he calls 'gift' purity of heart, for it is in proportion to our passionlessness that we are judged worthy of knowledge"; see Jeremy Driscoll, "*Apatheia* and Purity of Heart in Evagrius Ponticus," in *Purity of Heart,* ed. Luckman and Kulzer, 141–58, esp. 147.

19. Evagrius Ponticus, *Chapters on Prayer* nn. 67–70, in *Praktikos and Chapters on Prayer,* 66.

20. Cassian, *Conf.* 1.4, in *The Conferences,* trans. Boniface Ramsey (New York: Paulist, 1997), 43. For a discussion of Cassian's "purity of heart" see Columba Stewart, *Cassian the Monk* (New York: Oxford University Press, 1998), 42–47.

21. *Conf.* 1.6; *Conferences,* 45.

22. *Conf.* 1.7; ibid., 46.

23. *Conf.* 7.6; ibid., 253.

24. *Conf.* 12.7; ibid., 442–43.

25. *Conf.* 1.6; ibid., 45.

26. Cf. Stewart, *Cassian the Monk,* 90–99.

27. *Conf.* 14.9; in *Conferences,* 512.

28. *Conf.* 14.10; ibid., 513–14.

29. *Conf.* 1.10; ibid., 49.

30. Gregory of Nyssa, *Sermon on the Beatitudes* 6, in *The Lord's Prayer and The Beatitudes,* trans. Hilda Graef (Westminster, Md.: Newman, 1954), 148.

31. Ibid.

32. Ibid., 149.

33. Gregory of Nyssa, *Commentary on the Song of Songs,* trans. Casimir Mc-Cambley (Brookline, Mass.: Hellenic College Press, 1987), 92–93. In this passage, in connection with the image of the mirror, the Bridegroom also refers to the idea of beauty: "By approaching my archetypal beauty, you have yourself become beautiful. Just like a mirror you have taken on my appearance" (92).

34. *Tao-te-ching* 10, in *Lao-Tzu Te-Tao Ching: New Translation Based on the Recently Discovered Ma-Wang-Tui Texts,* trans. Robert Henricks (New York: Ballantine Books, 1989), 206. Some translations have "profound vision" instead of

"profound mirror." However, the Ma-wang-tui text (B) clearly shows the Chinese character *chien,* meaning "mirror."

35. *Tao-te-ching* 16; author's translation.

36. *Chuang Tzu* chapter 13, in *The Complete Works of Chuang Tzu,* trans. Burton Watson (New York: Columbia University Press, 1968), 142.

37. *Chuang Tzu* chapter 4; ibid., 58. For further discussion of Chuang Tzu see Joseph Wong's paper in this book (pp. 210–16).

38. See the "mirror" verses of the two patriarchs-to-be, Shen-hsiu and Hui-neng, in John C. Wu, *The Golden Age of Zen* (New York: Doubleday, 1996), 46–47; see also the papers of Heng Sure (p. 93) and Nicholas Koss (pp. 116–22). See also "mirror-wiping Zen" in Francis Cook (p. 127).

39. William Johnston, *The Mirror Mind: Spirituality and Transformation* (New York: Harper & Row, 1981), 36. For Hui-neng's teaching on "no-mind" see D. T. Suzuki, *The Zen Doctrine of No-Mind* (York Beach, Maine: Samuel Weiser, 1972), 22–30.

40. Cf. "Meditation," in *Encyclopedia of Religion,* 9:327. See also Pravrajika Vrajaprana's paper (pp. 28–30).

41. Cf. "Yoga," in *Encyclopedia of Religion,* 15:520.

42. "Seeing face to face" suggests a dualistic meaning. According to the biblical tradition, however, "seeing" is a unitive experience. This is better conveyed in the first letter of John: "When he [God] is revealed, we will be like him, for we will see him as he is" (1 Jn 3:2). "Seeing" implies the presence in the seer of the object seen and the transformation of the seer into what is seen.

43. Apophatic theology is centered in a "learned ignorance" or "knowing-in-unknowing." It insists upon the transcendence of human understanding and of conceptual and verbal expression by the Absolute. See Vladimir Lossky, *The Mystical Theology of the Eastern Church* (Crestwood, N.Y.: St. Vladimir's Seminary Press, 1976), chapter 2, "The Divine Darkness," 23–43, and Denys Turner, *The Darkness of God: Negativity in Christian Mysticism* (Cambridge: Cambridge University Press, 1995).

44. Recall Karl Rahner's reintroduction of the concept of "mystery" into the center of Catholic theology (cf. "The Concept of Mystery in Catholic Theology," in *Theological Investigations,* vol. 4 [New York: Seabury, 1974], 36–73) and Thomas Keating's explorations of the Christian apophatic tradition as a theological background for Centering Prayer.

45. Kataphatic theology or spirituality is an approach to God, or the Absolute, through the things of this world rather than by separation from the things of this world. Typical of this path is a poetic and imaginative relation to nature and—in the Christian mystical tradition—a use of sexual imagery for the personal relationship with God.

46. See section 2 above, "Paradox and Mystery … ", pp. 8–9.

47. Some traditions do regard desire more positively, however, especially the Tantric tradition.

48. David Loy, *Nonduality* (New Haven: Yale University Press, 1988).

49. See Aldous Huxley, *The Perennial Philosophy* (New York: Harper & Row, 1944); Bede Griffiths, *Return to the Center* (Springfield, Ill.: Templegate, 1976); Hajimi Nakamura, *Ways of Thinking of Eastern Peoples,* rev. ed. Philip F. Wiener (Honolulu: University of Hawaii Press, 1993), 67–72.

50. See chapter 18 of this book.

51. See section 1 above, p. 8.

52. See Jean Leclercq, *The Love of Learning and the Desire for God* (New York: Fordham University Press, 1961, rev. ed. 1974), 71–88; and Douglas Burton-Christie, *The Word in the Desert: Scripture and the Quest for Holiness in Early Christian Monasticism* (Oxford: Oxford University Press, 1993).

53. Mt 5:8.

54. Norman Fischer's contribution to the symposium, because of a prior publication commitment, does not appear in the present book. See, however, p. 16 below.

55. See chapter 2, pp. 39–40.

56. These words appear at the conclusion of Norman Fischer's introduction to the selections which he read from his translations of the biblical Psalms.

1. Pravrajika Vrajaprana: Regaining the Lost Kingdom

1. *Complete Works of Swami Vivekananda,* 9th ed. (Calcutta: Advaita Ashrama, 1972), 8:8. Swami Vivekananda was the foremost disciple of India's great nineteenth-century saint Sri Ramakrishna. Vivekananda brought Hinduism to the West when he represented Hinduism at the World's Parliament of Religions in Chicago in 1893. Vivekananda also founded the Ramakrishna Order, a monastic organization dedicated to the realization of God and service to humankind.

2. Katha Upanishad 2.1.1.

3. Raymond B. Blakney, trans., *Meister Eckhart: A Modern Translation* (New York: Harper and Row, 1941), 131.

4. Colm Luibheid, trans., *John Cassian: Conferences* (New York: Paulist Press, 1985), 40.

5. Bhagavad Gita 2.66.

6. Ibid., 2.67.

7. In its preliminary stages, hatha yoga deals extensively with physical fitness, though theoretically one is supposed to graduate to higher practices in the course of time. In practice, however, most people never move beyond the physical exercises and, as a result, only increase their body consciousness. For that reason, many spiritual teachers have cautioned against the practice of hatha yoga.

8. *Yoga Sutras* 3.2.

9. Ibid., 1.2.

10. See *Yoga Sutras* 2.30 and 2.32.

11. Bhagavad Gita 2.70.

12. St. John of the Cross, *Ascent of Mount Carmel,* trans. E. Allison Peers (Liguori, Mo.: Triumph Books, 1983), 270.

13. Swami Nikhilananda, trans., *The Gospel of Sri Ramakrishna,* 3d ed. (New York: Ramakrishna-Vivekananda Center, 1965), 277.

14. Swami Prabhavananda, trans., *Narada's Way of Divine Love: The Bhakti Sutras* (Hollywood: Vedanta Press, 1971), 13–39.

15. Bhagavad Gita 4.7.

16. Nikhilananda, *Gospel,* 680.

17. Bhagavad Gita 9.26.

18. Ibid., 9.27.

19. Ibid., 2.47.

20. Brother Lawrence [Nicolas Herman of Lorraine], *Practice of the Presence of God* (New York: Fleming H. Revell, 1958), 21–22.

21. Bhagavad Gita 6.30–31.

22. Katha Upanishad 1.3.12.

23. Kieran Kavanaugh, O.C.D., and Otilio Rodriguez, O.C.D., trans., *Sayings of Light and Love* (no. 49), in *The Collected Works of St. John of the Cross* (Washington, D.C.: ICS Publications, 1991), 89.

24. Katha Upanishad 2.3.14.

25. *Vivekacudamani* 20.

26. An excellent commentary on vairagya can be read in Sri Candrasekhara Bharati's commentary on the *Vivekacudamani* (Bombay: Bharatiya Vidya Bhavan, 1979), 36.

27. Kavanaugh and Rodriguez, *Sayings* (no. 22), 87.

28. A discussion of this is found in the *Vivekacudamani* 22–27 as well as in the much earlier Brihadaranyaka Upanishad 4.4.23.

29. Kavanaugh and Rodriguez, *Sayings* (no. 154), 96.

30. Swami Prabhavananda and Christopher Isherwood, trans., *Shankara's Crest-Jewel of Discrimination: Viveka-Chudamani* (Hollywood: Vedanta Press, 1947), 131–32.

31. Blakney, *Meister Eckhart*, 130.

2. Thomas Matus: Heart Yoga

1. St. Romuald, monastic reformer and initiator of the Camaldolese tradition of monks and nuns, lived in central Italy ca. 950–1027.

2. Jacques Dupuis, S.J., "Le dialogue interreligieux l'heure du pluralisme," in *Nouvelle revue théologique,* 120, no. 4 (October–December, 1998), 560. Cf. by the same author, *Vers une théologie chrétienne du pluralisme religieux,* Cogitatio fidei 200 (Paris: Cerf, 1997), and *Toward a Christian Theology of Religious Pluralism* (Maryknoll, N.Y.: Orbis, 1997).

3. Paramahansa Yogananda, *Autobiography of a Yogi* (Los Angeles: Self-Realization Fellowship, various editions), trans. into French, Italian, and many other languages.

4. Sri Kriyananda, an American who joined Yogananda in 1948 and who now lives in Italy, gathered a series of apothegms that illustrate the devotional thrust of his teacher's Yoga and the latter's constant effort to demonstrate the compatibility of Yoga practice and Vedanta philosophy with what Yogananda understood as "original Christianity." See Kriyananda (J. Donald Walters), *The Essence of Self-Realization: The Wisdom of Paramahansa Yogananda* (Nevada City, Calif.: Crystal Clarity Publishers, 1990).

5. See Mircea Eliade, *Yoga: Immortality and Freedom* (Princeton, N.J.: Princeton University Press, 1969), 204; and, by the same author, "Le problème des origines du Yoga," in Jacques Masui, ed., *Yoga, science de l'homme intégral* (Paris: Ed. Cahiers du Sud, 1953), 11–20; cf. also Eliade, *Patanjali et le Yoga* (Paris: Ed. du Seuil, 1962).

6. See Acts 17:28.

7. Written in Serampore, West Bengal, in 1894 and last published in Los Angeles: Self-Realization Fellowship, 1972.

8. Yogananda's work is being continued by his Self-Realization Fellowship, which associates a monastic order of men and women with lay disciples.

9. See Stanislav Grof and Christina Grof, eds., *Spiritual Emergency: When Personal Transformation Becomes a Crisis* (Los Angeles: Jeremy P. Tarcher, 1989). The two most significant types of these experiences are the near-death state (199–210) and the *kundalini* awakening (99–108).

10. This includes, of course, not a few monastics and other Catholic religious; see the document of the Benedictine-Cistercian joint commission for dialogue, the D.I.M. (*Dialogue Interreligieux Monastique*), "Contemplation et Dialogue Interreligieux." *Pro Dialogo* 84, no. 2 (1993): 250–70.

11. See Maurice Maupillier, *Le Yoga et l'homme d'occident* (Paris: Editions du Seuil, 1974), 262.

12. See B. K. S. Iyengar, *Light on Yoga: Yoga Dipika* (New York: Schocken, 1966).

13. See Bede Griffiths, *Return to the Centre* (London: William Collins Sons, 1976), especially the final chapter on "Yoga, the Way of Union," as well as Griffiths's many other works.

14. See John Main, *Christian Meditation* (Montreal: Benedictine Priory, 1977); *Word into Silence* (New York: Paulist Press, 1981).

15. See David Steindl-Rast and Robert Aitken-Roshi, *The Ground We Share: Everyday Practice, Christian and Buddhist* (Liguori, Mo.: Triumph Books, 1994).

16. D.I.M., "Contemplation et Dialogue Interreligieux," in *Pro Dialogo* 84, no. 2 (1993): 250–70.

17. See Maupillier, *Le Yoga,* 258.

18. In 1992 an excellent edition and commentary on this text was published in Italian: Massimo Vinti and Piera Scarabelli, *Patanjali Yoga Sutra con i commenti della tradizione* (Milan: Mimesis, 1992).

19. See Patanjali, *Yoga Sutras,* trans. James Haughton Woods, in *The Yoga System of Patanjali* [with the commentaries of Vyasa and Vachaspatimishra] (Harvard, 1914; reprint Delhi: Motilal Banarsidass, 1972), 3–12.

20. Ibid., 178–90.

21. See note 7. The following summary of Sri Yukteswar's teaching is based on a paper I delivered at the seminar of the Union européenne des fédérations de Yoga, held at Zinal, Switzerland, in August 1999, to be published in the Acts of the seminar.

22. Sri Yukteswar, *Kaivalya-darsanam* (see n. 7), 1.

23. Ibid., 2.

24. Ibid., 3.

25. Ibid., 3–4.

26. Ibid., 5–6.

27. Ibid., 15–18.

28. Ibid., 33–34.

29. Ibid.

30. Ibid., 35.

31. Ibid., cf. 38–39.

32. Ibid., 70–71.

33. Sir Walter Scott, *The Lay of the Last Minstrel,* canto 3, stanza 2.

34. Sri Yukteswar, *Kaivalya-darsanam,* 76.

35. Ibid., 76–77.

36. Thomas Matus, *Yoga and the Jesus Prayer Tradition: An Experiment in Faith* (New York: Paulist Press, 1984; reprint, Bangalore: Asian Trading, 1992).

37. *The Secret of Recognition (Pratyabhijnahrdayam): A Reviving Doctrine of Salvation of Medieval India,* Sanskrit text edited by the staff of the Adyar Li-

brary under the supervision of G. Srinivasa Murti, German translation and notes by Rev. Emil Baer, authorized translation into English by Kurt F. Leidecker (Madras: Adyar Library, 1938).

38. Inclusive language is not appropriate here, since in traditional Indian theater all actors are male.

39. See Kshemaraja, *The Secret of Recognition,* 40–41.

40. Ibid., 38 and passim.

41. Ibid., 71 and passim; Leidecker translates *cidananda* wrongly, in my opinion, as the separate words "spirit and bliss": as a compound the two terms mean more than the separate lexicographical sense of the roots and indeed imply the dialectic between the noetic and the affective. Hence our translation of *cidananda* as "All-knowing Love" is justified.

42. Ibid., 89.

43. Ibid., 71.

44. Ibid., 72.

45. Kshemaraja cites a *bhakti* text now and then: cf. p. 54.

46. Ibid., 73–74.

47. Ibid., 38 ff. Compare these with the "seven spheres or stages of creation" in Sri Yukteswar, *Kaivalya-darsanam* 12 ff.; 59 ff.

48. Kshemaraja, *The Secret of Recognition* (see n. 36), 77.

49. Ibid., 83.

50. Ibid., 138.

51. See Anand Nayak, *La méditation dans le Bhâgavata Purâna* (Paris: Dervy-Livres, 1978).

3. Cyprian Consiglio: The Space in the Lotus of the Heart

1. The anthropological ideas presented in this paper are explored more extensively, in their biblical and historical context, in Cyprian Consiglio, O.S.B. Cam., "The Space in the Heart of the Lotus: Spirit as an Anthropological Element Based on the Writings of Bede Griffiths," a thesis (unpublished at this date) submitted in partial fulfillment of the requirements for the Master of Arts in Theology at St. John's Seminary, Camarillo, California, Spring 1997.

2. All interpolations in brackets ([...]) will be my own.

3. Bede Griffiths, *The Marriage of East and West* [hereafter *MEW*] (Springfield, Ill.: Templegate, 1982), 46. I am grateful to Templegate Publishers for permission to use the extensive quotations from Bede Griffiths's books, published in the U.S. by Templegate (www.templegate.com), which are included in this paper.

4. Bede Griffiths, *A New Vision of Reality* [hereafter *NV*] (Springfield, Ill.: Templegate, 1989), 58.

5. *MEW,* 51.

6. *MEW,* 51.

7. Bede Griffiths, *Return to the Center* [hereafter *RTC*] (Springfield, Ill.: Templegate, 1976), 96.

8. *RTC,* 96.

9. *NV,* 59.

10. *NV,* 57.

11. Aldous Huxley, introduction to *Bhagavad Gita: The Song of God,* trans. Swami Prahavananda and Christopher Isherwood (Hollywood: Vedanta Press, 1987), 6.

12. Ibid., 7.

13. *Catechism of the Catholic Church* (Liguori, Mo.: United States Catholic Conference: 1994), n. 367, 93–94.

14. Bede Griffiths, "Integration of Mind, Body, and Spirit," An Occasional Paper of the Fetzer Institute (Kalamazoo, Mich.: 1994), 1.

15. *NV,* 97.

16. *NV,* 97.

17. *NV,* 70–71.

18. Bede Griffiths, *The Cosmic Revelation* [hereafter CR] (Springfield, Ill.: Templegate, 1983), 44–45; also Bede Griffiths, *Vedanta and Christian Faith* [hereafter VCF] (Los Angeles: Dawn Horse Press, 1973), 25.

19. *Chandogya Upanishad,* III.14.1, in *The Upanishads,* trans. Eknath Easwaren (Petaluma, Calif.: Nilgiri Press, 1987). References to the *Chandogya Upanishad* below are from this volume.

20. *RTC,* 126.

21. Bede Griffiths, *River of Compassion* [hereafter ROC] (Springfield, Ill.: Templegate, 1995), 110; *CR,* 44–45.

22. Baldev Raj Sharma, *The Concept of Atman in the Principal Upanishads* (New Delhi: Dinesh Publications, 1972), 13–14.

23. Sharma, *The Concept of Atman,* 11.

24. This term is borrowed from Robert Jewett, meaning "the divine spirit apportioned to the individual Christian . . . whose manifestations were visible in prophecy, ecstasy, wonders and the new life of faith, hope and love" (*Paul's Anthropological Terms* [Leiden: Brill, 1971], 182).

25. *CR,* 110.

26. *CR,* 104–5.

27. See, for example, 1 Cor 2:11; 14:14; Gal 6:18.

28. *Chandogya Upanishad,* VII.26.1–2, p. 190.

29. Bede Griffiths, "How I Pray," in *The Inner Directions Journal* 2, no. 3 (Summer 1996): 14.

30. *The Upanishads,* trans. Easwaran, 25.

31. *Chandogya Upanishad,* IV.13.3, p. 187.

32. *VCF,* 8.

33. *Chandogya Upanishad,* VIII.1.1, p. 191.

34. Sharma, *The Concept of Atman,* 19–20.

35. *NV,* 60; *RC,* 108.

36. *NV,* 29.

37. *ROC,* 108 (see *Bhagavad Gita* 6:5–6).

38. *ROC,* 108–109. Zaehner is one of two translators, along with Mascaró, whose texts Griffiths uses for his commentary on the *Bhagavad Gita.*

39. *RTC,* 93.

40. Sharma, *The Concept of Atman,* 108–9.

41. *NV,* 222–23.

42. Huxley, introduction to *Bhagavad Gita,* 10.

43. Bede Griffiths quoted in Rene Weber, *Dialogues with Saints and Sages* (London: Routledge and Kegan Paul, 1986), 171.

44. Weber, *Dialogues with Saints and Sages,* 172.

45. *RTC,* 16.

46. *CR,* 73, 110.

47. *CR,* 84.

48. Weber, *Dialogues with Saints and Sages,* 173.

49. Bede Griffiths, "Dzogchen and Christian Contemplation," *A.I.M. (Alliance for International Monasticism)* no. 55 (1993): 122–25.

50. See Hugo M. Enomiya-Lassalle, *The Practice of Zen Meditation* (San Francisco and London: Aquarian Press, 1990), 33.

51. *CR,* 84.

52. Ibid.

53. *RTC,* 28.

54. Ibid., 49–50.

55. Enomiya-Lassalle, *The Practice of Zen Meditation,* 33.

56. Paul Evdokimov, *Woman and the Salvation of the World: A Christian Anthropology on the Charisms of Women,* trans. Anthony P. Gythiel (Crestwood, N.Y.: St. Vladimir's Seminary Press, 1994), 43.

57. *Chandogya Upanishad,* VIII.1.1. p. 191.

58. See Evagrius Ponticus, *The Praktikos and Chapters on Prayer,* trans., with an introduction and notes, by John Eudes Bamberger, O.C.S.O. (Spencer, Mass.: Cistercian Publications, 1970), 10.

59. Simon Tugwell, *Ways of Imperfection: An Exploration of Christian Spirituality* (Springfield, Ill.: Templegate Publishers, 1985), 28.

60. *RTC,* 93.

61. Bede Griffiths, *The New Creation in Christ: Christian Meditation and Community* (hereafter *NCC*), ed. Robert Kiely and Laurence Freeman, O.S.B. (London: Darton, Longman and Todd, 1992), 33.

62. *NCC,* 99.

63. *ROC,* 305.

64. *NCC,* 32–33.

65. *NCC,* 99.

66. *ROC,* 19.

67. *Praktikos* (n. 81), 36.

68. *ROC,* 19.

69. *NCC,* 99 (see also *ROC,* 7).

70. *NV,* 241.

71. *ROC,* 98.

72. *Praktikos* (n. 64), 33–34.

73. *Praktikos* (n. 81), 36.

74. *NCC,* 99.

75. Ps 73:24.

76. *ROC,* 305.

4. Martin Verhoeven: Glistening Frost and Cooking Sand

1. Han-shan, *Cold Mountain, 101 Chinese Poems,* trans. Burton Watson (New York: Columbia University Press, 1970), no. 70.

2. Although the term "Dharma" in Brahmanism also meant the socioreligious duty appropriate to one's caste, it was also a more comprehensive concept that meant the true essence of things, righteousness, the way we should act morally, and the ordered nature of the universe. This eternal truth was not "religion," but constituted the basis of all religion.

3. *The Sixth Patriarch's Dharma Jewel Platform Sutra,* with commentary of Tripitaka Master Hua (San Francisco: Buddhist Texts Translation Society, 1977), 105, 169.

4. Ibid., 167.

5. Ibid., 68, 90.

6. Ibid., 108–9.

7. Arthur Waley, *The Way and Its Power: A Study of the Tao Te Ching and Its Place in Chinese Thought* (New York: Grove Press, 1958), 47.

8. Ibid., 58.

9. For a detailed explanation of this transformation of the ordinary mind into the Buddha-mind, or ordinary consciousness into enlightened wisdom, see *The Sixth Patriarch's Dharma Jewel Platform Sutra,* 215–20.

10. *The Shurangama-sutra,* translated into Chinese by Shramana Paramiti, Commentary by Tripitaka Master Hua (Talmage: BTTS, 1981), 7:1–60.

11. *The Dhammapada,* trans. Irving Babbitt (New York: Oxford University Press, 1936), 27, 43–44.

12. From "The Autobiography of Chan Master Han Shan (1546–1623)," in Charles Luk, *Practical Buddhism* (London: Rider, 1971), 81–83.

13. Ibid., 147–48.

14. Ibid.

15. Xu Yun, *Empty Cloud: The Autobiography of the Chinese Zen Master, Xu Yun,* trans. Charles Luk (Rochester, N.Y.: Empty Cloud Press, 1974), 6–7.

16. Ibid., 37–39.

17. St. Bruno of Querfurt, *The Life of the Five Brothers,* ch. 19; in *The Mystery of Romuald and The Five Brothers,* trans. from the Latin by Thomas Matus (Trabuco Canyon, Calif.: Source Books, 1994), 158.

18. *The Sixth Patriarch's Dharma Jewel Platform Sutra,* 86.

19. For the writings and insights of Paulo Giustiniani I am indebted to Father Thomas Hart, O.S.B., who provided me with the relevant passages from Jean Leclercq's *Alone with God,* trans. from *Seul avec Dieu* (London: Hodder & Stoughton, 1962), 162–81.

20. Ibid., 166–67.

21. Ibid., 165.

22. Ibid., 167–68.

23. *The Shurangama-sutra,* 6:45–48.

24. Leclercq, *Alone with God,* 181.

25. Ibid., 167.

5. Heng Sure: Cleansing the Heart

1. *Bodhimanda:* Sanskrit for "field of practice," "place of Bodhi (awakening)."

2. Father Thomas Hand proposes the word "psyche" for *xin.*

3. "Stopping" and "contemplating" correspond to the dual meaning of the Sanskrit word *dhyana.* Dhyana in Chinese is *Chan* (*Zen* in Japanese and *Son* in Korean) and has two definitions: "calming the mind" (*jing lyu*) and "cultivating thoughts" (*siwei xiu*). Calming the mind is *shamatha* "stopping," and cultivating thoughts is *vipassana,* or contemplating.

4. Master Hsuan Hua, *Sixth Patriarch's Dharma Jewel Platform Sutra* (San Francisco: Buddhist Texts Translation Society, 1977), 52.

5. Ibid., 57.

6. Ch'eng-kuan, *Huayenching Suchao* (an Exegesis and Subcommentary to the Flower Adornment Sutra), 10 vols. (Taipei: Huayen Lienshe, 1966), 2:14.

7. "Elite Buddhists have redefined Buddhism as synonymous with the practice of meditation. Those Buddhist groups that do not focus on teaching of meditation, therefore, are viewed as not really Buddhist at all." Jan Nattier, "Visible and Invisible: Buddhism and the Politics of Identity," *Tricycle: The Buddhist Review* 5, no. 1 (Fall 1995): 48. See also Paul David Numrich, *Old Wisdom in the New World: Americanization of Two Immigrant Theravada Buddhist Temples* (Knoxville: University of Tennessee Press, 1996), 119–25.

8. Eric Reinders, "The Iconoclasm of Obeisance: Protestant Images of Chinese Religion and the Catholic Church," *Numen: The International Review For the History of Religions* 44 (1997): 296–322.

9. Judith Lief, "On Practice: Bowing," in *Tricycle: The Buddhist Review* 9, no. 1 (Fall 1994): 33.

10. Reinders paints the picture: "On one end of the yardstick of obeisance was aversion to full prostration, and the implications of self-mortification, ritual nudity, despotism, militarism, deception, slavishness, China, Siam, Japan, primitives, Catholics, idolators and dogs. On the other positive end of attraction was Herbert Spencer's world: faint echoes of obeisance (growing fainter every day), freedom, industry, free-market capitalism, honesty, dignity, Britain, Protestantism (and perhaps even God.)" (Reinders, "The Iconoclasm of Obeisance," 314.)

11. Samuel E. Loewenstamm, "Prostration from Afar in Ugaritic, Accadian and Hebrew," in *Bulletin of the American Schools of Oriental Research* 188 (December 1967): 41–43.

12. Ibid., 42.

13. I am grateful to Dr. Yoel Kahn for his kindness in making available to me these materials on bowing in Judaism.

14. The situation regarding bowing is complex in Judaism. Prostration was a common act of self-abasement performed before relatives, strangers, superiors, and especially before royalty. Abraham bowed himself before the Hittites of Hebron (Gen 23:7, 12). He also bowed before the three strangers who visited him at Mamre (Gen 18:2), as did Lot before the two angelic visitors who came to him at Sodom (Gen 19:1). The verb, however, is used less frequently of an individual's worship of the Lord. Abraham on his way to sacrifice Isaac says that he is going to worship (Gen 22:5). It is used most often of particular acts of worship, e.g., of Abraham's servant who "bowed his head and worshipped" (Gen 24:26, 48), and of Gideon (Jud 7:15) upon experiencing God's grace. Such acts often involved actual prostration "to the earth" as in the case of Abraham's servant (Gen 24:52), Moses (Ex 34:8), Joshua (Josh 5:14), and Job (Job 1:20). Yet, while one is compelled to observe the rules for proper bowing, at the same time the second commandment forbids the worship of any graven images or other gods (Ex 20:5; 34:14; Deut 5:9). The Israelites were warned not to worship the gods of the Amorites, Hittites, etc. (Ex 23:24; Ps 81:9 [H 10]). Nevertheless the Israelites repeatedly worshiped other gods (Deut 29:26 [H 25]; Judg 2:12, 17; Jer 13:10; 16:11; 22:9). See *Theological Wordbook of the Old Testament*, vol. 1, ed. R. Laird Harris et al. (Chicago: Moody Press, 1980), 267–69.

15. Moses Maimonides, *Mishneh Torah: Laws of Prayer*, chap. 5; par. 10 and 12: Yad Hilkhot tefila 5:9–15) http://orthodoxinfo.com/inquirers/prostration_heb.htm.

16. Uri Ehrlich published a revised edition of his dissertation on the gestures and physical aspects of Jewish prayer in Hebrew as *Kol Atzmatai Tomarna* (Jerusalem: Magnes Press, 1999). Chapter 2 of his book deals explicitly with bowing.

17. Surah xxiii. 2. *Salat* doesn't mean "prayer"; another Arabic word *dua* corresponds to the concept of prayer. It doesn't occur in pre-Qur'anic literature. Muhammed took it, like the ceremony, from the Jews and Christians in Arabia. See also Surah ii. 83, 110, 172, 277; iv. 77, 162; v. 12, 55.

18. *Qur'an* xcvi. 19.

19. Ibid., 499.

20. Al-Ghazali, *Mysteries of Worship in Islam,* trans. E. E. Calverley (Chicago: Kazi Publications, 1981), 12–13.

21. "Why We Are Not to Kneel on Sundays," from "Living An Orthodox Life," Orthodox Christian Information Center, http://orthodoxinfo.com/praxis/kneeling .htm. See also Orthodox America, http://www.roca.org/oa/150/150e.htm.

22. *Rubrics of the Roman Breviary and Missal Translated from Acta Apostolicae Sedis* 52, no. 10 (August 15, 1960), trans. Leonard Doyle (Collegeville, Minn.: Liturgical Press, 1960).

23. Elizabeth T. Knuth, *Nine Ways of Prayer of St. Dominic:* Prostrations/Rev. December 12, 1998. URL: http://www.users.csbsju.edu/eknuth/nineways/9ways2.html.

24. *The Rule of St. Benedict,* chapters 44, 53, 58, 67, 71; in Timothy Fry, ed., *RB 1980,* abr. ed. (Collegeville, Minn.: Liturgical Press, 1981), 95, 105, 117, 137, 141.

25. Edward Said, *Orientalism* (New York: Vintage, 1979). See also Immanuel Wallerstein, "Eurocentrism and its Avatars: The Dilemmas of Social Science," 1997 [Keynote Address at ISA East Asian Regional Colloquium, "The Future of Sociology in East Asia," November 22–23, 1996, Seoul, Korea, cosponsored by Korean Sociological Association and International Sociological Association], http:// fbc.binghamton.edu/iweuroc.htm.

26. Gregory Schopen, "Archaeology and Protestant Presuppositions in the Study of Indian Buddhism," *History of Religions* 31, no. 1 (August 1991): 1–23. The study of Indian religions is dominated by a search in written sources for a logocentrism that typifies the Protestant traditions of most Western Indologists and Buddhologists. Evaluations of the quality and authenticity of their conclusions and foci of that scholarship must be reinterpreted in that light.

27. "The Ten Thousand Buddhas Repentance Liturgy" is bowed every spring at the City of Ten Thousand Buddhas in Northern California and requires 11,111 bows in all. The ceremony requires three weeks to complete.

28. More on bowing in Tibetan Buddhism can be found in an on-line article by Lama Surya Das: www.suryadas.org.

29. Master Hsuan Hua, *Records of a Life* (Hong Kong: BTTS, 1958), 1:4–5.

30. *Datang Xiyuji* (Journey to the Western Regions during the Great Tang Dynasty), chapter 2, "An Extensive Discussion of Indian Customs."

31. Antaiji moved to Hyogo Prefecture in 1976.

32. Shasta Abbey, in the Soto Zen lineage, under the tutelage of the late Jiyu Kennett Roshi, developed a full monastic liturgy that has been said to resemble Anglican church music. Kennett Roshi was an accomplished organist; her Protestant religious background, university training in music, and love for liturgy informed her translations of Japanese Zen ceremonies into Western modes.

33. "On Practice: Bowing," *Tricycle: The Buddhist Review* 4, no. 1 (Fall 1994): 32.

34. Norman Fischer, "Why Do We Bow?," *Tricycle: The Buddhist Review* 6, no. 3 (Spring 1997): 58–59.

35. Ibid.

36. Ibid., 59.

37. Takakusu and Watanabe, eds., *Taisho-shinshu-daizokyo* (Tokyo, 1922–33), 46:956a2.

38. I am indebted to Professor Dan Stevenson for this information.

39. For more on Samantabhadra, I refer the reader to Taigen Daniel Leighton's *Bodhisattva Archetypes: Classic Buddhist Guides to Awakening and their Modern Expression* (New York: Penguin Arkana, 1998).

40. The Buddha taught the "Three Dharma-seals," i.e., all dharmas made of components, arising from conditions, are (1) *dukkha*: subject to decay and destruction and thus inherently unsatisfactory, tending to suffering; (2) *anatta*: not-self; (3) *anitta*: transient and impermanent.

41. Four Stations of Mindfulness: (1) the body is impure; (2) feelings lead to suffering; (3) thoughts are transient; (4) all dharmas are no-self.

42. I have been unsuccessful in locating Hindu sources on bowing, and I will leave that rich tradition for an expanded analysis at a later time.

43. From the *Flower Adornment Sutra Preface*.

6. Nicholas Koss: The Historical Hui-neng

1. Yampolsky, in the Introduction of Hui-neng, *The Platform Sutra of the Sixth Patriarch: The Text of the Tun-huang Manuscript,* trans., with intro. and notes, by Philip B. Yampolsky (New York: Columbia University Press, 1967), 77.

2. Ibid., 90.

3. This essay, because of the nature of the volume of which it is part, will not discuss the original Chinese text of *The Platform Sutra*. A revised, expanded version of this study is being prepared that will examine the original Chinese text. Suffice it to say for now that the Chinese version of this sutra offers no inconsistencies with my interpretation of this text. The author also wishes to thank Dr. John J. Deeney and Dr. Steven Berkowitz for their careful reading of an earlier version of this essay.

4. *The Platform Sutra*, 113.

5. Another version of Hui-neng's enlightenment at the end of his autobiography appears in the later part of the sermon:

> Good Friends, when I was at Priest Jen's place, hearing it [the Diamond Sutra] just once, I immediately gained the great awakening and saw suddenly that True Reality was my original nature. Therefore, I have taken this teaching and, passing it on to later generations, shall make you students of the Way suddenly awaken to enlightenment . . . (ibid., 153).

6. Ibid., 127.

7. Here I am referring with much gratitude to Rev. Taigen Dan Leighton and Rev. Heng Sure.

8. Mt 14:13–21; 15:32–39.

9. *The Platform Sutra*, 125.

10. Ibid, 126.

11. Ibid.

12. Ibid., 128.

13. Ibid.

14. Ibid., 134.
15. Ibid., 128.
16. Ibid., 129.
17. Ibid., 130.
18. Ibid., 127.
19. Ibid.
20. Ibid., 128.
21. Ibid., 131.
22. Ibid., 129.
23. Ibid., 132.
24. Ibid., 131.
25. *The Cloud of Unknowing and Other Works,* trans. into modern English by Clifton Wolters (London: Penguin, 1978).
26. Ibid., Introduction, 12–13.
27. Besides being of help to understand aspects of Hui-neng, *The Cloud* can also be used as a commentary on the perplexities of Shen-hsiu when trying to decide what to do (*Platform Sutra,* 129), especially chapter 52, which expostulates on those who are "mad" in their approach to contemplation (*The Cloud,* 122). This passage in *The Cloud* explicitly presents what could very well have been the unexpressed dilemma of Shen-hsiu. Furthermore, passages from *The Cloud* can be given as possible explanations of what it is that the verse composed by Shen-hsiu does not understand (*Platform Sutra,* 130). See chapter 34, p. 101; chapter 51, p. 121; and chapter 57, p. 129.
28. *The Cloud,* 92.
29. Ibid., 125.
30. Ibid., 146.
31. Ibid., 62, 65.
32. *The Platform Sutra,* 127.
33. *The Cloud,* chapter 1, p. 59.
34. Ibid., chapter 34, p. 100.
35. Ibid., chapter 36, p. 103.
36. *The Platform Sutra,* 132.
37. *The Cloud,* 113.
38. Ibid., 116.
39. Ibid., 130.
40. Ibid., 133, 136.
41. Ibid., 140.

7. Francis Cook: Zen and the Impurity of Purity

1. Leo D. Lefebure, "Cardinal Ratzinger's Comments on Buddhism," *Buddhist-Christian Studies* 18 (1998): 221–23.
2. Ibid., 223.
3. *The Dhammapada,* trans. S. Radhakrishnan (New York: Oxford University Press, 1966).
4. *The Path of Purification,* trans. Bhikku Nanamoli (Columbo: R. Semage, 1956).
5. A readable translation with good commentary is *Yoga Sutras,* trans. Rammurti S. Mishra (Garden City, N.Y.: Anchor Books, 1973).

6. I am avoiding using the term "Hinayana" for this conservative form of Buddhism found in South and Southeast Asia because the term is pejorative and unkind. "Theravada" is an accurate term but it does not itself indicate that there are other schools that are of the same kind that the Mahayana was criticizing in using the term "Hinayana." As Roger Corless has pointed out, this criticism is similar to that used when Christians say that Judaism is all right as far as it goes but is merely a kind of anticipation of the real thing. Speaking of "Old Testament" and "New Testament" is similar to the Mahayana use of the term "Hinayana."

7. Cf. Edward Conze, *Buddhism: Its Essence and Development* (New York: Harper & Row, 1959), 123–35. According to Conze, the new form of Buddhism first surfaced in about 100 B.C.E. in the form of the *Prajnaparamita Sutras,* like the *Diamond Sutra,* which taught emptiness. It is not clear whether the appearance of these sutras indicates a new school of thought or whether that thought—universal emptiness—had existed from the very birth of Buddhism, coexisting side by side with the more conservative form.

8. *L'Enseignement de Vimalakirti,* trans. Etienne Lamotte (Louvain: Publications universitaires, 1962); Eng. trans. *The Teaching of Vimalakirti,* trans. Sara Boin (London: Pali Text Society, 1976). See also *The Vimalakirti Nirdesa Sutra,* trans. Charles Luk (Berkeley: Shambhala, 1972). My translation of Lamotte's work incorporates some of Luk's translation.

9. The five are: killing one's mother, killing one's father, killing an arhat, shedding the blood of a Buddha, and creating a schism in the Buddhist community of monks.

10. *L'Enseignement de Vimalakirti,* 285–87. My translation. I have abbreviated the passage somewhat, because it just prolongs the list of similar items.

11. Edward Conze, *Buddhist Wisdom Books* (London: George Allen and Unwin, 1958), 25.

12. *Three Texts on Consciousness Only,* trans. Francis H. Cook (Berkeley: Numata Center for Buddhist Translation and Research, 1999), 109.

13. Richard Robinson and Willard L. Johnson, *The Buddhist Religion,* 3d edition (Belmont, Calif.: Wadsworth Publishing Company, 1982), 69.

14. One was Hui-neng, in the *Platform Sutra of Hui-neng.* There, on several occasions, the author says that sitting meditation is not required, but it is most likely that the monks who practiced with him meditated. Cf. *The Platform Sutra of the Sixth Patriarch,* trans. Philip Yampolsky (New York: Columbia University Press, 1967), 82, 140–41.

15. This is not a contradiction with the basic Buddhist teaching of no-self (*anatman*), because one's "true nature" or "intrinsic nature" is no-nature. Consequently, one should not hypostasize this original nature or think of it as just a superior self such as is taught in Hindu religions. It is not a self or substance, but whatever it is called, it is impersonal, formless, faceless, and by no means a spiritual being.

16. The qualities I mention, such as generosity (*dana*), are the ten perfections of the ten stages of the bodhisattva's career. Each stage is correlated with a perfection (*paramita*).

17. In the *Platform Sutra* (cf. note 14) Hui-neng says, "If someone speaks of 'viewing purity' [then I would say] that man's nature is of itself pure, but because of false thoughts True Reality is obscured. If you exclude delusion, then the original nature reveals its purity" (139–41).

18. Thich Nhat Hanh, *Breathe! You are Alive* (Berkeley: Parallax Press, 1990.) Nhat Hanh translates the *Anapana-sati Sutra* (3ff.) and then discusses its meaning.

8. William Skudlarek: Zazen: A Path from Judgment to Love

1. Hugo M. Enomiya-Lassalle, *The Practice of Zen Meditation,* ed. Roland Ropers and Bogdan Snela, trans. Michelle Bromley (London and San Francisco: The Aquarian Press, 1992), 15.

2. The Rule of Benedict, chapter 58. *RB 1980. The Rule of St. Benedict,* ed. Timothy Fry (Collegeville, Minn.: Liturgical Press, 1980), 267.

3. Thomas Merton, *Zen and the Birds of Appetite* (New York: New Directions Publishing Corporation, 1968), 6–7.

4. Quotations from the Bible are taken from the New Revised Standard Version (Nashville: Thomas Nelson, 1990).

5. The *Shinkyôdôyaku* (New Common [i.e., ecumenical] Translation).

6. The way a command is heard depends, of course, on context, tone of voice, facial expression, and other nonverbal indicators. However, it can generally be said that this negative direct-style imperative is "extremely direct, aggressive, and not at all polite." Eleanor Harz Jorden, with Mari Noda, *Japanese: The Spoken Language,* Part III (Tokyo: Kodansha International, 1990), 173.

7. Max Zerwick, *Analysis Philologica Novi Testamenti Graeci* (Rome: Pontifical Biblical Institute, 1960), 15.

8. "The most ancient authorities lack 7.53–8.11; other authorities add the passage here or after 7.36 or after 21.25 or after Luke 21.38, with variations of text; some mark the passage as doubtful." Footnote in the New Revised Standard Version, 101.

Outside the Gospels, the principal texts dealing with judgment are Romans 2:1 ("Therefore you have no excuse, whoever you are, when you judge others; for in passing judgment on another you condemn yourself, because you, the judge, are doing the very same things") and 1 Corinthians 4:5 ("Therefore do not pronounce judgment before the time, before the Lord comes, who will bring to light the things now hidden in darkness and will disclose the purposes of the heart. Then each one will receive commendation from God").

9. Benedict T. Viviano, "The Gospel According to Matthew," *The New Jerome Biblical Commentary,* ed. Raymond Brown et al. (Englewood Cliffs, N.J.: Prentice-Hall, 1990), 646. Commenting on vv. 3–5 the author adds, "These verses contain a warning against hypocritical judges, which, however, presupposes some judging of others as necessary."

An exception to this mitigating approach to Jesus' words is found in a commentary by Wolfgang Trilling:

> Our distorted nature is inclined to pass judgment on others. And this judgment easily turns into one of condemnation. This is what Jesus means when he forbids us to judge our fellow men.... He who judges another arrogates to himself a right which he does not possess at all. He presumes to exercise a right which belongs to God, from whom alone a correct verdict is possible and legitimate. The man who judges has gone beyond the measure allotted to man, and is now sent back to his proper bounds.

Wolfgang Trilling, *The Gospel According to St. Matthew,* New Testament for Spiritual Reading, ed. John L. McKenzie, vol. 1 (New York: Crossroad, 1981), 128.

10. I. Howard Marshall, *The Gospel of Luke: A Commentary on the Greek Text* (Grand Rapids, Mich.: Eerdmans, 1978), 265f.

11. *The Sayings of the Desert Fathers: The Alphabetical Collection,* trans. and ed. Benedicta Ward, S.L.G., rev. ed. (Kalamazoo, Mich.: Cistercian Publications, 1984), xxv.

12. Ibid., 141.

13. Ibid.

14. Ibid., 142f.

15. Judith Simmer-Brown, in *Benedict's Dharma: Buddhists Reflect on the Rule of Saint Benedict,* ed. Patrick Henry with an afterword by David Steindl-Rast, O.S.B. (New York: Riverhead Books, 2001), 33.

16. Abba Poemen said that Abba Paphnutius used to say, "During the whole lifetime of the old men, I used to go to see them twice a month, although it was a distance of twelve miles. I told them each of my thoughts and they never answered me anything but this, 'Wherever you go, do not judge yourself and you will be at peace.' " *The Sayings of the Desert Fathers,* 202f.

17. When I prepared this paper, I was not yet familiar with the writings of Charlotte Joko Beck. She speaks frequently to the issue of judging in her books *Everyday Zen Love and Work,* ed. Steve Smith (San Francisco: HarperSanFrancisco, 1989) and *Nothing Special: Living Zen,* ed. Steve Smith (San Francisco: HarperSanFrancisco, 1993). In the latter book, in fact, there is a chapter entitled "Do Not Judge" (103–10).

18. Sister Kathleen Reilly, M.M., *dokusan,* September 28, 1998. Sister Kathleen describes her experience with Zen in an article entitled "Zen and Japanese Christians," *The Japan Mission Journal* 49, no. 1 (Spring 1995): 57–59.

19. Although the meaning of *teisho* is difficult to convey, it can briefly be described as a verbal expression of Zen realization, spoken by a Zen master in the presence of students, as an offering to the buddha.

20. In *Gateless Gate,* trans. with commentary by Zen Master Kôun Yamada, 2d ed. (Tucson: University of Arizona Press, 1979), 119, 131.

21. Shunryu Suzuki, *Zen Mind, Beginner's Mind* (New York and Tokyo: Weatherhill, 1970), 87.

22. Ibid., 136. Emphasis mine.

23. I was hoping the Dalai Lama would comment on this passage in his book *The Good Heart. A Buddhist Perspective on the Teachings of Jesus,* trans. Geshe Thupten Jinpa (Boston: Wisdom Publications, 1996), but unfortunately he does not.

24. Philip Kapleau, *The Three Pillars of Zen* (Tokyo: John Weatherhill, 1965), 96.

25. J.-M. Déchanet, *Christian Yoga* (New York: Harper & Brothers, 1960).

26. In *The Three Pillars of Zen,* 136.

27. Franco Sottocornola, S.X., "Zazen and Adoration of the Eucharist," *The Japan Mission Journal* 49, no. 1 (Spring 1995): 50.

28. Augustine Ichiro Okumura, *Awakening to Prayer,* trans. Theresa Kazue Hiraki and Albert Masaru Yamoto (Washington, D.C.: Institute of Carmelite Studies Publications, 1994), ix.

29. Ibid., 20.

30. Robert E. Kennedy, *Zen Spirit, Christian Spirit: The Place of Zen in Christian Life* (New York: Continuum, 1998), 14.

31. Eugene Boylan, *This Tremendous Lover* (Cork: Mercier Press, 1946), 296. Boylan bases the formulation "one Christ loving himself" on one of Augustine's homilies on the Gospel of John (*In Iohanne,* 108).

9. Taigen Dan Leighton: Sacred Fools and Monastic Rules

1. See Taigen Daniel Leighton and Shohaku Okumura, trans., *Dogen's Pure Standards for the Zen Community: A Translation of Eihei Shingi* (Albany: State University of New York Press, 1996).

2. For full translation and comment see Steven Heine, *Shifting Shape, Shaping Text: Philosophy and Folklore in the Fox Koan* (Honolulu: University of Hawaii Press, 1999), 217–22.

3. Thomas Cleary, trans., *Sayings and Doings of Pai-Chang* (Los Angeles: Center Publications, 1978), 26.

4. See Yifa, "The Rules of Purity for the Chan Monastery: An Annotated Translation and Study of the *Chanyuan qingui*" (Ph.D. Dissertation, Yale University, 1996).

5. Leighton and Okumura, *Dogen's Pure Standards for the Zen Community,* 141.

6. Ibid., 139.

7. Ibid.

8. Ibid., 140.

9. Ibid.

10. Ibid., 147.

11. Ibid.

12. Dogen criticized, for example, the view that it is enough to understand about Buddha nature without practice or observance of precepts in his writing *Bendowa* in 1231. See Shohaku Okumura and Taigen Daniel Leighton, trans., *The Whole-hearted Way: A Translation of Eihei Dogen's "Bendowa" with Commentary by Kosho Uchiyama Roshi* (Boston: Charles Tuttle, 1997), 32–34. Late in his career, Dogen again emphasized the importance of ethics, for example in his essay *Jinshin Inga,* "Deep Faith in Cause and Effect." See Francis Cook, *How to Raise an Ox: Zen Practice as Taught in Zen Master Dogen's "Shobogenzo"* (Los Angeles: Center Publications, 1978), 159–69.

13. For a treatment of the seven major archetypal bodhisattvas of East Asian Buddhism, including Maitreya, see Taigen Daniel Leighton, *Bodhisattva Archetypes: Classic Buddhist Guides to Awakening and Their Modern Expression* (New York: Penguin/Arkana, 1998). These bodhisattva figures are of questionable historicity, but have pervaded Mahayana Buddhism as objects of veneration and also as archetypal models of an approach to awakening to be incorporated and expressed by devotees.

14. See Burton Watson, trans., *The Lotus Sutra* (New York: Columbia University Press, 1993), 14–21.

15. I heard this in a wonderful course by Dr. Keene on Japanese literature that I attended at Columbia College in 1976. Perhaps a few Westerners may have transcended their anthropocentrism since then.

16. Taigen Daniel Leighton and Kazuaki Tanahashi, translations of poems by Ryokan in *Essential Zen,* ed. Tanahashi and Tensho David Schneider (HarperSanFrancisco, 1994), 132.

17. Taigen Dan Leighton and Kazuaki Tanahashi, translators, "Poetry of Ryokan," in "Udumbara," vol. 3, no. 1 (1985): 27.

10. Kevin Hunt: Doubt and Breakthrough in the Desert Fathers

1. St. Athanasius, *The Life of St. Antony,* trans. Robert T. Meyer (New York: Newman Press, 1950), 3, 7.

2. Ibid.

3. Ibid., 20.

4. Mk 1:12, 13.

5. St. Athanasius, *Life*, 29.

6. Ibid., 32.

7. *The Sayings of the Desert Fathers: The Alphabetical Collection,* trans. Benedicta Ward (Spencer, Mass.: Cistercian Publications, 1975), 4.

8. *Praktikos* Introduction; in *The Praktikos and Chapters on Prayer,* trans. John E. Bamberger (Kalamazoo, Mich.: Cistercian Publications, 1981), 14.

9. *Praktikos,* n. 81; ibid., 36.

10. *Praktikos,* n. 100; ibid., 41.

11. *Praktikos,* n. 79; ibid., 36.

12. *On Prayer,* nn. 66 and 70; ibid., 66.

13. *On Prayer,* nn. 117 and 120; ibid., 75.

14. *On Prayer,* n. 11; ibid., 57.

15. *Sayings,* 107.

16. Ibid., 143.

17. Poemen was considered one of the earliest and greatest of the desert abbas. He was at Scete toward the end of the life of Antony. Some think that the stories of Poemen formed the core around which the *Sayings* formed.

18. *Sayings,* 180.

19. Ibid.

20. Ibid., 142.

21. *Conf.* 1, XVII.1; *John Cassian: The Conferences,* trans. Boniface Ramsey (New York: Paulist Press, 1997), 56.

22. *Conf.* 1, VI; ibid., 45.

23. *Conf.* 1, VII; ibid., 46.

24. Lk 10:38–42.

25. *Conf.* 1, VIII; in *Conferences,* 46.

26. 1 Cor 13:8.

27. Mt 5:3.

28. *Conf.* 10, XI; in *Conferences,* 383–85.

11. Liu Xiaogan: The Taoist Tradition of Meditation

1. There are disputes about the date of the *Laozi.* The latest unearthed bamboo versions of the *Laozi* fully prove that it could be much earlier than A. C. Graham's theory allows. I argued that the main part of the *Laozi* could have been completed in the sixth century B.C.E. See Liu, *Laozi: niandai xinkao yu sixiang xinquan* (Laozi: A New Investigation of the Date and Interpretation of Thought) (Taipei: Grand East Book Co., 1997). A brief argument in English is available in the afterword of *Classifying the Zhuangzi Chapters* (Ann Arbor, Mich.: University of Michigan Center for Chinese Studies, 1994).

2. The citation of this chapter is rearranged in order to reveal the meaning of the text clearly. The translations of the *Laozi* in this paper are mostly adapted from Wing-tsit Chan and modified based on silken versions and bamboo versions of the *Laozi.* See Wing-tsit Chan, *A Source Book in Chinese Philosophy* (Princeton, N.J.: Princeton University Press, 1963), 139–76.

3. Burton Watson, trans., *The Complete Works of Chuang Tzu* (New York: Columbia University Press, 1968), 119–20. The translation is modified slightly.

4. Wang Ming compiled and edited a new and most complete version: *Taiping Jing Hejiao* (A Complete Edition of the Taiping Jing) (Beijing: Zhonghua Shuju, 1985). This paper is based on his book.

5. Ibid., 60.

6. See Livia Kohn, ed., *Taoist Meditation and Longevity Techniques* (Ann Arbor, Mich.: Center for Chinese Studies, the University of Michigan, 1989), 127–37.

7. Wang, *Taiping Jing Hejiao,* 12–13.

8. Ibid., 724.

9. Ibid., 716.

10. It could be rendered as "Keeping the Luminous One." See Isabelle Robinet, *Taoist Meditation* (Albany: State University of New York Press, 1993), 123.

11. For example, Yoshioka cited by Kohn in *Taoist Meditation and Longevity Techniques,* 140.

12. Wang, *Taiping Jing Hejiao,* 16, 739–40; Robinet, *Taoist Meditation,* 123.

13. Robinet, *Taoist Meditation,* 124.

14. Jao Tsung-I, *Laozi Xiang'erzhu Jiaozheng* (A Critical Edition of Xiang'er's Commentary on the Laozi) (Shanghai: Guji Chubanshe, 1991), 12; Robinet, *Taoist Meditation,* 124.

15. Robinet, *Taoist Meditation,* 64–66.

16. The translation is adapted from Kristofer Schipper, *The Taoist Body* (Berkeley: University of California Press, 1993), 130.

17. James Ware, trans., *Alchemy, Medicine, Religion in the China of A.D. 320* (Cambridge, Mass.: MIT Press, 1966), 302.

18. Ibid.

19. Ibid., 303–4.

20. Ibid., 304.

21. Ibid., 305.

22. Ibid., 305–6.

23. See Livia Kohn, "Guarding the One: Concentrative Meditation in Taoism," in *Taoist Meditation and Longevity Techniques,* 125–58.

24. Li Yangcheng, *Daojiao Shouce* (A Manual of Taoism) (Zhengzhou: Zhongzhong Guji Chubanshe, 1993), 299.

25. Kohn, *Taoist Meditation and Longevity Techniques,* 146–47.

26. Ibid., 149.

27. Ibid., 149–50.

28. Li, *Daojiao Shouce,* 300.

29. Kohn, *Taoist Meditation and Longevity Techniques,* 151–52.

30. Liu Xiaogan, "Taoism," in *Our Religions,* ed. Arvind Sharma (San Francisco: Harper, 1993), 277–78.

31. Robinet, "Original Contribution of *Neidan* to Taoism and Chinese Thought," in *Taoist Meditation and Longevity Techniques,* 299.

32. Ibid., 301.

33. Ibid., 301–2.

34. Kohn, *Taoist Meditation and Longevity Techniques,* 151–52.

35. The first version was published in 1914. I use a combined version of his first and second methods (*xubian*) published in Taiwan, 1977.

36. In this paper we discuss only his first method without the second one that follows Buddhist tradition.

37. Some parts of Jiang's book were translated into English. See Charles Luk (Lu K'uan Yü), *The Secrets of Chinese Meditation* (London: Rider and Company, 1964), 169, 174–75; and Jiang Weiqiao, *Yinshizi Jingzuofa* (Method of Sitting Still by Yinshizi) (Taipei: Xinwenfeng Press, 1977), 33, 42.

38. Eva Wong, *The Shambhala Guide to Taoism* (Boston and London: Shambhala, 1997), 201.

39. *Laozi* and *Zhuangzi* are well known nowadays. *Guanzi* is also an important book in Taoist meditative traditions. See Harold D. Roth, *Original Tao: Inward Training* (New York: Columbia University Press, 1999).

12. Paul Crowe: Chaos

1. Norman Girardot, *Myth and Meaning in Early Taoism: The Theme of Chaos (hun-tun)* (Berkeley: University of California Press, 1983), 276–78.

2. Ibid., 9.

3. Peter A. Angeles, *Dictionary of Philosophy* (New York: Barnes and Noble Books, 1981), s.v. chaos.

4. Given the context of this discussion, it is quite possible that Plato's views are not being represented in any straightforward way by Timaeus. Indeed Timaeus appears to be cast as something of a clown, with his grand ruminations on the origins of the cosmos. I would like to thank Brother Augustine Murray of New Camaldoli for a lively and enlightening discussion of this dialogue, prompting this qualifying note.

5. Plato, *Timaeus*, trans. Desmond Lee (1965; reprint London: Penguin Books, 1977), 30. References to the *Timaeus* will employ the standard page reference to the 1578 edition prepared by Stephanus. In the *Laws* Plato expresses a view concerning the soul which appears to be a modification of his earlier understanding of the rational soul. The account of creation in the *Timaeus* assumes that a primordial, chaotic matter was preexistent, perhaps eternal, and that the rational mind of the creator was brought to bear upon it. In Book 10 of the *Laws* Plato's desire to ensure the priority of the rational soul over the body and all things material causes him to suggest that the soul had always existed and existed prior to chaos. Plato, *Laws*, in *The Dialogues of Plato*, vol. 2, trans. Benjamin Jowett (1892; reprint, New York: Random House, 1937), 633–34.

6. Frederick Copleston notes that it is unlikely that Plato actually considered that there was an historical period during which chaos existed as an actual fact. He observes though that Aristotle's critique of the creation account in the *Timaeus* suggests that Aristotle did in fact read it this way. Frederick Copleston, *A History of Philosophy*, vol. 1: *Greece and Rome* (1946; reprint, New York: Image Books, 1985), 248.

7. Direct reference to the immortality of the soul can be found at *Timaeus*, 69.

8. Lee, *Timaeus*, 8.

9. St. Augustine offers the following comment on the meaning of the watery expanse: "He began with the heavens and the earth, itself, as Scripture adds, was at first invisible and formless, light not yet being as yet made, and darkness covering the face of the deep (that is to say covering an undefined chaos of earth and sea, for where light is not, darkness must needs be)." Augustine, *City of God*, trans. Marcus Dods, with an introduction by Thomas Merton (New York: Modern Library, 1950), 353.

10. Genesis 1:6–8. The role of division in the cosmogonic process is a persistent feature in Taoist accounts of the beginning of the world. A very clear example of this theme is found in the *Taishang laojun kaitian jing* (DZ 1059, TY 1424. For

an explanation of these abbreviations, *DZ* and *TY,* see note 12). An English translation of this text prepared by Edward H. Schafer, entitled "The Scripture of the Opening of Heaven by the Most High Lord Lao," can be found in the journal *Taoist Resources* 7, no. 2 (1977): 1–20. The opening section of this text contains the following lines: "Grand Antecedence first separated Heaven and Earth / And parted clear and turbid, / Split apart the boundless fog and vast haze" (ibid., 4).

11. A discussion of what Richard Rorty calls the "ontological gap" can be found in Richard Rorty, *Philosophy and the Mirror of Nature* (Princeton, N.J.: Princeton University Press, 1979), 22–32.

12. *Chungyang zhenren shou danyang ershisi jue* (Transmission of Twenty-Four Verses from Chongyang to Danyang), TY1149, DZ 796/1a. Texts from the *Daozang* will be cited using the system found in the *Daozang tiyao* (TY) and will include the fascicle number of the 1976 Shanghai reprint of the *Zhengtong Daozang* (DZ). These numbers will be provided only in the first reference to each work.

13. Traditional Taoist encyclopaedias such as the *Daojiao da cidian* and the *Daojiao wenhua cidian* maintain that there are two fundamentally divergent doctrinal positions on whether nature or life should be cultivated first. Isabelle Robinet points out that this is more a product of an impulse on the part of historians to retroactively assert doctrinal divisions where none appear to be. See her discussion of this in Isabelle Robinet, *Taoism: Growth of a Religion,* trans. Phyllis Brooks (Stanford: Stanford University Press, 1997), 225–27.

14. *Jindan sibai zi* (Four Hundred Words on the Golden Elixir), TY 1070, DZ 741/1a.

15. I have placed *energy* in quotation marks as I intend the term to be understood as a metaphor describing the function of the *jing-qi* rather than as a translation for this type of *qi.* I am here in accord with Paul Unschuld's observation that translating *qi* as "energy" is a mistake. Paul U. Unschuld, *Medicine in China: A History of Ideas* (Berkeley: University of California Press, 1985), 72.

16. *Jindan sibai zi* (Four Hundred Words on the Golden Elixir).

17. It is well worth reviewing Norman Girardot's detailed discussion of these themes in *Myth and Meaning in Early Taoism.* See especially chapters 2 and 3 which focus on the *Daode jing* and the *Zhuangzi* respectively.

18. *Yunji qiqian* (Seven Lots from the Bookbag of the Clouds), TY1023, DZ677–702, juan 2, 2b.

19. Robert G. Henricks, trans., *Lao-tzu Te-tao ching: A New Translation Based on the Recently Discovered Ma-wang-tui Texts* (New York: Ballantine Books, 1989), 106.

20. There is, perhaps, some room for ambiguity in Henrick's rendering of this line, as the Tao is not formed out of anything. On the contrary, the form of each thing emerges out of the Tao. Chapter 25 explains that there is nothing in the scheme of creation prior to Tao (see also chapter 42). Furthermore, Tao is independent in its completeness or self-containment. D. C. Lau translates this opening line by treating *hun* (chaos) adverbially: "There is a thing confusedly formed..." D.C. Lau, trans., *Tao Te Ching* (Hong Kong: Chinese University Press, 1963), 37. Girardot renders the same line as "There was something chaotic yet complete." Girardot, *Myth and Meaning in Early Taoism,* 49.

21. Henricks, *Te-tao ching,* 236. For some reason Henricks does not translate *yuan ming* as "original" or "primordial" name but only as "name."

22. Ibid., 194.

23. *Ziyang zhenren wuzhen pian zhizhi xiangshuo sansheng biyao* (A Direct and Detailed Discussion of the Abstruse and Important Points of the Three Vehicles Contained in the Realized Man Purple Yang's Chapters on Awakening to the Real), TY 143, DZ 64/1a.

24. *Wuzhen pian,* 27.8a.

25. Ibid., 27.2a.

26. Henricks, *Te-tao ching,* 104.

27. Ibid., 218. Henricks has elected not to translate *yuan,* "primal," probably because it does not appear in one of the texts he is using.

28. Ibid.

29. These two lines are inspired by chapter 16 of the *Tao-te ching:* "The ten thousand things—side-by-side they arise; And by this I see their return. Things [come forth] in great numbers; Each one returns to its root. This is called tranquillity. "Tranquillity"—This means to return to your fate." Henricks, *Te-tao ching,* 218.

30. *Wuzhen pian,* 28.14a.

31. Ibid., 26.9a.

32. Ibid., 26.32a–35a.

33. Burton Watson, trans. *The Complete Works of Chuang Tzu* (New York: Columbia University Press, 1968), 97.

34. Florian C. Reiter, "Ch'ung-yang Sets Forth His Teachings in Fifteen Discourses: A Concise Introduction to the Taoist Way of Life of Wang Che," *Monumenta Serica* 36 (1984–85): 48. The original text is found in section 7 of *Chongyang lijiao shiwu lun* (Zhongyang Sets Forth His Teachings in Fifteen Discourses), TY 1221, DZ 989/3b.

35. Henricks, *Te-tao ching,* 126, 134.

36. Ibid., 134.

37. I have chosen to translate this section myself rather than to use Watson's translation. Watson has chosen to translate *qi* as "spirit," a rendering usually reserved for *shen* in Taoist texts. By preserving the reference to *qi* the connection to the body is acknowledged rather than obfuscated.

38. Watson, *Chuang Tzu,* 76.

39. Ibid., 122.

13. Joseph Wong: Through Detachment to Vision

1. *Chuang-tzu* chapter 6, in Wing-tsit Chan, *A Source Book in Chinese Philosophy* (Princeton, N.J.: Princeton University Press, 1963), 191–92. In a poetic description Chuang Tzu calls a true person or perfect person a "spiritual being" who "mounts upon the clouds and forces of heaven, rides on the sun and the moon, and roams beyond the four seas" (*Chuang-tzu* chapter 2; ibid., 188). Quotations from chapters 6 and 2, "On the Equality of Things," of the *Chuang-tzu* are taken from Chan's translation, with some modifications.

2. *Chuang-tzu* chapter 6; ibid., 191.

3. Ibid.

4. Liu Xiaogan, *Chuang-tzu che-hsueh chi ch'i yen-pien* (Chuang Tzu's Philosophy and Its Development) (Peking: Chung-kuo hsie-hui ke-hsueh, 1987), 176.

5. *Chuang-tzu* chapter 22; cf. *The Complete Works of Chuang Tzu,* trans. Burton Watson (New York: Columbia University Press, 1968), 243. Quotations from the *Chuang-tzu,* other than from chapters 2 and 6, are from this translation, with modifications.

6. *Chuang-tzu* chapter 4; ibid., 58.

7. *Chuang-tzu* chapter 22; ibid., 234.

8. Ibid., 234–35.

9. *Chuang-tzu* chapter 6; Chan, *Source Book,* 201.

10. Cf. Ch'en Ku-ying, *Chuang-tzu chin-chu chin-i* (A Contemporary Commentary and Translation of Chuang-tzu), vol. 1 (Taipei: Shang-wu, 1985), 227–28.

11. Tseng Ch'ing-fan, ed., *Chuang-tzu chi-shih* (Collected Commentaries on Chuang-tzu), vol. 1 (Taipei: Chung-hua shu-chu, 1980), 153–54.

12. This knowledge through participation can be compared to a state of pure experience in which the individual is one with Tao and the universe; cf. Fung Yu-lan, *A History of Chinese Philosophy,* vol. 1 (Princeton, N.J.: Princeton University Press, 1952), 239–41.

13. *Chuang-tzu* chapter 6, in Chan, *Source Book,* 195–96.

14. Tseng, *Chuang-tzu chi-shih,* 1:136.

15. Ibid., 137.

16. Whereas Lao Tzu employs the term *tu* for Tao as an objective reality (e.g., *Tao-te ching,* chapter 25), Chuang Tzu often uses the term to convey the unique feeling of the subject, arising from encounter with Tao. Cf. Kwan Wing-chung, " 'Alone in the Intercourse with the Spirit of Heaven and Earth': Dialogue with Chuang Tzu's Epistemology of Mystical Experience" (in Chinese), 2–4; (paper delivered at the International Conference on "Dialogue between Christian Philosophy and Chinese Culture," November 23–25, 2000, sponsored by the Philosophy Faculty of Fujen Catholic University in Taiwan; publication of conference proceedings forthcoming).

17. Cf. ibid., 9–10.

18. Liu, *Chuang-tzu che-hsueh,* 176. For an appraisal of the *Chuang-tzu* as mystical text see Livia Kohn, *Early Chinese Mysticism: Philosophy and Soteriology in the Taoist Tradition* (Princeton, N.J.: Princeton University Press, 1992), 52–57.

19. *Chuang-tzu* chapter 4, in *Complete Works,* 58. Confucius gives the following explanation to "fasting of the mind": "Make your will one! Don't listen with your ears, listen with your mind. No, don't listen with your mind, but listen with your *ch'i.* Listening stops with the ears, the mind stops with recognition, but *ch'i* is empty and waits on all things. Tao gathers in emptiness alone. Emptiness is the fasting of the mind" (58).

20. Ibid.

21. Tseng, *Chuang-tzu chi-shih,* 1:82.

22. *Chuang-tzu* chapter 6; Chan, *Source Book,* 194.

23. *Chuang-tzu* chapter 22; *Complete Works,* 240–41. For the idea that Tao is at once transcendent and immanent, see John C. Wu, *Beyond East and West* (New York: Sheed and Ward, 1951), 158–59.

24. *Chuang-tzu* chapter 13; *Complete Works,* 142.

25. *Chuang-tzu* chapter 2; Chan, *Source Book,* 184.

26. Ibid., 186.

27. *Chuang-tzu* chapter 6; ibid., 195–96.

28. John Caputo, *The Mystical Element in Heidegger's Thought* (New York: Fordham University Press, 1986), 11.

29. For Cassian's "purity of heart" see Introduction to this book, p. 5; cf. also Columba Stewart, *Cassian the Monk* (New York: Oxford University Press, 1998), 42–47.

30. Cf. "Denys l'Aréopagite," in Charles Baumgartner, ed., *Dictionnaire de Spiritualité,* vol. 3 (Paris: Beauchesne, 1957), cols. 358–60.

31. Meister Eckhart, *On Detachment;* in *Sermons and Treatises,* trans. and ed. M. O'C. Walshe (Shaftesbury, Dorset: Element Books, 1990), 3:117.

32. Ibid., 117–18.

33. Ibid., 121.

34. In the only surviving part of the *Work of Propositions,* its prologue, Eckhart begins his systematic *Summa* with an analysis of the proposition *Esse Deus est* ("Existence is God"); see Josef Koch et al., eds., *Meister Eckhart: Die lateinische Werke Herausgegeben Auftrage der Deutschen Forschungsgemeinschaft,* vol. 1 (Stuttgart: Kohlhammer, 1936), 166–82. Cf. E. Colledge and B. McGinn, eds., *Meister Eckhart: The Essential Sermons, Commentaries, Treatises, and Defense* (New York: Paulist, 1981), 32.

35. Cf. Colledge and McGinn, *Meister Eckhart,* 34.

36. *On Detachment;* in *Sermons and Treatises,* 3:121.

37. Ibid., 123.

38. Ibid. The same idea is expressed by Eckhart in his other writings; e.g., *Sermon 53,* in *Sermons and Treatises,* 1:179. For the numbering of the German sermons I follow that of Quint, which is different from Walshe's. Thus *Sermon 53* becomes *Sermon 22* in Walshe; see "Concordances" in *Sermons and Treatises,* 3:150–60. For the idea of the "virtual existence" of all things in the Word from eternity, see Colledge and McGinn, *Meister Eckhart,* 40.

39. *On Detachment;* in *Sermons and Treatises,* 3:122.

40. Ibid., 120–21.

41. For Evagrius's *apatheia* see Introduction to this book, pp. 4–5. Cf. also Jeremy Driscoll, *The "Ad Monachos" of Evagrius Ponticus: Its Structure and a Select Commentary* (Rome: S. Anselmo, 1991), 11–15.

42. *On Detachment;* in *Sermons and Treatises,* 3:121.

43. Ibid., 120.

44. Ibid., 118.

45. Cf. Caputo, *Mystical Element,* 119.

46. *On Detachment;* in *Sermons and Treatises,* 3:126.

47. Ibid., 127.

48. Ibid., 128.

49. *Sermon 3;* in *Sermons and Treatises,* 1:197; cf. Thomas Aquinas, *Commentary on the Soul* 1, 4.

50. *Sermon 44;* ibid., 163. For a discussion on these two axioms as applied by Eckhart, see Reiner Schürmann, *Meister Eckhart: Mystic and Philosopher* (Bloomington: Indiana University Press, 1978), 17–25.

51. *The Nobleman;* in *Sermons and Treatises,* 3:105.

52. Ibid., 106.

53. Origen, *Homiliae in Gen.* 13, 4; ibid., 107.

54. *The Nobleman;* in *Sermon and Treatises,* 3:108–9; Origen is referring to Gen 26:15–22.

55. Ibid., 109.

56. Ibid.

57. Cf. Augustine, *De Trin.* XII, 7, 10; ibid.

58. *The Nobleman;* in *Sermon and Treatises* 3:109. Eckhart describes that in the soul which turns upward as "God's bare image, God's birth, bare and naked in the naked soul." "God's birth" here means the birth of the Son who is God's image.

59. *Sermon 6;* in *Sermons and Treatises,* 2:135.

60. Gabriel Théry, "Édition antique des pièces relatives au procès d'Eckhart contenues dans le manuscrit 33b de la Bibliothèque de Soest," *Archives d'histoire littéraire et doctrinal du moyen age* 1 (1926): 199, 243–44; quoted by Colledge and McGinn, *Meister Eckhart,* 52. Along with Eckhart's troublesome insistence on the identity of sonship between the just man and Christ, the only begotten Son of God, we often find statements that appeal to the more traditional distinction between our sonship and that of Christ, statements such as: the Word is Son by nature, we are sons by adoption.

61. *The Nobleman;* in *Sermons and Treatises,* 3:112.

62. *Sermon 3;* in *Sermons and Treatises,* 1:199. Eckhart points to Christ as the best illustration of this axiom of identity of being and knowing: "Since the Father is wholly present in the Son and the Son is wholly like him, none knows the Father save the Son" (ibid., 197).

63. *The Nobleman;* in *Sermons and Treatises,* 3:111–12.

64. Ibid., 112–13.

65. Ibid., 112.

66. Ibid., 114.

67. For a discussion on the theme of "breaking-through" in Eckhart, see Robert Forman, *Meister Eckhart: Mystic as Theologian* (Rockport, Mass.: Element, 1991), 167–92.

68. *Sermon 52;* in *Sermons and Treatises,* 2:272. Eckhart's idea is based on Thomas Aquinas's teaching on *resultatio* or *emanatio,* which means the origin of the powers from the substantial ground of the soul; cf. *Summa Theologiae* I, q. 77, a. 6 ad 3; a. 7, ad 1. This Thomistic teaching is one of the basic presuppositions for Karl Rahner's philosophical dissertation and his later formulation of the theory of "real symbol"; cf. *Spirit in the World* (New York: Sheed & Ward, 1968), 253–60; "The Theology of the Symbol," in *Theological Investigations,* vol. 4 (New York: Seabury, 1974), 232–35.

69. Cf. *Sermon 52;* in *Sermons and Treatises,* 2:275. There is utter poverty and nakedness in the "ground of the soul," where the soul "becomes ignorant with knowing, loveless with loving, and dark with enlightenment" (*On Detachment; Sermons and Treatises,* 3:126–27).

70. In his German works, Eckhart sometimes indicates the "Godhead" as beyond Father, Son, and the Holy Spirit; e.g., *Sermon 2,* in *Sermons and Treatises,* 1:76–77; *Sermon 48,* in 2:105. However, in *Sermon 26,* he identifies the "Godhead" with the "Father"; 1:99–100. This latter view, which is in harmony with the theology of the Greek Fathers, is in keeping with Eckhart's Latin works in general. For the two different formulations in Eckhart see Colledge and McGinn, *Meister Eckhart,* 35–39.

71. For an explanation of these two basic types of mysticism see Evelyn Underhill, *Mysticism: A Study in the Nature and Development of Man's Spiritual Consciousness* (New York: Meridian, 1955), 415–16; Oliver Davies, *God Within: The Mystical Tradition of Northern Europe* (New York: Paulist, 1988), 1–7. Davies translates *Wesensmystik* as "mysticism of being," and considers this as the most universal

form of mysticism, which can be found in the Christian tradition and other religions as well.

72. Davies, *God Within*, 4.

73. It would take us too long to discuss whether Tao is personal or not. For the view of Tao as a personal being in *Chuang-tzu* see Kwan Wing-chung, " 'Roaming about with the Creator': A Dialogue with Chuang Tzu on Mysticism," *Che-hsueh lun-ping* (Philosophical Review) 22 (January 1999): 137–72.

74. John C. Wu, *The Golden Age of Zen* (New York: Doubleday, 1996), 33.

14. Donald Corcoran: Benedictine Humility and Confucian "Sincerity"

1. The proceedings of the Gethsemani meeting are found in Donald Mitchell and James Wiseman, eds., *The Gethsemani Encounter: A Dialogue on the Spiritual Life by Buddhist and Christian Monastics* (New York: Continuum, 1998).

2. Aidan Kavanaugh, "Eastern Influences on the Rule of Saint Benedict," in Timothy Gregory Verdon, ed., *Monasticism and the Arts* (Syracuse: Syracuse University Press, 1984), 59.

3. Ibid., 61.

4. Terrence Kardong, "Editorial-Controversy Anyone?" *American Benedictine Review* 47:3 (September 1966): 224.

5. Terrence Kardong, *Benedict's Rule: A Translation and Commentary* (Collegeville, Minn.: Liturgical Press, 1981), 135–68.

6. For a beginning introduction to this theme, see James Finley, *Merton's Palace of Nowhere: A Search for God through Awareness of the True Self* (Notre Dame, Ind.: Ave Maria Press, 1978). See also Francis Dorf, *The Art of Passing-Over* (New York: Paulist, 1992).

7. See the great "kenotic hymn" in Philippians 2. For a full development of the theme, see, for example; Lucien Richard, *Christ the Self-Emptying of God* (New York: Paulist, 1997).

8. Alasdair MacIntyre, *After Virtue* (Notre Dame, Ind.: University of Notre Dame Press, 1984), 263.

9. Robert Bellah et al., *The Good Society* (New York: Vintage, 1992).

10. Confucianism is also a "spirituality," not merely a humanistic ethic. See for example, Rodney Taylor, *The Religious Dimensions of Confucianism* (Albany: State University of New York Press, 1989). Also John Berthrong, "Trends in Interpretation of Confucian Religiosity," in *All Under Heaven: Transforming Paradigms in Confucian-Christian Dialogue* (Albany: State University Press of New York, 1994). Also Tu-Wei Ming, *Confucian Thought: Selfhood as Creative Transformation* (Albany: State University of New York Press, 1985).

11. Herbert Fingarette, *Confucius: Secular as Sacred* (New York: Torchbooks, 1972), 16.

12. Dietrich von Hildebrand, *Liturgy and Personality* (Manchester, N.H.: Sophia Press, 1992).

13. Timothy Fry, ed. and trans., *RB 1980: The Rule of Benedict in Latin and English with Notes* (Collegeville, Minn.: Liturgical Press, 1980), 293–95. The title of this chapter of the Rule of Benedict is "The Good Zeal Monks Ought to Have." See especially line 4, "they should each try to be the first to show respect to the other."

14. William Theodore de Bary, *Neo-Confucian Orthodoxy and the Learning of the Mind-and-Heart* (New York: Columbia University Press, 1981), 76.

15. It is a reverent piety not in the modern sense of devotion but rather a rooted-ness in a deep Scriptural/liturgical sensibility, a total attitude out of which all living proceeds.

16. Rodney Taylor, *The Religious Dimensions of Confucianism,* 49.

17. Gregory Palamas, *The Triads,* trans. and ed. Nicholas Gendle, with an intro-duction by John Meyendorff (New York: Paulist Press, 1983). See section "Apophatic Theology as Positive Experience," 38–39. Palamas refers to Benedict as "another saint, one of the most perfect."

18. See John Levko, "Incessant Prayer and John Cassian," *Diakonia* 28 (Spring 1995): 71–90.

19. Jean Leclercq, "A propos du hesychasm en occident," in *Le Millenaire du Mont Athos 963–1963,* vol. 1 (Chevetogne, Belgium: Editions du Chevetogne, 1968), 253–64.

20. William Theodore de Bary, *Neo-Confucian Orthodoxy,* 101–2.

21. Hans Küng and Julia Ching, *Christianity and Chinese Religions* (New York: Doubleday, 1989).

22. See "Spiritual Dimensions: The Doctrine of the Mean," in Wing-tsit Chan, trans. and ed., *A Source Book in Chinese Philosophy* (Princeton, N.J.: Princeton University, 1963), 98–114.

23. Tu Wei-Ming, *Centrality and Commonality: An Essay on Confucian Reli-giousness* (Albany: State University of New York Press, 1989), 73.

24. Rodney Taylor, *The Religious Dimensions,* 34.

25. *The Mean* 1; in Chan, *Source Book,* 98.

26. *The Mean* 20; ibid., 107.

27. Mencius, VII B:25, quoted in Tu Wei-Ming, *Centrality and Commonality,* 86.

28. *The Mean* 22; in Chan, *Source Book,* 107–8.

29. Thomas Berry, "Affectivity in the Classical Confucian Tradition," Riverdale Papers (unpublished essay).

30. Bruno Barnhart, *Second Simplicity: The Inner Shape of Christianity* (New York: Paulist, 1999), 24, 33, and passim.

31. *The Mean* 13; in Chan, *Source Book,* 100. This is a key metaphysical insight—realignment of the self (*hsin*) brings realignment with heaven and earth forming the cosmic axis.

32. See P. Courcelle, " 'Habitare secum' selon Perse et Saint Grégoire le Grand," *Revue des études anciennes* 69 (1967): 266–79.

33. William Theodore de Bary, *Neo-Confucian Orthodoxy,* 56.

34. Timothy Fry, *RB 1980,* Ch. 31, "Qualifications of the Monastery Cellarer," 227–29.

35. Chang Tsai, "The Western Inscription"; in Chan, *Source Book,* 497.

36. Timothy Fry, *RB 1980,* 202–3.

37. Herbert Fingarette, *Confucius: Secular as Sacred,* 40.

38. Timothy Fry, *RB 1980,* 283.

39. Gregory the Great, *Life and Miracles of St. Benedict* (Book Two of *The Dia-logues*), trans. Odo Zimmerman and Benedict Avery (Collegeville, Minn.: Liturgical Press, 1952), Ch. 34, 71–73.

40. Ibid.

41. Ezra Pound, trans. and commentator, *Confucius: The Great Digest, The Unwobbling Pivot, The Analects* (New York: New Directions), 95–100.

42. Aidan Kavanaugh, "Eastern Influences on the Rule of Benedict," 63.

43. William Butler Yeats, "The Second Coming." See Stephen Maxfield Parrish, *A Concordance to the Poems of W. B. Yeats* (Ithaca, N.Y.: Cornell University Press, 1963), 350.

44. Tu Wei-Ming, *Centrality and Commonality,* 73.

45. Odo Casel, "Benedict of Nursia as Man of the Spirit," *Monastic Studies* 11 (Advent, 1975): 143–73.

46. Evagrius Ponticus, *The Mind's Long Journey to the Holy Trinity. The Ad Monachos of Evagrius Ponticus,* trans. with introduction by Jeremy Driscoll, O.S.B. (Collegeville, Minn.: Liturgical Press, 1993), 50.

47. Ibid., 51.

48. Terrence Kardong, *Benedict's Rule,* Prologue, 24.

49. Ibid., 11.

50. Evagrius Ponticus, *The Praktikos and Chapters on Prayer,* translated with introduction by John Eudes Bamberger (Spencer, Mass.: Cistercian Studies, 1970), lxxi–xcix.

51. Herbert Fingarette, *Confucius: Secular as Sacred,* 89.

52. André Louf, "The Word Beyond the Liturgy," *Cistercian Studies* 6 (1971): 353–68; 7 (1972): 63–76.

15. Laurence Freeman: Discovering What You Really Want

1. Helena Norbert Hodge, *Ancient Futures* (San Francisco: Sierra Club Books, 1991).

2. Letter to Richard Woodhouse, 27 October 1818; see R. Gittings, ed., *Letters of John Keats* (Oxford: Oxford University Press, 1970).

3. *Romeo and Juliet,* 2.6.

4. The Dalai Lama, *Transforming the Mind* (London: Thorsons, 2000).

5. Ibid.

6. Ibid.

7. Ibid., 31.

8. Ibid.

9. Jn 15:11.

10. Dalai Lama, *Transforming the Mind,* 52.

11. Shantideva, quoted by Dalai Lama, ibid., 77.

12. *The Philokalia* (London: Faber and Faber, 1979), vol. 1, 251–96

13. Ibid., 253, n. 2.

14. Ibid., 253, n. 3.

15. Rom 7:14–19.

16. Diadochos, 285, n. 85.

17. Ibid.

18. John Climacus, *The Ladder of Divine Ascent,* Step 30. See John Climacus, *The Ladder of Divine Ascent,* trans. Colm Lubheid and Norman Russell (New York: Paulist Press, 1982), 287.

19. Diadochos, 256, n. 14.

20. Simone Weil, *Waiting for God* (New York: Putnam, 1951).

21. Saying of Abba Anthony.

22. Weil, *Waiting for God,* 106.

23. Ibid., 107.

24. Ibid., 112.

25. Ibid., 110.

16. Bede Healey: On the Re-creating of Desire

1. Sebastian Moore, *The Crucified Jesus is No Stranger* (New York: Seabury, 1977).

2. Ibid, 80.

3. In the psychoanalytic literature, Object Relations is a technical term that refers to human relations. Specifically, it refers to the inner, largely unconscious web of relationships developed early in life with our significant caregivers, which then tend to color and shape our current "real" external relationships. From this perspective, human beings are not looking for sexual and aggressive drive discharge, but are (human) object-seeking from birth. This relational drive, if you will, is the hallmark of this radical break with Freudian psychoanalytic approaches. A recent book that provides a useful and accessible introduction to this area is by Lavinia Gomez, *An Introduction to Object Relations* (New York: New York University Press, 1997).

4. *The Random House Dictionary of the English Language, College Edition* (New York: Random House, 1968).

5. The Rule of Benedict (hereafter RB) 7:10.

6. RB 7:67; see also 1 Jn 4:18.

7. Neatly defining purity of heart seems to be an impossibility. Columba Stewart says, " 'Purity of heart' is a theological prism refracting an extraordinary spectrum of biblical, philosophical and ascetic themes" (Harriet Luckman and Linda Kulzer, eds., *Purity of Heart in Early Ascetic and Monastic Literature* [Collegeville, Minn.: Liturgical Press, 1999], 2). According to Stewart, purity of heart involves elements of "ritual and bodily purity, moral purity, and metaphysical purity" (ibid., 4). The book's index, under "purity of heart," refers to *apatheia*, clarity of vision, gift, goal, *katharos*, sincerity of speech, spirit-bearers, and as wisdom, as well as connecting it with the body, chastity, conversion, discipline, fear of the Lord, health of soul, innocence, love, monastic purity, moral purity, prayer, repentance, ritual, and vision of God. In many ways this word, like "desire," defies definitions that might limit its full meaning.

8. Acts 17:28.

9. Rev 21:5.

10. Sebastian Moore, *Let This Mind Be In You* (Minneapolis: Winston Press, 1985), 85.

11. I will use "Desire" (with a capital "D") to refer to the transcendent divine Desire, given to us at baptism. It is, among other things, the indwelling of Divinity within us, and the simultaneous call to become united with that Desire. Our desire is to be Desire. This is not meant to limit God to being categorized as simply desire, or to say that our concept of desire, and that which we ascribe to God, even comes close to capturing the reality of divine Desiring. Words fail, but they are the best tools we have. A quotation from Moore's, *Jesus the Liberator of Desire* (New York: Crossroad, 1989) may help. "People say to me, 'You are talking about a certain *kind* of desire, aren't you?' I answer, 'No, I am trying to talk about that of which all desires are kinds' " (13).

12. We can imagine our ontological identity as a transcendent self, fully present in its essence, but awaiting development and birth as we participate in the process of our own, particular re-creation. We are to become complete joy (Jn 16:23–24).

13. D. W. Winnicott, *The Maturational Processes and the Facilitating Environment* (New York: International Universities Press, 1965), 140–52.

14. Ibid.

15. Quoted in A. W. Richard Sipe, *Celibacy: A Way of Loving, Living, and Serving* (Liguori, Mo.: Triumph Books, 1996), 67.

16. In the field of psychoanalysis, it is common to talk about "following the red thread" of the patient's associations to get to the deeper level of the patient's world. Bede Griffiths, quoting William Blake, wrote of the "golden string." See also Bernard Faure, *The Red Thread: Buddhist Approaches to Sexuality* (Princeton, N.J.: Princeton University Press, 1998).

17. See, for example, the recent book edited by Bjorn Krondorfer, *Men's Bodies, Men's Gods: Male Identities in a (Post-)Christian Culture* (New York: New York University Press, 1996).

18. Terrence G. Kardong, *Benedict's Rule: A Translation and Commentary* (Collegeville, Minn.: Liturgical Press, 1996), 208.

19. Esther de Waal, *A Life-Giving Way: A Commentary on the Rule of St. Benedict* (Collegeville, Minn.: Liturgical Press, 1994), 194.

20. William Johnston, *"Arise, my love . . . ": Mysticism for a New Era* (Maryknoll, N.Y.: Orbis, 2000), 114.

21. Esther de Waal, *A Life-Giving Way,* 194.

22. Mark Epstein, *Thoughts without a Thinker: Psychotherapy from a Buddhist Perspective* (New York: Basic Books, 1995), 65.

23. Ibid., 72.

24. Ibid.

25. Guy Claxton, ed., *Beyond Therapy: The Impact of Eastern Religions on Psychological Theory and Practice* (Dorset, England: Prism Press, 1986/1996).

26. Ibid., 19–29.

27. John Cassian, *Conf.* 1.4.3.

28. RB Prologue: 49.

29. John McDargh, "The Life of the Self in Christian Spirituality and Contemporary Psychoanalysis," *Horizons* 11, no. 2 (1984), 344–60. I am indebted to this author for introducing me, years ago, to a rich and vital approach to understanding the interplay of psychoanalytic theory and spirituality.

17. Mary Margaret Funk: Purity of Heart: A Dialogue

1. Rob Baker and Gray Henry, eds., *Merton and Sufism: The Untold Story* (Louisville: Fons Vitae, 1999).

2. Timothy Fry, O.S.B., ed., *Rule of Benedict* (Collegeville, Minn.: Liturgical Press, 1982), 165.

3. Baker and Henry, *Merton and Sufism,* 51.

4. Ibid., 52.

5. Thomas Merton, *Conjectures of a Guilty Bystander* (New York: Doubleday, 1966), 136.

6. "Then it was as if I suddenly saw the secret beauty of their hearts, the depths of their hearts where neither sin nor desire nor self-knowledge can reach, the core of their reality, the person that each one is in God's eyes. . . . Again, that expression, *le point vierge* (I cannot translate it) comes in here. At the center of our being is a point of nothingness, which is untouched by sin and by illusion, a point of pure truth, a point or spark which belongs entirely to God, which is never at our disposal, from which God disposes of our lives, which is inaccessible to the fantasies of our own mind or the brutalities of our own will. This little point of nothingness and of *absolute poverty* is the pure glory of God in us. It is so to speak His name written

in us, as our poverty, as our indigence, as our dependence, as our sonship. It is like a pure diamond, blazing with the invisible light of heaven. It is in everybody, and if we could see it we would see these billions of points of light coming together in the face and blaze of a sun that would make all the darkness and cruelty of life vanish completely.... I have no program for this seeing. It is only given. But the gate of heaven is everywhere." *Conjectures,* 142.

7. Ibid.

8. Ibid.

9. Ibid.

10. Baker and Henry, *Merton and Sufism,* 65.

11. Ibid., 64–65, citing Massignon, *The Passion of al-Hallaj: Mystic and Martyr of Islam,* trans. Herbert Mason, vol. 3 (Princeton: Princeton University Press, 1982), 17–19.

12. Baker and Henry, *Merton and Sufism,* 65.

13. Merton, *Conjectures,* 141.

14. Ibid.

15. Ibid.

16. Ibid.

17. Ibid., 141–42.

18. Ibid., 142.

19. Baker and Henry, *Merton and Sufism,* 65.

20. Ibid., 65, quoting Massignon, *L'Hospitalité sacrée,* ed. Jacques Keryell (Paris: Nouvelle Cité, 1987), 257.

21. Merton, *Conjectures,* 142.

22. Baker and Henry, *Merton and Sufism,* 66, citing Herbert Mason, ed., *Testimonies and Reflections: Essays of Louis Massignon* (Notre Dame, Ind.: University of Notre Dame Press, 1988), 127.

23. Søren Kierkegaard, *Purity of Heart Is to Will One Thing* (New York: Harper and Row, 1965).

24. Baker and Henry, *Merton and Sufism,* 66, citing Herbert Mason, *Testimonies and Reflections,* 127.

25. Baker and Henry, *Merton and Sufism,* 66, citing Louis Massignon to Robert Caspar, November 12, 1955, quoted in Caspar, "La vision de l'islam chez L. Massignon et son influence sur l'église," in *Massignon,* ed. J.-F. Six (Paris: Cahiers de l'Herne, 1970), 126–47.

26. Baker and Henry, ibid., 64, from Merton, *Conjectures,* 151.

27. Thomas Merton, "Final Integration: Toward a 'Monastic Therapy,' " in Baker and Henry, ibid., 271.

28. Ibid., 271–72.

29. Ibid., 272.

30. Ibid.

31. Ibid.

32. Ibid., 272–73.

33. Ibid., 270.

34. Ibid., 269.

35. Ibid., 270.

36. Ibid., 274.

37. Ibid.

38. Ibid., 67, citing an undated letter to Merton (at Thomas Merton Center).

39. Ibid., 67.

40. Merton, *Conjectures*, 117.

18. Bruno Barnhart: Christian Self-Understanding in the Light of the East

1. For purity of heart, see Juana Raasch, O.S.B., "The Monastic Concept of Purity of Heart and its Sources," *Studia Monastica* 8, no. 1 (1966): 7–33, 8, no. 2 (1966): 183–213; 10, no. 1 (1968), 7–55; 11, no. 2 (1969), 269–314; 12, no. 1 (1970), 7–41; Harriet A. Luckman and Linda Kulzer, O.S.B., eds., *Purity of Heart in Early Ascetic and Monastic Literature* (Collegeville, Minn.: Liturgical Press, 1999). For contemplation see Andrew Louth, *The Origins of the Christian Mystical Tradition from Plato to Denys* (Oxford: Oxford University Press, 1981).

2. See, for example, the Gospel and First Letter of John, passim, and "The Odes of Solomon," ed. J. H. Charlesworth, in *The Old Testament Pseudepigrapha*, vol. 2 (Garden City, N.Y.: Doubleday, 1985), 725–71.

3. Here we include the "Deuteropauline" letters to the Colossians and Ephesians.

4. See, for example, Abhishiktananda, *Hindu-Christian Meeting Point* (Delhi: ISPCK, 1976), chapter 6, "The Johannine Upanishads," 77–93; Bede Griffiths, *Return to the Center* (Springfield, Ill.: Templegate, 1976), 143–46; *The Marriage of East and West* (Springfield, Ill.: Templegate, 1982), 94–99, 189–90; *The Cosmic Revelation* (Springfield, Ill.: Templegate, 1983), 131; and *A New Vision of Reality* (Springfield, Ill.: Templegate, 1989), 125–27, 219–21.

5. See David Loy, *Nonduality* (New Haven: Yale University Press, 1988).

6. "Identity" is to be understood here in both senses: (1) sameness, unity, and (2) personal identity, the constitution and awareness of self. In Hindu Vedanta particularly, the transcendent Self, or Atman, is the center and the goal of spiritual life.

7. "Word" here is intended to denote not only the biblical word but the divine Word (of the Christian Trinity) which is incarnate in Jesus Christ.

8. See, for example, Aldous Huxley, *The Perennial Philosophy* (New York: Harper & Row, 1944); Bede Griffiths, *Return to the Center*; Ken Wilber, *The Atman Project* (Wheaton, Ill.: Theosophical Publ., 1980).

9. Bede Griffiths, *Universal Wisdom: A Journey through the Sacred Wisdom of the World* (London: HarperCollins, 1994), Introduction, p. 8.

10. See Col 1:19–22; Eph 1:10; 2:13–16.

11. The *event* of Christ is presupposed everywhere in the New Testament, and explicitly appears in texts like Heb 1:1–3; Jn 1:1–18; 1 Jn 1:1–3. The various implications of this event are Paul's continual subject in his letters. See, for example, Rom 5:6, 8; 1 Cor 1:2, 15; 2 Cor 3:4; Gal passim; Col 1–2; Eph 1–3.

12. See Basil Studer, *Trinity and Incarnation: The Faith of the Early Church,* trans. Matthias Westerhoff, ed. Andrew Louth (Collegeville, Minn.: Liturgical Press, 1993).

13. See 1 Cor 1:17–24.

14. "Nonduality of the end": see, e.g., Gal 3:28; Eph 1:10; 4:4–6; Col 1:19–20.

15. See 1 Cor 10:17, 12:13; Col 1:19–20; Eph 1:23; 2:16.

16. See Hugo Rahner, "The Christian Mystery and the Pagan Mysteries," in *The Mysteries: Papers from the Eranos Yearbooks*, vol. 2, ed. Joseph Campbell (Princeton, N.J.: Princeton University Press, 1955), especially "The Mystery of the Cross," 369–87.

17. See Col 1:19–22; Eph 1:10; 2:13–16; and Hugo Rahner article cited in note 16.

18. Irenaeus, "Against Heresies," in *The Ante-Nicene Fathers* (reprint, Grand Rapids, Mich.: Eerdmans, 1981), vol. 1: III, 11, n. 8, pp. 428–29; IV, 20, n. 1–4, pp. 487–88; V, 17, n. 3, pp. 545–46.; Irenaeus, *Proof of the Apostolic Preaching,* trans. Joseph P. Smith, *Ancient Christian Writers* 16 (New York: Newman [Paulist], 1952), chapter 34, pp. 69–70.

19. See Bruno Barnhart, *Second Simplicity: The Inner Structure of Christianity* (New York: Paulist, 1999), passim.

20. The four yogas (the conception of four yogas derives from Vivekananda in the nineteenth century) have been explained more fully by Pravrajika Vrajaprana in her paper; see pp. 27–38 above. See also *The Encyclopedia of Eastern Philosophy and Religion: Buddhism, Hinduism, Taoism, Zen,* by Ingrid Fischer-Schreiber et al., ed. Stephan Schuhmacher and Gert Woerner (Boston: Shambhala, 1994), s. v. *yoga, dhyana, jnana, bhakti, karma.*

21. See Catherine Mowry Lacugna, *God for Us: The Trinity and Christian Life* (New York: HarperCollins, 1991).

22. See Harold Coward, *Jung and Eastern Thought* (Albany: State University of New York Press, 1985).

23. See Jesus' words to Nicodemus in Jn 3:3–5.

24. Bede Griffiths, *Return to the Center,* 16.

25. See 2 Cor 4:16 and (differently) Rom 7:11–23.

26. See Rom 7:14–18; 8:1–10; Gal 5:16–25; 6:8.

27. See Eph 4:1–6; Jn 17:11, 21; 1 Jn 1:3; 3:1–2; 4:16–17.

28. See Jn 3:1–8; 14:25–26; 16:12–15; 1 Cor 2:7–16; 2 Cor 3:16–18; 4:6; Gal 4:6–9; 1 Jn 2:20–27.

29. See 1 Cor 4:7; Col 2:1–7, 8–10; 1 Jn 2:20–27.

30. See Jn 1:1–18; Rom 8:14–23; Col 1:15–22, 26–27; Eph 1:9–10; 4:8–10.

31. See Jer 31:31–34; Ezek 26:24–28; Jn 7:37–39; Rom 5:5; Gal 4:6.

32. See the previous section "Unitive Self and Baptism."

33. See Cassian, *Conference* 1, 8.1, in *John Cassian: The Conferences,* trans. and annotated by Boniface Ramsey, O.P., Ancient Christian Writers 57 (New York: Paulist, 1997), 47–48.

34. *Conf.* 1, 8.1, ibid., 46–48.

35. *Conf.* 1, ibid., 43–52.

36. Besides those papers included in this symposium volume which involve such a confrontation, see the dialogue between Thomas Merton and D. T. Suzuki in Merton's *Zen and the Birds of Appetite* (New York: New Directions, 1968), 99–138.

37. For the biblical meaning of "heart," see Xavier Leon-Dufour, S.J., ed., *Dictionary of Biblical Theology,* 2d ed. (New York: Seabury, 1973).

38. These conceptions of a return to an original nondual reality have been abundantly brought forth in the papers on Hindu, Buddhist, and (especially) Taoist spiritualities in this volume.

39. See for example Rom 5:1–5; 6:3–6; 8:9–16, 26; 2 Cor 3:15–18; 4:6; Gal 3:1–5; 1 Jn 2:20–27; 3:1–3; 3:24; 4:13.

40. See for example 2 Cor 4:6; Gal 2:20; Phil 3:7–11; Col 3:1–4; and Paul's frequent use of "in Christ" or "in him": e.g., in Ephesians 1.

41. 2 Cor 4:6; Phil 3:7–8; see also Eph 1:17–23; 3:17–19.

42. Gal 2:20; Phil 3:7–11.

43. See 1 Cor 13:2–13; Eph 3:17–19.

44. Identity and relationship: see above, p. 296.

45. See 2 Cor 4:6; Rom 8:18–23.

46. See the "first and second Axial periods" proposed by Ewert Cousins in his *Christ of the Twenty-First Century* (Rockport, Mass.: Element, 1992).

47. I am using the word "fontality" here (from Latin *fons,* fountain) to denote a single vital movement which embraces the three modalities of faith, hope, and love. One draws from the Invisible in faith, stands upon this invisible ground (hope), and gives from the invisible inner store, without discrimination and without expecting a return of one's gift (love). In each of these three acts the *person* is realized in bringing forth something new into this world. This "bringing forth" parallels the progression from "contemplation" to "action" and from "baptism" to "eucharist." In Jesus' teaching in the Sermon on the Mount (Matthew, chapters 5–7) we have a long lesson in fontality, moving continually from one to another of its three moments (corresponding to faith, hope, and love). Fontality, in nontheological language, might be called creativity or, better, generativity.

Contributors

Bruno Barnhart, O.S.B. Cam., is a monk of New Camaldoli Hermitage, Big Sur, California. After entering the Big Sur monastery in 1959, he studied theology at Sant' Anselmo in Rome during the years of the Second Vatican Council (1962–66) and then returned to his monastery in California to work in formation. He served as prior of the Big Sur community from 1970 through 1987. Since then Bruno (aside from teaching and other duties in the monastery) has been largely occupied with study and writing on the Christian sapiential (wisdom) tradition and its rebirth in our time. He is author of *The Good Wine: Reading John from the Center* (1993) and *Second Simplicity: The Inner Shape of Christianity* (1999), and editor of *The One Light: Bede Griffiths' Principal Writings* (2001).

Cyprian Consiglio, O.S.B. Cam., is a monk and priest of New Camaldoli Hermitage. He received his master's degree in theology at St. John's Seminary in Camarillo, California, with a thesis on the writings of Bede Griffiths. Father Cyprian recently traveled to South India, where he studied Indian music while living and working with the community of Saccidananda Ashram, Shantivanam. He is also a composer, recording artist, and speaker, currently recording and publishing with Oregon Catholic Press. Father Cyprian serves as choirmaster and liturgist for his community, as well as Postulant Master and teacher.

Francis H. Cook, Ph.D., has devoted much of his life to the study and practice of Buddhism, including a year and a half in Kyoto as a Fulbright Fellow. He has taught Buddhism at the University of California, Riverside, where he is Emeritus Professor. He has been director of translations at the Institute for Transcultural Studies in Los Angeles. Married and father of four children, Professor Cook is the author of *Hua-yen Buddhism: The Jewel Net of Indra,* of *How to Raise an Ox* (Dr. Cook's translation of ten chapters of Dogen's *Shobogenzo*), and a number of articles on Buddhism in scholarly journals.

Donald Corcoran, O.S.B. Cam., is prioress of Transfiguration Monastery in Windsor, New York, affiliated with the Camaldolese Benedictine Nuns. She entered the Benedictines in 1959, and earned a Ph.D. at Fordham in the history of religions, with an emphasis on spirituality. She taught for three years at St. Louis University before helping to found the monastery in Windsor. She has taught occasional courses at St. John's (Collegeville),

SUNY Binghamton, and Fordham. She is a widely recognized presenter of retreats and workshops.

Paul Crowe is a doctoral candidate in the Department of Asian Studies at The University of British Columbia in Vancouver. He holds a master's degree in religion from the University of Calgary and a master's degree in Asian studies from the University of British Columbia. In addition to his academic studies he has practiced and taught *Taiji* for almost twenty years. Paul is also a member of the Fung Loy Kok Institute of Taoism founded by his teachers, the Taoist monk Moy Lin-shin, and the Taoist priest Mui Ming-to, both of whom provided him with guidance in his practice of Taoist meditation. He currently resides in Vancouver, British Columbia, with his wife and son.

Laurence Freeman, O.S.B., entered the monastic life at Ealing Abbey in London, where John Main was his spiritual guide. Father Laurence helped John Main with the establishment of the first Christian Meditation Center in London in 1975, and then followed him to Canada in 1977, where they began the Montreal Priory. Since John Main's death in 1982, Father Laurence has continued his work. When the World Community for Christian Meditation was formed in 1991, Father Laurence became its Director. Father Laurence is a monk of the Monastery of Christ the King, Cockfosters, London. He serves a worldwide network of meditation groups. Father Laurence Freeman is the editor of John Main's works and the editor of *Monastic Studies*. He is also the author of *Christian Meditation: Your Daily Practice, Light Within, The Selfless Self, Short Span of Days, Common Ground, Jesus the Teacher Within,* and many sets of tapes and articles on meditation.

Mary Margaret Funk, O.S.B., is a member of Our Lady of Grace Monastery in Beech Grove, Indiana, since 1961. She was prioress from 1985 to 1993 and has been the Executive Director of Monastic Interreligious Dialogue since 1994. In that capacity she coordinated the Gethsemani Encounter in 1996 and traveled to India and Tibet on the 6th Spiritual Exchange Program. She has engaged in formal dialogue with the Hindu, Zen Buddhist, and Islamic traditions. Sister Mary Margaret's book, *Thoughts Matter,* was published in 1998 by Continuum. It is a teaching based on the eight "evil thoughts" or afflictions of John Cassian's Institutes. She has codirected Lectio retreats with Bruno Barnhart. Sister Mary Margaret has served on the Board of Trustees of *Contemplative Outreach* and the board of Weston School of Theology in Cambridge, and is currently a member of the Board of Overseers of St. Meinrad School of Theology. She collaborated with Dr. Patrick Henry and Brother David Steindl-Rast on the book *Benedict's Dharma* that will be published by Riverhead in 2001.

Thomas G. Hand, S.J., holds an S.T.L. from Santa Clara University. Father Hand spent twenty-nine years in Japan, where he was engaged in teaching, directing retreats, and providing spiritual direction. While in Japan he received formal Zen training for six years. He is currently on the staff of the

Mercy Center Institute of Contemporary Spirituality in Burlingame, California. He is coauthor, with Chinese Sister Chwen Jiuan Lee, of *A Taste of Water: Christianity through Taoist-Buddhist Eyes.*

Bede J. Healey, O.S.B. Cam., Ph.D., is a monk of New Camaldoli Hermitage at Big Sur, where he is Novice Master and Vocation Director and serves on the Formation Team. Prior to transferring to the hermitage, he was a monk of St. Benedict's Abbey in Atchison, Kansas. While there he was the Director of Religion and Psychiatry at the Menninger Clinic in Topeka. He has written and presented in the areas of religion, spirituality, and psychology.

Kevin Hunt, O.C.S.O., entered St. Joseph's Abbey (a Trappist monastery) in 1953. He helped in the construction of several monasteries here and abroad. He has been a Zen student since the early 1970s and participated in interreligious dialogue since that time. In the 1990s he was a member of Monastic Interreligious Dialogue and has participated in a number of international conferences. Currently he is residing at his monastery in Massachusetts.

Nicholas Koss, O.S.B., a monk of St. Vincent Archabbey, Latrobe, Pennsylvania, has been assigned to Wimmer Priory in Taipei, Taiwan, since 1966. He holds a Ph.D. in Comparative Literature from Indiana University and has taught at Fu Jen Catholic University for over twenty years. His publications include *The Best and the Fairest Land: Medieval Images of China* (Taipei, 1999) and numerous translations for *The Chinese Pen* (Taiwan).

Rev. Taigen Dan Leighton is a Soto Zen priest and Dharma successor in the lineage of Shunryu Suzuki Roshi. He has practiced and resided at San Francisco Zen Center, Tassajara Monastery, and Green Gulch Farm Zen Center. He has also practiced for two years in Kyoto, Japan. Taigen is author of *Bodhisattva Archetypes,* and he is cotranslator and editor of several Zen texts, including *Cultivating the Empty Field, The Wholehearted Way,* and *Dogen's Pure Standards for the Zen Community,* as well as contributor to many other books and journals. He teaches at the Graduate Theological Union in Berkeley and has taught at the California Institute of Integral Studies, Saint Mary's College, and the University of San Francisco. Taigen leads meditation groups in Bolinas, San Rafael, and San Francisco and has been active in interfaith dialogues, as well as in Engaged Buddhist programs for social action.

Dr. Liu Xiaogan, Professor of Philosophy at the Chinese University of Hong Kong, since receiving his Ph.D. from Peking (Beijing) University in 1985, has taught and conducted research at Peking, Harvard, Princeton, and the National University of Singapore, in addition to serving as visiting professor at Pacific School of Religion (Berkeley). His books include *Classifying the Zhuangzi Chapters,* and he is a contributor to many books and journals, such as *Our Religions, Taoism and Ecology, Lao-tzu and the Tao-te-ching, Religious and Philosophical Aspects of the Laozi, What Men Owe* *to Women, Journal of Chinese Philosophy, Taoist Resources.* He has also published books and many papers in Chinese.

Thomas Matus, O.S.B. Cam., was born in Hollywood, California, in 1940 and has been a Camaldolese monk since 1962. He has earned degrees in music (Occidental College, 1961), theology (Anselmianum, Rome, 1972) and the history of religion (Fordham University, 1977). Not raised in any particular religious denomination, he discovered yoga and the spiritual traditions of India through the writings of Paramahansa Yogananda, and in 1960 he became a Roman Catholic. He is author of *Yoga and the Jesus Prayer Tradition* (1984) and *The Mystery of Romuald and the Five Brothers* (1994) and coauthor, with Fritjof Capra and David Steindl-Rast, of *Belonging to the Universe* (1991).

William Skudlarek, O.S.B., entered St. John's Abbey, Collegeville, Minnesota, in 1958 and was ordained to the priesthood in 1964. He completed a doctoral program in homiletics at Princeton Theological Seminary. For almost twenty years he taught and held administrative positions at St. John's University and Seminary. From 1985 to 1990 he lived and worked in Brazil as an associate of the Maryknoll Missionary Society. At present he is a member of Holy Trinity Monastery, a priory of St. John's Abbey, in Japan (Nagano Province), where he practices *zazen,* ministers to Brazilians living in the province, serves as a prison chaplain, and plays cello in a nearby orchestra. He is the current chairman of the board of Monastic Interreligious Dialogue.

David Steindl-Rast, O.S.B., was born in Vienna, where he studied art, anthropology, and psychology. He holds degrees from the Vienna Academy of the Fine Arts and the Psychological Institute, and received his Ph.D. in experimental psychology from the University of Vienna. In 1953, he joined the newly founded Benedictine monastery of Mount Saviour in Elmira, New York. There he received training in philosophy and theology. He has lectured in the United States, Europe, and Asia. Brother David has been involved in monastic renewal and in East-West dialogue (particularly the Buddhist-Christian dialogue) for nearly forty years. His books include *A Listening Heart: The Art of Contemplative Living, Gratefulness, the Heart of Prayer,* and (with Aitken Roshi) *The Ground We Share: Everyday Practice, Buddhist and Christian,* and (with Fritjof Capra and Thomas Matus) *Belonging to the Universe: Explorations on the Frontier of Science and Spirituality.*

Rev. Heng Sure was ordained as a Buddhist Bhikshu (monk) at the City of Ten Thousand Buddhas, in Almage, California, in 1976. A native of Toledo, Ohio, he met his teacher, the late Ven. Master Hsüan Hua, while finishing his M.A. in Oriental Languages at the University of California, Berkeley. After receiving full ordination in the Mahayana tradition of Chinese Buddhism, he commenced a "three steps, one bow" pilgrimage, dedicating his efforts to world peace. He traveled up the California Coast Highway from South Pasadena to Ukiah, a distance of over six hundred miles, in two years and nine months. During the pilgrimage and for two years following, he kept a strict vow of silence. Rev. Heng Sure currently serves as Director of the Berkeley Buddhist Monastery and recently advanced to candidacy in the doctoral program at the Graduate Theological Union in Berkeley. He also represents Buddhism on the Board of Directors of the United Religions Initiative and the Interfaith Center at the Presidio.

Dr. Martin Verhoeven received his M.A. in history (1971) from the University of Wisconsin-Madison, was a Visiting Scholar at Stanford under a Ford Fellowship, and completed his Ph.D. at the University of Wisconsin-Madison on the American encounter with Asian religions. He was a Buddhist monk for eighteen years, and is currently Associate Professor of History and Asian Religions at the Institute for World Religions in Berkeley, California, as well as Adjunct Professor of History and Religion at the Pacific School of Religion, Graduate Theological Union, in Berkeley. His most recent publication, "Americanising the Buddha: Paul Carus and the Transformation of Asian Thought," appears in *The Faces of Buddhism in America,* ed. Charles S. Prebish and Kenneth K. Tanaka, published by the University of California Press (Berkeley), 1998.

Pravrajika Vrajaprana has been a nun of Sarada Convent at Santa Barbara's Vedanta Society (the Western branch of the Ramakrishna Order of India) since 1977. She is the author of *Vedanta: A Simple Introduction* (Vedanta Press, 1999), *A Portrait of Sister Christine* (Ramakrishna Mission Institute of Culture, 1996), and *My Faithful Goodwin* (Advaita Ashrama, 1994), as well as the editor of *Seeing God Everywhere* (Vedanta Press, 1996) and *Living Wisdom: Vedanta in the West* (Vedanta Press, 1994). She has written numerous articles for journals both in the United States and India; her writings have been translated into German, Japanese, and various Indian languages.

Joseph H. Wong, O.S.B. Cam., a Chinese from Hong Kong, is a monk of New Camaldoli Hermitage and director of junior monks there. After obtaining a master's degree in theology from Heythrop College, University of London, he completed his doctorate in theology at the Gregorian University in Rome with a dissertation on K. Rahner, published as *Logos-Symbol in the Christology of Karl Rahner.* He taught systematic theology and spirituality in Rome and is the author of many articles. He is the Chairman of the Camaldolese Institute for East-West Dialogue and a board member for Monastic Interreligious Dialogue. As a research associate of the Ricci Institute for Chinese-Western Cultural History at the University of San Francisco, Father Joseph is working in the area of an inculturated Chinese theology and spirituality, with special interest in Christian-Taoist dialogue. Periodically he teaches theology at Sheshan Seminary in Shanghai, China.

Two of the symposium papers are not included in this book.

Dr. Chung-ying Cheng, Professor of Philosophy at the University of Hawaii at Manoa, presented a paper entitled "A Confucian Theory of the Human Self: Self-Cultivation and Free Will in Confucian Philosophy." Because of other commitments, it was not possible for Dr. Cheng to prepare his paper for publication.

Norman Fischer, Green Dragon Temple, Sausalito, California, former abbot of the San Francisco Zen Center and author of several books of poetry, presented a selection of his versions of the biblical Psalms, under the title "Zen Songs: The Psalms as the Music of Enlightenment." He introduced the Psalm versions with personal and theological reflections on the significance both of these poems and of interreligious dialogue in our time. Because of a prior publication commitment, his paper could not be included in the present volume.

Discussants

These participants responded to the presentations and moderated the discussions.

Father Peter-Damian Belisle, O.S.B. Cam., New Camaldoli Hermitage, Big Sur, California.

Dr. John Borelli, of the Secretariat for Ecumenical and Interreligious Affairs of the National Conference of Catholic Bishops.

Sister Pascaline Coff, O.S.B., Osage Monastery, Sand Springs, Oklahoma.

Father Thomas Hand, S.J., Mercy Center, Burlingame, California (biographical account above).

Father Thomas Hart, O.S.B., St. Vincent's Archabbey, Latrobe, Pennsylvania.

Dr. Emily John, Evanston, Illinois.

Rev. Myo Lahey, Zen Mountain Center, Tassajara, California.

Dr. Patrick Mitchell, St. John's Seminary, Camarillo, California.

Brother David Steindl-Rast, O.S.B., Mount Saviour Monastery, Elmira, New York (biographical account above).

Steven Tainer, Institute for World Religions, Berkeley, California.

Index